EASY PCs
2ND EDITION

Suzanne Weixel

Illustrations by

Kathy Hanley

EASY PCS, 2ND EDITION

Library of Congress Catalog No.: 93-85885

ISBN: 1-56529-276-6

95 94   6 5 4 3 2

Interpretation of the printing code: the rightmost double-digit number is the year of the book's printing; the rightmost single-digit number, the number of the book's printing. For example, a printing code of 93-1 shows that the first printing of the book occurred in 1993.

Screen reproductions in this book were created using Collage Plus from Inner Media, Inc., Hollis, NH.

Publisher: David P. Ewing

Director of Publishing: Mike Miller

Managing Editor: Corinne Walls

Publishing Manager

Shelley O'Hara

Production Editors

Don Eamon

Chris Haidri

Editors

Tom Hayes

Patrick Kanouse

Technical Editor

James C. Goetz

Book Design

University Graphics

Indexer

Joy Dean Lee

Production Team

Claudia Bell

Danielle Bird

Anne Dickerson

Donna Winter

Novice Reviewer

Paul J. Marchesseault

About the Author

Suzanne Weixel is the revision author of *MS-DOS 6 Quick Start* and author of *Everyday DOS*, both published by Que Corporation.

Table of Contents

Understanding Your Operating System 63

Getting Started   97

Task/Review   111

INTRODUCTION

WHY YOU NEED THIS BOOK

It's easy to be intimidated by computers. You hear words like chip and processor, and acronyms like VGA and DOS, and may decide that being computer ignorant is easier than being computer literate. However, a lot of learning about a PC is seeing the machine for what it is — a tool. A tool you can use to get ahead in your job, keep your household more organized, write letters, or just have fun.

Keep in mind that behind all the confusing lingo and inside all those thick computer manuals, you can find something worth learning.

This book shows you the magic behind the computer screen. It teaches you how to understand computers and how to take control of the great technology on your desktop.

HOW THIS BOOK IS ORGANIZED

This book is designed to give you all the information you need, without you having to flip through a large number of pages. The text is supported by clear graphics that help you visualize the content for better understanding.

The book is divided into sections that completely explore specific topics, all on a few pages. Each page is marked clearly at the top with the section's name.

You can read the book from start to finish, or you can jump around to look for the topics you need.

The last section is called Task/Review. This section provides simple, step-by-step instructions for using a computer to accomplish basic commands and everyday tasks.

WHERE TO GET MORE HELP

As you become more comfortable with a computer, you may need a more complete reference book. Que offers several books to suit your needs.

Que also offers several books on specific software programs.

Here are some of the other Easy books published by Que:

- *Easy DOS*
- *Easy Excel*
- *Easy Lotus 1-2-3*
- *Easy Windows*, 3.1 Edition
- *Easy WordPerfect*

Some of the most popular titles include the following:

- *Using 1-2-3 Release 2.4*, Special Edition
- *Using Excel 4 for Windows*, Special Edition
- *Using WordPerfect 6*, Special Edition

Here are some additional books on DOS and Windows:

- *MS-DOS 6 Quick Reference*
- *MS-DOS 6 QuickStart*
- *Using MS-DOS 6*
- *Windows 3.1 Quick Reference*
- *Windows 3.1 QuickStart*
- *Using Windows 3.1*, Special Edition

Also of interest:

- *Introduction to Personal Computers*, 4th Edition
- *Que's Computer User's Dictionary*, 3rd Edition

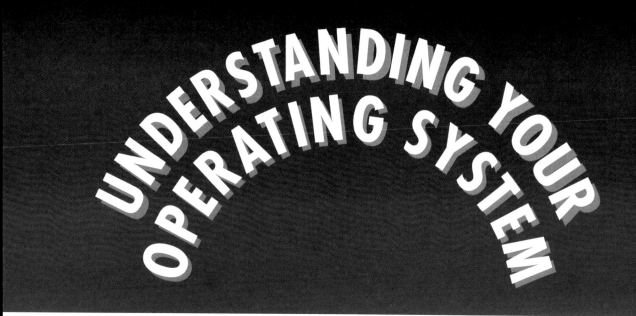

UNDERSTANDING YOUR OPERATING SYSTEM

WHAT IS A COMPUTER?

Believe it or not, a computer is just an appliance— a machine built from plastic and metal, designed to automate routine tasks. Some appliances, like toaster ovens and vacuum cleaners, relieve the tedium of everyday chores. Some appliances, like televisions and CD players, add enjoyment to everyday life. Computers do both.

Of course, a computer is a bit more complicated than a toaster oven, but that's what makes it interesting and fun. With a toaster oven, you can bake, broil, or toast. With a computer, you can organize, calculate, design, educate, schedule, illustrate, edit, communicate... the list is nearly endless!

Inside all appliances there are wires and cables and nuts and bolts that you probably will never see, let alone touch. The same is true for computers, but the more you know, the better off you are when it comes to buying new equipment or getting old equipment repaired.

WHAT IS HARDWARE?

The physical parts of the computer—the parts that you can see and touch—are called *hardware*. The keyboard, the monitor, and the box that houses the system unit are all hardware. So are the cables that connect them, the electronics that make them work, and the screws that hold them together.

Computer hardware also includes other machines that are attached to the computer, called *peripherals*. Some peripherals that you might have include printers, modems, and mice.

NOTE:

You will also hear the word *compatible* used to describe software programs and hardware devices. If one piece of the computer system is compatible with another, it means that they can work together without causing problems. If they are not compatible, chances are they won't work at all. So, software designed to run on an IBM PC cannot run on an Apple Macintosh.

Monitor

Keyboard

System Unit

Mouse

A (BRIEF) HISTORY OF PERSONAL COMPUTERS

The earliest computers were impractical. They filled entire rooms, cost a small fortune, and were incapable of performing many useful functions. Like dinosaurs—big and bulky, and not too bright—they were more suited to science fiction than to homes and businesses.

The promise was there, however, and researchers worked hard to find ways to fit more and more processing power into smaller and smaller boxes. In 1981, IBM introduced a microcomputer—a machine designed to fit on a desktop and provide information processing for one—and called it the IBM Personal Computer (PC).

The IBM PC is no longer the only microcomputer on the block. Other manufacturers make PCs that are compatible with the IBM PC. Compatible means that the computers are based on the same technology as the IBM machines, and can run the same programs. Sometimes, compatibles are called clones, because they have been built to perform the same as the IBM products.

WHAT IS SOFTWARE?

Software refers to the programs that you run on a computer. The programs are made up of coded instructions that tell the hardware how to process information. There are two types of software programs:

- System software determines how the different pieces of hardware will operate, and how the PC responds to commands. Some people like to think of the system software as the traffic cop that controls and coordinates the flow of information within the computer system. MS-DOS (which stands for disk operating system), NetWare, Windows, and OS/2 are examples of common system software programs.

- Application software lets you perform specific tasks, such as word processing and desktop publishing. Lotus 1-2-3 and Word-Perfect are two common application programs.

NOTE:

The concept of "software" can be difficult to grasp because you cannot actually see software or touch it. System software is usually installed on your computer by someone else, either before you buy the computer, or when it is attached to a network. Applications are installed using floppy disks or transferred from other computers attached to the same network.

Some manufacturers have developed personal computers that use completely different technology. These computers, such as Apple's Macintosh series, are not compatible with IBM PCs, and although they are personal computers, they are not generally referred to as PCs. That's not to say they aren't as good—just different. You have to decide which type is better for you.

All PCs require hardware and software in order to work. Hardware provides the foundation, and software provides the information. You can think of the software as the brains and the hardware as the brawn.

BASIC HARDWARE COMPONENTS

Most PCs sold today are built around the same basic hardware components:

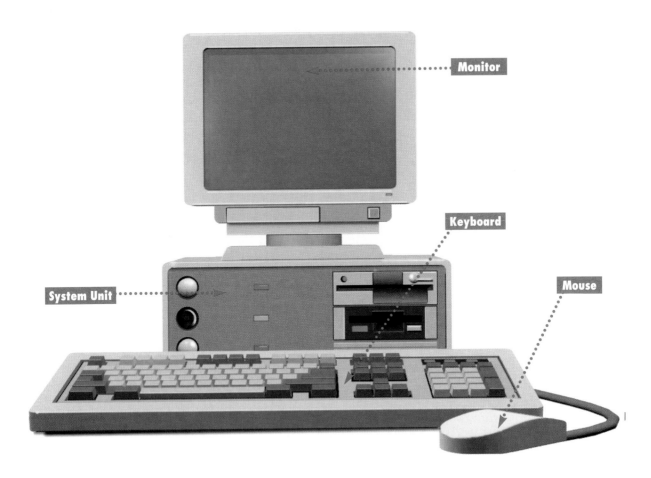

With the earliest PCs, you could get only one model — often called the "plain vanilla" model because of its lack of options. Now, advancements in technology have made it possible to package these basic components in different ways. As long as you have the basic system components, the size and shape of a PC is a matter of personal preference or necessity.

SYSTEM UNIT

The system unit is the heart of the computer. It is the box, or case, that holds the electrical components — the chips, wires, and circuits — that actually do the information processing.

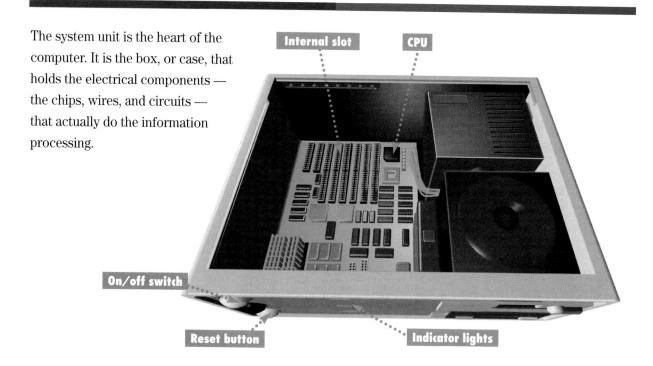

Internal slot **CPU**

On/off switch

Reset button **Indicator lights**

The computer's *on/off switch* is located on the system unit. The *main power cord* is attached to the system unit. *Indicator lights* show you which options are turned on.

Most system units also have a *reset button* so that you can restart the computer without shutting it off, and a *turbo button* that lets you switch between two different speeds.

Inside the system unit, you find the most important piece of the computer, the *central processing unit* (CPU), as well as the computer's memory.

NOTE:

Be careful that you don't press the reset button accidentally. You might damage your software programs or lose the information you have worked with.

NOTE:

You probably will never need to open the system unit. If you do, be very careful. Only a tiny amount of dirt or disruption can damage the components inside the box, but it may take a lot of time and money to repair them!

All peripherals are attached to the system unit. Some peripherals, such as internal modem cards, fit into sockets inside the box, called *slots*. Other peripherals, such as printers, are attached with cables to sockets, called *ports*, on the outside of the system unit.

For more detailed information on the system unit, see the section *More on System Units*.

THE MONITOR

The *monitor*, also called the screen or the display, shows both the information you type on the keyboard and the computer's response to this information. When you press a key on the keyboard, for example, the typed letter appears on the monitor. When you enter a command, you see the computer's response to the command.

Monitors can be *monochrome*, which means that you see one color on a background, or *color*, which means that you see a range of colors. Like a TV, most monitors have an on/off switch and knobs to control brightness and contrast. For more information, see the section *More about Monitors*.

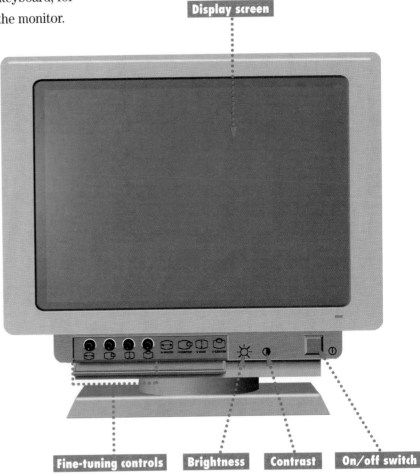

Display screen

Fine-tuning controls   Brightness   Contrast   On/off switch

THE KEYBOARD

You use the *keyboard* to input information into the computer. The keyboard has all the keys that a typewriter keyboard has, plus some keys unique to computers. For example, your keyboard probably has *special purpose keys*, such as Ctrl (Control) and Alt (Alternate) keys. With these keys, you input commands specific to the software you are using. Likewise, in most application programs, if the information you are looking at does not all fit on-screen at the same time, press the key labeled PgDn (Page Down). The monitor displays the next

screen of information. Try doing this on a typewriter!

You can choose from a wide variety of keyboard styles, depending on the PC you have or the applications you usually use. Most laptop-sized portable PC keyboards, for example, are smaller than desktop PC keyboards, but even desktop PCs can have different keyboards. For more information, see the section *More about Keyboards*.

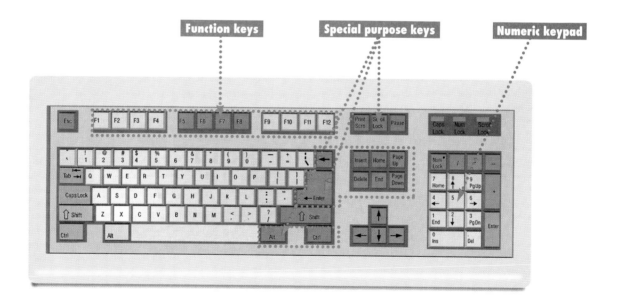

THE DISK DRIVES

Disk drives are devices that the computer uses to store information when not in use. Disk drives hold disks that the computer can write information on or read information from. Disk drives are similar to phonographs or CD players — the disk rotates inside the drive as an arm moves across the disk and a head on the end of the arm interprets electrical signals between the computer and the disk.

Floppy disk drives are usually built into the system unit. You insert and remove floppy disks via disk drive doors, which look like mail slots in the box. Floppy disks are used to install application programs, store information, and read stored information.

Hard disk drives are either built into the system unit or attached to it via cables. Because most hard disks cannot be removed, they are sometimes called *fixed disks*.

Hard disks can hold far more information than floppy disks, and they are not as easily damaged. Before hard disks were available, people spent a lot of time inserting and removing floppy disks and waiting while the computer either read the information from, or wrote information onto, the floppy. Hard disks made PCs much easier and faster to use. Most PCs sold today have at least one internal hard disk. For more information on drives, see the section *More about Storage*.

NOTE:

Most disk drives have in-use lights on the front of the system unit. When the PC is reading or writing information to a disk in that drive, the light shines. Don't turn off the computer when the in-use light is on.

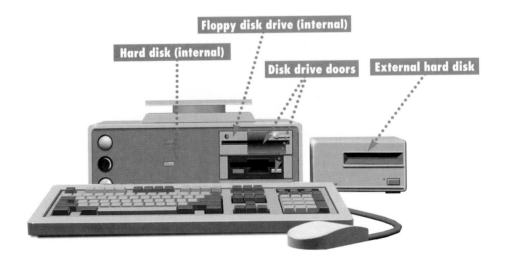

Floppy disk drive (internal)

Hard disk (internal)

Disk drive doors

External hard disk

OTHER COMPONENTS

You can use the *mouse* — a small, hand-held pointing device — instead of, or in conjunction with, a keyboard to input commands. A mouse, for example, is a useful way to select menu options in Microsoft Windows.

You use a *printer* to print copies of the computer data. After you see the information on the monitor, you can print the data for other uses. The printed material is often called *hard copy*, to differentiate it from the data stored on a disk or held in the computer's memory.

You use a *modem* to connect the computer to a telephone. You can use the modem to call other computers and to exchange information with them. For example, a modem lets you connect with an on-line service such as CompuServe. Some modems have built-in fax capabilities that let you connect with facsimile machines.

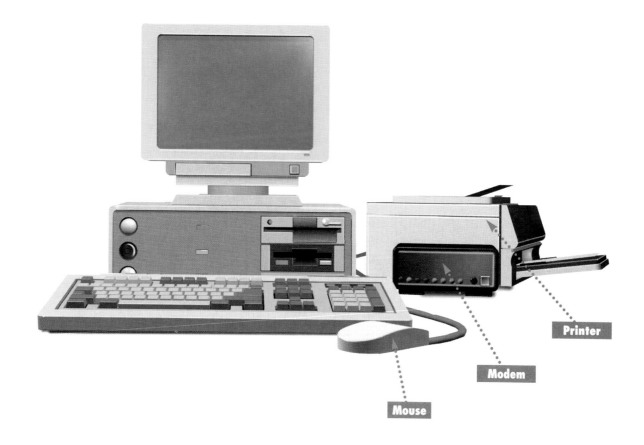

Mouse

Modem

Printer

COMPUTER STYLES

The traditional PC is called a *desktop model* because it fits nicely on most desks and is suitable for most people to use at work or at home. Some desktop models have a *small footprint* case, which means the case is designed to take up less space. Small footprint models usually stand higher than other desktop models, so that they still have room inside for the same basic components, despite the shorter length and width.

A *tower model* looks like a desktop model standing on its side. Tower PCs can stand on the floor under the desk, leaving the desktop free and providing easy access to controls such as the on/off switch, as well as to the interior components.

Tower models are larger than desktop models and have a lot of room inside for future growth. They also usually cost more than desktop models.

A *portable PC* lets you use a computer when you are away from your desk. All the basic components are built into the unit, not attached with cables. Most portables have no room for future growth, although some can be attached to external peripherals such as disk drives, and even to so-called docking units, which transform the portable into a desktop model on your desk. Portables are

Tower-style system unit

classified by weight, ranging from laptops (8 to 10 pounds) to notebooks (6 to 8 pounds) to sub-notebooks (2 to 6 pounds). Portables usually are a trade-off between convenience and ease-of-use. Because these computers are so small, the basic components also must be small.

Portable computer

- If you do most of your computing at your desk, and you don't plan to add a lot of peripherals or memory, you can buy a basic desktop PC.

- If you need to access information or draft memos while flying home from a sales call, you can buy a portable PC that fits in a briefcase.

- If you need a lot of space on your desktop, or you plan to attach lots of peripherals to the PC, you can buy a tower model.

HOW COMPUTERS WORK

Like most appliances, computers run on electricity and plug right into the outlets in your home or office, or — in the case of portables — have batteries. After a computer is plugged in and turned on, its electronic circuitry is ready to go. All it needs is your command. Using a computer requires three basic steps:

1. You enter data.

You can enter data using any input device, such as the keyboard, a mouse, or a scanner, or from files stored on disks. Some computers even recognize spoken words.

2. The computer processes the data.

The computer translates the data into electrical signals that it can process, using its memory and circuitry. The way the computer processes the signals depends on the software program you are using. Different programs contain different instructions. The computer interprets the instructions and performs the required task. For example, a word processing program contains instructions for which key controls inserting or overwriting text. A spreadsheet program contains instructions for performing calculations.

3. The computer outputs the result as new data.

The electrical signals are then sent to an output device, which translates the signals back into a data format that you can understand. The data, for example, may appear on the display screen, print on a printer, or be saved on a disk for storage. Sometimes output is simply held in the computer's memory until you need it.

NOTE:

Data is any kind of information you can imagine. Most commonly, we use PCs to process data in the form of words, numbers, or pictures.

MORE ABOUT THE *SYSTEM UNIT*

The *system unit* is the box that contains the electronic components that make the computer work. System units generally contain power supplies, one or more disk drives, and circuit cards that control the system peripherals.

If you take the top off a basic desktop PC system unit, you see some of the following things:

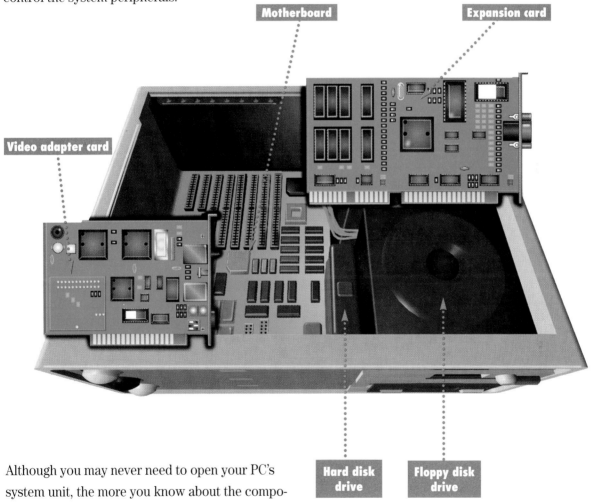

Motherboard

Expansion card

Video adapter card

Hard disk drive

Floppy disk drive

Although you may never need to open your PC's system unit, the more you know about the components in it, the better off you are when buying new equipment or getting old equipment repaired.

THE MOTHERBOARD

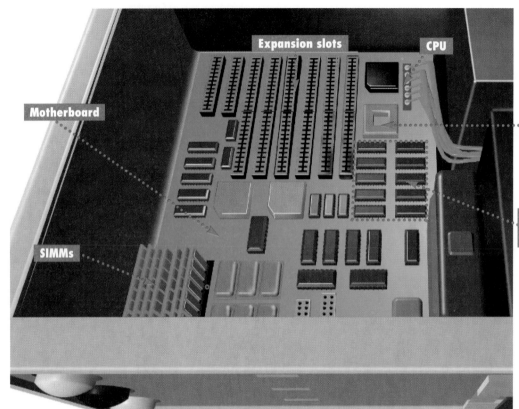

Expansion slots

CPU

Motherboard

Math coprocessor
chip slot

Computer chips
(integrated circuits)

SIMMs

The system unit is the heart of the computer. It is the box, or case, that holds the electrical components — the chips, wires, and circuits — that actually do the information processing.

The *motherboard* is the main circuit board in the system unit. The most important electronic components, such as the central processing unit (CPU) and the RAM, are attached to the motherboard.

The *CPU*, or "computer brain," is the electronic circuit that performs the actual computing. The

CPU is part of the computer's *microprocessor* — a chip installed on the motherboard that controls every computer instruction performed by the PC. When you press keys on the keyboard, the CPU interprets the keystrokes and takes the appropriate action — for example, the CPU might display on-screen the character that you typed, enter a command, or restart the computer. Sometimes, the terms CPU and microprocessor are used interchangeably.

The motherboard also has sockets, called *expansion slots*, where you can plug in additional circuit boards, called *expansion cards*. For example, most system units have a disk controller card and a video adapter card. The number of expansion slots depends on the size of the system unit. Your system may have an internal modem card, an internal fax card, or a sound board.

The motherboard usually has slots where you can plug in memory expansion cards, called *SIMMs* (Single Inline Memory Modules), and a slot for a *math coprocessor* chip, an electronic circuit which helps programs that use a lot of graphics or math equations run faster.

RAM stands for *random-access memory*. RAM is the electronic memory where the computer can store information until it is needed or stored on a disk. RAM is not permanent; when the computer is turned off, all information stored in RAM is lost.

Chips are the tiny integrated circuits that control computer functions. The microprocessor is a chip. The math coprocessor is a chip. Memory is contained on chips. Chips are built into circuit boards, or can be plugged into expansion slots on the circuit boards.

THE POWER SUPPLY

The *power supply* converts the AC electricity from the outlet in your home or office to the DC electricity the PC uses. The computer's on/off switch is connected to the power supply. Like lightbulbs, the capacity of a power supply is measured in watts. 200 watts is just about right for the average PC, although some may need only 150 watts, and some may need up to 350 watts. A fan keeps the power supply and other components in the system unit from overheating.

Because most PCs plug into a standard electrical outlet, they are affected by changes in the electrical current. It is a good idea to plug the PC into a surge suppressor instead of plugging directly into the wall outlet. Power protection is discussed in greater detail in the section *Caring for Your Computer*.

NOTE:

Some PCs, notably portables, run on internal batteries. Two types of batteries are used: Nickel Cadmium (often abbreviated Ni-Cad) and Metal Hydride. Metal Hydride batteries are newer, and usually are more reliable and easier to recharge. Of course, Metal Hydride batteries cost more than Ni-Cads.

MICROPROCESSORS

Microprocessors, the chips that control the computer, are identified with numbers. Usually, the chips with the higher numbers are newer and more powerful. The more powerful the chip, the faster the computer will process information, which means that software programs will run better. Of course, the newer, more powerful chips also cost more. It is a good idea to buy a PC with the most powerful microprocessor you can afford. Chip technology evolves quickly, and even the second most powerful microprocessor can soon be obsolete.

If you think your processing needs are going to grow, you should examine the possibility of purchasing a PC that can be upgraded.

DECODING THE CHIP NUMBER	Processor type	Usage
	8086 and 8088	The first PCs ran on these CPUs.
	80286	Still running a vast number of installed PCs, IBM based its AT-class PCs on the 80286.
	80386	PCs manufactured today have at least an 80386 CPU.
	80486	Currently, PCs based on the 80486 are considered the standard.
	80586	The newest generation of microprocessors more than doubles the performance of the fastest 80486 microprocessors. Computers built around the 80586 are not generally available yet. Intel Corporation is marketing its 80586 by the name Pentium.

WHAT ARE SX, DX, AND SO ON?

Microprocessors also are differentiated by type, or version. The different versions are suitable for different uses, because they may process information in a certain way or they may have more built-in features. The letters that designate the chip type help describe the applications for which the chip should be used.

SX SX chips usually run slower than DX chips. For example, 386SX chips use a 16-wire bus instead of a 32-wire bus. SX chips usually are less expensive, so they are better suited to casual or home use.

DX DX chips usually process information faster than SX chips. 386DX chips use a 32-wire bus, which is more efficient than a 16-wire bus. 486 DX chips have a built-in math coprocessor for enhancing the performance of scientific or spreadsheet calculations. DX chips are suitable for most business uses.

Other chip designations include DX2 and SL. SL chips, which are designed to conserve power consumption, usually are used in portable PCs, and DX2 chips usually are used for heavy-duty information processing.

NOTE:

Newer chips usually are downwardly compatible with the older chips, which means that you can run software programs written to run on computers with the older chips on newer computers with the newer chips. The older chips, however, may not be upwardly compatible, or able to run programs written for the newer chips.

A WORD ABOUT SPEED

Computer speed refers to how fast the CPU can process information — or turn input into output. Each microprocessor contains a clock. The faster the clock ticks, the faster the computer functions are processed. Microprocessor speeds are measured in megahertz (MHz).

CPUs can run at different speeds. An 80486 microprocessor, for example, may run at 25 MHz, 33 MHz, or 66 MHz. Because newer chips are designed to outperform earlier models, they can run at slower speeds than older chips, and still process information at a faster rate, which means that an 80486 running at 25 MHz processes information faster than an 80386 running at 33 MHz.

How fast a computer processes information depends on the microprocessor, the clock speed, and the amount of available memory. Sometimes, the difference in speed is barely noticeable, but most software programs run better on a PC with a faster processor and a faster clock speed. If you try to run Windows on a PC with a 286 processor, you will spend a lot of time waiting for a task to be accomplished. When you run Windows on a PC with a 486DX, however, programs move smoothly.

NOTE:

Some programs run faster if your computer has a math coprocessor chip installed on the motherboard. Math coprocessors are designed specifically to boost the performance of the CPU when it is processing calculations for graphics and scientific software programs.

Here are some things to keep in mind when selecting a microprocessor:

- What kinds of software will you run? Some software programs, such as Windows, run better on a faster processor.

- Will you do a lot of number crunching? Scientific and mathematical calculations require a math coprocessor to run efficiently.

- How much can you afford? Even if you don't think you need the most powerful chip available today, you should buy the most advanced computer that you can afford. Developments in technology quickly make older, slower chips obsolete.

TIP:

If you think your processing needs are going to increase, or you just want to be ready to take advantage of improvements in technology, you should consider buying a PC that can be upgraded to a new microprocessor.

ABOUT MEMORY

Memory is the electronic circuitry where the PC stores information that it is not currently using. There are two types of memory: RAM and ROM.

RAM stands for *random-access memory*, which is memory that is constantly being written, erased, and written again, like a blackboard.

ROM stands for *read-only memory*, which is memory that you cannot erase or write on.

ROM provides the instructions a computer needs to get started each time you turn it on.

PCs come with different amounts of RAM, and you can add more RAM if needed. For practical purposes, the only kind of memory you need to be concerned with is RAM. ROM is determined by the hardware manufacturer. You cannot increase the existing amount of ROM.

WHY RAM IS IMPORTANT

RAM is contained on memory chips installed on the motherboard. For most applications, the more RAM you have installed, the faster your PC can process information, because it has room in memory to hold a lot of working information at any one time. The faster the PC processes information, the better the software operates. The PC does not waste time reading and writing data to and from a disk.

When you type data for a document in a word processing program, for example, the PC holds this information in RAM. When you enter the command to save the document, the PC copies the document data from RAM onto a disk.

If you continue adding information to the document until it is so large it cannot all fit into RAM at once, the PC has to leave some information on-disk. You have to wait while the PC swaps data from the disk to memory, and vice versa.

Different programs require different amounts of memory in order to run correctly. Check the software package or the documentation to find out how much memory a program needs before you buy it. Microsoft, for example, recommends that to run Windows 3.1 on an 80286-based PC, you should have a minimum of 640K of conventional memory and 256K of extended memory. On an 80386-based PC, you should have a minimum of 640K of conventional memory and 1024K (or 1M) of extended memory.

NOTE:

As you will see, there are many different ways to classify RAM. Don't let it confuse you! The most important thing to remember is that the amount of available memory directly affects the way your software programs perform. When memory is available, your PC can swap information faster, so programs run faster. You spend less time waiting and more time working!

SAVE YOUR WORK!

Data stored in the computer's memory is always at risk. To permanently save information, you need a hardware storage device. That's where disk drives are important. When you save your data to disk, it is copied out of memory. Even if the data is lost from RAM, you can recall it from disk.

CAUTION:

RAM is not permanent! All data currently stored in RAM is lost when:

- You shut off your PC.
- You reset your PC.
- You close the current application program.
- You lose power.

MEASURING MEMORY

Memory (and storage space) is measured in bytes. Each *byte* is roughly the equivalent of one character you might type on a keyboard. A *kilobyte* (K) equals a thousand characters. A *megabyte* (M) equals a million characters. A *gigabyte* (G) equals a billion characters.

Measurements in bytes are rounded off to make keeping track of memory and storage space easier. When someone says his computer has 1M of

memory, for example, it is not exactly the same as saying it has 1,000,000 bytes of memory. A computer with 1M of memory actually has 1,048,576 bytes.

TIP:

You can upgrade memory in your PC by plugging memory chips or SIMM boards into the motherboard. If the motherboard has no memory slots, you can plug a memory expansion card into an open expansion slot. By adding memory, you might be able to run more software programs, or run the ones you have faster, because the PC won't spend time swapping data to and from the disks.

HOW PCs USE MEMORY

No matter which processor you have — or how much memory there is in your PC — all information is processed in the first 640K. That's the way software instructions are currently designed.

However, many programs have too many instructions to fit into 640K at one time. Waiting for the instructions to be swapped back and forth from a disk is not practical, so computer technicians figured out how to let your PC use memory over the 640K limit for temporarily storing information. When the information is needed, the PC can swap it down into the 640K where processing takes

place, and move other, unneeded information into the higher, available memory.

However, adding memory is not the only answer to boosting performance. The way a PC uses memory also depends on the type of microprocessor in the PC and the software program (or programs) the PC is running.

Processor	Use of Memory	Typical Memory Configuration
8088	Can access up to 640K of RAM	512K to 640K of RAM installed
80286	Can access up to 16M of RAM	640K to 1M of RAM installed
80386 and 80486	Can access up to 4G of RAM	4M to 32M of RAM installed

TYPES OF MEMORY

To help you understand how PCs and software programs use memory, RAM is classified in three categories:

- Conventional memory
- Upper memory
- Extended or high memory

Conventional memory is the first 640K of RAM. All PCs use conventional memory for running the operating system and application programs, and for storing data. The less conventional memory that is available for processing, the slower programs will run. For instance, if the operating system is using a percentage of available conventional memory, applications programs will run slower because more of the instructions must be stored on disk. Today, most PCs have the maximum 640K of conventional memory installed, but they can have less.

Upper memory is all the memory between conventional memory and 1024K (1M). PCs based on an 80286 or higher microprocessor can use upper memory for temporarily storing information. The operating system and some memory resident

utilities, for instance, can be moved into upper memory, freeing conventional memory for running applications.

Extended (or high) memory is all memory over 1M. It is called *extended memory* because it extends the amount of memory available to the PC. Currently, some PCs can use up to 4G of memory, although 16M or 32M is more common.

MORE TYPES OF MEMORY

The preceding section defines the amount of RAM installed on your PC according to the order in which it is used (first 640K, 640K to 1M, over 1M). The performace of some PC hardware and software may be improved by making memory available in other ways:

- *Expanded* memory is a combination of hardware and software that lets PCs based on the 8088 microprocessor access memory over the 640K conventional memory limit, up to 32M. It tricks the PC into thinking that extended (or high) memory is really conventional memory. You can add expanded memory hardware and software to any PC built around any microprocessor. Some software programs, such as the R2.X versions of Lotus 1-2-3, use expanded memory instead of extended memory.

- *Cache* memory is made up of additional memory chips that are built right into the CPU, or added externally to the CPU. Cache memory can boost the PC's processing speed because it

makes commonly used instructions available to the CPU at all times. You do not have to wait while the CPU swaps information in and out of RAM. How much cache memory will improve your PC's performance depends mostly on the type of applications you are running. All programs will benefit somewhat, but large, complex programs will benefit the most. 80486 processors generally come with at least 8K of built-in cache memory. If you plan to run large spreadsheets or relational database programs, you may want to consider 16K or 32K of cache.

- *Video* memory is made up of additional memory chips that are built right into the video display adapter card that controls your monitor. The amount of video memory determines how many colors can be displayed, and how fast images will appear. If you plan to run applications that display graphics, you should purchase a video adapter card that comes with built-in memory, or that has room for memory to be added.

FIGURING OUT HOW MUCH MEMORY YOU HAVE

To find out how much memory your computer has, do one of the following:

● Watch the monitor when you start up. As the PC checks the memory, it displays the number of bytes installed.

● Use the operating system's MEM command. It displays a chart of all types of memory installed, used, and available.

```
C:\>MEM

Memory Type       Total = Used  + Free
----------------  ------  ------  ------
Conventional       640K    119K    521K
Upper              155K     27K    128K
Adapter RAM/ROM    384K    384K      0K
Extended (XMS)    2917K   1241K   1676K
----------------  ------  ------  ------
Total memory      4096K   1770K   2326K

Total under 1 MB   795K    145K    650K

Largest executable program size    521K   (533696 bytes)
Largest free upper memory block    128K   (131248 bytes)
MS-DOS is resident in the high memory area.

C:\>
```

● Use the operating system's CHKDSK command. It displays information about the current disk, including the amount of conventional memory installed and available.

```
C:\>CHKDSK

Volume MS-DOS_6    created 06-05-1993 2:16p
Volume Serial Number is 1AC5-73E4

  85018624 bytes total disk space
  12648448 bytes in 3 hidden files
     40960 bytes in 16 directories
  22159360 bytes in 643 user files
  50169856 bytes available on disk

      2048 bytes in each allocation unit
     41513 total allocation units on disk
     24497 available allocation units on disk

    655360 total bytes memory
    533824 bytes free

C:\>
```

ABOUT EXPANSION

Expandability is the amount of room available in a computer for adding peripherals or memory.

Most people want to buy computers that have a lot of expandability because, chances are, you will need more computing power in the future than you need now. Because predicting how much computing power you will need, or even what kind of computing power will be available, is hard, you can hedge your bets by purchasing a computer that has room for expansion.

Sound board

FAX/modem card

For example, you can attach internal modems, fax boards, sound boards, and network controllers. Also, as new technologies become available, you may be able to add them to your computer, rather than purchasing a new computer.

EXPANDING YOUR COMPUTER?

The expandability of a system unit depends on three things:

- The number and type of internal expansion slots.

- The number and type of external ports.

- The number of available RAM and VRAM expansion SIMM slots.

EXPANSION SLOTS AND EXPANSION CARDS

Expansion slots are sockets on the motherboard where you can attach expansion cards. *Expansion cards* are circuit boards that contain the electronics that control peripherals or add memory. The words *board* and *card* are used interchangeably.

Some slots hold cards that control the basic system components, such as the video adapter card for the monitor and the disk controller card for the disk drives. These slots are not available for other cards.

Depending on the size of your system unit, however, there may be slots left open, even after the basic controller cards are installed. These open slots are the key to your computer's expandability.

Disk drive
controller card

Video adapter
card

WHAT IS A BUS?

Expansion slots are sometimes called the expansion bus. An *expansion bus* is a set of wires or conductors over which the microprocessor sends data. There are different types of buses, and so there are different types of expansion bus slots. When you buy an expansion card, make sure the card is compatible with the type of expansion bus in your computer. To discover what kind of bus you have, check the original packing slip that came with your PC. It should list which bus you have. If it doesn't, contact your dealer.

Expansion buses and expansion cards are characterized by size and speed, which are determined by the number of wires used to connect the PC's electrical components. The more wires in a bus, the faster the bus can transfer data. Cards and slots come in different sizes, as well. Full-size cards fit in full-size slots; half-size cards fit in half-size slots.

ISA (*Industry Standard Architecture*) slots transfer data at speeds up to 16M per second. ISA is the most common PC bus. ISA expansion slots come in two sizes. Full-size, or long slots, and half-height, or short slots.

EISA (*Enhanced Industry Standard Architecture*) slots transfer data at speeds up to 32M per second. ISA cards can fit in EISA expansion slots, but they do not provide the EISA speed or features.

MCA (*Micro Channel Architecture*) slots transfer data at speeds up to 40M per second. Neither ISA nor EISA cards can fit into MCA slots.

EXPANSION PORTS

Ports are electrical sockets on the outside of the system unit that are connected to expansion cards on the inside of the system unit. You use cables to plug peripheral devices into ports. Inside the system unit, an expansion card, such as the card that controls the video display, also is connected to the port. This way, peripherals and the PC can communicate.

Most PCs come with at least one parallel port, one serial port, one game port, and one video adapter port. Some PCs come with more than this number of ports.

You cannot attach peripherals to just any port that happens to be available. For example, your monitor attaches to the video adapter port. You cannot plug a printer into the video adapter port. Even if the plug fits (it won't), the printer won't work. The port on the system unit and the plug on the peripheral's cable must be compatible, which means both the size and type must match.

NOTE:

One way to tell with which port the plug works is by counting the number of connectors, or pins, it has. Look on the system unit for a port that corresponds in size to the plug on the cable. Also, look to see if the pins stick out or in. Ports with pins sticking out are called male, and ports that have sockets are called female. Connections are always between males and females. You cannot plug a male cable into a male port, or a female cable into a female port. So, if the pins on the plug stick out, the pins on the port must stick in, and vice versa.

Port type	Usage
Parallel	Parallel ports send all data synchronously, one character at a time through eight separate wires in a cable. Parallel ports usually are designated LPT (an abbreviation for line printer). If the computer has one parallel port, it is called LPT1; a second parallel port is called LPT2; and so on. Parallel ports are used primarily for attaching printers. They only transmit data efficiently up to 15 feet.
Serial	Serial ports send data through one wire. These ports transfer data more slowly than parallel ports, but more effectively over long distances. Some serial ports have 9-pin connectors; some have 25-pin connectors. Serial ports are sometimes called RS-232 ports and usually are designated COM (short for communications). If your computer has one serial port, it is called COM1; a second serial port is called COM2; and so on. Serial ports are commonly used for attaching serial printers, modems, and mice.
Video Adapter	Video Adapter ports are used for attaching monitors to the video adapter card inside the system unit. Video adapter ports are designed for a specific type of video display adapter card. Some ports have 9-pin connectors and some have 15-pin connectors. The plug from a monitor must be compatible with the type of video adapter card you have.
SCSI	SCSI ports let you transfer data at high speeds. SCSI ports are used to attach SCSI-compatible devices such as external hard disks, tape backup units, or CD-ROM drives. You can attach up to eight SCSI devices to one SCSI port. SCSI ports are not as common as the other port types, partly because SCSI devices usually are expensive.
Game	Game ports are used for attaching a joystick device to the system unit. Joysticks are commonly used for playing games.

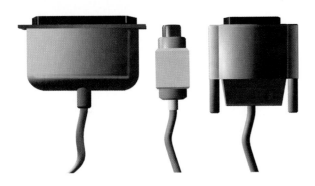

Examples of plugs and expansion ports commonly found on most PCs are shown here.

MORE ABOUT STORAGE

If computers could keep data only in RAM, they would not be much use. When you shut off the PC or changed applications, all the current data would be erased. You would quickly decide that returning to a pencil and paper was easier — and safer!

Storage devices enable you to store programs and data for future use. When you enter the correct command, the PC writes the data it has in memory onto the storage device. The data stays there until you enter the command to read it back into memory, overwrite it, or erase it.

The most common type of storage device is a magnetic disk, either hard or floppy, as shown on the following page.

Most PCs come with at least one hard disk drive and one floppy disk drive. A standard configuration, for example, includes one 3 ½-inch floppy drive and one hard disk drive. PCs can contain more than one disk drive and more than one disk drive type. Your PC, for example, might have one hard drive, one 5 ¼-inch floppy drive, and one 3 ½-inch floppy drive. Your co-worker's PC might have one hard drive and two 5 ¼-inch floppy drives. There are many possibilities.

Disk drives usually are installed inside the system unit, although some are attached externally with cables.

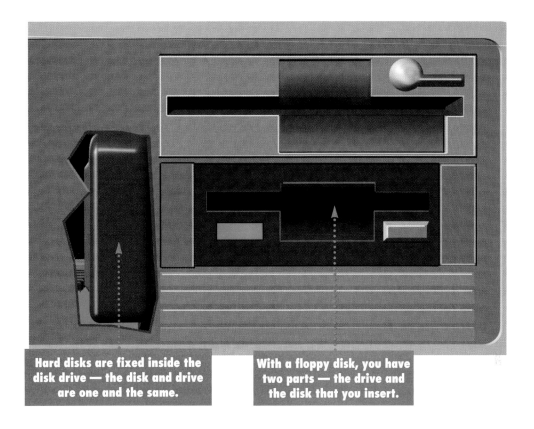

Hard disks are fixed inside the disk drive — the disk and drive are one and the same.

With a floppy disk, you have two parts — the drive and the disk that you insert.

HOW DRIVES WORK

Hard disks and floppy disks work in a similar manner. Each disk is coated with a magnetic material. Inside the drive, heads move across the rotating disk, reading and writing magnetic data.

Before you can use a disk, it must be formatted. *Formatting* divides disks into tracks and sectors so that the drive can locate data for reading and writing. Formatting is kind of like painting lines in a parking lot. Hard disks should be formatted before you buy your PC. Floppy disks can be purchased formatted, or you can format them before you use them.

Tracks

Sectors

A formatted disk is divided into circular *tracks* and wedge-shaped *sectors*. When you save data, it is copied on the disk into a particular track and sector. The location is recorded on the disk as well. When you recall the data you need, the drive references the correct track and sector. In a parking garage, for example, you find your car by remembering the floor level and section, maybe Blue E. On a disk, the drive finds your file by remembering the track and sector.

HOW MUCH YOU CAN STORE

The amount of data you can store on a disk is *storage capacity*. Capacity, like memory, is measured in bytes. Hard disks hold from 20M to more than 200M. Floppy disks hold from 360K to 2.88M. (See the section *More about Floppy Disks* for more information about floppy disk sizes and capacities.)

Remember that 1 byte equals about 1 character. So, assuming that you can fit 1,000 typed characters on a page, each 1K of storage space can hold about 1 page of information, which means that an 80M hard drive can hold about 80,000 pages!

CAUTION:

To safeguard information on the computer, you should make a backup copy of the information. Hard disks are mechanical and can fail, plus users sometimes make mistakes and delete or destroy information accidentally. Floppy disks also can fail. For this reason, make a backup. You might choose to back up just your important files, all files, all programs and files, or any other data items. For more information about backups, see the section *Caring for Your Computer*.

DRIVE NAMES

No matter how many drives your PC has, or which type, they follow the same naming scheme. Drives are identified by letters of the alphabet. The first floppy drive is drive A; if you have a second floppy drive, it is drive B; the first hard drive is drive C; and so on.

NOTE:

Even if you don't have a second floppy drive (B), the first hard drive is always called drive C.

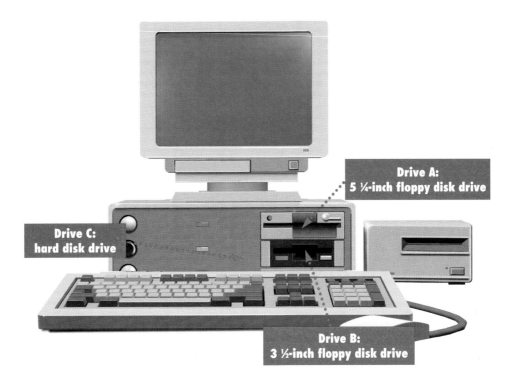

Drive A:
5 ¼-inch floppy disk drive

Drive C:
hard disk drive

Drive B:
3 ½-inch floppy disk drive

MORE ABOUT HARD DRIVES

Hard disks can hold more information than floppy disks. Each hard disk drive contains many disks, or *platters*, all of which are used to store data. Hard disks also are less easily damaged than floppies because they are fixed inside the drive, and therefore are less susceptible to heat, dirt, and other external conditions.

Most PC hard drives are based on the IDE standard. IDE drive controllers attach to an IDE connector built directly into most motherboards, eliminating the need for an expansion card or special software. Each IDE controller can support

up to two hard drives, which is more than enough for most home and business applications.

Some PC hard drives are based on the SCSI standard. In order to use a SCSI drive, the PC must be equipped with a SCSI controller. Installing a SCSI controller requires an expansion card and special software drivers. However, SCSI controllers can be used to operate up to seven peripherals, including tape backup units and CD-ROM drives. SCSI devices are, generally, significantly more expensive than IDE devices, but they offer more power.

Hard disks are differentiated primarily by capacity. The amount of storage space is the most important factor to consider when you are buying a hard disk drive. A good rule of thumb is to buy a hard drive that can hold at least twice as much as you think you need. Chances are your storage requirements are going to increase, not decrease!

Here are some things to keep in mind when you use a hard drive:

- Avoid bumping or moving your computer when the disk drive in-use light is on. Hard disks can be damaged if the read and write heads in the drive touch the disk.

- Lock your computer to prevent unauthorized use of the information stored on your hard disk.

- Back up the data from your hard disk to floppy disks or to tape. If something happens to your hard disk, at least your data will be safe.

- Don't try to format a hard disk yourself unless you are very confident about your computer skills. Take it to a professional computer technician.

The speed with which a disk drive can find information stored on disk is called *average access time*. Average access time is measured in milliseconds (ms). One millisecond equals 1/1000 of a second. Most hard drives have average access times between 15ms and 20ms.

TIP:

You can speed up a hard drive's average access time by using a disk cache program. A disk cache program is software that tells the PC to keep a portion of RAM available so that data from the hard disk can be stored until the CPU needs it. That way, the CPU doesn't have to wait for the drive to find the data from the hard disk. MS-DOS and Windows both come with disk cache programs.

MORE ABOUT FLOPPY DISKS

Floppy disks, also called diskettes or floppies, can be confusing. First, they come in two sizes — 5 ¼ inch and 3 ½ inch. Disk drives are designed for one size or the other — you cannot put a 5 ¼-inch disk into a 3 ½-inch disk drive, or vice versa. Telling a 5 ¼-inch disk or drive from a 3 ½-inch disk or drive is easy — the 5 ¼-inch disk and the 5 ¼-inch drive are bigger.

However, each size of disk comes in two densities — double density and high density — and in varying capacities. High-density drives can format, read, and write double-density disks, but double-density drives cannot format, read, or write high-density disks. You cannot tell what the density of a disk is just by looking at it — you must check the label.

NOTE:

When you buy disks, read the box carefully to make sure that you are buying disks that you can use with your PC!

CAUTION:

If you use a double-density disk in a high-density drive, the risk of losing data doubles. Make sure that the disks you buy are the correct ones for your PC!

COMMON DISK TYPES AND CAPACITIES:	Disk Type	Capacity
	5 ¼-inch	
	Double-density (DD)	360K
	High-density (HD)	1.2M
	3 ½-inch	
	Double-density (DD)	720K
	High-density (HD)	1.44M or 2.88M

PARTS OF A FLOPPY

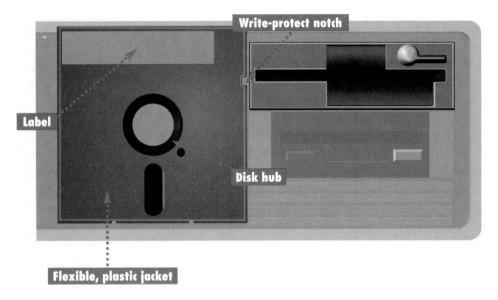

Write-protect notch

Label

Disk hub

Flexible, plastic jacket

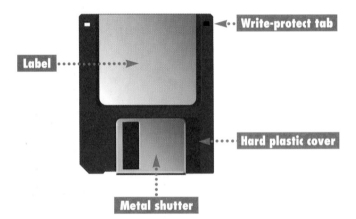

Write-protect tab

Label

Hard plastic cover

Metal shutter

5 ¼-inch disks are truly *floppy* — the magnetic disk is sealed inside a flexible, plastic jacket.

3 ½-inch disks are sturdier than 5 ¼-inch disks and are not as flexible because they are encased in a sturdy plastic-and-metal cover. This cover helps to protect 3 ½-inch disks from dirt and everyday handling. When the disk is in the drive, the metal shutter slides to the side so that the drive can access the disk. The drive uses the disk spindle to spin the disk.

TIPS ON FLOPPY DISK CARE

• The 5 ¼-inch disk can be bent, torn, or ripped if you are not careful. Do not touch the areas, such as the disk hub, where the disk is not covered by the protective jacket!

• Keep disks away from heat and dirt and do not store them too close to magnetic sources (including the PC if it has a hard drive in it!). Paper clips also can become magnetized if you have a magnetic paper clip holder.

• Attach your own label to each disk so that you always know what is stored on it. Use a felt-tip pen to record information such as the date, the file and program names, and whether the disk is formatted or not.

WRITE-PROTECTING DATA

You can protect the data on a 5 ¼-inch disk from being erased or overwritten, by covering the notch with a *write-protection* sticker.

3 ½-inch disks have a built-in write-protect tab located at the top right corner. When the tab is in the protected position, a small window is open. When the tab is in the not protected position, the window is closed. Use a finger to slide the tab back and forth.

If you try to write or save data to a disk that has been write-protected, this message appears on-screen:

```
Write protect error writing devicename
Abort, Retry, Fail?
```

Remove the disk and make sure that it is the one you want. If it is, remove any write-protection, reinsert the disk, and press R. Otherwise, use a different disk.

INSERTING DISKS

When you insert a 5 ¼-inch disk in the disk drive, be careful that it doesn't bend. Hold the disk with the label toward you, facing up. Slide it all the way in, then close the drive door. To remove the disk, open the drive door and slide the disk out.

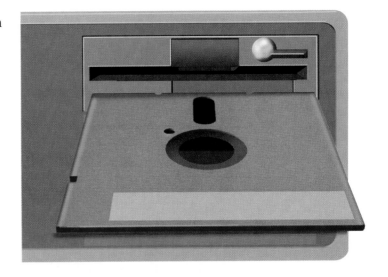

Insert 3 ½-inch disks into the disk drive, metal shutter first, with the label facing up. 3 ½-inch drives do not have drive doors. Slide the disk in all the way, until you hear a click, and the disk removal button pops out. To remove the disk, press the disk removal button in so that the disk slides easily out of the drive.

CAUTION:

A disk should slide easily into the drive. If it doesn't, don't force it! Make sure that you are holding the disk the right way, and that another disk isn't already in the drive. Also, never try to insert or remove a disk if the drive in-use light is on.

DECODING A DISKETTE BOX

When you purchase diskettes, make sure you buy the disks that are compatible with your disk drive. Remember to check:

- Size
- Number of sides
- Density
- Formatted or unformatted

Sometimes, manufacturers use codes or abbreviations on the diskette box. Read the box carefully, using the following chart as a guide:

On the box	What it means
DD	Double-density.
HD	High-density.
2 or DS	Double-sided.
1 or SS	Single-sided.
Pre-formatted IBM	The disks have been formatted for use with IBM-compatible PCs.
Pre-formatted Apple	The disks have been formatted for use with personal computers manufactured by Apple.
Mini-floppy	For use in 5 ¼-inch drives.
Micro-floppy	For use in 3 ½-inch drives.

OTHER TYPES OF STORAGE DEVICES

PCs can store and access data on storage devices other than magnetic disks. Two other storage devices — sometimes called storage media — are tape and CD-ROM.

TAPE BACKUP UNITS

You can use *tape backup units* to store a lot of data quickly and easily. You can remove the tapes and put them in a safe place, so that if something happens to your disks, you still have all your data.

You can attach tape backup units internally, inside the system unit, to an existing floppy disk drive controller card or to an expansion card. External units are connected by cables to a port on the system unit. External backup units look much like external hard disk drives.

Tape backup units come in different sizes — depending on the size of the actual tape cartridge — and in different capacities. Units that conform to the quarter-inch cartridge standards (QIC-40 or QIC-80) generally are appropriate for use with PCs.

The tape cartridges look like cassette tapes. Like disks, they must be formatted before they can hold data. You can buy tapes pre-formatted.

NOTE:

Most tape backup units are designed for backup purposes. Unlike disk drives, you cannot easily access information stored on a tape.

Tape drive

CD-ROM DRIVES

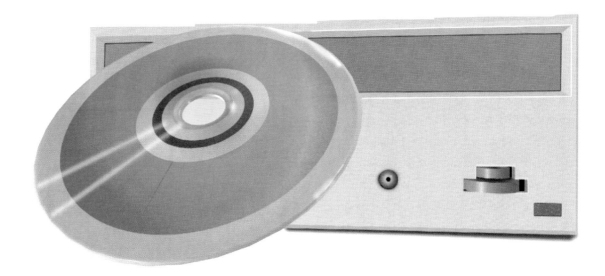

CD-ROM stands for Compact Disk-Read Only Memory. CD-ROM drives let you access large amounts of data stored on 5 ¼-inch platters, called *CD-ROMs*. One CD-ROM can hold up to 650M of data, which is much more than a typical hard disk can hold.

PCs can access the data on CD-ROMs, but cannot write anything on them, which means that you cannot use a CD-ROM drive for backing up or storing your own files on CD-ROMs.

CD-ROM drives can be installed internally or externally.

Because CD-ROMs can hold so much data, they usually are used to store large amounts of text, such as encyclopedias, telephone books, magazines, and periodicals. CD-ROMs also can be used for multimedia applications, which means that they can store and play back information in forms other than simple text. A CD-ROM, for example, can hold audio (such as music), animation, and computer-generated graphics. A CD-ROM drive and your PC must have special hardware and software to run multimedia applications.

Some reasons why you might want to purchase a CD-ROM drive with your PC include:

- The ability to run multimedia applications.

- The ability to access large amounts of information from one source.

- The future potential for more applications — CD-ROM technology is expanding at a rapid pace.

MORE ABOUT KEYBOARDS

Before you can store data, or even process data, you must input data. The most common method of inputting is with the keyboard.

PC keyboards take their basic design straight from the familiar QWERTY typewriter layout — you will recognize the letter, number, and punctuation keys. The resemblance to a typewriter, however, is only skin deep. The PC keyboard is easier and more forgiving to use than a typewriter. Don't be put off just because it has many more keys!

NOTE:

Regular touch keyboards click when you press a key. *Soft touch* keyboards press down more easily and make very little noise. You should test both kinds before you decide which feels right for you.

The *typewriter keys* let you type letters and numbers. When you press a key, you see the character on your monitor. The Tab, Caps Lock, and Shift keys, and the space bar perform the same functions as on a typewriter. (When you press the Caps Lock key, a status light is on, indicating that all keystrokes appear in uppercase until you press the Caps Lock key again.) The Del key (delete) and the Backspace key (sometimes indicated by a small, left-pointing arrow) are special function keys that let you erase mistakes.

The *function keys* are labeled with the letter F and a number, such as F1. Some keyboards have ten function keys; some keyboards have more. The function keys perform different tasks, depending

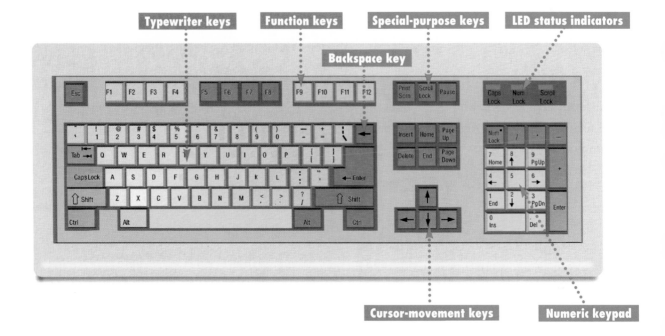

Typewriter keys   Function keys   Special-purpose keys   LED status indicators

Backspace key

Cursor-movement keys   Numeric keypad

on the software program you are using. In many programs, including Windows 3.1 and Word 5.5, you can press the F1 function key to display a help screen.

The *cursor-movement keys* are used to move around a document or file displayed on the monitor. The arrow keys move the cursor up, down, left, or right. The PgUp (Page Up) and PgDn (Page Down) keys move, or scroll, the cursor one page at a time. Depending on the software program you

are using, the Home and End keys respectively may move you to the top and bottom of the page, or to the beginning and end of the current line. The Ins (Insert) key changes back and forth between overwriting and inserting text.

The keys on the numeric keypad have two uses: the number keys each correspond to a cursor-movement key, but, if the Num Lock status light is on, they let you type the numbers. People accustomed to calculators or adding machines find it easier to enter numbers using the numeric keypad rather than the number keys at the top of the typewriter keyboard. To turn the Num Lock light on or off, press the Num Lock key.

Standard 101-key enhanced keyboard

84-key enhanced keyboard

DIFFERENCES IN KEYBOARDS

Not all keyboards look the same or have the same keys. The 101-key extended keyboard is the most common for desktop PCs, but you may have a different version.

The 84-key enhanced keyboard was introduced with AT-model PCs.

Keyboards designed for portable computers must fit in a small package. Some use different layouts, and some have fewer keys. Most portables do not have a separate numeric keypad.

The *special-purpose keys* perform functions unique to computers. Backspace, Del, and Ins are special-purpose keys used to control the cursor and text on the monitor. Some other commonly used special-purpose keys are Enter, Esc, Alt, and Ctrl. You can use Enter like a carriage return to move the cursor to the next line, or, in some programs, to enter commands. On some keyboards, the Enter key is labeled Return, or is marked with a long arrow pointing down and left. Esc, short for escape, is used by most software programs to cancel the current activity. In Windows 3.1, for example, pressing Esc clears a menu from the screen. Alt, short for alternate, and Ctrl, short for control, are used in combination with other keys to perform other functions. For example, pressing Ctrl, Alt, and Del at the same time resets, or reboots, a PC.

The *LED status indicators* show you if a keyboard function is on or off. For example, if the Caps Lock light is on, all the keys you press appear as uppercase.

MORE ABOUT MICE

A mouse, like a keyboard, is an input device. The mouse can be easier to use than a keyboard because you don't have to remember commands or key combinations; you simply point at an object or command on-screen and press a button on the mouse to make a selection. As the mouse becomes more popular, more software programs are designed with the mouse in mind. Although you can get by with just a keyboard using Windows 3.1, it is much easier and more fun if you have a mouse.

NOTE:
You do not have to choose exclusively between a keyboard and a mouse. You may find that many programs are easiest to use when you combine the two.

CONNECTING A MOUSE

To use a mouse, you need the following:

- A mouse
- A software application designed for use with a mouse, such as Windows 3.1 or WordPerfect 6.
- Software — called a device driver — that tells the PC how to use the mouse
- An open mouse port or an expansion slot for connecting a bus mouse adapter

- An open serial port for connecting a serial mouse.

- A mouse pad (optional).

A mouse is attached to a port on the PC with a cable. A serial mouse connects directly to a serial port which on some, but not all, computers is built into the system unit. A bus mouse connects to a special mouse port and may require an adapter card that plugs into an expansion slot. Both types of mice appear and function in basically the same manner.

In addition, the PC must have a mouse device driver software program to tell the PC the type of mouse it is and the type of signals the mouse uses.

ANATOMY OF A MOUSE

Although mice come in different shapes and sizes, all are designed to fit easily into the palm of your hand. A mouse gets its name from its shape. Notice that the cable that connects the mouse to the system unit looks like a tail.

Most mice have either two or three buttons. Most software programs use the left button to perform common functions, and the right button or middle button for special purposes. Your mouse may have only one button. Don't worry—you still can use it for most actions. On the underside of the mouse is a tracking ball, which translates the mouse movements into input signals that the PC can understand.

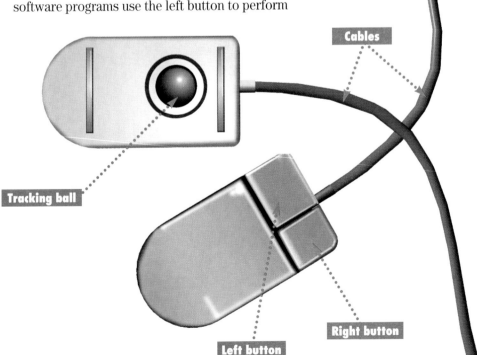

Cables

Tracking ball

Left button

Right button

When you hold the mouse correctly, your pointer finger sits gently on top of the left button. Your other fingers can rest on the other buttons, or guide the mouse around the desktop.

A mouse pad is a rubber pad that provides a uniform surface for the mouse to slide on. Your desk may work just fine, but often a mouse pad adds a bit of traction that makes the mouse more accurate, or easier to point.

NOTE:

If you are left-handed, you may find the mouse awkward to use. Luckily, most software programs, including Windows 3.1, let you reverse the mouse buttons so that you can use the right button to perform most functions and the left or middle buttons for special purposes.

USING A MOUSE

Software programs designed for use with a mouse display a *mouse pointer* on-screen. The pointer may be an arrow, a small rectangle, an I-beam, or even a hand with a pointed finger. Occasionally, the pointer changes to indicate the current action. For example, an arrow can change to an I-beam to indicate that the current action is entering text.

To move the pointer, you gently slide the mouse around the desktop. When you slide the mouse left, the pointer moves left. When you slide the mouse toward the back of your desk, the pointer moves toward the top of the screen. To move the mouse without moving the pointer, pick it up.

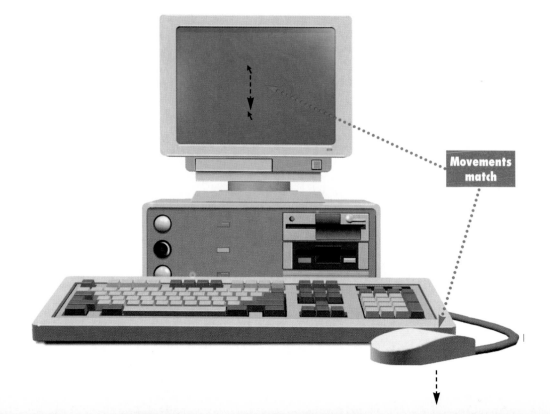

Movements match

NOTE:

If the software program does not display a pointer, it may not be designed for use with a mouse. Or, you may not have installed the mouse device driver correctly. Check the instructions that came with the mouse, or contact the store where you purchased it.

Mouse use has a language all its own. The following chart defines some common mouse terms:

Term	Definition
Point	Move the pointer to the desired spot on the screen.
Click	Press and release the left mouse button.
Double-click	Press and release the left mouse button twice, as quickly as possible.
Drag	Press and hold the left mouse button, while moving the pointer to another location.
Drop	Release the mouse button after dragging.
Point-and-shoot	Point, then click.

Trackball

Joystick

Scanner

OTHER INPUT DEVICES

A *trackball* looks like a mouse turned upside down and can be used like a mouse to move a pointer around the screen. Rather than sliding the mouse around a desktop or a mouse pad, you rotate the trackball with your fingertips. Trackballs are suited to small spaces, and are often used with portable PCs in place of a mouse.

A *joystick* is a pointing device often used with games that benefit from realistic interaction. A flight simulator, for example, is more lifelike if you use a joystick to control it than if you use a keyboard. Joysticks connect to a game port on the system unit.

A *scanner* lets you input information already on a piece of paper directly to the PC. You insert the page in the scanner the same way you insert it in a copy machine. Rather than copying the information on the page to another piece of paper, the scanner translates the information into signals that the computer stores as a file. You can use the file as you use any file, which means that you can display it on a monitor, print it, or edit it. You can scan text or pictures, but if you want to edit or display scanned pictures, your PC and monitor must be able to display graphics. In addition, scanners require special software.

Voice and handwriting recognition are still developing technologies. However, devices are available that let you input information into PCs just by talking or writing.

MORE ABOUT MONITORS

The monitor lets you see the information you are exchanging with the computer. As you input information, it is displayed on the monitor. As the PC processes the information and responds, the output is displayed on the monitor. During virtually all the time you spend with your PC, you are looking at something displayed on a monitor.

NOTE:

The words *monitor, screen,* and *display* are used interchangeably.

Monitors can be either *monochrome* or *color*. Monochrome monitors can display only two colors, usually black and white, amber and white, or green and black. Color monitors can display anywhere from 16 colors to 16.7 million colors. Today, most PCs are sold with color monitors, and are easier and nicer to look at, and most applications developed are designed to be displayed in color.

The size of the monitor screen is measured like a TV screen: diagonally, in inches. 14-inch screens are common for desktop PCs. Portables have smaller screens. If you use the PC to display graphics, such as for desktop publishing, you may want a monitor with a larger screen.

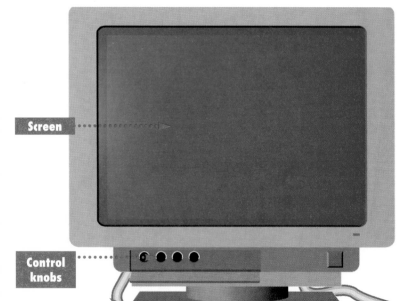

Screen

Control knobs

Stand

Cables

The *control knobs* enable you to adjust brightness, contrast, and the position of the information on-screen.

The monitor sits on a *stand*. A tilt-and-swivel stand lets you adjust the monitor to the position most comfortable for you to look at.

A monitor has two *cables* — one connects it to the video adapter port on the system unit; the other plugs into a regular electrical outlet.

MONITOR MODES

Monitors can display information in two modes:

- In *text mode*, basic characters, such as letters and numbers, are displayed. The quality of the image depends in part on how many columns and rows of text are displayed. Columns measure the width of the screen; rows measure the height. For example, most screens display 25 rows of text and 80 columns. That means that each row can hold up to 80 characters.

- In graphics mode, pictures, such as graphs, icons, and drawings, can be displayed as well. The quality of the displayed image depends in part on its resolution. The resolution is the number of horizontal and vertical pixels that a

monitor can display. It is written as an equation, like this: horizontal pixels × vertical pixels. The more pixels, the higher the resolution. Higher resolution produces a better quality display. So, a monitor that displays graphics in 800×600 resolution displays a higher quality image than a monitor with 640×480 resolution.

Pixel is short for picture element. Each pixel is a dot on-screen where information can be displayed.

NOTE:

All monitors can display information as text. Only certain monitors can also display graphics.

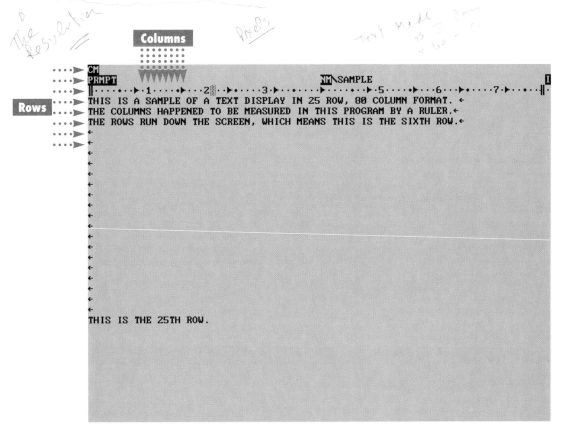

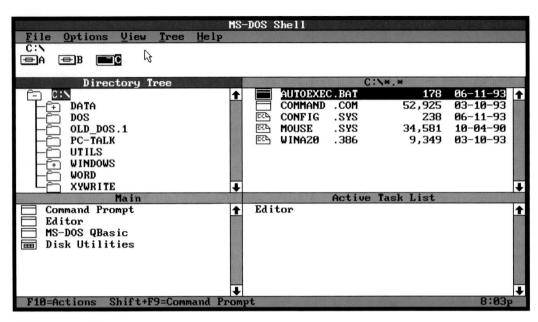

25 lines, low resolution

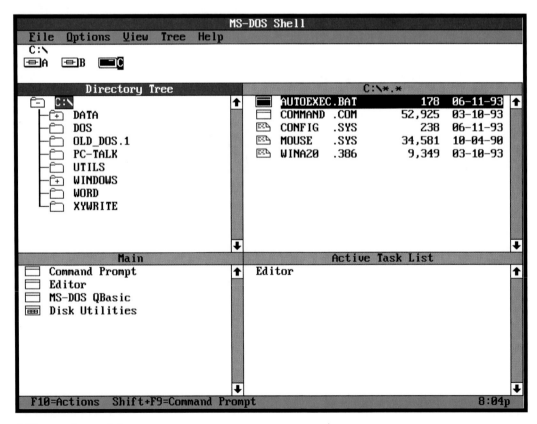

34 lines, medium resolution

VIDEO DISPLAY ADAPTERS

To display any kind of information, a monitor needs a *video display adapter*. The video display adapter is an expansion card that translates the signals processed by the CPU into a format that the monitor can display. Usually, the video display adapter is built right into the motherboard, but it sometimes is an expansion card that fits in an expansion slot.

The video display adapter controls the resolution, the number of colors, and how fast images appear on-screen. The video display adapter and the monitor must be compatible for the images to be displayed correctly.

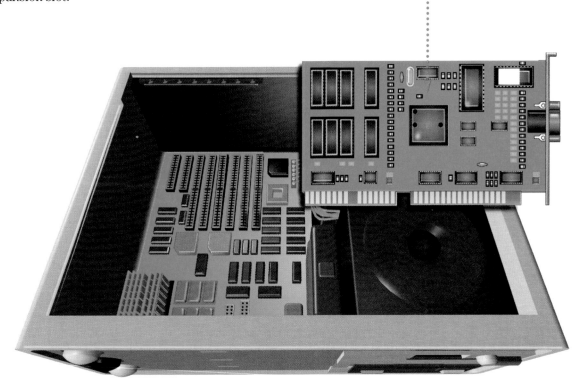

Video adapter card

The following chart describes the different types of video display adapters that are available:

Type	Description
Monochrome Display Adapter (MDA)	MDA cards are designed for use with monochrome monitors. They do not support color.
Color Graphics Adapter (CGA)	CGA cards can be used with either monochrome or color monitors. They support a 25-row, 80-column text mode with 16 foreground and 8 background colors.
Enhanced Graphics Adapter (EGA)	EGA cards can also be used with either monochrome or color monitors. In text mode, EGA cards display 25 or 43 rows of text. In graphics mode, EGA cards support the two CGA resolutions as well as a 640×350 16-color mode.
Multi-Color Graphics Array (MCGA)	MCGA cards were designed for IBM's PS/2 models 25 and 30. They support the same modes as EGA cards, as well as a 640×480 two-color mode and a 320×200 256-color mode.
Video Graphics Array (VGA)	VGA cards support the most common video standards available today. They display up to 50 rows and 80 columns in text mode. In graphics mode, they support 640×480 with 16 colors and 320×200 with 256 colors.
Super Video Graphics Array (SVGA)	SVGA, also known as AVGA, for Advanced VGA, adds an 800×600 graphics mode and a 1024×768 graphics mode.

NOTE:

Video display adapters have their own memory chips for controlling how fast images are displayed. How fast the card can process the images determines how many colors it can display. Video display adapters come with anywhere from 256K of memory, which easily supports 16 colors, to 1M or more, which can support up to 16.7 million colors.

Many of these standards are already out-of-date. Only the oldest monitors use MDA or CGA, while most new monitors use VGA or SVGA standards.

As with other hardware devices, you should buy the best quality you can afford. Even if you think

you don't need a color monitor with an SVGA adapter, you might want that later.

Here are some of the things you should consider when selecting a monitor and display adapter:

● *Color or monochrome.* Most software is now developed for use on color monitors, and color is nicer to look at for long periods of time.

● *Resolution.* The types of software you use will dictate the resolution quality you need. Text-based applications, such as word processing, don't require as high a resolution as graphics-based applications, such as desktop publishing.

● *Compatibility.* There are two issues related to compatability: your software must be compatible with the monitor and display adapter type, and your monitor and video display adapter must be compatible with each other. If you have existing software, check to be sure that it can work with a new adapter. If you are changing just your monitor, or just the video adapter card, make sure the new component is compatible with the old.

● *Monitor size.* 14-inch monitors are suitable for most home and business applications, but some applications, such as desktop publishing, are easier to use on a larger monitor.

● *Video memory.* If the software you plan to run requires a large number of colors, you should consider a video display adapter card that comes with at least 1M of video RAM.

MORE ABOUT PRINTERS

After you put information into the PC, you will probably want to get it out. A printer lets you output (print) the information stored in your PC onto paper. That part is easy to understand. The hard part is that there are so many different kinds of printers, all with different capabilities, that it can be hard to decide which kind is best for you.

Printers fall into two basic categories: impact and nonimpact.

IMPACT PRINTERS
(DOT-MATRIX AND DAISYWHEEL)

Impact printers are similar to typewriters. They use a print head to strike a ribbon against paper, leaving the image of a character. Two common types of impact printers are *dot-matrix printers*, which form characters out of a series of dots, and *daisywheel printers*, which print with individual character keys attached to a wheel. Daisywheel printers cannot print graphics. Dot-matrix printers usually print at about 150 to 300 characters per second. Daisywheel printers usually print at about 10 to 75 characters per second.

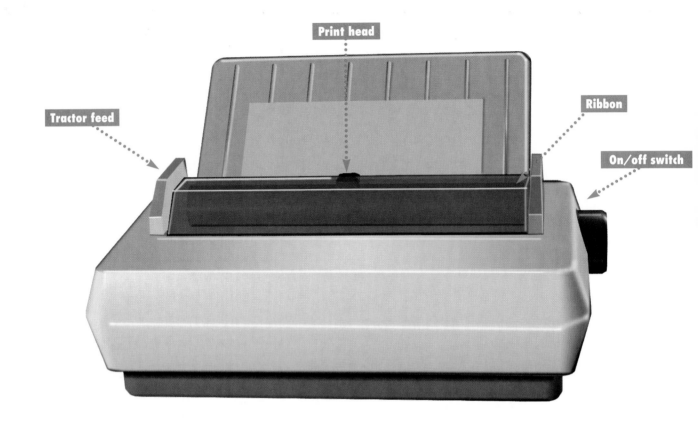

Print head

Ribbon

On/off switch

Tractor feed

NONIMPACT PRINTERS
(LASER AND INKJET)

Nonimpact printers use different methods to adhere ink or toner (powder) to the paper. Two common types of nonimpact printers are *laser printers*, which combine a magnetic roller with toner to form characters or images on a page, and *inkjet printers*, which spray ink through holes in a matrix. Laser printers are similar to copy machines, and can print at speeds ranging from 6 to 20 pages per minute. Inkjet printers can print at about 120 to 240 characters per second.

In general, impact printers are slower, noisier, and less expensive than nonimpact printers, and they have a poorer output quality. Impact printers, however, can print on continuous-feed, multipart, or cut-sheet paper, while nonimpact printers typically use only cut-sheet paper.

PostScript is the name of a printer language that has become a standard for graphics printing with laser printers. Printers that use PostScript are simply called PostScript printers. Many programs

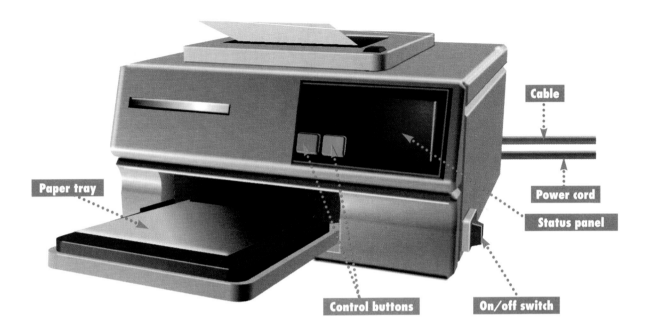

Cable

Paper tray

Power cord

Status panel

Control buttons

On/off switch

support PostScript printing. Usually, PostScript printers cost more than other laser printers, but if you do a lot of graphics printing or need to share files with other users, PostScript is worth the price. Many printers can be upgraded to support the PostScript language.

Another standard laser printer language is printer control language (PCL). PCL printers can output at resolutions and speeds similar to PostScript printers, but they are not as common.

SOME THINGS YOU SHOULD CONSIDER WHEN SELECTING A PRINTER

- *Speed.* Printers are rated by how many characters they can print in a second or how many pages they can print in a minute. CPS stands for characters per second. PPM stands for pages per minute. The higher the number, the faster the printer.

- *Quality.* Quality is measured by how many dots per inch (DPI) the printer can print. The more dots per inch, the higher the resolution of the printed image. The higher the resolution, the better the quality. Sometimes print quality is described as draft mode (low resolution), near-letter-quality mode (medium resolution), letter-quality mode, or graphics mode (high resolution). Currently, a standard resolution for a dot matrix printer is 300DPI, although 600DPI is becoming more common. Very high quality printers can output at resolutions as high as 3,386DPI.

- *Noise.* Some printers are noisier than others. Impact printers, for example, are louder than nonimpact printers. You should decide how loud a printer you want to put into your office environment.

- *Software support.* Printers are controlled by software programs called printer drivers. You should make sure that the software programs you use support the printer driver for your printer.

- *Paper, ink, and so on.* Consumables are the parts of the printer that must be replaced periodically in order to keep the printer working. For instance, printer ribbons, ink cartridges, and toners are all consumables. Different types of printers use different consumables. You should consider the cost of the consumables as well as how easy it is to change or replace them.

- *Available fonts.* A font is a specific size and style of character that can be printed or displayed by your PC. Some printers come with built-in fonts, some let you download fonts stored on the PC, and some let you insert cartridges containing fonts directly into the printer. To discover which fonts your printer supports, check your printer manual.

- *Other features.* Some printers come with options, such as color, or extra-wide carriage widths for printing on wide paper.

MORE ABOUT MODEMS

Modem is short for MOdulator-DEModulator. A modem lets a PC connect to another PC, using a plain telephone line. After the PCs are connected, you can transfer files or input any data that the other PC can output. You can use a modem to connect to a bulletin board service such as CompuServe, to check your E-mail if you are traveling, or to connect to an office if you work at home.

Communications via modems over telephone lines are called telecommunications.

A modem sends data by translating the signals it receives from the CPU into signals that the telephone line can transmit. It receives data by translating the signals from the telephone line back into signals that the CPU can use.

TYPES OF MODEMS

If you have an external modem, it connects to the PC via a cable to a serial port. The modem has two telephone jacks: one connects the modem to the phone line and the other connects the modem to a telephone. The modem also plugs into an electrical outlet. You must turn on the modem before you use it to call another computer.

If you have an internal modem, it attaches to an expansion slot on the motherboard in your PC. The modem uses the computer's power supply, so it is on whenever the PC is on. On the back of the system unit are the phone jacks that let you attach a telephone and a telephone line.

NOTE:
If you use the phone jack on the modem to attach a telephone, you can, on the same line that the modem uses, make regular telephone calls when you are not using the modem.

External modem

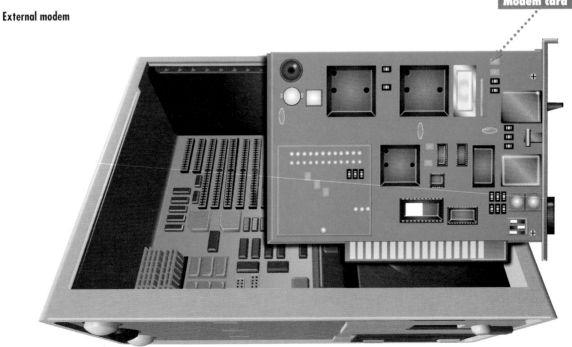

Modem card

SPEED

A modem's speed, called *baud rate*, is measured in bits per second (bps or bit/sec). Speeds range from 300 bps to 14.4K bps. Common speeds for PC-to-PC communications are 2400 bps, 4800 bps, and 9600 bps. The higher the number, the faster the data is transmitted.

Some modems can compress data before transmitting it. Data compression actually shrinks the size of the signals so that they can be transmitted faster. Two common compression standards are MNP 5, which doubles transmission speed, and CCITT V.42bis, which quadruples transmission speed.

In addition, modems use one of three transmission standards:

V.22bis   Maximum transmission speed: 2400 bps

V.32   Maximum transmission speed: 9600 bps

V.32bis   Maximum transmission speed: 14.4K bps

Fall-back speed is a slower speed that the modem can use if the telephone lines, or the modem on the other end, require it. Faster transmission is desirable for two reasons: you don't spend as much time waiting, and, because you usually pay telephone charges, the transmission costs less.

COMMUNICATIONS SOFTWARE

To use a modem, you must have a communications software program. Many different programs are available. Windows 3.1 comes with one program, called Terminal.

You use the communications program to set communications parameters, which are the rules the modem will use to make the call and transmit the data. Communications parameters include the transmission speed to use, the data format to use, and the compression standard to use, if any.

NOTE:
To establish a connection between two computers, both modems must use the same communications parameters!

Making a call with a modem is just like making a call with a telephone. You use the communications program to tell the computer what number to dial when it hears a dial tone, and at the end of the call, you use the communications program to tell the computer to hang up. If you are calling long distance, you must remember to tell the computer to dial 1 and the area code. Some communications programs even make provisions for time delays needed for entering calling card numbers!

FAX/MODEMS

A *fax/modem* is an internal modem card that also provides fax capabilities. If you have a fax/modem and the necessary software, you can transmit files from your PC to a fax machine, and you can receive data from a fax machine to save as a file on your PC. You cannot transmit data from a printed page using a fax/modem card. The transfer doesn't happen directly as on a fax machine — here, data is translated into a graphic format file, and then sent.

SOUND BOARDS

Another output device worth mentioning is a *sound board*. A sound board, which plugs into an expansion slot, lets the computer make more noise. Instead of the beeps and alarms that all computers can make, a PC equipped with a sound board can generate high-quality sound effects and music.

Sound boards are used most often for games and multimedia applications. They can emit digitized sound effects, such as an engine's roar. Some sound boards can be used to record sounds and imitate speech.

Most sound boards can be connected to microphones, speakers, and instruments that are compatible with the Musical Instrument Digital Interface (MIDI) standard.

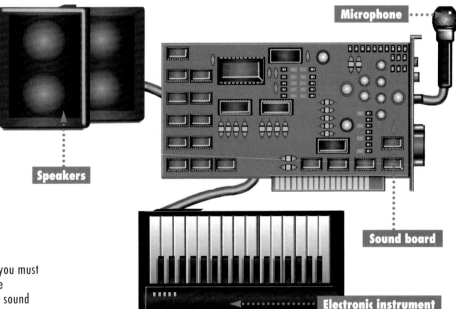

Microphone

Speakers

Sound board

Electronic instrument

NOTE:
In order to use a sound board, you must have the correct software device driver. Windows 3.1 comes with sound device drivers, as do many games.

MORE ABOUT NETWORKS

Once, all personal computers were unique unto themselves. They were designed to be used by one person at a time, for one task at a time. That's why they were called personal computers. Today, many computers are still stand-alone systems, which means that the computers are self-sufficient units, standing alone on their desktops.

However, just as the world has grown into a so-called global village, and we live in a so-called wired society, our PCs can be connected, linking us into groups, or *networks*.

When two or more computers are connected, it is called a network. PCs on a network can share data, applications, and peripherals. Businesses have found that by connecting computers into networks, productivity is increased, and overhead is reduced. Everyone on the network uses the same tools, and can communicate easily. Networks mean fewer expenditures for costly resources, such as printers, and important data can be kept safe by practicing company-wide policies for security and file backups.

A STAR NETWORK

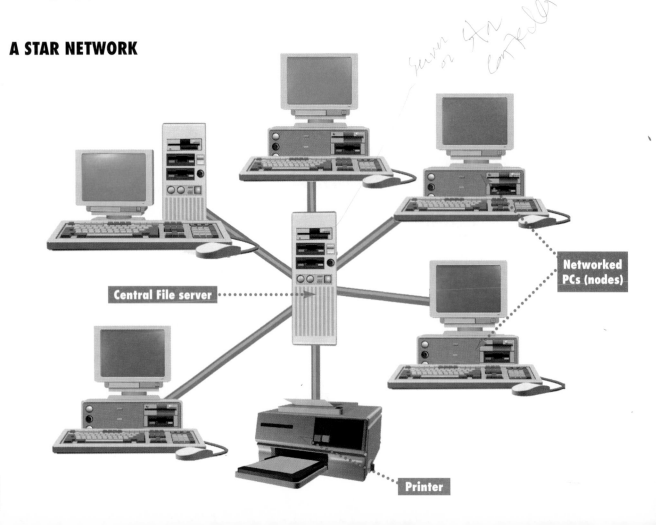

Central File server

Networked PCs (nodes)

Printer

KINDS OF NETWORKS

There are two basic kinds of networks: *Local area networks (LANs)* and *wide area networks (WANs)*. LANs can be connected to each other, and to WANs. A wide variety of networking and internetworking devices are available for connecting computers into networks and networks into larger networks.

LANs usually are smaller than WANs and usually are contained within one building or department.

WANs cover more territory, and can be linked across several buildings, even in different cities or localities.

Most PCs, however, are connected to local area networks (LANs) via cables and network adapter cards. Each computer on a network is called a *node*. Sometimes, computers on a network are called *workstations*.

THE FILE SERVER

PCs on a LAN are managed by a more powerful PC, called a *server*. The server stores the software programs and files that everyone shares, and it controls the flow of data. Security systems, such as assigned passwords, make sure that only the

people who are supposed to access certain data can do so. A network administrator makes sure that the network is running smoothly, and that everyone has access to the information they need.

WHAT'S DIFFERENT FOR THE USER?

If you are connected to a PC network, you may not even notice. You still have a PC on your desk. The PC looks and acts the same as if it were not connected to a network. The difference is that if you are connected to a network, you can communicate with other people on the network. You can use electronic mail (E-mail). You can share the same

data files for projects you are working on together, and you can be sure that everyone is using the most up-to-date information and programs.

NOTE:

Some networked PCs do not have all of the basic system components. For example, because devices can be shared, some networked PCs may not have hard disk drives. They can store files on floppy disks or on the file server. Also, networked PCs probably don't have individual printers, because printers are easily shared.

TYPES OF LOCAL AREA NETWORKS

- There are three basic types of LANs:

- In a *token-ring network*, PCs and peripherals are attached in a loop, or ring.

- In a *star network*, each PC and peripheral is attached directly to a central device — either a file server or a star controller.

- In a *bus network*, all PCs and peripherals are attached to one cable, called a bus.

A TOKEN-RING NETWORK

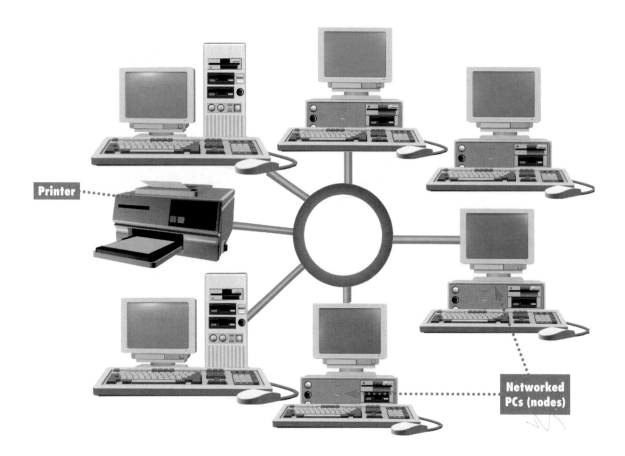

Printer

Networked
PCs (nodes)

WHAT IS AN OPERATING SYSTEM?

An *operating system* is a group of software programs that provides the instructions you need to control a PC. If you didn't have an operating system, you would need to know how to program your hardware peripherals and software applications directly.

Think of an operating system as a general contractor at a building site. The general contractor makes sure that all other service providers—the electrician, the plasterer, the roofer—show up at the right time, do the job that's expected of them, and don't get in each other's way. The workers communicate through the general contractor, and the job gets done to specification.

The operating system makes sure that all parts of the PC work together to get the job done, according to the specifications you enter as commands. The operating system controls the flow of input and output, and calls in the hardware and software to perform the necessary services at the right time.

Without an operating system, you would have to speak and understand the signals used by every piece of hardware connected to the PC. You would have to input instructions detailing every action you want the PC to perform, from how to load a program into memory, to copying disks and printing files.

WHAT'S AN INTERFACE?

Graphical User Interface

GUI

An *interface* is a point of connection between parts of the PC. A user interface is the point at which you interact with the computer. With software, such as an operating system, interface refers to the way you enter commands and the way the PC displays its response so that you can understand.

DOS, the most common operating system, uses a *command line interface*. You type the command you want, and DOS responds by executing it.

Some programs, such as Windows, have a *graphical user interface (GUI)*, which means the programs use pictures, called *icons*, to help you understand the commands and actions you need to take.

Most people find that using a graphical interface is easier because they don't have to remember commands.

Point of connection between parts of the PC

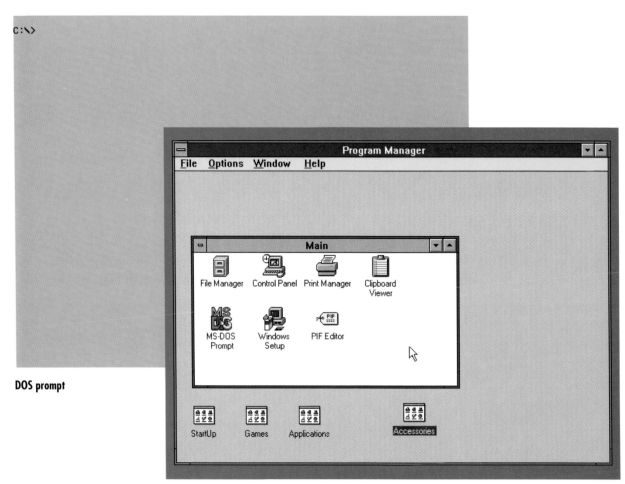

DOS prompt

Windows

OPERATING SYSTEM SERVICES

Some of the services provided by an operating system include:

- *Disk management.* The operating system helps you control your storage devices. For example, you can use the operating system to format, label, copy, and organize hard and floppy disks.

- *File management.* The operating system helps you organize the data you store in files. For example, the operating system keeps track of where a file is stored, what the file is named, how big the file is, and when the file was created or changed. You can use the operating system to list all file information.

- *Device management.* The operating system provides the instructions needed to control peripherals such as keyboards, printers, mice, and modems. For example, the operating system interprets mouse movements and keystrokes into commands.

- *Program management.* The operating system provides the interface a software application-program needs to communicate with the PC. For example, the operating system controls the input and output between a word processing program and the keyboard, and between a communications program and the modem.

- *User management.* The operating system provides an easy-to-use interface that lets you communicate with the PC in a language you understand. Because of the operating system, you do not need to know a cryptic programming language to start an application program. You can type a word in English, or select a menu item, or click on an icon on the monitor screen.

NOTE:

An operating system usually comes installed on a PC's hard disk, but you are given the original program floppy disks. Keep the disks in a safe place, in case you need them in the future.

ABOUT DOS

The most common PC operating system is *DOS*, which stands for *disk operating system*. Microsoft's version of DOS is MS-DOS. IBM's version of DOS is PC-DOS. The two operating systems are virtually the same and generally are referred to simply as DOS.

DOS COMMANDS

DOS has more than 100 commands you can use to control a PC. Most of these commands have names that indicate their functions. The COPY command, for example, lets you copy files, and the FORMAT command lets you format floppy disks. You probably will use fewer than ten DOS commands frequently. Some of the most useful DOS commands are covered in this book's *Task/Review* section.

If you use DOS 4 or higher, you can enter commands into DOS by using either of the two DOS user interfaces: the DOS command line prompt or the DOS Shell. With earlier DOS versions, you are limited to the command line.

THE DOS PROMPT

DOS identifies the line on your monitor where you can type commands by displaying a greater than symbol (>), called the *DOS command line prompt*. You know that DOS is ready to process a command when you see the DOS prompt on your screen. In addition to the > symbol, DOS can include some useful information in the DOS prompt. For example, DOS usually includes the name of the disk drive it is working from (the current drive) and the name of the directory it is working in (the current directory).

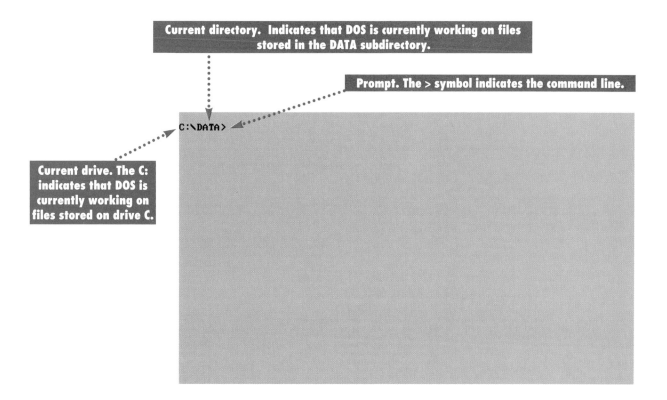

Current directory. Indicates that DOS is currently working on files stored in the DATA subdirectory.

Prompt. The > symbol indicates the command line.

C:\DATA>

Current drive. The C: indicates that DOS is currently working on files stored on drive C.

TYPING A COMMAND AT THE DOS PROMPT

You type a command to the right of the DOS prompt, then press the Enter key. DOS processes the command and displays the result.

DOS is particular about the way you type a command. If you don't get it exactly right, DOS cannot process the command. For example, if you leave a space between the prompt and the command, DOS does not recognize the command. When you press Enter, DOS responds with the message, Bad command or file name. If you make a mistake typing a command, you can press the Backspace key to delete the mistake, then continue typing. If you press Enter before you notice the mistake, you can

press Esc to try to stop the command before it is executed.

Each DOS command has a special name and format, called *syntax*. You must type the command, using the correct name and syntax, or DOS cannot process the command correctly. Most command names indicate their use clearly, such as COPY and FORMAT, but some are abbreviations, such as MD for Make Directory and CLS for Clear Screen.

Some commands have switches, which change the way DOS displays the output, and some have parameters, which specify how the command should be executed. The DIR command, for example, displays a listing of all files in the current directory. You can type a parameter to specify a listing of all files in a different directory, or type switches to specify the order in which the files are displayed. For information about the correct names and syntax for all DOS commands, see *Using MS-DOS 6*, Special Edition.

Some common DOS commands include:

Command	Result
DIR	List files in a directory
COPY	Copy files from one location to another
CD	Change the current directory
MD	Make a directory
DEL	Delete a file
RENAME	Rename a file
FORMAT	Format a disk

For information about using some common DOS commands, see the *Task/Review* section of this book.

USING THE DOS SHELL

The Dos Shell contains these elements:

The Mouse Pointer. You can use a mouse or keyboard with the Shell. You can only use the keyboard with the prompt.

The Menu Bar. You can select DOS commands from one of the Shell's menus. When you select a menu from the menu bar, the command options drop down into the screen.

The Disk Drive Area. All available disk drives are displayed so that you can easily select the one you want to work on. The current drive is highlighted.

The Directory Tree. All directories stored on the current drive are displayed on the top left side of

the Shell. Folder icons indicate directories. The current directory is highlighted.

The File List. All files stored in the current directory or folder are listed on the top right side of the Shell. Document icons are used to indicate files.

The Program List. Application software programs and groups of related programs are listed in the Program List area.

Active Task List. The Shell lets you start more than one program at a time, and switch back and forth between them. Programs that have been started during the current session are listed in the Active Task List.

Icons.

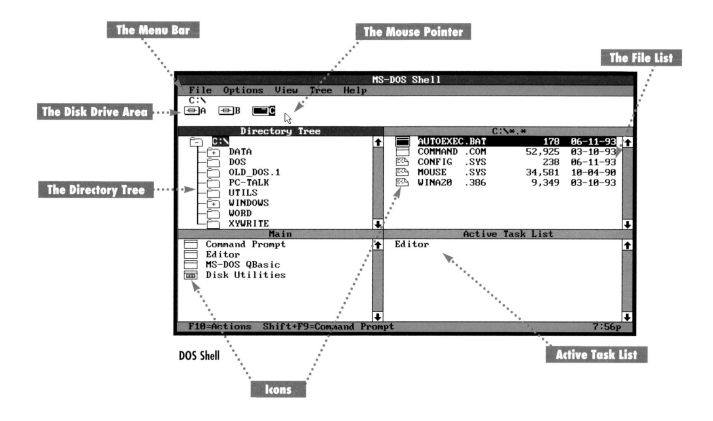

The Menu Bar

The Mouse Pointer

The File List

The Disk Drive Area

The Directory Tree

DOS Shell

Icons

Active Task List

THE DOS SHELL INTERFACE

The DOS Shell is a graphical user interface. The Shell lets you use icons, menus, and plain English to enter the same commands that you type at the DOS prompt.

For information on how to start the DOS Shell, see the *Task/Review* section of this book.

DOS SPECIAL FILES

DOS is made up of more than 150 files. There are three special files that you should know about: COMMAND.COM, , CONFIG.SYS and AUTOEXEC.BAT.

- *COMMAND.COM*. This file processes the DOS commands. When you enter a

command into DOS, you are entering it into COMMAND.COM.

- *CONFIG.SYS*. This DOS file can contain commands. The CONFIG.SYS commands tell DOS if the peripherals or application programs need to be set up in a certain way. For example,

CONFIG.SYS includes a command about how many files DOS must set aside to run programs. CONFIG.SYS also might include a command telling DOS how to allocate memory resources.

- *AUTOEXEC.BAT*. This file can contain commands you want DOS to perform each time you start the computer. DOS always looks for the AUTOEXEC.BAT file when it starts, and then executes all the commands it finds there. For

example, AUTOEXEC.BAT might include the command for making a certain directory current, or it might include the command to start the DOS Shell.

CAUTION:

You must be careful never to delete these three files. If you understand what you are doing, you can edit AUTOEXEC.BAT and CONFIG.SYS, but you should never try to edit COMMAND.COM.

DOS VERSIONS

DOS Version 1.0 was introduced along with the first PCs. Since then, DOS has been improved considerably. Each time a new version of a software program is released, it gets a new number.

For example, in Version 4.0, the Shell was introduced; in Version 5.0, the Shell was enhanced. The most current version of DOS is Version 6.0.

DECODING THE VERSION NUMBER

If changes are minor, such as fixing a small problem, called a *bug*, only the number to the right of the decimal point changes.

If the changes are significant, such as adding a lot of new features or completely rewriting the existing program, the number to the left of the decimal point changes.

Sometimes, the number to the right of the decimal point is replaced by an X, such as DOS 5.X. There isn't really a DOS Version 5.X. The X means that whatever is said about the software is true for all of the versions of DOS since the major upgrade to DOS 5, but before the major upgrade to DOS 6. This list would include DOS 5.1, DOS 5.2, and so on.

OTHER PC OPERATING SYSTEMS

DOS may be the most common PC operating system, but not the only one. Some of the other operating systems are compatible with DOS, which

means they can control applications written for DOS. Some operating systems are not DOS-compatible, which means that you must use applications that were written for that particular operating system. Trying to run a DOS program with a non-DOS operating system is like trying to play an eight-track tape in your cassette player, or a 45 RPM record at 33 RPM.

Operating system	Compatible with DOS?
OS/2	Yes
DR DOS	Yes
Unix	No
Xenix	No
CP/M	No

WHAT ABOUT WINDOWS?

Noticeably missing from the list of PC operating systems is Microsoft Windows. That's because Windows is an operating environment, not an operating system.

Operating environment is a fancy way of saying user interface. The DOS Shell, the command prompt, and Windows are three operating environments for DOS. You can use these operating environments to enter commands and control the PC.

The Windows environment is a GUI (*graphical user interface*). A GUI is very easy to use because it uses icons, menus, and plain English to present everything you need clearly on-screen.

BENEFITS OF WINDOWS

With Microsoft Windows you can do the following:

- *Start programs*. Rather than memorize and type commands to start a program, you point to the program you want and click the mouse. The program opens on-screen in a window.

- *Manage files*. You can use Windows to perform file management tasks. You can select commands from a menu rather than typing them and you can display files in a window on-screen. Displaying several windows of files at once makes it easier to copy, move, and rename files without making costly mistakes.

- *Accessorize*. The built-in Windows accessories make add-on utilities obsolete.

- *Run multiple programs*. If you have enough memory, you can run more than one program at a time, switching between them and even exchanging data between programs.

● *Use Windows programs.* Although with Windows you can use programs written for DOS, programs written specifically for Windows use the same basic keystrokes and mouse actions to accomplish similar tasks. Once you learn one Windows program, you essentially know how to use them all!

Of course, Windows isn't the answer for everyone. For one thing, it requires tremendous computer resources to work efficiently. Without a 386-based PC and 4M of RAM, you spend a lot of time waiting in front of the Windows screen. Also, if you have a lot of DOS applications already, it may not be worthwhile to switch to Windows.

THE WINDOWS DESKTOP

Windows is based on the idea that the monitor screen is just like your desk top. You can have more than one project on the desk at once, and on the desk, you probably have the papers, books, calculators, notepads, and other accessories that you need to do the job. Windows lets you keep the tools you need available on-screen.

The *desktop* is the whole screen on which Windows is displayed.

Icons are pictures of items you can select, such as files and application programs.

Windows open on the desktop to reveal groups of programs, or to run applications. You control the way windows appear on the desktop: you can rearrange, resize, or temporarily reduce windows to an icon whenever you want. The *Task/Review* section of this book covers some common Windows tasks.

Multiple programs can run at the same time, because multiple windows can be open on the desktop. You can select the window you want to be active, moving another window into the background until you need it. You even can copy and paste, or drag and drop, information from one window into another. The more extended memory you have access to, the more windows you can open.

Menus drop down so that you can select commands.

With a mouse, you can use the *mouse pointer* (the on-screen symbol—usually an arrow) to point and click your way through many tasks that were made tedious by DOS commands. You also can take advantage of Windows' graphics capabilities. Of course, even with a keyboard, you can benefit from the Windows environment.

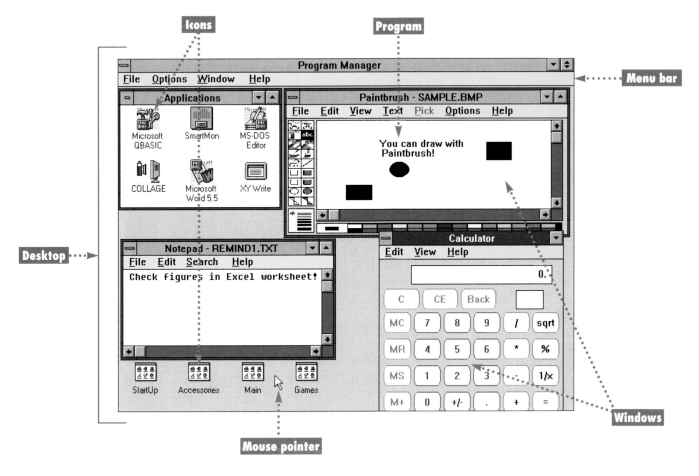

WINDOWS GOODIES

Windows is more than just a pretty face for DOS. Windows comes with built-in programs, called *accessories*, for doing just about every application you can think of.

Some of the Windows accessories are:

Accessory	Use
Write	Word processing
Paintbrush	Graphics
Calendar	Scheduling
Terminal	Communications
Cardfile	Database
Clipboard	Copying data from one application to another

Although with Windows you can use software written for DOS, many applications are written specifically for Windows. Not only do Windows applications take advantage of Windows features, but these applications are designed to look and work the same way, which means that when you learn the basic skills for using Windows, you know the basic skills for using all Windows applications.

NOTE:

Windows and Windows applications use far more memory than DOS and DOS applications. You should have at least 4M of RAM for Windows to run well. Also, although Windows can run on any PC, it performs best on machines equipped with at least an 80386 microprocessor.

DOS AND DATA STORAGE

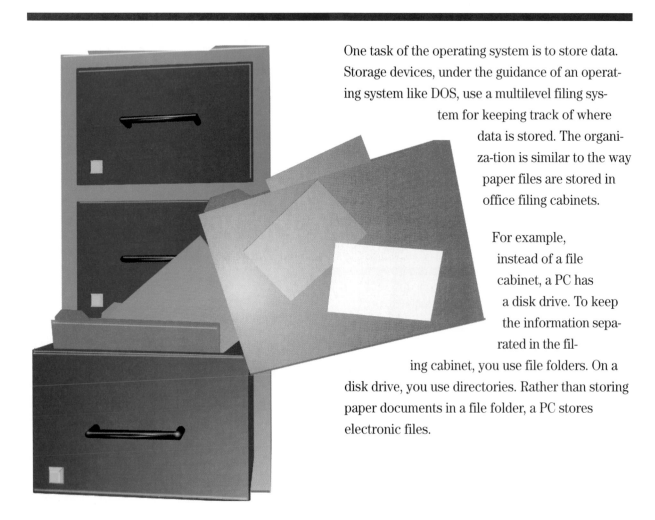

One task of the operating system is to store data. Storage devices, under the guidance of an operating system like DOS, use a multilevel filing system for keeping track of where data is stored. The organization is similar to the way paper files are stored in office filing cabinets.

For example, instead of a file cabinet, a PC has a disk drive. To keep the information separated in the filing cabinet, you use file folders. On a disk drive, you use directories. Rather than storing paper documents in a file folder, a PC stores electronic files.

THE DIRECTORY STRUCTURE

The organization of directories is *hierarchical*, which means that layers of directories grow out of one main directory. Because the directories on a disk look like the connected branches of a tree, a diagram of the directories is called a *directory tree*. The main directory is called the *root directory*.

Directories can contain files or other subdirectories. Because all directories are subdirectories of the root, the terms directory and subdirectory are used interchangeably.

NOTE:

Files should be stored in subdirectories, not in the root directory.

You can create directories by using the DOS Make Directory command. See the *Task/Review* section for more information. Some programs automatically create the directories they need during installation.

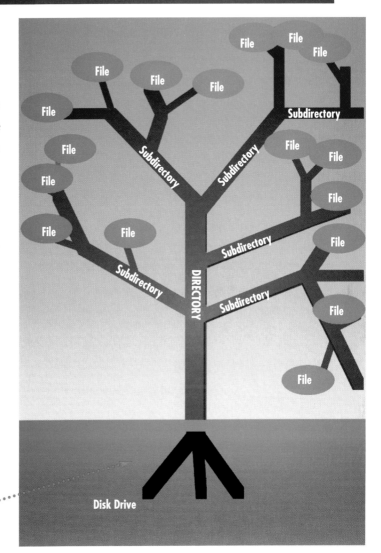

NAMING DIRECTORIES

To identify the root directory, the backslash symbol is used alone. To identify a directory other than the root, the backslash symbol is followed by the directory name. You assign a name by using DOS and by following DOS rules.

A DOS directory name can contain up to eight characters. You can use the letters A through Z, the numbers 0 through 9, and the symbols ! @ # $ % ^ & ( ) - _ and ~.

NAMING FILES

You usually name files when you are using an application program. For example, if you are typing a letter in WordPerfect, when you save the file, you assign a name through WordPerfect. WordPerfect still must follow the following DOS file name rules:

- File names, like directory names, can contain up to eight characters.

- Files can also have a three-character file extension. The extension usually indicates the type of file. For example, DOC files are document files, BAK files are backup files. Often, an application program will define a file by automatically adding a certain extension.

- The file extension is separated from the file name by a period (.).

- You can use the same characters in file names and extensions that you use in directory names.

 TIP:

Give some thought to the names you give files and directories. A good name will identify the contents clearly.

EXAMPLE FILE NAMES

Here are a few examples of valid and invalid file names:

REPORT.DOC	Valid
REPORT.BAK	Valid
TAXES.WKS	Valid
MY NOTES.DOS	Invalid. You cannot leave a space in a file name.
EASYDOSBOOK.DOC	Invalid. You cannot have more than eight characters in a file name.
R*E*M.DOC	Invalid. You cannot use the character * in a file name.

FILE EXTENSIONS

You can use file extensions to help identify the file. The following list shows some common extensions and what they mean:

Extension	Meaning
BAK	Backup file
BAT	Batch file
COM	Program file
DOC	Document file
EXE	Program (executable file)
WKS	Worksheet file

FINDING FILES

If you need a copy of a particular letter in your office, you find it by going to the file cabinet, looking through the file folder, and pulling out the letter.

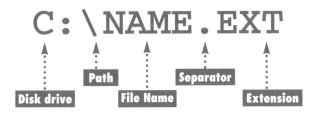

When you want DOS to locate a file on a disk, you must specify exactly which file you want by identifying the disk drive (file cabinet), the path from the root through other directories (file folders) to the file, and the file name and extension (file). All of these identifiers listed together are called the *file specification*.

FILE PATHS

A *file path* tells DOS where to find a particular file. It includes the drive where the file is stored, the series of directories between the root and the file, and the complete file name.

Telling DOS to execute a command without specifying a complete file path is like telling someone to look up a phone number for Mr. Smith, without specifying Mr. Smith's first name or address. Calling a lot of Mr. Smiths may be a nuisance, but deleting the wrong file can be disastrous!

If you have problems finding a file, do the following:

- *Check your typing.* You may have typed the wrong file or directory name.

- *Check the directory.* Make sure that you include the complete path from the root to the file.

- *Check the file name.* You may not remember the exact file name. See if you have the file name written down somewhere (like on a floppy disk label), or use the DOS DIR command to list all the files in the directory.

- *Check the floppy disk.* If you are using a floppy disk, be sure that the disk is inserted correctly in the drive.

As an example, you may have more than one file called MEMO.DOC stored on drive C. One may be in the \DATAsubdirectory, and one may be in the \LETTERS subdirectory. If you decide to delete one, and you type DEL MEMO.DOC, DOS doesn't know which of the two files you are referring to. If you include the file path in the command, DOS correctly deletes the file:

DEL C:\DATA\MEMO.DOC

NOTE:

A path must include all subdirectories between the root and the file in order for DOS to find the correct file. Remember to separate directory names and file names using a backslash (\).

WILD CARDS

Sometimes you may not be able to remember a complete file name. DOS uses two wild-card characters to help you find files, or to execute a command on a series or group of files.

In DOS, you can use a question mark (?) in place of any single character in a file name or extension. You can use an asterisk (*) in place of a single character and all the characters that follow it in a file name or extension.

Wild cards are particularly useful in listing files with the DIR command. For example, to see all files in the directory, you can type the command:

    DIR *.*

The first * means that you want to list all file names and the second * means that you want to list all file extensions. To see all files with any name and a DOC extension, you would type the command:

    DIR *.DOC

APPLICATION SOFTWARE

APPLICATION SOFTWARE

DOS usually is the worst part of dealing with a computer — learning all the rules and typing the command just right. Luckily, you don't spend much time at the DOS prompt. Most of the time you use a computer, you use an application program.

Applications are the programs designed to accomplish specific tasks.

If you think of an operating system as a general contractor hired to control your PC worksite, then applications are the professionals or specialists that you call in to perform a particular service. Just as you call in a plumber to take care of installing a bathroom, you can call in a word processing application to take care of typing.

The words *application*, *software*, and *program* are often used interchangeably.

TYPES OF APPLICATIONS

Some of the most commonly used types of applications include:

- Word Processors
- Spreadsheets

- Databases
- Graphics
- Desktop Publishing
- Communications

BUYING APPLICATIONS

Take the time to decide which software programs you will need. Ending up with a program that doesn't perform the way you expected can be very frustrating, not to mention costly.

Here are some questions to ask when planning a new software purchase:

- Make a list of the things you want to do with the program. Do you want to type letters? Set up a budget? Send out mass mailings? All three?

- Next, make a list of the things you might want to do in the future. For example, all you want to do today is type a form letter, but next year you might want to send out a newsletter.

- Write down how much money you want to spend. Software programs vary in price, depending on how many features they offer, so you should have a budget in mind.

- Shop around. Pick up a computer publication, and read the ads and the product reviews. Talk to friends and coworkers about their programs. Go into a software store and ask to see a demonstration.

After you decide on a program, make sure that it is compatible with your PC. Most software packages list the system requirements, which means that they tell you what hardware and software you must have in order to use the program. If you are still unsure, ask a salesperson or call the manufacturer. Here are the things you should look for:

- Which microprocessors does the application work with?

- How much memory do you need to run this program?

- How much disk space do you need to run this program?

- What versions of DOS does it work with?

- Does the application work with Windows?

- Is the application compatible with software you already have?

- Is the application compatible with hardware you already have?

- Does the application require additional hardware devices, such as a mouse?

- Does the application come with technical support or training?

- Can the application be returned?

WORD PROCESSORS

A *word processor* is just a computerized typewriter. It lets you enter, edit, arrange, and print text. You can use one to create memos, letters, reports, brochures... any printed material!

Word processing applications vary in the features they offer. Some are simple — they are used just to type, edit, and print. Some word processors are complex — they let you select fonts, include graphics, and format pages in many ways.

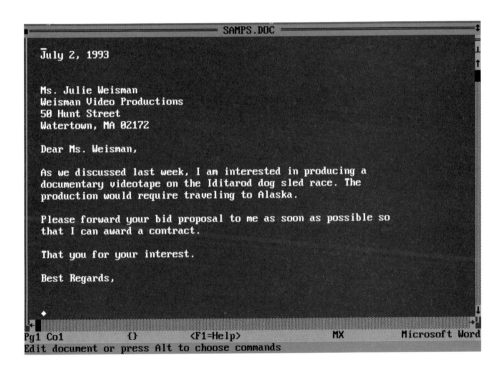

WORD PROCESSOR FEATURES

Some features to consider in a word processing package include:

- With word processors, you don't need to press Enter at the end of each line (unlike a typewriter, where you hit Return). The program uses a feature called *word wrap*, which wraps text at the end of a line to the next line. This makes it easy to insert or delete text. The word processor automatically adjusts the line breaks.

- Most word processors enable you to *copy* and *move* text from one place in a document to another, or to another document. This makes rearranging the text easy.

- *Search and replace* features enable you to look for a particular word or phrase within a document, and if you want, you can search and replace all instances of a word or phrase. Suppose that you use the name Smith throughout a document, and then you find out that the correct spelling is Smythe. You can search for all instances of Smith and replace them with Smythe.

- Unlike a typewriter, a word processing program gives you more control over the look of a document. You can add emphasis-style attributes— bold, italic, and underline. You can change the font and the font size. Most word processors display on-screen how the document will look when printed. This feature is called *WYSIWYG* — what you see is what you get.

- If you are a poor typist or speller, you will love the spell check feature, which flags misspelled words and double words. You still need to proofread the document, however, because the speller doesn't know whether you mean "to" or "too" or "two."

- *Grammar checkers* also are available to help you become a better writer.

- If you send the same letter to lots of people, look for a word processor with a merge feature. *Merge* enables you to take a mailing list and merge it with a template letter, creating a unique letter for each name on the mailing list.

- More complex programs include features that enable you to create an index or table of contents automatically, create and rearrange an outline easily, or add footnotes and endnotes.

IS A WORD PROCESSOR FOR YOU?

A word processor is for you if you:

- Spend a lot of time typing.

- Send out mailings.

- Write documents of any kind.

POPULAR WORD PROCESSORS

Some popular word processing packages include:

- WordPerfect for Windows.
- WordPerfect for DOS.
- Word for DOS.

- Word for Windows.
- Ami Pro for Windows.
- WordStar.

SPREADSHEETS

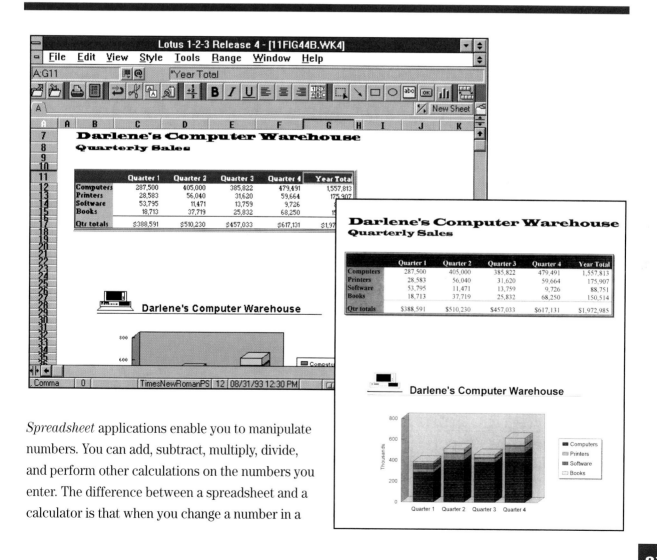

Spreadsheet applications enable you to manipulate numbers. You can add, subtract, multiply, divide, and perform other calculations on the numbers you enter. The difference between a spreadsheet and a calculator is that when you change a number in a spreadsheet, any formulas that use that number are automatically updated. No more totaling the numbers again when you make a change, as you do with a calculator.

Spreadsheets help you organize your data and analyze the results. Spreadsheets are commonly used for creating financial reports, graphs and charts, and for tracking personal finances.

SPREADSHEET FEATURES

Some features to consider in a spreadsheet package include:

- You can use built-in *functions* (predefined formulas) to set up and perform common calculations. Most spreadsheets include a function that calculates loan payments.

- *What-if analysis* lets you see what the results would be if you changed certain data. If we raise the price by 10 percent, what effect does this raise have?

- To show trends or overall relationships between the numbers, you can create a *graph*. A pie graph of sales by product, for example, would show how much each product contributed to the whole amount of sales.

- *Formatting* for spreadsheets may be as simple as displaying numbers as dollar values, percentages, or dates, or it may mean positioning text, using different fonts, and adding effects such as shading or borders.

DO YOU NEED A SPREADSHEET?

You will find a spreadsheet useful if you:

- Spend a lot of time with a calculator or adding machine.

- Prepare financial reports of any kind.

- Like to play around with numbers.

POPULAR SPREADSHEETS

Some popular spreadsheet packages include:

- Lotus 1-2-3.

- 1-2-3 for Windows.

- Microsoft Excel for Windows.

- Quattro Pro.

- Quattro Pro for Windows.

DATABASES

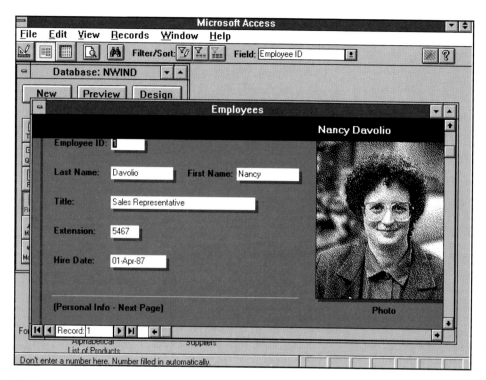

A *database* application lets you collect, organize, and analyze any information you enter into the PC. You can keep track of employees, mailing lists, recipes, clients, and a vast range of other subjects. After the information is entered into the database, you can use it in many ways. With a database of clients, for example, you can create a mailing list. With a database of employees, you can track vacation days.

Witanowski's East-West Market
7775 S.W. Clinton Ave.
Lewiston ID 83501
USA

Always Open Quick Mart
77 Overpass Ave.
Provo UT 84604
USA

Fujiwara Asian Specialties
72 Dowlin Pkwy.
Phoenix AZ 85306
USA

Cactus Pete's Family Market
87 Yuca Dr.
Albuquerque NM 87123
USA

Village Food Boutique
2782 - 92nd Ave.
Suite 1
Los Angeles CA 90071
USA

Rite-Buy Supermarket
P.O. Box 4421
Berkeley CA 92701
USA

Save-a-lot Markets
187 Suffolk Ln.
Boise ID 83720
USA

Pedro's Bodega
7 Nachoes Way
Phoenix AZ 85021
USA

Rattlesnake Canyon Grocery
2817 Milton Dr.
Albuquerque NM 87110
USA

Top of the Food Chain
488 Sacajawea Ct.
Santa Fe NM 87501
USA

La Tienda Granda
12345 - 6th St.
Los Angeles CA 91406
USA

Dollarwise Convenience Store
98 N. Hyde Dr.
San Francisco CA 94103
USA

TYPES OF DATABASES

In a *Relational database*, information entered on one database file can be related to, or combined with, the information from another database file.

In a *Flat File database*, information from different files cannot be related to, or combined with, records from other database files.

DATABASE FEATURES

Some features to consider in a database package include:

- *Search* enables you to scan through the records in the database to find the information you need.

- *Sort* allows you to organize and arrange the records within the database.

- *Query* functions specify the information you want the database to search or sort. For instance, you might want to display all entries with a certain ZIP code.

- *Built-in reports* allow you to organize the information from the records for analysis or distribution.

IS A DATABASE FOR YOU?

You will find a database program useful if you:

- Keep records of any kind.

- Use records to assemble lists or reports.

POPULAR DATABASES

Some popular database packages include:

- dBASE
- Paradox.
- Paradox for Windows.

- R:BASE.
- FoxPro.
- Q&A.

GRAPHICS

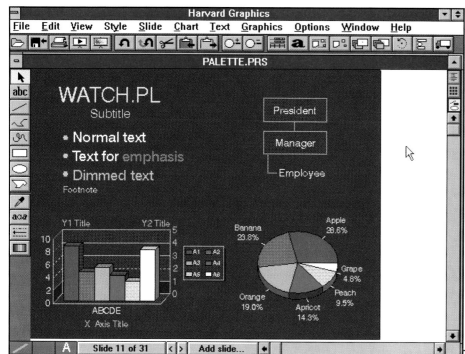

Example of on-screen graphics and the final printed version.

Graphics applications enable you to create artwork that you can print or use with other applications, such as desktop publishing packages.

You can use graphics software for everything from simple line drawings to complex graphs, charts, and presentations.

GRAPHICS FEATURES

Some of the features you should consider in a graphics package include:

- *Drawing tools*, which select the method you use for creating an image. With some tools you draw free hand; others create perfect geometric shapes, or add text to an image. Tools also determine the effects you can achieve, such as a paintbrush or a spray can.

- *Image editing* allows you to modify a drawing without starting over. You should be able to erase a part of the image, or move a piece, without changing the rest.

- *Compatibility* with other programs is important if you want to save the image in a file you can use with another application.

DO YOU NEED A GRAPHICS PROGRAM?

You will find a graphics program useful if you:

- Create documents that can be improved with artwork.

- Create artwork that can be used on its own.

- Like to play around with graphic messages.

POPULAR GRAPHICS PROGRAMS

Some popular graphics programs include:

- Harvard Graphics for DOS or Windows.

- Animator (Draw).

- CorelDRAW! (Draw).

- AutoCAD (CAD).

- PowerPoint for Windows.

- PC Paintbrush for DOS or Windows.

- Generic CADD (CAD).

TYPES OF GRAPHICS PROGRAMS

There are several types of graphics programs:

- *Clip art programs* are disks full of different images that you can copy into your own files.

- *Paint* and *draw* programs let you create your own artwork.

- *Computer-aided design (CAD)* programs are more sophisticated than print and draw programs, but essentially allow you to accomplish the same tasks — drawing and illustrating designs and images.

- *Presentation programs* let you develop presentations to be used on slides or overhead transparencies.

DESKTOP PUBLISHING

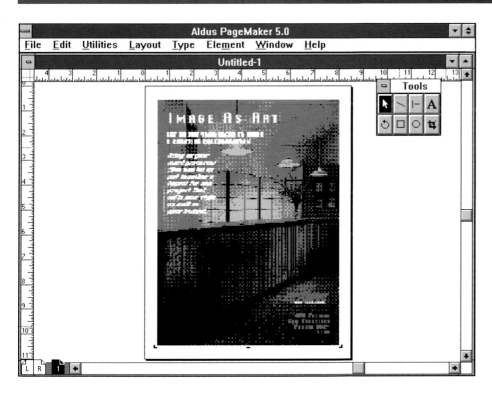

Desktop publishing applications allow you to use a PC to create documents that look typeset or published. You can use a desktop publishing application to create newsletters, reports, books, annual reports, and any other document that may require page layout.

Usually, desktop publishing applications combine data from other applications, such as text from a word processor and artwork from a graphics package. Even scanned images such as photographs or line art can be included in desktop published documents.

DESKTOP PUBLISHING FEATURES

Although some word processors include simple desktop publishing features, true desktop publishing programs can be very complex and powerful.

Some features to consider in a desktop publishing package include:

● Flexible control for setting margins, headers, footers, columns, and other page design features.

- *Templates*, for saving a page layout for use in other documents.

- *Text editing*, for making changes to text, setting fonts and styles, and moving and positioning text on a page.

- *Graphics editing*, for creating and changing

DO YOU NEED A DESKTOP PUBLISHING PROGRAM?

You will find a desktop publishing program useful if you:

- Produce many documents for publication, such as reports and newsletters.

- Want to incorporate graphics in your documents.

- Find a word processor too limiting in its functions.

POPULAR DESKTOP PUBLISHING PROGRAMS

Popular desktop publishing programs include:

- PageMaker for Windows.

- Ventura Publisher for DOS or Windows.

- PFS: First Publisher.

COMMUNICATIONS

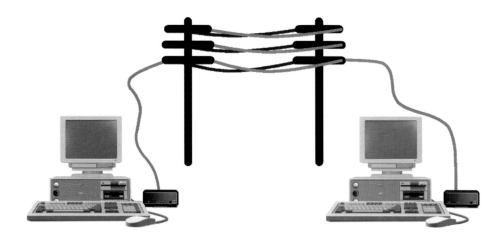

With *communications* applications you use a modem to communicate with other computers via telephone lines. You can *call* other PCs, on-line services, bulletin boards, or mainframe host computers, and then exchange files.

The basic purpose of communications programs is to transmit and receive files. Most programs also allow you to keep a directory of telephone numbers, to automatically dial calls, and to save communications settings for different connections that you make frequently.

To use a communications program, you need a modem and a telephone line.

COMMUNICATIONS FEATURES

Some features to consider in a communications applications include:

- Most communications packages include a *telephone directory* that lets you save telephone numbers, and an *automatic dialer* that allows you to dial a number entered in the telephone directory. This feature saves you the trouble of entering the same numbers again and again.

- *Automatic answerers* tell the modem to answer incoming calls.

- Built-in *error correction* checks files for errors as they are sent or received. There are different error-correction standards, so make sure that you get one you can use.

- Built-in *data compression* compresses or decompresses data as it is sent or received.

Several data-compression standards exist, so make sure that you get one you can use. Just ask your supplier, or read the documentation, to make sure that you have the correct one.

- *Graphics* support lets you send or receive files stored in a non-text — or graphics — format.

On-line services and *bulletin boards* are not applications, but they let you use a computer to tap into a wide range of services. For a monthly fee, a usage charge, and telephone expenses, services such as CompuServe and Prodigy let you exchange electronic mail with other PC users around the world,

take part in on-line talk forums, shop at home, check news, weather, and stock market information, and make airline reservations.

Bulletin boards generally let you exchange information about a specific topic with other people interested in the topic. Most computer user groups, for example, have bulletin boards. Your PC must have a modem and communications software to access on-line services or bulletin boards.

DO YOU NEED COMMUNICATIONS SOFTWARE?

You will find communications software useful if you:

- Exchange data regularly.

- Want E-mail.

- Are interested in accessing on-line services.

TYPES OF COMMUNICATIONS PROGRAMS

Some popular communications programs include:

- ProComm Plus.

- XTalk.

- PC Talk.

- Terminal.

OTHER SOFTWARE

There are too many types of applications to count or to list here. Someone has written a program for pretty much anything you can imagine doing with a computer.

TIP:

To get an idea of the possibilities, look through some computer software catalogs, or browse through a software store.

Here are some examples of other software applications you may be interested in:

- With *financial programs* you perform finance-related tasks such as creating tax returns, balancing your checkbook, and setting up an accounting system.

- *Integrated programs* combine many applications into one package, allowing you to mix and match the data to more easily accomplish a specific task. You can create a form letter, for example, with the integrated word processor, using the mailing list from the integrated database.

- *Utility programs* are designed to enhance a computer system by helping you manage your hardware and software. Many packages come with built-in utilities. DOS 6, for example, comes with a utility for backing up disks, and Windows comes with all of its accessories.

- *Educational programs* are developed for all ages and in all subjects, such as typing, spelling, reading, and planning a travel route.

- *Games* are designed for fun. They, too, are developed for all ages and in all subjects, such as card games, golf, baseball, war, and flight simulation.

SOFTWARE INSTALLATION

When you purchase a software program, it comes on floppy disks.

You must install the program, either on your hard disk or on other floppy disks, before you can use it. You cannot just put most original program floppy disks in the disk drive, or copy the files from the floppy disk onto a hard disk.

Most programs come with an installation utility program and instructions. Read the instructions carefully before you install the program. You may need to know certain information about your PC, such as the kind and model of printer you have, or to which port the printer is connected. Or, you may discover that the installation disk is a 3½-inch floppy disk, and you have a 5¼-inch disk drive.

When you are ready, follow the installation instructions carefully. When you have completely installed the program, put the original floppy disks in a safe place and send in the product registration card.

TROUBLESHOOTING CHECKLIST

If you encounter problems while using a software application, take the following steps:

1. Watch to see if the disk drive in-use lights are flashing. You may think the program is not responding, when it is just taking a long time to process your most recent command.

2. If an error message is displayed, write it down. Look in the user's manual for information about the message, and have it with you if you need to call the customer support line.

3. Press F1, or the appropriate Help function key, to see if a help screen is available.

4. If something is displayed on the on-screen that you did not expect, press the Esc key once or twice. Usually, the Esc key cancels the current action and returns you to where you were before.

5. If the computer really is hung up and does not respond to anything you do, press Ctrl, Alt, and Del at the same time to restart the computer.

GETTING STARTED

SETTING UP YOUR COMPUTER

Before you ever buy a computer, technicians at the dealership usually install all expansion boards, the operating system, device drivers, and maybe even some applications. They put the computer through a *burn-in* period to make sure that everything works. The burn-in period consists of running a nonstop series of tests called *diagnostics*. After they determine that the computer works properly, they take it apart, pack it up, and send it to you.

Once you have the computer, you need to set up a work area and connect the components.

SETTING UP THE WORK AREA

Before you can use your stereo or CD player, you have to decide where to place it, attach the receiver, hook up and position the speakers, and, finally, plug it in. The same is true for a computer.

You should give some thought to what constitutes a good work area. If you are at work, you probably are limited to your desk. If you have a choice, however, here are some things to consider:

The *lighting* should make it easy to see the screen clearly without causing a glare. Bright sunlight can completely block out everything on the display, so windows should be equipped with shades.

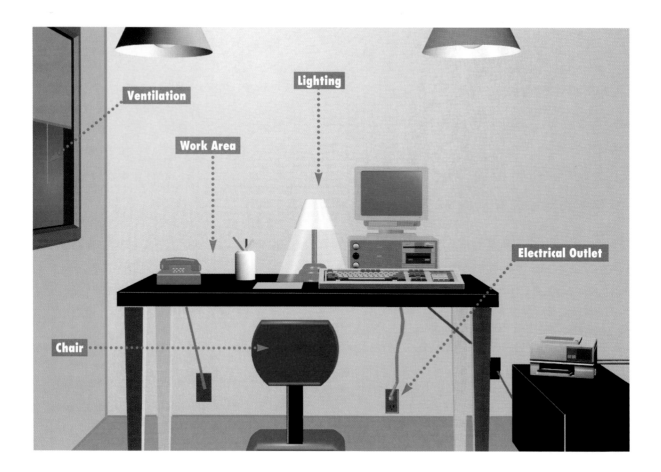

The *desktop* or *tabletop* where you put the PC must provide plenty of room. Besides the computer, you need space for a mouse, a telephone, pens, pencils, notebooks, and any other items you usually keep handy.

PCs need access to *electrical outlets*. The system unit, as well as most external peripherals, have their own plugs.

The PC should be arranged for *accessibility*. You do not want to fumble for disk drives or worry about someone bumping into a power switch.

PCs require lots of *room for cables*, so make sure that enough space exists between the furniture and walls.

Ventilation is very important. You need room for air to circulate around the PC. Both the system unit and the monitor have vents that should not be blocked. If there is not enough air flow, the unit may overheat.

Your *chair* should be comfortable and adjustable. Ideally, you should be seated so that your lower arms are perpendicular to the floor when you type, and your eyes are level with the screen.

NOTE:

Rather than plugging the components directly into a wall outlet, use a surge suppressor or other device which can help protect your computer equipment from fluctuations in the electrical current. If you have a modem, a modem/phone line surge suppressor can help protect the modem from fluctuations in the phone line.

MAKING THE HARDWARE CONNECTIONS

When you unpack the PC, put the components near the place where you intend to set them up. Leave room to reach and adjust all of the ports and cables. Most ports are on the back of the system unit, but on some units certain peripherals, such as a keyboard, plug into the front.

NOTE:

As you unpack the components, check to be sure that you received the correct equipment. Also, compare the packing slips to your invoice or order form to make sure that the internal components are the ones you ordered.

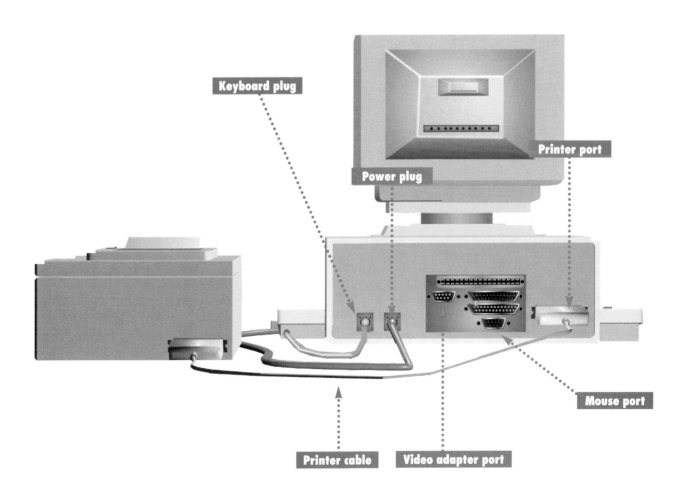

Keyboard plug

Printer port

Power plug

Mouse port

Printer cable

Video adapter port

Screws

Connectors

Most peripherals can plug into only one particular port. To find the right one, look at the plug and compare it with the ports. When you find the right port, use a small screwdriver to tighten the screws on both sides of the port, which keep the cable firmly attached.

NOTE:

Do not plug anything into an electrical outlet until you have connected all of the components.

CONNECTING THE CABLES

- Only one cable comes from the system unit — the power cord.

- Two cables come from the monitor: one goes to an electrical outlet; the other goes to the video adapter port on the system unit.

- Two cables come from the printer: one goes to an electrical outlet; the other goes to the printer port on the system unit.

- One cable comes from the keyboard. Attach it to the keyboard port on the system unit. Make sure that the connectors are aligned correctly.

- One cable comes from the mouse. Attach it to a port on the system unit.

- If you have an internal modem, plug one end of a phone wire to the line jack on the system unit and the other end to the phone jack in the wall. If you want to use a telephone on the same line, plug one end of another phone wire to the phone jack on the system unit and the other end to a telephone.

- When all of the other connections have been made, plug the monitor, printer, and system unit into a surge suppressor. Plug the surge suppressor into an electrical wall outlet. Now, you are ready for action!

STARTING YOUR COMPUTER

Before you turn on your PC, take a minute to check a few things:

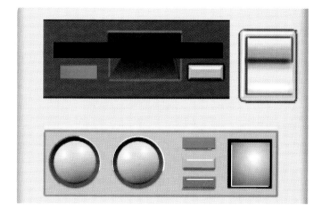

- Locate the power switches on the system unit and all peripherals.

  Most power switches are marked on one side with a straight line like this: |. This character means On, and on the other side with a circle like this: ○, which means Off. Some may have power buttons, which push in to turn on and push out to turn off.

- Make sure that the brightness and contrast controls on the monitor were not turned all the way down (to the right). If you cannot see the display when you start the PC, you will think something is wrong with the computer.

- Make sure that the operating system (usually DOS) is on a disk where your PC can find it. If the operating system was installed on drive C, make sure that there are no floppy disks in drive A or B. If the operating system is installed on a floppy disk, make sure that it is correctly inserted in drive A.

- Make sure that the surge suppressor or other power device is turned on.

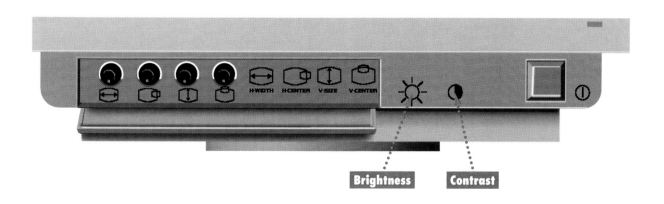

Brightness   Contrast

NOTE:

If the operating system is not yet installed, contact your dealer or computer technician, or consult a book that explains how to install it correctly.

After everything is plugged in and double-checked, go ahead and turn on the system unit by gently pressing the power switch until it clicks into the On position. If the setup instructions that came with your computer differ, follow them.

Gently press the power switches on the monitor, the printer, and other external peripherals until they click into the On position.

WHAT HAPPENS DURING STARTUP?

As soon as the power is on, the PC begins running a power-on self-test (POST) to make sure that all components are in working order. You probably will hear the system come to life with some hums, clicks, and whirrs as the power supply's fan starts and as the CPU counts the memory, checks components, and accesses the disk drives.

On the monitor, the CPU may display the name of some of the components it finds and how much memory is available.

When the POST is complete, the CPU looks for the operating system. It always looks in drive A first, so the drive A in-use light will go on. If there is no disk in drive A, it looks on hard drive C, so the hard disk in-use light will go on.

NOTE:

If the CPU finds any problems during the POST, it may display an error message. If it does, write down the message and call your dealer or a computer technician.

NOTE:

When the computer finds DOS, you may see the message, Starting DOS.... If the PC doesn't find DOS, you may see the message:

```
Non-System disk or disk error
Replace and strike any key when ready
```

If DOS is installed on the hard disk, make sure that there is no floppy disk inserted. If DOS is installed on a floppy disk, make sure that you inserted the correct disk. Try to start DOS again by pressing any key. If you see a message that says no operating system was found, contact the dealer or a computer technician. You must install an operating system before you can use your PC.

What you see next depends on how the PC was set up.

- If your PC does not have an internal clock/calendar, you are asked to enter the date and time. Use the format indicated in the parentheses.

- If device drivers or other commands were included in the DOS AUTOEXEC.BAT file, the PC displays a message as it processes each one.

- If DOS loads successfully, you see the DOS prompt:

    C:\>

NOTE:

If someone added a command to your AUTOEXEC.BAT file to display a different operating environment, the specified environment is displayed instead of the DOS prompt. Some PCs load into the DOS Shell, some load into Windows, and some load into a customized menu screen.

```
003712 KB OK
Wait.......
```

```
Starting MS-DOS...

Microsoft (R) Mouse Driver Version 7.05
Copyright (C) Microsoft Corp. 1988-1989. All rights reserved.
Mouse driver installed
```

TROUBLESHOOTING STARTUP

Here are some of the things to do if you have problems starting your computer:

- Check that all components are connected correctly to their ports.

- Check that all components are plugged into a power source.

- Check that the power source is on.

- Check that all components are turned on.

- Check the brightness and contrast adjustments on the monitor.

If the above fails, shut everything off, wait a few minutes, and try turning it all on again. Watch and listen to see if you can pinpoint the problem. Things to watch and listen for are:

- If you do not hear the hum of the system unit's fan, the power supply may be bad.

- If you do not see anything on the monitor, the monitor may be broken, or the controls may need adjusting.

- If you do not see the memory count displayed, the CPU is not completing the POST correctly.

- If you do not see the disk drive in-use lights go on, the CPU is not completing the POST correctly, or the drives are damaged.

- If you do not see the keyboard on-line light go on, the CPU is not completing the POST correctly, or the keyboard is damaged.

- If an error message is displayed, write it down. You can look in a computer manual or Que's book, *Using DOS 6*, Special Edition, to see what the message means, which may help the computer technician find the problem.

TROUBLESHOOTING PERIPHERALS

If you have problems with a peripheral, here are some things to check:

- Check that all cables are correctly attached.

- Check that everything is plugged in.

- Check that all power switches are turned on.

- Check to see if the device's on-line light is on.

- For a printer, check that the paper is loaded correctly.

- For a modem, check that the telephone lines are correctly connected.

CARING FOR YOUR COMPUTER

You should care for your PC the same way you care for any sensitive, high-priced appliance.

Here is a list of some of the things you can do to make sure that it lasts for a long time:

- Use a power protection device.
- Unplug all components when they are not in use.
- Keep it away from food and drinks.
- Keep it away from extreme temperatures.
- Keep it clean. A cover helps keep dust from building up inside the system unit or peripherals
- Insure the computer.
- Keep records of the serial numbers of all components, including software.

- Send in all warranty and registration cards.
- Take care of your disks. Don't leave them in the heat, don't get them wet, and don't store them near electrical devices that have a magnetic field. Label disks by using a felt-tip pen, so that you always know what they contain. Write-protect disks so that you do not accidentally copy data over data that you may need.

NOTE:

You can clean a computer by using a clean cloth for dusting and glass cleaner for removing smudges from the monitor screen. You also can vacuum dust from a keyboard and from peripherals.

- For a keyboard, if it beeps incessantly during startup, wait or shut the system off and try again. Something may have been pressing down on a key.
- Check the software program that controls the peripheral to be sure that it has the correct set up. For example, make sure that the program knows the port to which you connected the printer or modem.
- Check to make sure that the device driver is installed correctly.

MOVING YOUR COMPUTER

If you have to move the computer, carefully follow these steps:

1. Make sure that every device is turned off. This includes external peripherals such as modems, printers, and CD-ROM drives.

2. Unplug every device.

3. Carefully disconnect all of the cables that connect devices to the system unit. If you want, label the plugs and ports with masking tape so you can easily reconnect them.

4. Put an unused disk into the floppy drive(s) to protect the drive head from sudden jolts.

5. If your hard disk does not automatically *park* itself in a safe position, use a disk-parking utility to be sure that the drive head will not damage data on the disk. To find out if your computer's hard disk needs to be parked, refer to the instructions that came with your computer, usually found in the setup section.

6. If you are moving far, pack each device securely in a well-padded box.

POWER SOURCES

Like all electrical appliances, a PC can be damaged by changes to the power source. Here are a few things you can do to keep it safe:

- Unplug all components, including phone lines, during thunder and lightning storms. If lightning strikes the house or the power lines, the equipment can be ruined.

- When you turn on your computer, turn on the devices that use the most power first to avoid a power drain on smaller devices. This is the most common order:

1. Turn on external peripherals.

2. Turn on the system unit.

3. Turn on the monitor.

4. Turn on the printer.

- When you turn off the computer, follow the reverse order to avoid a power surge to smaller devices.

- Always use a power protection device.

TYPES OF POWER DEVICES

Type	Benefits
Surge Suppressor	A surge, or spike, suppressor prevents damage from sudden changes in voltage by filtering the current coming from the wall outlet. It does not protect the equipment from power outages. Phone/modem line suppressors do the same for the telephone lines.
Uninterruptible Power Supply (UPS)	Besides protecting a computer from power surges, a UPS has its own battery which is activated in the event of a power failure. Before you lose data, you can save, and then shut off the equipment.
Power Bars	A power bar simply provides additional outlet connections. It offers no protection from power surges or power outages.

SAVING YOUR WORK

When a PC's power supply is interrupted, you lose all the data in memory. The only assurance against losing data from RAM is to save your work often.

It is a good idea to establish a schedule for saving data. You may want to save every half hour, then you know the most work you can lose at a time can be re-created in half an hour. You may want to save every page. Some applications come with built-in saving utilities that automatically save or prompt you to save at certain intervals.

Even if you save religiously, there are other potential threats to data. Storage devices are not foolproof. Disks and disk drives can be damaged or destroyed, taking valuable data with them.

PROTECTING DATA

Here are some things you can do to protect your data:

Backup! Backup! Backup! There is no way to know how important having backup disks is until you face a crisis. If you do not have backups, you will spend hours, maybe even days, trying to re-create lost data. You can use disks or tapes to create backups. You can copy individual files, or you can copy entire portions of a hard disk. DOS comes with a built-in backup utility, and other backup utilities are available. You should make a habit of copying data files at least once a day, and you should make backup copies of all software program disks that you buy. For added security, keep backup copies of important data and programs in a safe place, such as a safety deposit box.

Be Aware of Viruses. One of the most insipid problems facing computer data today is the software virus. Software viruses are programs that have been written deliberately to wreak havoc on your computer system. The results of a virus may be as benign as displaying an unwanted message on your screen or as malignant as destroying everything on your hard disk. You can protect your PC from viruses by only using software you buy from a reputable dealer. Don't download programs from a bulletin board service, and don't use programs that you get on a disk from another user. You can also use an anti-virus software utility program to remove viruses from disks and memory. DOS 6 comes with an anti-virus utility, and others are available.

DO'S AND DON'TS Here is a brief reminder of some of the most important PC Do's and Don'ts:

Do put some thought into the type of PC you need before you buy one.

Do check the system requirements for a software program before you buy it.

Do save your work frequently.

Do create backups of your data.

Do use descriptive file names.

Do use directories to organize your files.

Do turn off your computer only at the DOS prompt.

Do write down all error messages displayed on your screen.

Do label your disks.

Do use a power protection device.

Do make sure that the brightness and contrast controls on your monitor are adjusted.

Do register your software.

Do return all warranty cards.

Do use a user's manual or other book.

Do store your disks in a safe place.

Do keep your computer clean and dry.

Do be careful if you ever open the system unit.

Don't try to attach any peripherals to your computer when it is turned on.

Don't open the system unit if the computer is turned on.

Don't take a disk out of a drive when the drive in-use light is on.

Don't turn off the computer if a software application is running.

Don't force a disk into a disk drive.

Don't leave disks in the heat.

Don't spill anything on a disk or on the PC.

Don't open the metal shutter of a floppy disk.

Don't use the original program disks to install or run a software program.

Don't use borrowed disks, or downloaded programs.

Don't move the computer when it is turned on.

Don't leave your monitor on for long periods of time unless you are using it or have a screen-saver utility.

WORKING WITH DOS

THIS SECTION COVERS THE FOLLOWING TASKS:

Turn on the computer

Turn off the computer

Restart DOS

See what is in the current directory

Clear the screen

Change the current date

Change the current time

Change to a different drive

Make a directory

Change to a different directory

Change to the root directory

Copy a file

Copy a file to another directory or disk

Rename a file

Delete a file

Delete all files

Remove a directory

Format a floppy disk

Start the DOS Shell

Start a DOS program

Exit a DOS program

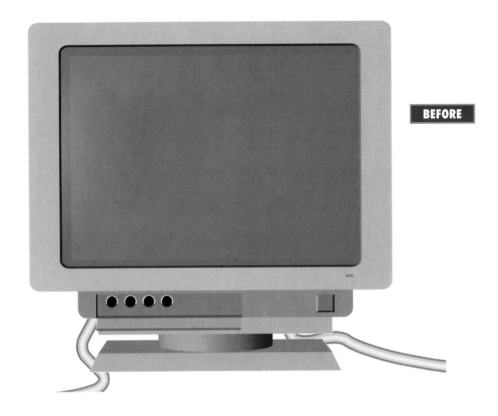

BEFORE

1. Turn on the computer.

A computer's power switch may be on the front, side, or back of the system unit. Most power switches are marked with a I for On and ○ for Off. Some computers have a power button that you push in to turn on the system.

2. Turn on the monitor.

You probably have to turn on the monitor. Look for the monitor's on/off switch under the screen, on the right side, or near the back.

If the PC has an internal clock/calendar, it displays the DOS prompt (usually C:). If the DOS prompt appears, skip the next two steps.

3. If prompted, type the current date, and press Enter.

See *TASK: Change the current date* for more information.

4. If prompted, type the current time, and press Enter.

See *TASK: Change the current time* for more information.

The standard DOS prompt includes the current drive (C:) and the current directory (called the root, represented by \). Your DOS prompt may be different. You can change the prompt. For more information, see *Easy DOS* or *Using MS-DOS 6*, Special Edition, published by Que Corporation.

OOPS!

If the DOS prompt does not appear on-screen, be sure that you turned on both the system unit and the monitor. Be sure that all components are attached and plugged in correctly. If a surge suppressor is used, be sure that it is plugged in and turned on.

c:\>

AFTER

REVIEW

1. Turn on the computer.

2. Turn on the monitor, if it has its own power switch.

3. If you are prompted, type the current date and press Enter.

4. If you are prompted, type the current time and press Enter.

STILL DON'T SEE ANYTHING?

Check to be sure that the brightness and contrast controls on the monitor are correctly adjusted so that you can see the screen display.

NON-SYSTEM DISK

If your PC displays the message, Non-System disk or disk error. Replace and press any key when ready, there is a disk in a floppy drive that does not contain DOS. If DOS is on the hard drive, just eject the disk from the floppy drive and press any key. If DOS is on a floppy disk, eject the other disk from the floppy drive and insert the DOS disk, then press any key. If DOS still will not load, there may be a problem with the DOS installation. See *Using MS-DOS 6, Special Edition*, for more information.

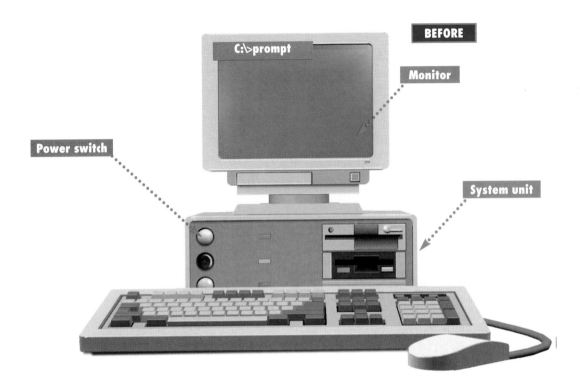

BEFORE

C:\>prompt

Monitor

Power switch

System unit

1. Exit all application programs.

Turn off the computer only when you see the DOS prompt on-screen. If you are working in a program, save all desired files and exit the program before you turn off the computer. See *TASK: Exit a DOS program* or the application's user manual for more information.

2. Turn off the monitor.

Most monitors have their own on/off switches.

3. Turn off the computer.

The power switch may be on the front, on the side, or even on the back of the system unit.

Some people think that leaving the computer on most of the time is best, even when you are not using it. Others think you should always turn off the computer when you are not using it. You should decide for yourself which you think is best, based on how long you will be leaving the computer, how many times a day you leave the computer, and how much energy you think your computer consumes. In any case, it is a good idea to turn off the monitor while it is not in use.

To turn the computer on, see *TASK: Turn on the computer.*

AFTER

REVIEW

1. Exit all application programs so that a DOS prompt appears.

2. Turn off the monitor, if it has its own power switch.

3. Turn off the computer.

BEFORE

```
MOUSE    SYS     34581 10-04-90   3:09p
       32 file(s)       754145 bytes
                      53041152 bytes free

C:\>dir

 Volume in drive C is MS-DOS_6
 Volume Serial Number is 1AC5-73E4
 Directory of C:\

OLD_DOS  1    <DIR>      06-05-93   2:17p
DOS          <DIR>      06-05-93   2:17p
COMMAND  COM    52925 03-10-93   6:00a
WINA20   386     9349 03-10-93   6:00a
PC-TALK      <DIR>      06-05-93   3:08p
UTILS        <DIR>      06-05-93   3:08p
WORD         <DIR>      06-05-93   3:09p
XYWRITE      <DIR>      06-05-93   3:11p
WINDOWS      <DIR>      06-05-93   3:18p
CONFIG   SYS      238 06-11-93   5:21p
AUTOEXEC BAT      178 06-11-93   5:21p
       11 file(s)        62690 bytes
                      53041152 bytes free


C:\>
```

1. Press Ctrl, Alt, and Del.

You must press all three keys at the same time to restart (reboot) DOS. This means that you should press the Ctrl key and hold it down, then press the Alt key and hold both down, then press the Del key. Pressing more than one key at a time is called a key combination, and often is indicated in instructions by plus signs between the keys, as in Ctrl+Alt+Del.

2. Release all three keys simultaneously.

Ctrl+Alt+Del often is called a warm boot or a soft boot, because you do not turn off the PC in order to restart it. A cold boot occurs whenever you turn on the computer with the power switch. In a warm boot, DOS runs through the startup routine and executes the commands in the CONFIG.SYS and AUTOEXEC.BAT files. In a cold boot, the computer runs through its power-on self test (POST) startup routine as well.

Use the Ctrl+Alt+Del combination if your system is frozen and doesn't respond to your commands. If the computer still doesn't respond, try a cold boot by shutting off everything, then turning it back on. Restarting DOS erases all information currently in RAM.

OOPS!

If nothing happens when you press Ctrl+Alt+Del, turn off the computer, wait a few minutes, and then turn it on again; or press the Reset button.

AFTER

c:\>

REVIEW

1. Press Ctrl+Alt+Del.
2. Release all three keys.

WHY RESTART?

If the system hangs up (doesn't respond to your commands), you may need to restart. Also, if you make changes to the CONFIG.SYS or AUTOEXEC.BAT file, you must restart to make the changes effective.

BE CAREFUL!

Restarting DOS deletes all data currently in memory. Only restart if your system is frozen and does not respond to your commands.

BEFORE

`C:\>DIR`

1. At the DOS prompt, type DIR.

DIR, the directory command, tells DOS to list all files in the directory in which DOS is currently working). In this case, the current directory is the root (\ ) . See *TASK: Change to a different directory* for information on changing the current directory.

2. Press Enter.

Pressing Enter sends your command to the microprocessor. After DOS processes it, you see on-screen a list of the files and directories contained in the root. The list has the following information:

File name	The first part of the file name — up to eight characters long — appears in the first column.
File Extension	The file extension — up to three characters long — appears in the second column. Directories do not have file extensions.
<DIR>	To indicate a directory, <DIR> is displayed in the third column.
File size	The size of a file in bytes is listed in the third column. Directories do not include a size.
Date	The date the file was created or modified is listed in the next column.
Time	The time the file was created or last modified is listed in the last column.

The two lines after the listing display the number of files, the total number of bytes used, and the number of bytes remaining unused (free).

The DOS prompt after the file listing shows that DOS is ready to accept another command.

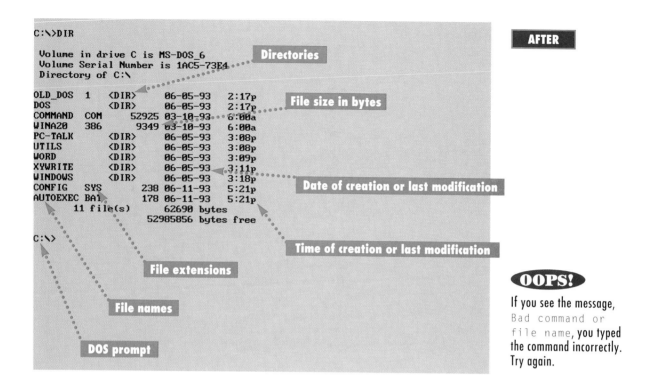

AFTER

```
C:\>DIR

 Volume in drive C is MS-DOS_6
 Volume Serial Number is 1AC5-73E4
 Directory of C:\

OLD_DOS   1    <DIR>      06-05-93   2:17p
DOS            <DIR>      06-05-93   2:17p
COMMAND   COM      52925  03-10-93   6:00a
WINA20    386       9349  03-10-93   6:00a
PC-TALK        <DIR>      06-05-93   3:08p
UTILS          <DIR>      06-05-93   3:08p
WORD           <DIR>      06-05-93   3:09p
XYWRITE        <DIR>      06-05-93   3:11p
WINDOWS        <DIR>      06-05-93   3:18p
CONFIG    SYS        238  06-11-93   5:21p
AUTOEXEC  BA1        178  06-11-93   5:21p
        11 file(s)         62690 bytes
                        52985856 bytes free

C:\>
```

Directories

File size in bytes

Date of creation or last modification

Time of creation or last modification

File extensions

File names

DOS prompt

OOPS!

If you see the message,
Bad command or
file name, you typed
the command incorrectly.
Try again.

REVIEW

1. At the DOS prompt, type DIR.
2. Press Enter.

FILES SCROLL OFF THE SCREEN?

If you have too many files to display on one screen, you can use a DIR command switch to change the display format. Type DIR /W to display a wide listing, or DIR /P to display one page at a time. See *Easy DOS* for more information.

CHANGE DRIVES OR DIRECTORIES

To see the contents of another drive, change to that drive before typing the DIR command. See *TASK: Change to a different drive*. To see the contents of another directory, change to that directory before typing the command. See *TASK: Change to a different directory*.

TRY A SHORTCUT

To see the contents of a different disk or directory, use the DIR command and the full path name to the desired drive or directory.

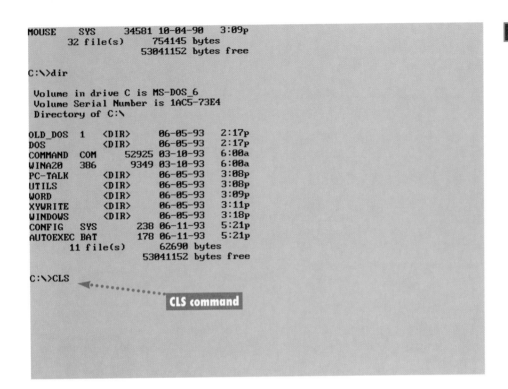

```
MOUSE    SYS      34581 10-04-90   3:09p
         32 file(s)       754145 bytes
                        53041152 bytes free

C:\>dir

 Volume in drive C is MS-DOS_6
 Volume Serial Number is 1AC5-73E4
 Directory of C:\

OLD_DOS   1   <DIR>      06-05-93   2:17p
DOS           <DIR>      06-05-93   2:17p
COMMAND   COM      52925 03-10-93   6:00a
WINA20    386       9349 03-10-93   6:00a
PC-TALK       <DIR>      06-05-93   3:08p
UTILS         <DIR>      06-05-93   3:08p
WORD          <DIR>      06-05-93   3:09p
XYWRITE       <DIR>      06-05-93   3:11p
WINDOWS       <DIR>      06-05-93   3:18p
CONFIG    SYS        238 06-11-93   5:21p
AUTOEXEC  BAT        178 06-11-93   5:21p
         11 file(s)       62690 bytes
                        53041152 bytes free

C:\>CLS
```

CLS command

1. At the DOS prompt, type CLS.

CLS is the clear screen command.

2. Press Enter.

Pressing Enter inputs the command. DOS
clears all information displayed on the current
screen, then displays the DOS prompt at the top
of the empty screen.

OOPS!

If you see the message, Bad command or file name,
you typed the command incorrectly. Try again.

AFTER

`c:\>`

REVIEW

1. At the DOS prompt, type CLS.
2. Press Enter.

```
C:\>DATE
```

OOPS!

If you see the message, Bad command or file name, **you typed the command incorrectly. Try again. If you see the message**, Invalid date, **you typed the date incorrectly. Try again.**

1. **At the DOS prompt, type DATE.**

   DOS marks each file with a date stamp. When you list the files, you can see when they were created or last modified. This is useful for keeping track of the most current version, or when you last worked on the file. It is important to note that once you modify a file, only the date of the most recent modification is listed. The date of creation will not be available through DIR even after one modification.

   If the PC has an internal clock/calendar, it automatically sets the date at startup. Otherwise, DOS prompts you to enter the date each time you start up DOS. You can change or simply verify the date by using the DATE command.

2. **Press Enter.**

   Pressing Enter inputs the command. After DOS displays the current date, you are prompted to enter a new date. If you do not want to change the date, skip step 3.

3. **Type the current date; for example, 07-24-93.**

   Type the new date in the format mm-dd-yy: the month, then a hyphen, then the day, then a hyphen, then the year.

4. **Press Enter.**

   Pressing Enter inputs the new date, or (if you did not type a date) accepts the old date.

```
C:\>DATE
Current date is Thu 07-22-1993
Enter new date (mm-dd-yy): 07-24-93
```

REVIEW

1. At the DOS prompt, type DATE.

2. Press Enter.

3. Type the new date in mm-dd-yy format.

4. Press Enter.

CHECK THE NEW DATE

To see the new date, or to change the date again, reuse the DATE command.

`C:\>TIME`

BEFORE

OOPS!

If you see the message, `Bad command or file name`, **you typed the command incorrectly. Try again.** If you see the message, `Invalid time`, **you typed the time incorrectly. Try again.**

---

1. At the DOS prompt, type TIME.

DOS marks each file with a time stamp. When you list the files, you can see what time they were created or modified, which is useful for tracking the most current version or when you last worked on the file.

If the PC has an internal clock/calendar, the time is set automatically at startup. Otherwise, DOS prompts you to enter the time each time you start up DOS. You can change or simply verify the time using the TIME command.

2. Press Enter.

Pressing Enter executes the command. After DOS displays the current time — including hours, minutes, seconds, and, sometimes,

tenths of seconds — you are prompted to enter a new time. If you do not want to change the time, skip step 3.

3. Type the current time; for example, 1:22.

Type the new time in the correct format: the hour, a colon, the minutes, and another colon. You do not have to type the seconds or the tenths of a second because DOS adds them. Add a "p" to indicate the time is p.m.

4. Press Enter.

Pressing Enter inputs the new time into DOS, or (if you did not type a time) accepts the old time.

```
C:\>TIME
Current time is  2:14:40.74p
Enter new time: 1:22
```

AFTER

REVIEW

1. At the DOS prompt, type TIME.

2. Press Enter.

3. Type the new time in hh:mm:ss format.

4. Press Enter.

CHECK THE TIME

To see the new time, or to change the time again, reuse the TIME command.

A.M. OR P.M.

DOS uses a 24-hour clock, so unless you are used to military time, you should add an "a" in step 3 to indicate morning or a "p" to indicate afternoon.

C:\>A:

1. Insert a formatted disk into drive A.

If you have only one floppy disk drive, it is drive A. If you have more than one floppy disk drive, the one on top (if arranged vertically) or the one on the right (if arranged horizontally) usually is drive A.

See *TASK: Format a disk* for information on formatting a blank disk.

2. Type A:.

Typing A: specifies that you want to change to drive A. Type the name of any drive you want to make current. For example, to change to drive B, type B:. You must type the letter of the drive and the colon without leaving a space.

3. Press Enter.

Pressing Enter sends the command to the microprocessor. DOS makes drive A current, as indicated by the DOS prompt A:> or A:\>.

To change back to drive C, type C: at the DOS prompt and press Enter.

OOPS!

If you see the message, Not ready reading drive A Abort, Retry, Fail?, you may not have a disk in drive A, or you may have inserted a disk incorrectly. Insert a disk correctly and press R to retry the command.

```
C:\>A:
A:\>
```

REVIEW

1. Insert a disk into the drive, if you are changing to a floppy disk drive.

2. Type the drive letter, followed by a colon, like this: A:, B:, or C:.

3. Press Enter.

DISK NOT FORMATTING?

If the disk in the specified drive is not formatted, you see the message, `General failure reading drive A Abort, Retry, Fail?`. Insert a formatted disk into the drive and press R to retry the command. If R doesn't work, press A to cancel the command and return to the DOS prompt. If A doesn't work, press F and then change to a valid drive.

WHY CHANGE DRIVES?

DOS works on the current drive. Although you can tell DOS to execute a command on a different drive, it is easier to change drives and work on the current drive because you don't have to type the full path name (the drive letter and all directories that lead to the file or files with which you are working) each time you use a DOS command.

MAKE A DIRECTORY

```
C:\>MD \DATA
```

1. At the DOS prompt, type MKDIR or MD.

MKDIR is the make directory command. MD is a short form of MKDIR. This command tells DOS to create a new directory.

2. Type \DATA.

After the command, you must type in the name and path to the new directory. The path includes all of the directories between the root and the new directory. You can use any valid new directory name, up to eight characters long. In this case, the complete command line is MD\DATA.

3. Press Enter.

Pressing Enter inputs the command, and DOS creates the new directory. Keep in mind that you remain in the current directory. You created a new directory but you did not make

the new directory current. To change directories, see *TASK: Change to a different directory.*

After you create a directory, you cannot rename it from the DOS prompt, so give some thought to the directory name, and be sure to type the name correctly before you press Enter. A good naming scheme helps to keep your disks organized.

4. Type DIR and press Enter.

Use the DIR command to see that the directory was created. You can see the new directory in the list.

OOPS!

If you see the message, Directory already exists, a directory was already created with the same name as the directory that you are trying to create. Use the make directory command to create a directory with a different name.

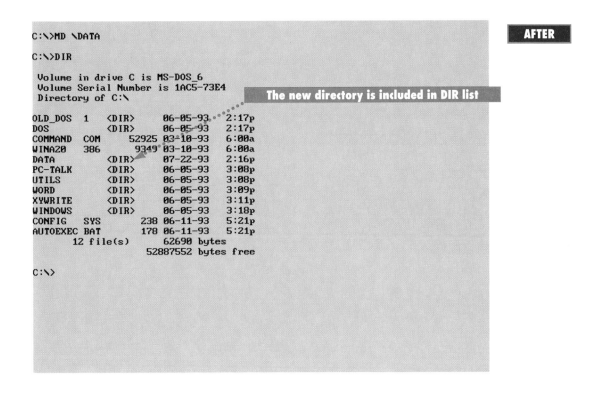

AFTER

```
C:\>MD \DATA

C:\>DIR

 Volume in drive C is MS-DOS_6
 Volume Serial Number is 1AC5-73E4
 Directory of C:\
```

The new directory is included in DIR list

```
OLD_DOS   1    <DIR>      06-05-93    2:17p
DOS            <DIR>      06-05-93    2:17p
COMMAND   COM    52925 03-10-93      6:00a
WINA20    386     9349 03-10-93      6:00a
DATA           <DIR>      07-22-93    2:16p
PC-TALK        <DIR>      06-05-93    3:08p
UTILS          <DIR>      06-05-93    3:08p
WORD           <DIR>      06-05-93    3:09p
XYWRITE        <DIR>      06-05-93    3:11p
WINDOWS        <DIR>      06-05-93    3:18p
CONFIG    SYS      238 06-11-93      5:21p
AUTOEXEC  BAT      178 06-11-93      5:21p
        12 file(s)      62690 bytes
                     52887552 bytes free

C:\>
```

REVIEW

1. At the DOS prompt, type MD.

2. Type the complete name of the directory, including the backslash and the path.

3. Press Enter.

WHY MAKE A DIRECTORY?

Directories are similar to file folders; directories let you organize the files on a disk. Rather than have all files jumbled together in the root, you can create directories to contain related files. For example, you can create a directory for storing all letters, all memos, or all financial information.

WHAT IS A PATH?

A path is the route to a directory or file. Starting from the disk drive, the path tells DOS which directories to go through to reach the specified directory or file.

CHANGE TO A DIFFERENT DIRECTORY

```
C:\>CD \DATA
```

1. At the DOS prompt, type CHDIR or CD.

CHDIR, the change directory command, tells DOS to make the specified directory the current directory. CD is an abbreviated version of the command.

2. Type \DATA.

After the command, type the name and path to the directory that you want to make current. In this case, the complete command is CD\DATA .

Remember that the path tells DOS where to find the directory, so you must type the entire path on the command line. For example, if \DATA is a subdirectory of \WORD, you must specify CD\WORD\DATA . If you omit the path through \WORD, DOS cannot find \DATA.

3. Press Enter.

Pressing Enter inputs the command. If your prompt is set to display the current directory, it now looks like this: C:\DATA>. This prompt tells you that C is the current drive and that DATA, one level below the root (\), is the current directory. (Your prompt may show different information. To learn how to change the prompt, see *Easy DOS* or *Using MS-DOS 6, Special Edition*.)

OOPS!

If you see the message, Invalid directory, you either mistyped the directory name or included in the path a directory name that doesn't exist. Try typing the command again.

```
C:\>CD \DATA
C:\DATA>
```

REVIEW

1. At the DOS prompt, type CD.
2. Type the directory name and path.
3. Press Enter.

WHY CHANGE DIRECTORIES?

DOS works in the current directory. Although you can tell DOS to execute a command on a file in a different directory, working in the directory that contains the files is an easier method, because when working from another directory, you must use the full path name each time you issue a DOS command. The CD command gives you the power to navigate a disk structure.

TRY THIS

To move to the directory that contains the current directory, type CD.. (two periods). The two dots tell DOS to move back one directory. If you are in the C:\WORD\DATA directory, for example, you can type CD.. to change to the C:\WORD directory.

`C:\DATA>CD\`

BEFORE

1. At the DOS prompt, type CD.

CD is the change directory command. CD tells DOS to make current the specified directory.

2. Press \.

The backslash is the symbol for the root directory. The complete command is CD\.

3. Press Enter.

Pressing Enter inputs the command. DOS makes the root directory current, as indicated by the prompt, `C:>` or `C:\>`.

OOPS!

If you see the message, `Bad command or file name`, you may have typed the command incorrectly. Try retyping it.

AFTER

c:\>

REVIEW

1. At the DOS prompt, type CD\.

2. Press Enter.

RETURN FROM ANYWHERE

The CD\ command lets you change to the root directory from any other directory on the drive.

```
C:\>COPY AUTOEXEC.BAT AUTOEXEC.OLD
```

1. Type CD\ and press Enter to change to the root directory.

The root directory contains the file that you want to copy.

2. Type COPY.

COPY tells DOS to duplicate the file.

3. Press the space bar once.

You must leave a space between the COPY command and the name of the file to be copied.

4. Type AUTOEXEC.BAT.

This step shows the name of the file to copy.

5. Press the spacebar once.

Leave a space between the name of the file to copy and the name of the duplicate file.

6. Type AUTOEXEC.OLD.

The COPY command makes a duplicate of an existing file. You must specify the name you want to give to the new file. The original file remains unchanged.

If the name you specify for the duplicate file is the name of an existing file, the COPY command copies the requested information onto any existing information in the file, destroying the existing information.

7. Press Enter.

Pressing Enter inputs the command. DOS displays the message, 1 file(s) copied.

8. Type DIR and press Enter.

DIR displays a directory listing. Now, you have two copies of the file, each with a different name.

AFTER

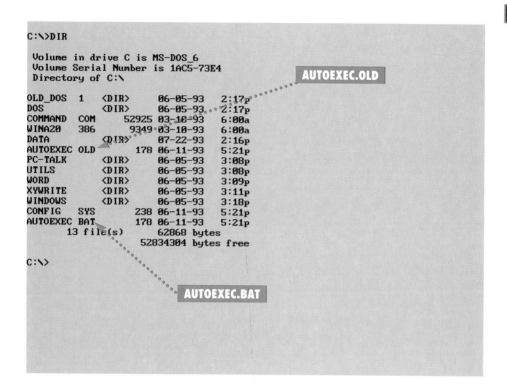

```
C:\>DIR

 Volume in drive C is MS-DOS_6
 Volume Serial Number is 1AC5-73E4
 Directory of C:\

OLD_DOS  1    <DIR>        06-05-93    2:17p
DOS           <DIR>        06-05-93    2:17p
COMMAND  COM     52925     03-10-93    6:00a
WINA20   386      9349     03-10-93    6:00a
DATA          <DIR>        07-22-93    2:16p
AUTOEXEC OLD       178     06-11-93    5:21p
PC-TALK       <DIR>        06-05-93    3:08p
UTILS         <DIR>        06-05-93    3:08p
WORD          <DIR>        06-05-93    3:09p
XYWRITE       <DIR>        06-05-93    3:11p
WINDOWS       <DIR>        06-05-93    3:18p
CONFIG   SYS       238     06-11-93    5:21p
AUTOEXEC BAT       178     06-11-93    5:21p
        13 file(s)       62868 bytes
                      52834304 bytes free

C:\>
```

AUTOEXEC.OLD

AUTOEXEC.BAT

REVIEW

1. Change to the directory that contains the file that you want to copy.

2. Type COPY.

3. Press the space bar once.

4. Type the name of the file that you want to copy.

5. Press the space bar once.

6. Type the name that you want to give to the duplicate file.

7. Press Enter.

OOPS!

If you see the message, `File cannot be copied onto itself`, you either forgot to specify the new file name, or you typed the same name for the new file as for the original file. Try retyping the command.

COPY A FILE TO ANOTHER DIRECTORY

To copy a file to another directory, see *TASK: Copy a file to another directory or disk.*

START FROM THE CORRECT PLACE

If you see the message, `File not found`, DOS cannot find the file which you specified to copy. Remember that DOS works on the current disk in the current directory. If the file that you want to copy is in a different directory, or on a different disk, you must change disks or directories, or include the file's full path name in the command. Try again. For information on changing disks, see *TASK: Change to a different drive.* For information on changing directories, see *TASK: Change to a different directory.*

```
C:\>COPY AUTOEXEC.OLD C:\DATA
```

BEFORE

1. **Type CD\ and press Enter to change to the root.**

2. **Type COPY.**

   COPY tells DOS that you want to duplicate the file.

3. **Press the space bar once.**

4. **Type AUTOEXEC.OLD.**

   This step enters the complete file name and extension of the file that you want to copy.

5. **Press the space bar once.**

   Leave a space between the name of the file to be copied and the name of the duplicate file.

6. **Type C:\DATA.**

   This step enters the complete path to the directory or disk to store the duplicate file. To copy the file to a directory on the same drive,

type the directory name. To copy the file to the current directory on a different disk, type the disk name, like this: A:.

To copy the file to a directory on a different disk, follow steps 2 through 5, and then type both the drive and directory, like this: A:\DATA.

If you specify no new name, DOS stores the file with the same name as the original file. The original file remains unchanged. COPY AUTOEXEC.OLD C:\DATA is the complete command to copy the AUTOEXEC.OLD file to the \DATA directory on drive C.

7. **Press Enter.**

   Pressing Enter inputs the command. DOS copies the specified file to the specified drive and directory and displays the message,
   ```
   1 file(s) copied.
   ```

```
C:\>DIR AUTOEXEC.*

 Volume in drive C is MS-DOS_6
 Volume Serial Number is 1AC5-73E4
 Directory of C:\

AUTOEXEC OLD        178 06-11-93   5:21p
AUTOEXEC BAT        178 06-11-93   5:21p
        2 file(s)          356 bytes
                     52580352 bytes free

C:\>DIR \DATA ◄············································ New file locations

 Volume in drive C is MS-DOS_6
 Volume Serial Number is 1AC5-73E4
 Directory of C:\DATA

.              <DIR>        07-22-93   2:57p
..             <DIR>        07-22-93   2:57p
AUTOEXEC OLD        178 06-11-93   5:21p
        3 file(s)          178 bytes
                     52580352 bytes free

C:\>
```

REVIEW

1. Change to the directory that contains the file that you want to copy.

2. Type COPY.

3. Press the space bar once.

4. Type the name of the file that you want to copy.

5. Press the space bar once.

6. Type the path to the disk or directory where you want to store the duplicate file. If you want to give the duplicate file a new name, type the path plus the new file name.

7. Press Enter.

OOPS!

If you see the message, File not found, **DOS cannot** find the file you specified to copy. Remember that DOS works on the current disk in the current directory. If the file that you want to copy is in a different directory, or on a different disk, you must change disks or directories, or include the file's path in the command. Try again.

USE A DIFFERENT FILE NAME

You can give the duplicate file a different name by including the new file name as part of the path in step 6.

RENAME A FILE

BEFORE

```
C:\DATA>RENAME AUTOEXEC.OLD AUTOEXEC.BAK
```

---

1. **Type CD\DATA and press Enter.**

   This step changes to the directory that contains the file that you want to rename.

2. **Type RENAME or REN.**

   RENAME is the DOS command for renaming a file. REN is its abbreviation.

3. **Press the space bar once.**

   You must leave a space between the command and the old file name.

4. **Type AUTOEXEC.OLD.**

   This step specifies the file you want to rename.

5. **Press the space bar once.**

   You must leave a space between the old file name and the new file name.

6. **Type AUTOEXEC.BAK.**

   This step enters the new name for the file. The complete command line is:
   RENAME AUTOEXEC.OLD AUTOEXEC.BAK.

7. **Press Enter.**

   Pressing Enter inputs the command. DOS renames the file.

8. **Type DIR and press Enter.**

   Use the DIR command to confirm that the file is renamed.

OOPS!

If you see the message, Duplicate file name or file not found, the new name you specified already exists, or DOS cannot find the file you specified to rename. Try again.

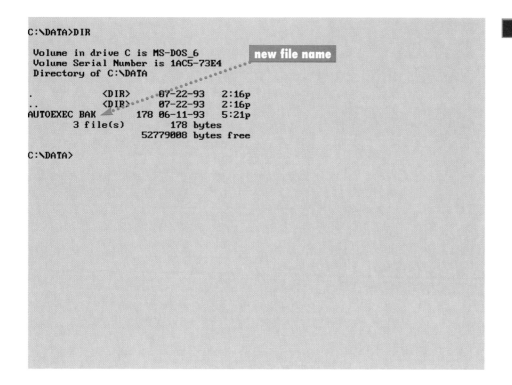

```
C:\DATA>DIR

 Volume in drive C is MS-DOS_6        new file name
 Volume Serial Number is 1AC5-73E4
 Directory of C:\DATA

 .              <DIR>       07-22-93    2:16p
 ..             <DIR>       07-22-93    2:16p
AUTOEXEC BAK          178 06-11-93    5:21p
       3 file(s)            178 bytes
                       52779008 bytes free

C:\DATA>
```

REVIEW

1. Change to the directory that contains the file that you want to rename.

2. Type REN.

3. Press the space bar once.

4. Type the old file name.

5. Press the space bar once.

6. Type the new file name.

7. Press Enter.

NAME A GROUP OF FILES

You can use DOS wild-card characters to rename more than one file at a time. For information on using wild cards, see *Easy DOS* or *Using MS-DOS 6*, Special Edition.

WHY RENAME A FILE?

Rename a file if the original file name is not descriptive of the file's contents.

```
C:\DATA>DIR

 Volume in drive C is MS-DOS_6
 Volume Serial Number is 1AC5-73E4
 Directory of C:\DATA

 .            <DIR>      07-22-93    2:16p
 ..           <DIR>      07-22-93    2:16p
AUTOEXEC BAK      178 06-11-93    5:21p
         3 file(s)         178 bytes
                      52779008 bytes free

C:\DATA>DEL AUTOEXEC.BAK
```

1. **Type CD\DATA and press Enter.**

   This step changes to the directory that contains the file that you want to delete.

2. **Type DEL.**

   The DEL command tells DOS to delete the specified file.

3. **Press the space bar once.**

   You must leave a space between the command and the file name.

4. **Type AUTOEXEC.BAK.**

   This step enters the complete name of the file that you want to delete. Remember to include the file extension. The complete command is: DEL AUTOEXEC.BAK.

5. **Press Enter.**

   Pressing Enter inputs the command. DOS deletes the specified file.

6. **Type DIR and press Enter.**

   Use the DIR command to confirm that the file was deleted.

OOPS!

If you see the message, File not found, DOS cannot find the file that you specified. Make sure that the current disk and directory are correct, then check your typing and try again.

```
C:\DATA>DIR

 Volume in drive C is MS-DOS_6
 Volume Serial Number is 1AC5-73E4
 Directory of C:\DATA

 .              <DIR>      07-22-93   2:16p
 ..             <DIR>      07-22-93   2:16p
        2 file(s)             0 bytes
                      52752384 bytes free

C:\DATA>
```

REVIEW

1. Change to the directory that contains the file that you want to delete.

2. Type DEL.

3. Press the space bar once.

4. Type the complete name and extension of the file that you want to delete.

5. Press Enter.

BE CAREFUL!

Using the DEL command is easy, but re-creating an accidentally deleted file is difficult. Be sure that you check the command line before you press Enter. Also, you may want to use DIR to check the directory list before you delete a file.

CAN YOU UNDELETE A FILE?

An undelete utility was added to DOS 5, and enhanced in DOS 6. Previous versions of DOS do not have undelete. If you have DOS 5 or higher, you may be able to recover all or part of a deleted file. See *Using MS-DOS 5* or *Using MS-DOS 6*, Special Edition, for more information.

WHY DELETE A FILE?

Delete files that you no longer need, because storing files takes a lot of space. If you don't periodically delete unneeded files, you may use up all the storage space on your disks.

```
C:\DATA>DIR

Volume in drive C is MS-DOS_6
Volume Serial Number is 1AC5-73E4
Directory of C:\DATA

.              <DIR>    07-22-93  2:57p
..             <DIR>    07-22-93  2:57p
README   NOW      429 06-05-93  2:57p
PORT     DOC    14336 05-13-93  2:19p
REFERENCE DOC     989 04-25-93  9:08p
53MEMO   DOC     2048 05-31-93  3:07p
DISKS    DOC     2048 08-22-93  2:06p
ORDER    DOC     4701 03-15-90  1:10a
        8 file(s)    24551 bytes
                  47368192 bytes free

C:\DATA>DEL *.*
All files in directory will be deleted!
Are you sure (Y/N)?
```

BEFORE

---

1. **To delete all files in the directory, type CD\DATA.**

   This step changes to the directory or disk that contains the files that you want to delete. If the directory that contains the files is on a different disk, include the drive letter in the path.

    TIP

   It is a good idea to use the DIR command before continuing!

2. **Type DEL.**

   The DEL command tells DOS to delete files, which you will specify.

3. **Press the space bar once.**

   You must leave a space between the command and the file name.

4. **Type *.*.**

   The asterisk (*) is the wild-card character that represents any set of characters. In this case, you use the asterisk to mean all file names and all file extensions. The complete command is

   DEL *.*. The command does not delete subdirectories.

   This command deletes all files in the directory. If you do not want to delete these files, do not press Enter!

5. **Press Enter.**

   Pressing Enter inputs the command. DOS confirms the command before deleting the files. You see the message, All files in directory will be deleted! Are you sure (Y/N)?.

6. **Type Y and press Enter to delete all files.**

   This step confirms that you want to delete all files.

7. **Type DIR and press Enter.**

   Use the DIR command to confirm that the files were deleted. Only subdirectories remain.

```
README    NOW      429 06-05-93  2:57p
PORT      DOC    14336 05-13-93  2:19p
REFERENCE DOC      989 04-25-93  9:08p
53MEMO    DOC     2048 05-31-93  3:07p
DISKS     DOC     2048 08-22-93  2:06p
ORDER     DOC     4701 03-15-90  1:10a
            8 file(s)    24551 bytes
                     47368192 bytes free

C:\DATA>DEL *.*
All files in directory will be deleted!
Are you sure (Y/N)?

C:\DATA>DIR

Volume in drive C is MS-DOS_6
Volume Serial Number is 1AC5-73E4
Directory of C:\DATA

.              <DIR>    07-22-93  2:57p
..             <DIR>    07-22-93  2:57p
        2 file(s)         0 bytes
                   47384576 bytes free

C:\DATA>
```

AFTER

REVIEW

1. Change to the directory that contains the files that you want to delete.

2. Type DEL.

3. Press the space bar once.

4. Type *.*.

5. Press Enter.

6. Type Y.

7. Press Enter.

OOPS!

If you change your mind, type N instead of Y in step 6.

BE CAREFUL!

Using the DEL command is easy, but re-creating accidentally deleted files is difficult. Be sure that you check the command line before pressing Enter. Also, you may want to use DIR to check the directory list before you delete all files.

```
C:\DATA>CD\
C:\>RD \DATA
```

1. Type CD\ and press Enter.

This step changes to the directory (in this case, the root) that contains the directory that you want to remove. You cannot remove the current directory.

2. Type RMDIR or RD.

RMDIR is the remove directory command. It tells DOS to remove the specified directory from the disk. RD is an abbreviation of the remove directory command.

3. Type \DATA.

This step enters the complete path name of the directory that you want to remove. The entire command line is RD\DATA.

4. Press Enter.

Pressing Enter inputs the command. DOS removes the specified directory.

5. Type DIR and press Enter.

Use the DIR command to confirm that the directory was removed.

OOPS!

If you see the message, `Invalid path, not directory, or directory not empty`, you probably tried to remove a directory that contains files or other directories. Use the DEL command to delete all files in the directory that you want to remove (see *TASK: Delete all files,* earlier in this section), then try again.

AFTER

```
C:\>RD \DATA

C:\>DIR

 Volume in drive C is MS-DOS_6
 Volume Serial Number is 1AC5-73E4
 Directory of C:\

OLD_DOS  1    <DIR>        06-05-93   2:17p
DOS           <DIR>        06-05-93   2:17p
COMMAND  COM      52925 03-10-93   6:00a
WINA20   386       9349 03-10-93   6:00a
AUTOEXEC OLD        178 06-11-93   5:21p
PC-TALK       <DIR>        06-05-93   3:08p
UTILS         <DIR>        06-05-93   3:08p
WORD          <DIR>        06-05-93   3:09p
XYWRITE       <DIR>        06-05-93   3:11p
WINDOWS       <DIR>        06-05-93   3:18p
CONFIG   SYS        238 06-11-93   5:21p
AUTOEXEC BAT        178 06-11-93   5:21p
        12 file(s)      62868 bytes
                     52711424 bytes free

C:\>
```

REVIEW

1. Change to whichever directory contains the directory that you want to remove.
2. Type RD.
3. Type the complete path name of the directory that you want to remove.
4. Press Enter.

YOU CANNOT REMOVE THE CURRENT DIRECTORY

You must change to the directory that contains the directory that you want to remove. Removing the current directory would be like sawing off the tree branch you're sitting on! See *TASK: Change to a different directory* earlier in this section for information on changing directories.

STUCK WITH SUBDIRECTORIES?

If the directory that you want to remove contains subdirectories, you must remove these subdirectories first! After you use DEL *.* to delete all files, use RD to delete each subdirectory. Use DIR to list the names of all subdirectories.

```
C:\>FORMAT A:
```

OOPS!

If you mistype the command, press the Backspace key to erase it, then retype it.

1. Insert a disk in drive A.

Formatting a disk prepares it for use with DOS. All information on the disk is erased during formatting, so be sure that either the disk is blank, or you do not want any of the files it contains.

2. At the DOS prompt, type FORMAT.

This tells DOS that you want to format a disk.

3. Press the space bar once.

4. Type A:.

This tells DOS that you want to format a disk in drive A. You must include the colon. To format a disk in drive B, you would type B:.

5. Press Enter.

Even if you have already inserted a disk, DOS prompts you to do so. Take this opportunity

to make sure that you have inserted the correct disk.

6. Press any key to continue.

DOS formats the disk, displaying on-screen how much is currently formatted. At the end of formatting, DOS displays how much storage space is on the disk and whether or not any bad sectors were found. Then DOS asks you to enter a label.

7. Type DATADISK and press Enter.

A label is an electronic name up to 11 characters long. If you do not want to label the disk, press Enter without typing anything.

DOS asks if you want to format another disk.

8. Type N and press Enter.

```
C:\>FORMAT A:
Insert new diskette for drive A:
and press ENTER when ready...

Checking existing disk format.
Saving UNFORMAT information.
Verifying 1.2M
Format complete.

Volume label (11 characters, ENTER for none)? DRIVE A

    1213952 bytes total disk space
    1213952 bytes available on disk

        512 bytes in each allocation unit.
       2371 allocation units available on disk.

Volume Serial Number is 426A-14FF

Format another (Y/N)?
```

REVIEW

1. Insert a disk in the appropriate drive.

2. Type FORMAT.

3. Press the space bar once.

4. Type the drive letter, followed by a colon.

5. Press Enter.

6. Press any key when you are ready to continue.

7. Type an 11-character disk label and press Enter, or just press Enter.

8. Type Y to format another disk, or type N to return to the DOS prompt.

9. Press Enter.

LABEL DISKS!

Put a paper label on each formatted disk so that you know which disks are formatted.

CAREFUL!

Be sure that each disk you format is blank, or that you do not need the files on the disk. If you format the wrong disk, immediately try typing UNFOR-MAT A: (or the appropriate drive letter) to see if the UNFORMAT command can recover any of the data that was stored on the disk. Then press Enter.

If you receive a `Bad command or filename` message, try typing C:\DOS\FORMAT in step 2. To add the \DOS directory to the PATH command in your AUTOEXEC.BAT file, see *Using MS-DOS 6*, Special Edition.

```
C:\>DOSSHELL
```

1. At the command prompt, type DOSSHELL.

The DOSSHELL command loads the DOS Shell user interface. Usually, you can load the DOS Shell from any current directory. If you receive a Bad command or filename message, try typing C:\DOS\DOSSHELL in step 1. For more information about adding the \DOS directory to the PATH command in your AUTOEXEC.BAT file, see *Using MS-DOS 6*, Special Edition.

2. Press Enter.

Pressing Enter inputs the command. DOS loads the DOS Shell and displays it on-screen.

OOPS!

If you see the message, Bad command or file name, try typing the command again. If it still doesn't work, type CD\ and press Enter to change to the root, then try the command again.

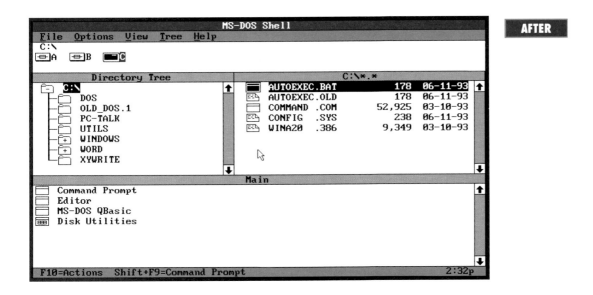

AFTER

REVIEW

1. At the DOS prompt, type DOSSHELL.

2. Press Enter.

RETURN TO THE DOS PROMPT?

To return to the DOS prompt from the DOS Shell, press F3.

MORE INFORMATION

For more information on using the DOS Shell, see *Easy DOS* or *MS-DOS 6 QuickStart*.

```
C:\>CD \WORD
C:\WORD>WORD
```

BEFORE

1. Type CD\WORD.

This step changes to the directory that contains the application program files. This example uses Microsoft Word. Many application programs cannot start unless the program file directory is the current directory. A program file directory is created when you install an application. The name of the program file directory usually includes the full or abbreviated name of the application. Check the application's user manual to find the name of the program file directory.

2. Type WORD.

This step enters the command that starts the program. Most programs use the full or abbrevi-

ated program name as the command to start. Check the application's user manual to find the correct command.

3. Press Enter.

Pressing Enter inputs the command. DOS starts the application.

OOPS!

If you see the message, Bad command or file name, you either typed the command incorrectly or used the wrong command. Check your typing or check the application's user manual to find the correct command, then try again.

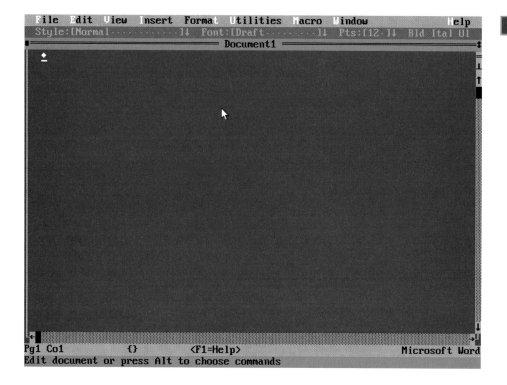

REVIEW

1. Change to the directory that contains the program files.
2. Type the command that starts the program. Here are some common DOS program commands:

Application	Startup command
Harvard Graphics	HG
Lotus 1-2-3	123
Q&A	QA
Quattro Pro	Q
Quicken	Q
Windows	WIN
Word	WORD
WordPerfect	WP
WordStar	WS

3. Press Enter.

TRY THIS

Use the DIR command with a wild card to list all program files. Program files usually have the extension EXE. Type DIR *.EXE and press ENTER. When the directory list is displayed, see if you recognize the name of the program that you want to start. Type the file name without the extension at the DOS prompt, and press Enter to start the program.

DON'T WANT TO CHANGE DIRECTORIES?

Some programs are set up to start from any directory, so that you don't have to change to the directory that contains the program files. Check the application's user manual for information about adding the program file directory name to the PATH command in the AUTOEXEC.BAT file.

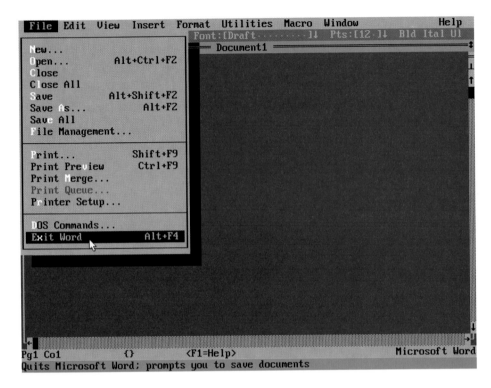

OOPS!

If you have trouble exiting, read the application's user manual.

1. Start the program.

For help with this step, see the preceding section, *TASK: Start a DOS program*. This example uses Microsoft Word. Your program may require different steps for exiting.

2. Press Alt.

In most DOS programs, pressing Alt activates the menu bar so that you can make a menu selection. If the program doesn't use this kind of menu, consult the application's user manual for information on exiting.

3. Press F.

In most DOS programs, pressing F activates the File menu. You see a list of File commands.

4. Press X.

In most DOS programs, pressing X activates the Exit command. The program closes and the DOS prompt appears on-screen.

Some programs have different commands. Here are some tips on exiting:

Look for a Quit menu or an Exit menu.

Look for a Quit command or an Exit command on the File menu.

Try pressing Esc. Sometimes, the Esc key exits the program or displays information on exiting.

If a command line is present, type QUIT and press Enter, or type EXIT and press Enter.

Press F1 to display Help.

AFTER

C:\WORD>

REVIEW

1. Open the File menu.
2. Select the Exit command.

SAVE YOUR WORK!

Before you exit an application, use the program's Save command to save the data to disk, or all your work may be lost.

REMEMBER

Some programs use a different exit procedure. If you cannot figure out how to exit the application, read the application's user manual.

WORKING WITH MICROSOFT WINDOWS

THIS SECTION COVERS THE FOLLOWING TASKS:

Start Microsoft Windows

Select a menu command

Close a window

Open a window

Select a window

Maximize a window

Restore a window

Minimize a window

Move a window

Resize a window

Start a Microsoft Windows program

Exit a Microsoft Windows program

Get help for Microsoft Windows

Exit Microsoft Windows

C:\>WIN

BEFORE

OOPS!
To exit Microsoft Windows, see *TASK: Exit Microsoft Windows.*

1. At the DOS prompt, type WIN.

WIN is the DOS command that starts Windows. (If you do not see the DOS prompt on-screen, you need to start DOS. See *TASK: Start DOS.*)

If you receive a Bad command or filename message, try typing C:\DOS\WIN in step 1. For more information about adding the directory to the PATH command in the AUTOEXEC.BAT file, consult *Using MS-DOS 6*, Special Edition, published by Que Corporation.

2. Press Enter.

Pressing Enter inputs the command. DOS loads Windows. An hourglass-shaped mouse pointer appears on-screen, indicating that Windows is performing the requested task. The Program Manager window then appears. The first time you start Windows, the Main group window is

open on top of the Program Manager.

Program Manager is a Windows application program. When Windows is running, the Program Manager window is open. The Main group window contains icons that represent programs you can run in Windows. These graphics are called *program item icons*.

For information about the parts of the window displayed on-screen, see *What About Windows*, earlier in this book.

CHANGE THE DESKTOP

You can change the way the Windows Desktop appears on-screen. See the other tasks in this section for more information. Also, the desktop may not look exactly like the desktop in this illustration, because you may have different programs installed, or different windows opened.

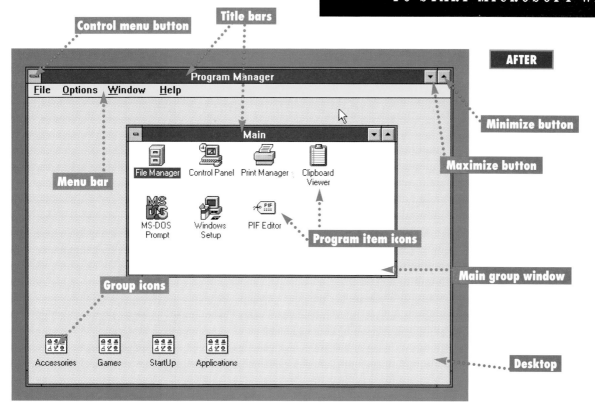

Control menu button

Title bars

AFTER

Minimize button

Maximize button

Menu bar

Program item icons

Main group window

Group icons

Desktop

REVIEW

1. At the DOS prompt, type WIN.
2. Press Enter.

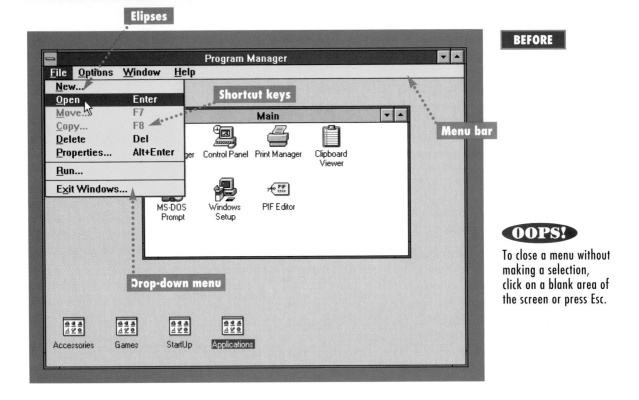

Elipses

BEFORE

Shortcut keys

Menu bar

Drop-down menu

OOPS!

To close a menu without making a selection, click on a blank area of the screen or press Esc.

1. **Point to File.**

   When you use a mouse, actions consist of moving the mouse around until the mouse pointer touches the item you want. In this case, point the mouse pointer at a menu name, such as File.

2. **Click the left mouse button.**

   Clicking the left mouse button inputs the command. In this case, the File menu *drops down* onto the desktop.

3. **Point to Open.**

   Use the mouse pointer to point at the command you want to choose—in this case, Open.

   Some menu commands have shortcut keys that you can use to execute the command. Shortcut keys are listed on the menu, to the right of the commands.

4. **Click the left mouse button, or select a menu command with the keyboard.**

   Again, click the left mouse button to input the command. A new window opens on the desktop.

   To select a command with the keyboard, press Alt to activate the menu bar. Press the highlighted letter of the menu name. After the menu appears, press the highlighted letter in the command name, or use the up - or down-arrow key to highlight the command you want to select, and press Enter.

   ### WHAT DO THE ELLIPSES MEAN?

   Some commands are followed by ellipses (...), which means that a dialog box opens if you select this command, because you must specify additional options before the command can be fully executed. See *Easy Windows*, 3.1 Edition, or *Using Windows 3.1*, Special Edition, for more information.

AFTER

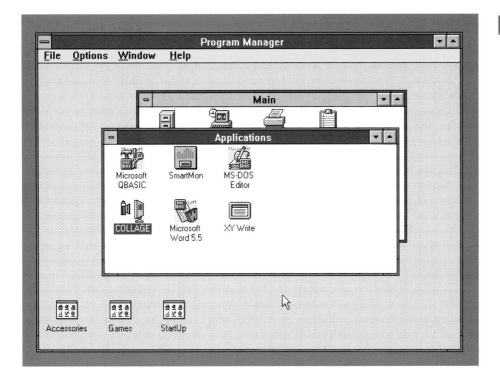

REVIEW

1. Point and click on the menu name in the menu bar.

2. Point and click on the command.

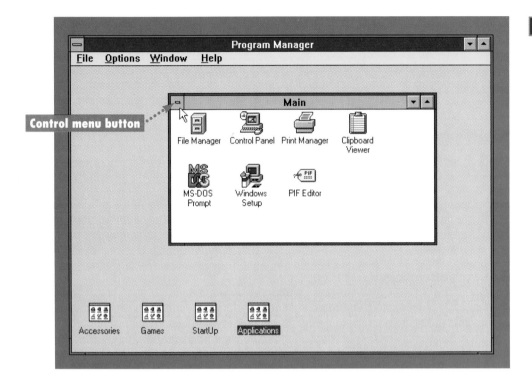

BEFORE

Control menu button

1. Click on the Control menu button for the Main window.

Each window has a Control menu. To drop down a window's Control menu, point at the Control menu button in the upper left corner of the window and click the left mouse button.

USE A KEYBOARD?

You can drop down a Control menu with a keyboard, too. In a group window, like Accessories, press Alt+hyphen. In an application window, like the Program Manager, press Alt+space bar.

2. Click on Close.

This step chooses the Close command (with the keyboard, you press C). The window closes.

If you have more than one window open at a time, be sure that you select the Control menu for the window you want to close.

TRY A SHORTCUT

With a mouse, double-click the Control menu button to close the window quickly. Double-click means to click the button two times, quickly. With a keyboard, press Ctrl+F4.

AFTER

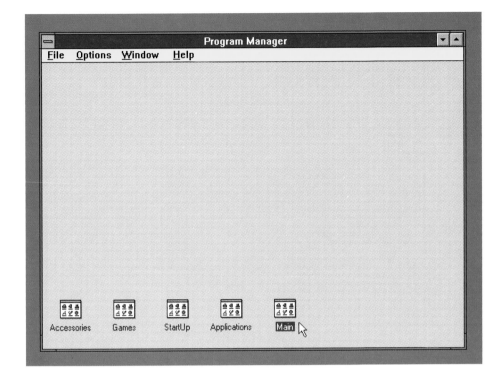

REVIEW

1. Click on the Control menu for the window you want to close.

2. Click on the Close command.

EXITING WINDOWS?

Closing the Program Manager window closes Windows.

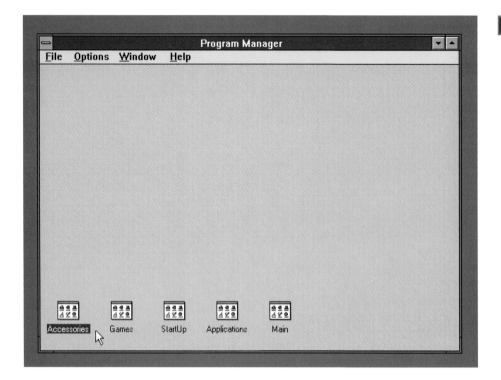

BEFORE

1. Point to the Accessories icon.

This step selects the icon for the window you want to open.

2. Double-click the icon.

To double-click, press the left mouse button two times, quickly. The window opens.

There are two types of windows: Group windows and Application windows. Group windows display the icons for each program item in the group. Application windows display programs when they are running.

In the Program Manager, the icons are group icons; each icon opens a group window.

In a group window, such as Accessories or Main, the icons are typically program item icons; each icon opens an application window.

To close a window, see *TASK: Close a window.*

OPEN OTHER WINDOWS

You can open more than one window at a time. Just follow the *TASK: Open a window* procedure without closing any windows. Use other tasks in this section to arrange the windows on-screen.

AFTER

REVIEW

1. Point to the icon for the window you want to open.
2. Double-click the mouse button.

USE THE CONTROL MENU

You also can use the icon's Control menu to open the window. Click once on the icon to display the Control menu or press Tab enough times to highlight the icon, then press Alt+hyphen. From the Control menu, select Restore to open the window.

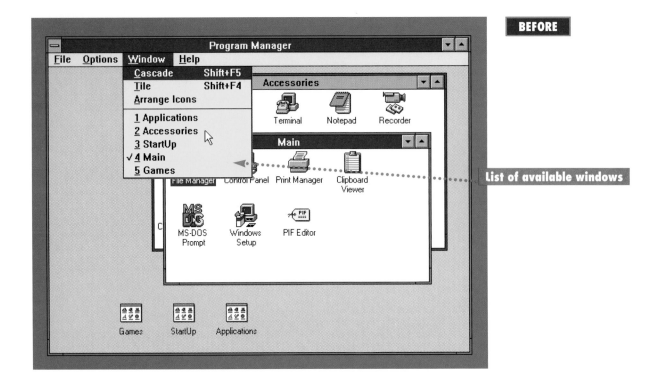

BEFORE

List of available windows

---

1. **Click on Window in the menu bar.**

   From the Window menu, you can select from a list of available windows. The current window has a check mark to the left of the window's title.

2. **Click on the Accessories selection.**

   This step chooses the window in which you want to work. The chosen window moves to the top of the desktop and becomes the active, or current, window.

   No matter how many windows you have open at once, only one window can be the active window.

The active window appears at the top of the desktop, possibly overlapping other windows. The active window usually has a different color border and menu bar than the other, inactive windows.

 OOPS!

You can make any open window active simply by clicking on its name in step 2.

TRY A SHORTCUT

If you can see the window you want on-screen, even if the window is somewhat hidden, point to any part of the window and click the left mouse button. The window becomes active.

AFTER

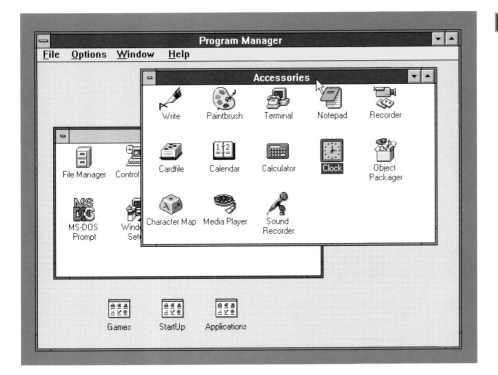

1. Click on Window in the menu bar.
2. From the list of open windows, click on the name of the window you want to make active.

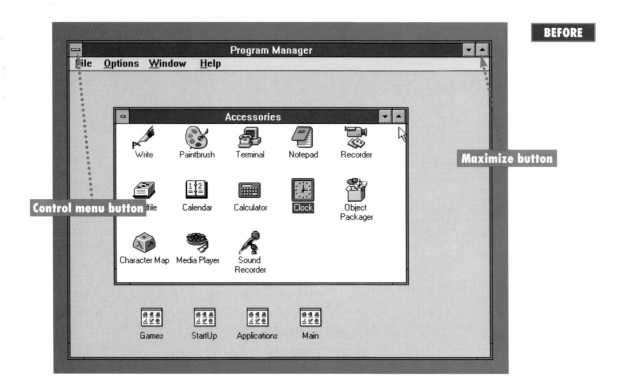

BEFORE

Control menu button

Maximize button

1. **Click on the Maximize button for the Accessories window.**

   The Maximize command causes the window to fill the entire desktop. You can no longer see any other open windows. When the window is maximized, the Maximize button is replaced by the Restore button, a two-headed arrow, pointing up and down.

OOPS!

To restore the window to its previous size, see *TASK: Restore a window.*

USE THE CONTROL MENU

You also can open the Control menu of a window, and select Maximize.

Program Manager - [Accessories]

File   Options   Window   Help

Write   Paintbrush   Terminal   Notepad   Recorder

Cardfile   Calendar   Calculator   Clock   Object Packager

Character Map   Media Player   Sound Recorder

REVIEW

1. Click on the Maximize button.

MAXIMIZE, MINIMIZE, AND RESTORE

Keep in mind the differences between Maximize, Minimize, and Restore. Maximize expands the window to fill the desktop. Minimize reduces the window to an icon. Restore returns the window to its last displayed size and location.

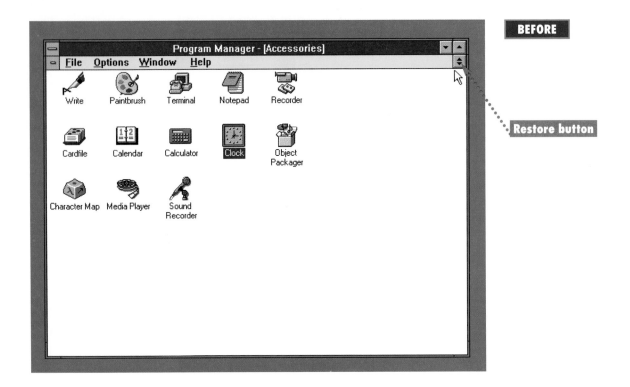

BEFORE

Restore button

---

1. **Click on the Restore button for the Accessories window.**

   The window is restored to its previous size and location. When the window is restored, the Restore button changes to a Maximize button, an arrow pointing up.

USE THE CONTROL MENU

You also can open the Control menu and select Restore to restore a window.

OOPS!

You cannot restore a window unless it has been maximized or minimized.

MAXIMIZE, MINIMIZE, AND RESTORE

Keep in mind the differences between Maximize, Minimize, and Restore. Maximize expands the window to fill the desktop. Minimize reduces the window to an icon. Restore returns the window to its last displayed size and location.

AFTER

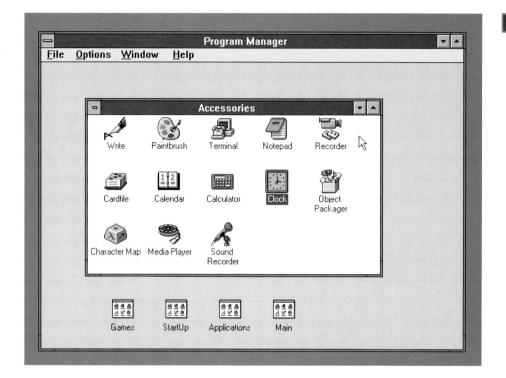

REVIEW

1. Click on the Restore button.

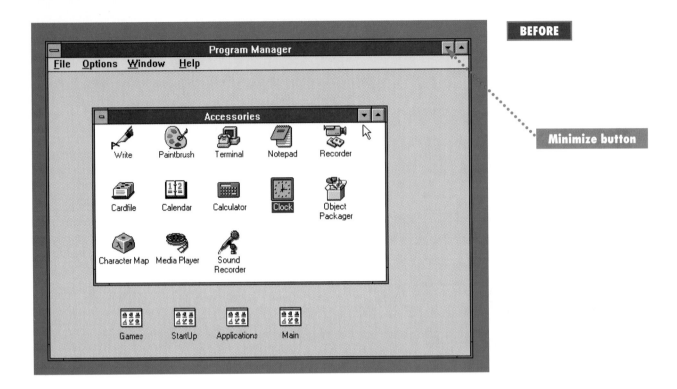

BEFORE

Minimize button

---

1. **Click on the Minimize button for the Accessories window.**

   If this window isn't open, open it; to do so, see *TASK: Open a window*. The Minimize button reduces the window to an icon at the bottom of the desktop.

USE THE CONTROL MENU

You also can use the Control menu and select Minimize, to minimized a window.

OOPS!

To restore the window, see *TASK: Restore a window*.

AFTER

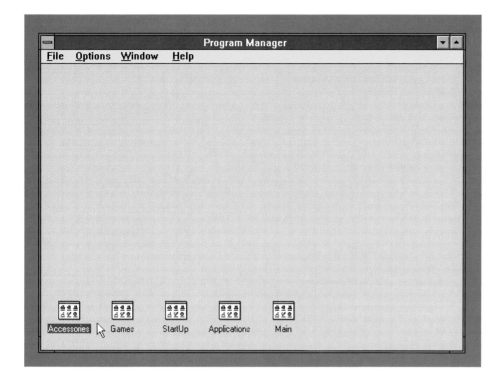

REVIEW

1. Click on the Minimize button.

MAXIMIZE, MINIMIZE, AND RESTORE

Keep in mind the differences between Maximize, Minimize, and Restore. Maximize expands the window to fill the desktop. Minimize reduces the window to an icon. Restore returns the window to its last displayed size and location.

BEFORE

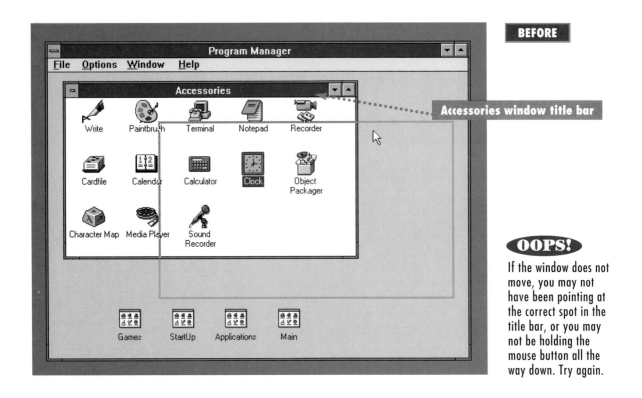

Accessories window title bar

OOPS!

If the window does not move, you may not have been pointing at the correct spot in the title bar, or you may not be holding the mouse button all the way down. Try again.

1. Point to the title bar of the window you want to use.

This step selects the window you want to move. The title bar is the bar across the top of the window that displays the window's name. Be sure that you are pointing at the title bar, not at the window's border.

2. Press and hold the left mouse button.

When you press and hold the left mouse button, notice that the window's border changes color.

3. Drag the mouse pointer to the new location.

When you drag the window, you see the outline of the window move along with the mouse pointer.

4. Release the mouse button.

When you release the mouse button, the window moves to the new location.

If you exit Windows, the program remembers the size and location of all open windows. When you re-enter Windows, all of the windows on-screen are displayed exactly as they were in the preceding session.

USE A KEYBOARD?

You can move a window with the keyboard. Drop down the Control menu, then select Move. Use the arrow keys to move the window to the new location, then press Enter.

AFTER

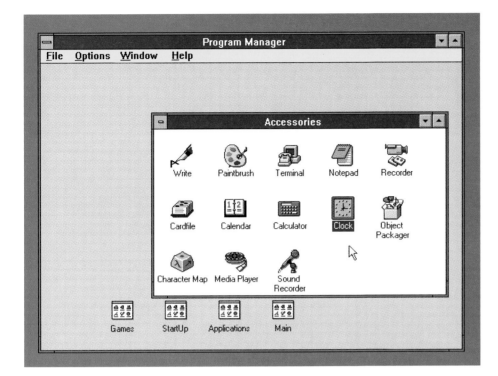

REVIEW

1. Point to the window's title bar.

2. Press and hold the left mouse button.

3. Drag the window to its new location.

4. Release the mouse button.

ARRANGE ALL WINDOWS

You can automatically arrange the way windows are displayed on the desktop. Drop down the Window menu and select Tile to arrange the windows side by side. Select Cascade to arrange the windows so that they overlap neatly.

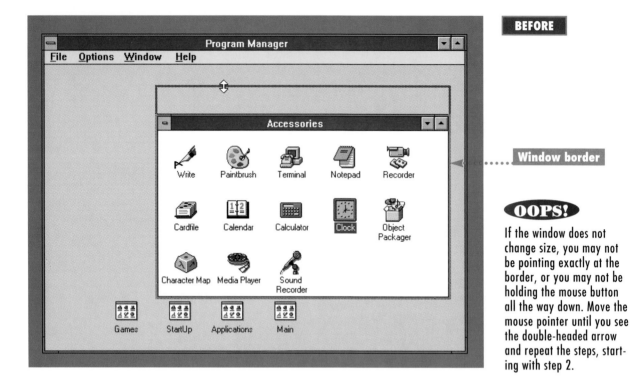

BEFORE

Window border

OOPS!

If the window does not change size, you may not be pointing exactly at the border, or you may not be holding the mouse button all the way down. Move the mouse pointer until you see the double-headed arrow and repeat the steps, starting with step 2.

1. Point to the border of the window that you want to resize.

You must point to the border. You will know you are pointing at the correct spot when the pointer changes to a two-headed arrow.

2. Press and hold the left mouse button.

When you press and hold the left mouse button, the border changes color.

3. Drag the border as far as you want, to resize the window.

As you drag, you see the outline of the border move. You can drag the top, bottom, left, or right border. You can drag it to the center of the screen to make the window smaller or toward the edge of the screen to make the window larger.

4. Release the left mouse button.

When you release the button, the window assumes the new size.

If you exit Windows, the program remembers the size and location of all open windows, and, when you re-enter Windows, displays them exactly as they were in the previous session.

USE A KEYBOARD?

You can resize windows with the keyboard. Drop down the window's Control Menu and select Size. Then use the arrow keys to move the borders, and press Enter to resize the window.

TRY A SHORTCUT

To quickly resize a window, point directly to a corner. Drag the corner out to make the window larger; drag the corner in to make the window smaller.

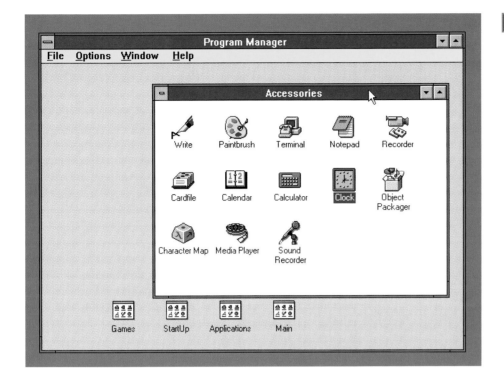

AFTER

REVIEW

1. Point at the border of the window so that the pointer changes to a double-headed arrow.

2. Press and hold the left mouse button.

3. Drag the border as far in or out as you want.

4. Release the left mouse button.

BEFORE

1. Open the window that contains the program item icon for the program you want to start.

Remember, Group windows contain the icons for groups of programs. To open Windows Paintbrush, for instance, first open the Accessories group window.

2. Double-click the program item icon.

This step chooses and starts the program. With the keyboard, use the arrow keys to highlight the icon, and press Enter. As the program starts, an hourglass indicates that Windows is processing the command.

There are many other ways to start and run programs with Windows. For more information see *Using Windows 3.1*, Special Edition.

OOPS!

If the program doesn't start, you may not have clicked twice. Point to the icon and try again.

EXIT THE PROGRAM

To exit the program, see *TASK: Exit a Microsoft Windows program*.

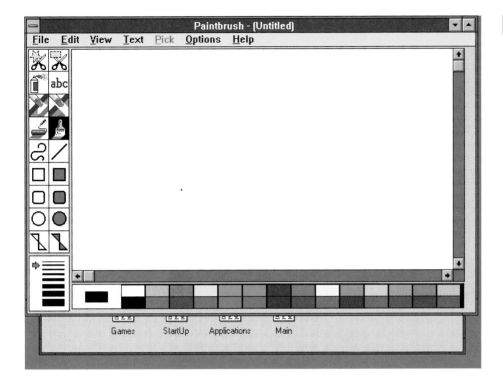

AFTER

REVIEW

1. Open the group window that contains the program item icon.

2. Double-click the program item icon. With the keyboard, highlight the icon and press Enter.

EXIT A MICROSOFT WINDOWS PROGRAM

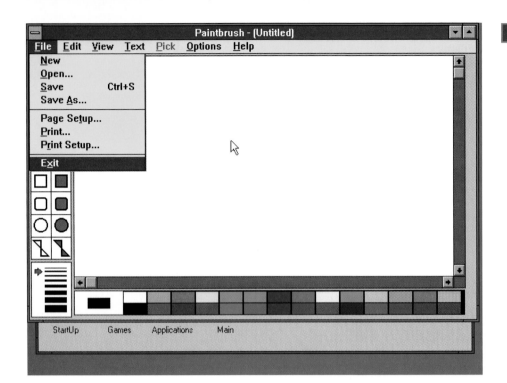

BEFORE

1. **In the program window, click on File in the menu bar.**

   This step opens the File menu. You see a list of File commands.

2. **Click on the Exit command.**

   Selecting Exit closes the program window, reducing it to an icon.

OOPS!

To restart the program, see *TASK: Start a Microsoft Windows program*.

TRY A SHORTCUT

To exit a program quickly, double-click on the program window's Control menu button.

AFTER

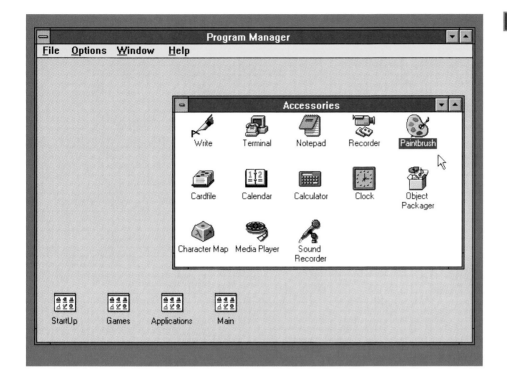

REVIEW

1. Drop down the program window's File menu.

2. Select the Exit command.

SAVE YOUR WORK!

Before you exit an application, be sure that you save all current data in a file on a disk. If you don't save before you exit, all your work will be lost. Some programs prompt you to save, before closing the window.

BEFORE

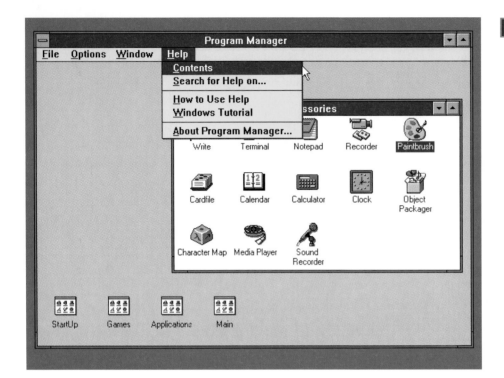

1. **Click on Help in the menu bar.**

   This step opens the Help menu and displays a list of help commands.

2. **Click on Contents.**

   This step chooses the Contents command. The Help window opens, displaying a table of contents.

3. **Click on the desired topic.**

   This step chooses a topic from the Table of Contents menu. After you choose a topic, information about that topic is displayed. Each application in Windows has help topics.

When you are finished using the help feature, close the Help window. For more information about closing a window, see *TASK: Close a window.*

For more information about using Windows Help, see *Using Microsoft Windows 3.1*, Special Edition.

SCROLL THE HELP WINDOW

To scroll through information in the Help window, click on the up and down scroll arrows along the right side of the window, or press the PgUp and PgDn keys.

To close the Help window quickly, double-click on its Control menu button.

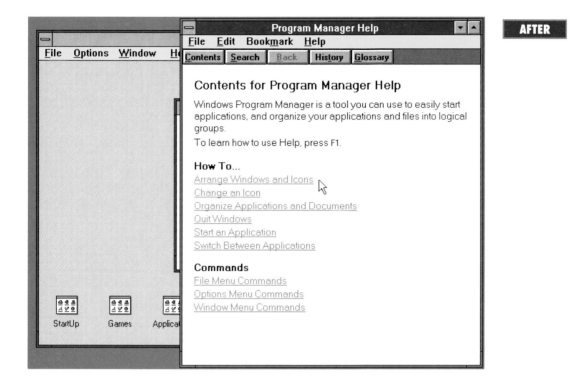

AFTER

REVIEW

1. Click on Help in the menu bar.

2. Click on the Contents command.

3. Click on the topic for which you need information.

TRY A SHORTCUT

Press the F1 key as a shortcut for steps 1 and 2.

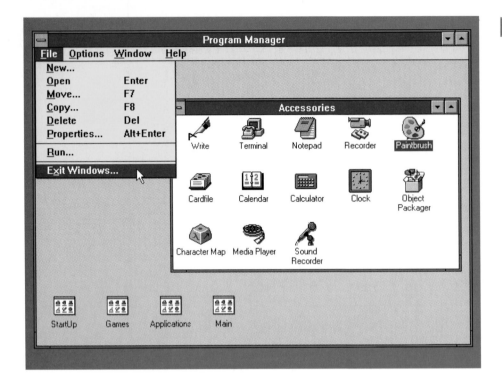

BEFORE

---

1. **In the Program Manager window, click on File in the menu bar.**

   This opens the File menu on the desktop.

2. **Click on the Exit Windows command.**

   A dialog box opens on the desktop. The box asks you to confirm that you want to exit Windows.

3. **Click on the OK button.**

   Windows closes, and the DOS prompt is displayed on-screen.

OOPS!

If you change your mind about leaving Windows, select Cancel in step 3.

RESTART MICROSOFT WINDOWS

To restart Windows, see *TASK: Start Microsoft Windows.*

c:\>

AFTER

REVIEW

1. Click on File in the menu bar.
2. Click on the Exit Windows command.
3. Click on OK in the Exit Windows dialog box.

TRY A SHORTCUT

As a shortcut for steps 1 and 2, double-click the Control menu button in the Program Manager window. Remember, the Control menu button is the small box with a hyphen in the upper left corner of the screen.

GLOSSARY

3½-inch disk A floppy disk enclosed in a hard plastic case. These disks come in two capacities — double density (720K) and high density (1.44M or 2.88M).

5¼-inch disk A floppy disk enclosed in a flexible plastic case. These disks come in two capacities — double density (360K) and high density (1.2M).

Application A software program designed to help you perform a specific task. Word processors and spreadsheets are two common application programs.

AUTOEXEC.BAT A file that DOS executes each time you start a PC. The file may include commands that control the way the computer runs. For example, it may tell DOS where to find certain files, or what directory to make current.

Back up To copy the files from a hard disk to a removable storage medium, such as floppy disk or DA tape. The copied files are called backups.

Batch file A file that contains a series of DOS commands. The commands are executed when you run the batch file. You may use DOS to create a batch file that changes to a certain directory and starts a program.

Baud rate The speed at which data is transmitted by a modem. Baud rate is usually measured in bits per second (bps).

Boot The process of starting a computer and loading the operating system.

Bus A set of wires or conductors that carry signals among the different computer components.

Byte   A measure of information stored on a disk. One byte is approximately equal to one character.

Cache   A type of memory that the CPU can use to store frequently needed information.

Capacity   The amount of data that can be stored on a disk or in memory. Capacity is measured in bytes, kilobytes (K), megabytes (M), and gigabytes (G).

CD-ROM   An acronym for compact disk-read-only memory. CD-ROMs are storage devices that can contain a large amount of data. CD-ROM drives are used to read the data from a CD-ROM into the PC. The PC cannot write onto a CD-ROM.

CD-ROM drive   A device used by the PC to read data from CD-ROMs.

Central Processing Unit (CPU)   The main microprocessor chip controlling the computer; in other words, the brain of the computer. The CPU is stored inside the system unit. CPUs are given numbers so that you can tell them apart. Examples are 8088, 8086, 80286, 80386, and 80486. The higher the number, the newer and faster the CPU.

Chip   A tiny integrated circuit, built into the circuit board, or plugged into expansion slots, that either controls computer functions or stores information. The microprocessor and math coprocessor are chips, and read-only memory storage units are chips.

Click   To press and release a mouse button.

Clone   An IBM PC-compatible computer built by another manufacturer.

COMMAND.COM   An essential DOS file, containing the command processor.

Compatible   Having the capability to work with other components. Both software and hardware are said to be compatible if they work with other PC components.

CONFIG.SYS   A special DOS file that determines configuration settings. DOS executes the commands in this file every time it starts.

Continuous-feed paper   Perforated computer paper that runs through the sprockets on impact printers so that paper is always available. Also called tractor-feed or fan-fold.

Conventional memory   All of the random-access memory in a PC up to 640K.

CPU   See *Central Processing Unit.*

Current directory   The directory DOS is working in. Also called the active directory.

Current disk   The disk DOS is working from. Also called the active disk.

Cursor   A marker used to indicate the current position of input or output on a monitor display.

Database   An application used to store and retrieve related sets of information. For example, a mailing list can be stored in a database.

Density   A term used to describe the amount of information you can store on a disk. Double-density disks store 360K or 720K of data; high-density disks store 1.2M, 1.44M, or 2.88M of data.

Desktop   A type of system unit case, designed to fit conveniently on the top of a desk. Also, in Windows 3.1, the monitor screen where windows are displayed.

Desktop publishing program   An application that combines text formatting and graphics manipulation to create professional-looking documents.

Dialog box   A window that opens on-screen. A dialog box either provides information about the current action or asks you to enter additional information to complete the action.

Directory   A grouping of files and other directories on a hard disk. DOS uses directories the way you might use file folders to organize data on a disk.

Disk drive   A hardware device that reads and writes information to and from magnetic storage disks. Disk drive types include hard disks, floppy disks, and CD-ROMs.

Docking station   A component that allows you to use a portable computer as a desktop system.

DOS   Disk Operating System. DOS is the most common PC operating system. It manages the PC's resources, including files, disks, and programs.

DOS prompt   The user interface that appears on-screen when DOS is waiting for a command. Minimally, the DOS prompt displays the current drive like this: `A>` or `C:\>`.

DOS Shell   A graphical user interface built into DOS to provide an alternative to the DOS prompt.

Dot matrix   An impact printer that arranges dots in rows and columns to print text and graphics on a page.

Double-click   The act of pressing and releasing a mouse button twice in rapid succession.

Double-density   A measurement of disk capacity.

Drag   The act of pressing and holding down a mouse button and then sliding the mouse pointer to another location.

Draw   An application used to draw computer graphics.

Drop   The act of releasing the mouse button after completing a drag.

E-mail   Electronic mail that you can transmit to other computer users on a network or by way of a modem.

Escape   The act of pressing the Esc key. Usually used to cancel the previous action.

Expandability   The amount of room available in a computer for adding peripherals or memory.

Expanded memory   A combination of hardware and software that tricks some computers and programs into accessing more than 1M of memory.

Expansion card   A printed circuit board that fits into an expansion slot in the system unit for controlling peripherals or adding memory. Also called an expansion board.

Expansion slot   A slot on the motherboard where an expansion card is attached.

Extended memory   Memory above 1M used by PCs based on 80286, 80386, or 80486 microprocessors.

Fax   Short for facsimile. A way of transmitting data over telephone lines.

File   A collection of data stored on a disk for future use. For example, a letter or a worksheet can be stored as a file.

File name   The name you give a file so that you and DOS can find the file on the disk. A file name has two parts: the name can be up to eight characters long; the extension can be three characters long.

File specification   The complete name and path to a file stored on a disk. The file specification tells DOS where to find the file.

Floppy disk   A removable magnetic device, used to store computer files. Also called a disk, a floppy, or a diskette. Floppy disks come in two sizes: 3½-inch or 5¼-inch.

Floppy disk drive   A device that reads and writes information on a floppy disk.

Font   A specific size and style of character that can be printed or displayed by a PC.

Format   The process that prepares a disk for use. Also, the layout of information on a page, and additionally, the particular way a PC stores data. For example, graphics files are stored in a graphics format; text files are stored in a text format.

Function keys   The keys on a PC keyboard that are labeled with the letter F and a number from 1 to 15 (some keyboards have fewer function keys). Function keys perform tasks or execute commands specific to the application being used.

Gigabyte (G)   One billion bytes.

Graphical User Interface (GUI)   An easy-to-use user interface that combines graphics, menus, and plain English commands to let the user communicate with the PC. For example, Microsoft Windows is a GUI.

Group   In Microsoft Windows, a group is a collection of related programs. These programs are stored together in a group window represented by a group icon.

GUI   An abbreviation for graphical user interface. It is pronounced "gooey."

Hard copy   Printed information. Hard copy is sometimes called computer printout.

Hard disk   A data storage device usually fixed inside the system unit. Hard disks range in size from 20M to over 250M.

Hardware   The physical parts of the computer that you can see and touch. For example, the keyboard, the monitor, and the case that houses the system unit are all hardware.

High density   A measurement of disk capacity.

Icon   A picture used in a graphical user interface to represent an element within the program. In Microsoft Windows, some common icons represent files, disks, programs, and groups.

Input   Data put into the computer for processing.

Interface   A point of communication between parts of the PC.

Joystick   A pointing or input device used mostly for playing computer games.

Keyboard   An input device used to enter data or commands by typing.

Kilobyte (K)   1,024 bytes. 1K is usually rounded to equal one thousand bytes. Kilobytes are used to measure disk capacity and memory.

LAN   See *Local area network*.

Laser printer   A nonimpact printer that uses a laser beam and toner to create an image on paper.

Local area network (LAN)   A group of computers linked by cables in a small area, such as one office building.

Math coprocessor   A computer chip designed to perform complex calculations. A math coprocessor usually is built into the microprocessor or is added to the motherboard.

Megabyte (M)   One million bytes.

Memory   The electronic circuitry where a PC stores information that it is not currently using.

Memory resident software   A software program that stays in RAM while you are using it.

Microprocessor   The main chip that contains all the elements of the PC's central processing unit.

Microsoft Windows   An operating environment developed by Microsoft Corporation for use with DOS. Windows uses a graphical user interface to simplify using a PC.

Modem   A device used for transmitting data over telephone lines. Short for *mo*dulator/*dem*odulator.

Monitor   The hardware that displays the information you type on the keyboard and the PC's response to commands. The monitor also is called a display or screen.

Motherboard   The main circuit board in the system unit. It usually holds the CPU and the RAM and has slots for attaching expansion boards.

Mouse   A pointing device used with some programs to input data.

Mouse pad   A rubber pad that provides a uniform surface for a mouse to slide on.

Mouse pointer   The symbol that indicates the location of the mouse on-screen.

MS-DOS   A version of DOS developed by Microsoft Corporation.

Multimedia   Applications that use a combination of graphics, text, sound, and video.

Multitasking   The capability of running more than one application at the same time.

Network   A group of computers linked together by cables to share data and resources.

Notebook   A portable PC small enough to fit in a briefcase.

Operating system   A group of software programs that provides the instructions you need to control a PC.

OS/2   A PC operating system.

Output   Data after it is processed by the computer and returned to a format the user can understand.

Parallel port   A type of port on the system unit, usually used to attach printers.

Path   The route the operating system must follow to find a file stored on a disk. Usually, a path includes the disk drive, all directories between the root directory and the file, and the complete file name.

PC   An acronym for personal computer. Usually, PC refers to an IBM-compatible personal computer.

Peripherals   Hardware devices attached to the main system unit. A printer, modem, and mouse are all peripherals.

Pixel   A unit of measurement. Each pixel is one of many dots on the screen that forms information to be displayed. Short for picture element.

Point   The act of moving the mouse pointer so that it is touching the desired element on-screen. Also a measure of type size.

Port   An electrical socket on the outside of the system unit that connects external peripherals to expansion cards on the inside of the system unit. Most PCs come with at least one parallel port, one serial port, one game port, and one video adapter port.

Portable   A small PC that can be carried easily. Often, a portable runs on batteries. Different types of portables include notebooks and laptops.

PostScript   The name of a printer control language that has become a standard for graphics printing.

Program   A set of instructions that tells the computer what to do. Also called *application* or *software*.

Protocol   The language that sets the rules for communication between hardware devices.

RAM   An acronym for random-access memory. RAM is the electronic memory where the computer can store information until it is needed or stored on a disk.

Resolution   A measurement of the quality or the sharpness of a monitor, the image on a monitor, or a printed image. Resolution usually is measured by the number of dots used to make the image.

ROM   An acronym for read-only memory. ROM is memory that cannot be erased or added to. ROM provides the instructions the computer needs to get started each time you turn it on.

Root directory   The main directory on a disk. All other directories grow out of the root.

Scanner   A device used to input printed information into the PC.

SCSI   An acronym for *small computer systems interface*. SCSI is a standard used for connecting some devices to a PC.

Serial port   A type of port on the system unit, usually used for attaching communications devices.

Shell   An interface between the operating system and the user.

Software   Programs comprised of coded instructions that you run on the computer to tell the hardware how to process information. Two basic types of software exist — system software and application software.

Spreadsheet   An application used to manipulate numbers and perform calculations.

Storage device   A hardware device used by the PC to store data. For example, hard disks, floppy disks, and DA tapes are storage devices.

Subdirectory   A directory that is created in another directory. Technically speaking, all directories on a disk are subdirectories of the root.

Surge suppressor   A power-protection device that filters the voltage between an outlet and a hardware component to prevent damage from sudden voltage changes.

Syntax   The format and rules used to issue a DOS command.

System software   Software that instructs the different pieces of hardware how to operate and how to respond to your commands. For example, an operating system is a system software program.

Telecommunications   Using modems to exchange data between computers over telephone lines.

Uninterruptible Power Supply (UPS)   A power protection device that has a built-in battery to protect the computer components from a power outage.

User interface   A point of communication between the user and the PC. The DOS prompt, the DOS Shell, and Microsoft Windows are examples of user interfaces.

Video adapter   The circuit that controls the monitor. The video adapter is built into the motherboard or installed as an expansion card. The monitor connects to the video adapter via the video adapter port on the system unit. Common types include CGA, EGA, VGA, and SVGA.

Video Graphics Array (VGA)   A common video graphics adapter standard that provides high resolution.

Virus   A software program, maliciously designed to damage existing files, programs, and disks, and surreptitiously transferred to the PCs of unsuspecting owners.

What you see is what you get (WYSIWYG)   A term that describes software programs that display information on the monitor exactly as it prints on the page.

Wild card   A character used by DOS to represent other characters. For example, a question mark (?) represents any single character. An asterisk (*) represents any group of characters.

Window   An area on-screen used by some programs, such as Microsoft Windows, to display information. Some windows contain applications, some contain icons that represent the applications, and some contain documents created with the applications.

Word processor   An application used for entering and manipulating text.

Write-protection   The process of protecting the files stored on a disk from being overwritten with new data.

WYSIWYG   An acronym for *what you see is what you get*, pronounced "wizzywig."

INDEX

Symbols

A

B

INDEX

F

INDEX

Volume 1 Topics 1–7

Authors

Randall I. Charles
Professor Emeritus
Department of Mathematics
San Jose State University
San Jose, California

Jennifer Bay-Williams
Professor of Mathematics
Education
College of Education and Human
Development
University of Louisville
Louisville, Kentucky

Robert Q. Berry, III
Associate Professor of
Mathematics Education
Department of Curriculum,
Instruction and Special Education
University of Virginia
Charlottesville, Virginia

Janet H. Caldwell
Professor of Mathematics
Rowan University
Glassboro, New Jersey

Zachary Champagne
Assistant in Research
Florida Center for Research in
Science, Technology, Engineering,
and Mathematics (FCR-STEM)
Jacksonville, Florida

Juanita Copley
Professor Emerita, College
of Education
University of Houston
Houston, Texas

Warren Crown
Professor Emeritus of Mathematics
Education
Graduate School of Education
Rutgers University
New Brunswick, New Jersey

Francis (Skip) Fennell
L. Stanley Bowlsbey Professor
of Education and Graduate and
Professional Studies
McDaniel College
Westminster, Maryland

Karen Karp
Professor of Mathematics
Education
Department of Early Childhood
and Elementary Education
University of Louisville
Louisville, Kentucky

Stuart J. Murphy
Visual Learning Specialist
Boston, Massachusetts

Jane F. Schielack
Professor of Mathematics
Associate Dean for Assessment
and Pre K-12 Education,
College of Science
Texas A&M University
College Station, Texas

Jennifer M. Suh
Associate Professor for
Mathematics Education
George Mason University
Fairfax, Virginia

Jonathan A. Wray
Mathematics Instructional
Facilitator
Howard County Public Schools
Ellicott City, Maryland

SAVVAS
LEARNING COMPANY

Mathematicians

Roger Howe
Professor of Mathematics
Yale University
New Haven, Connecticut

Gary Lippman
Professor of Mathematics and
Computer Science
California State University,
East Bay
Hayward, California

ELL Consultants

Janice R. Corona
Independent Education Consultant
Dallas, Texas

Jim Cummins
Professor
The University of Toronto
Toronto, Canada

ISBN-13: 978-0-328-96833-6
ISBN-10:   0-328-96833-1
8 2022

Digital Resources

You'll be using these digital resources throughout the year!

Go to SavvasRealize.com

MP
Math Practices Animations to play anytime

Learn
Visual Learning Animation Plus with animation, interaction, and math tools

Practice Buddy
Online Personalized Practice for each lesson

Assessment
Quick Check for each lesson

Games
Math Games to help you learn

ACTIVe-book
Student Edition online for showing your work

Solve
Solve & Share problems plus math tools

Glossary
Animated Glossary in English and Spanish

Tools
Math Tools to help you understand

Help
Another Look Homework Video for extra help

eText
Student Edition online

SAVVAS realize.™ Everything you need for math anytime, anywhere

Contents

And remember your eText is available at SavvasRealize.com!

TOPICS

TOPIC 1 Understand Multiplication and Division of Whole Numbers

*Lesson exclusively for Virginia at the end of this volume

You can represent multiplication as an array with equal rows and columns.

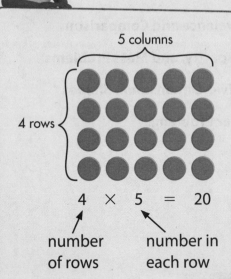

5 columns

4 rows

$$4 \times 5 = 20$$

number of rows · number in each row

TOPIC 2 Multiplication Facts: Use Patterns

You can use patterns to help remember multiplication facts.

DATA

9s Facts

$0 \times 9 = 0$

$1 \times 9 = 9$

$2 \times 9 = 18$

$3 \times 9 = 27$

$4 \times 9 = 36$

$5 \times 9 = 45$

$6 \times 9 = 54$

$7 \times 9 = $

$8 \times 9 = $

$9 \times 9 = $

*Lesson exclusively for Virginia at the end of this volume

TOPIC 3 Apply Properties: Multiplication Facts for 3, 4, 6, 7, 8

Properties can help you use known facts to find unknown facts.

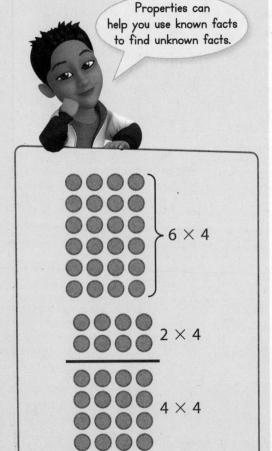

6×4

2×4

4×4

TOPIC 4 Use Multiplication to Divide: Division Facts

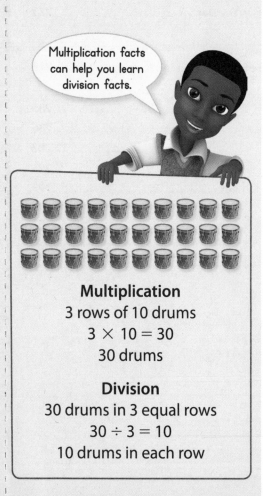

Multiplication facts can help you learn division facts.

Multiplication
3 rows of 10 drums
$3 \times 10 = 30$
30 drums

Division
30 drums in 3 equal rows
$30 \div 3 = 10$
10 drums in each row

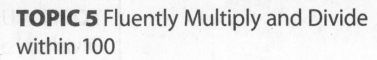

TOPIC 5 Fluently Multiply and Divide within 100

You can use a multiplication table to find missing factors.

$3 \times 5 = 15$ $15 \div 3 = 5$

TOPIC 6 Connect Area to Multiplication and Addition

You can find the area of a shape by counting the number of unit squares needed to cover it.

TOPIC 7 Represent and Interpret Data

*Lesson exclusively for Virginia at the end of this volume

You can use a scaled bar graph to help compare data.

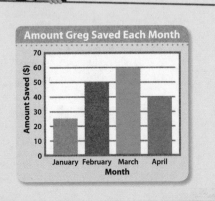

Amount Greg Saved Each Month

Virginia Mathematics Standards of Learning

NUMBER AND NUMBER SENSE

3.1 The student will

    a) read, write, and identify the place and value of each digit in a six-digit whole number, with and without models;

    b) round whole numbers, 9,999 or less, to the nearest ten, hundred, and thousand; and

    c) compare and order whole numbers, each 9,999 or less.

3.2 The student will

    a) name and write fractions and mixed numbers represented by a model;

    b) represent fractions and mixed numbers with models and symbols; and

    c) compare fractions having like and unlike denominators, using words and symbols ($>$, $<$, $=$, or $\neq$), with models.

Dear Families,

The standards on the following pages describe the math that students will learn this year.

Virginia Mathematics Standards of Learning (cont.)

COMPUTATION AND ESTIMATION

3.3 The student will

   a) estimate and determine the sum or difference of two whole numbers; and

   b) create and solve single-step and multistep practical problems involving sums or differences of two whole numbers, each 9,999 or less.

3.4 The student will

   a) represent multiplication and division through 10 × 10, using a variety of approaches and models;

   b) create and solve single-step practical problems that involve multiplication and division through 10 × 10; and

   c) demonstrate fluency with multiplication facts of 0, 1, 2, 5, and 10; and

   d) solve single-step practical problems involving multiplication of whole numbers, where one factor is 99 or less and the second factor is 5 or less.

3.5 The student will solve practical problems that involve addition and subtraction with proper fractions having like denominators of 12 or less.

Virginia Mathematics Standards of Learning (cont.)

MEASUREMENT AND GEOMETRY

3.6 The student will

    a) determine the value of a collection of bills and coins whose total value is $5.00 or less;

    b) compare the value of two sets of coins or two sets of coins and bills; and

    c) make change from $5.00 or less.

3.7 The student will estimate and use U.S. Customary and metric units to measure

    a) length to the nearest $\frac{1}{2}$ inch, inch, foot, yard, centimeter, and meter; and

    b) liquid volume in cups, pints, quarts, gallons, and liters.

3.8 The student will estimate and

    a) measure the distance around a polygon in order to determine its perimeter using U.S. Customary and metric units; and

    b) count the number of square units needed to cover a given surface in order to determine its area.

3.9 The student will

    a) tell time to the nearest minute, using analog and digital clocks;

    b) solve practical problems related to elapsed time in one-hour increments within a 12-hour period; and

    c) identify equivalent periods of time and solve practical problems related to equivalent periods of time.

3.10 The student will read temperature to the nearest degree.

3.11 The student will identify and draw representations of points, lines, line segments, rays, and angles.

3.12 The student will

    a) define polygon;

    b) identify and name polygons with 10 or fewer sides; and

    c) combine and subdivide polygons with three or four sides and name the resulting polygon(s).

3.13 The student will identify and describe congruent and noncongruent figures.

Virginia Mathematics Standards of Learning (cont.)

PROBABILITY AND STATISTICS

3.14 The student will investigate and describe the concept of probability as a measurement of chance and list possible outcomes for a single event.

3.15 The student will

  a) collect, organize, and represent data in pictographs or bar graphs; and

  b) read and interpret data represented in pictographs and bar graphs.

PATTERNS, FUNCTIONS, AND ALGEBRA

3.16 The student will identify, describe, create, and extend patterns found in objects, pictures, numbers and tables.

3.17 The student will create equations to represent equivalent mathematical relationships.

Virginia Mathematical Process Goals for Students

The content of the mathematics standards is intended to support the following five process goals for students: becoming mathematical problem solvers, communicating mathematically, reasoning mathematically, making mathematical connections, and using mathematical representations to model and interpret practical situations. Practical situations include real-world problems and problems that model real-world situations.

MATHEMATICAL PROBLEM SOLVING

Students will apply mathematical concepts and skills and the relationships among them to solve problem situations of varying complexities. Students also will recognize and create problems from real-world data and situations within and outside mathematics and then apply appropriate strategies to determine acceptable solutions. To accomplish this goal, students will need to develop a repertoire of skills and strategies for solving a variety of problem types. A major goal of the mathematics program is to help students apply mathematics concepts and skills to become mathematical problem solvers.

MATHEMATICAL COMMUNICATION

Students will communicate thinking and reasoning using the language of mathematics, including specialized vocabulary and symbolic notation, to express mathematical ideas with precision. Representing, discussing, justifying, conjecturing, reading, writing, presenting, and listening to mathematics will help students to clarify their thinking and deepen their understanding of the mathematics being studied. Mathematical communication becomes visible where learning involves participation in mathematical discussions.

Virginia Mathematical Process Goals for Students (cont.)

MATHEMATICAL REASONING

Students will recognize reasoning and proof as fundamental aspects of mathematics. Students will learn and apply inductive and deductive reasoning skills to make, test, and evaluate mathematical statements and to justify steps in mathematical procedures. Students will use logical reasoning to analyze an argument and to determine whether conclusions are valid. In addition, students will use number sense to apply proportional and spatial reasoning and to reason from a variety of representations.

MATHEMATICAL CONNECTIONS

Students will build upon prior knowledge to relate concepts and procedures from different topics within mathematics and see mathematics as an integrated field of study. Through the practical application of content and process skills, students will make connections among different areas of mathematics and between mathematics and other disciplines, and to real-world contexts. Science and mathematics teachers and curriculum writers are encouraged to develop mathematics and science curricula that support, apply, and reinforce each other.

MATHEMATICAL REPRESENTATIONS

Students will represent and describe mathematical ideas, generalizations, and relationships using a variety of methods. Students will understand that representations of mathematical ideas are an essential part of learning, doing, and communicating mathematics. Students should make connections among different representations—physical, visual, symbolic, verbal, and contextual—and recognize that representation is both a process and a product.

Problem Solving Handbook

Math Practices

1. Make sense of problems and persevere in solving them.

2. Reason abstractly and quantitatively.

3. Construct viable arguments and critique the reasoning of others.

4. Model with mathematics.

5. Use appropriate tools strategically.

6. Attend to precision.

7. Look for and make use of structure.

8. Look for and express regularity in repeated reasoning.

There are good Thinking Habits for each of these math practices.

Make sense of problems and persevere in solving them.

Good math thinkers make sense of problems and think of ways to solve them.

If they get stuck, they don't give up.

Mia has $36. Kate has $17 less than Mia. Do Mia and Kate together have enough money to buy a bike for $54?

Here I listed what I know and what I am trying to find.

What I Know:
- Mia has $36.
- Kate has $17 less than $36.
- The bike costs $54.

What I need to find:
- Whether Kate and Mia have at least $54 in all.

Thinking Habits

Be a good thinker! These questions can help you.

- What do I need to find?
- What do I know?
- What's my plan for solving the problem?
- What else can I try if I get stuck?
- How can I check that my solution makes sense?

2 Reason abstractly and quantitatively.

Good math thinkers know how to think about words and numbers to solve problems.

I drew a bar diagram that shows how things in the problem are related.

Jake bought a coat for $47. He also bought a shirt. Jake spent $71 in all. How much did he spend on the shirt?

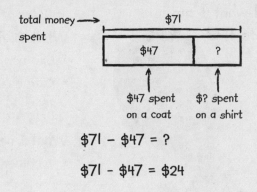

total money spent → | $71 |
$47 | ?

$47 spent on a coat

$? spent on a shirt

$71 – $47 = ?

$71 – $47 = $24

Thinking Habits

Be a good thinker! These questions can help you.

- What do the numbers and symbols in the problem mean?

- How are the numbers or quantities related?

- How can I represent a word problem using pictures, numbers, or equations?

3 Construct viable arguments and critique the reasoning of others.

> Good math thinkers use math to explain why they are right. They can talk about the math that others do, too.

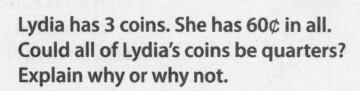

> I wrote a clear argument with words, numbers, and symbols.

Lydia has 3 coins. She has 60¢ in all. Could all of Lydia's coins be quarters? Explain why or why not.

Marta's Work

Lydia's coins cannot all be quarters.

1 quarter is 25¢.

3 quarters is 25¢, 50¢, 75¢.

75¢ > 60¢

So, 3 quarters is more money than Lydia actually has.

Thinking Habits

Be a good thinker! These questions can help you.

- How can I use numbers, objects, drawings, or actions to justify my argument?

- Am I using numbers and symbols correctly?

- Is my explanation clear and complete?

- What questions can I ask to understand other people's thinking?

- Are there mistakes in other people's thinking?

- Can I improve other people's thinking?

4 Model with mathematics.

Good math thinkers choose and apply math they know to show and solve problems from everyday life.

Harry has carrots in his garden. Harry has 5 rows of carrots with 4 carrots in each row. How many carrots are in Harry's garden?

$4 + 4 + 4 + 4 + 4 = 20$

There are 20 carrots in Harry's garden.

I used what I know about arrays and addition. I drew a picture to help.

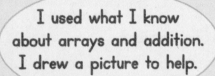

Thinking Habits

Be a good thinker! These questions can help you.

- How can I use math I know to help solve this problem?

- How can I use pictures, objects, or an equation to represent the problem?

- How can I use numbers, words, and symbols to solve the problem?

5 Use appropriate tools strategically.

Good math thinkers know how to pick the right tools to solve math problems.

I decided to use place-value blocks to help me compare. I can use them to show the hundreds, the tens, and the ones.

Carla has 234 stickers. Dan has 242 stickers. Who has more stickers?

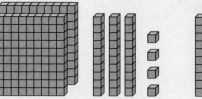
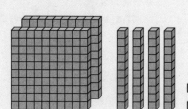

242 is greater than 234.
Dan has more stickers.

Thinking Habits

Be a good thinker! These questions can help you.

- Which tools can I use?

- Why should I use this tool to help me solve the problem?

- Is there a different tool I could use?

- Am I using the tool appropriately?

Attend to precision.

Good math thinkers are careful about what they write and say, so their ideas about math are clear.

I was precise with my measurements and the way that I wrote my solution.

Which of these two paths is longer? How much longer?

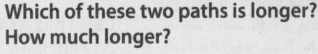

Blue path: 3 cm + 3 cm = 6 cm

Yellow path: 4 cm + 1 cm = 5 cm

6 cm - 5 cm = 1 cm

The blue path is 1 cm longer than the yellow path.

Thinking Habits

Be a good thinker! These questions can help you.

- Am I using numbers, units, and symbols appropriately?

- Am I using the correct definitions?

- Am I calculating accurately?

- Is my answer clear?

7 Look for and make use of structure.

Good math thinkers look for patterns or relationships in math to help solve problems.

A store has 123 apples. 67 apples are sold. How many apples does the store have left?

123 - 67 = ?

I know 67 = 60 + 7.
123 - 60 = 63
63 - 7 = 56

So, 123 - 67 = 56.
The store has 56 apples left.

I broke apart 67 to solve 123 - 67.

Thinking Habits

Be a good thinker! These questions can help you.

- What patterns can I see and describe?

- How can I use the patterns to solve the problem?

- Can I see expressions and objects in different ways?

8 Look for and express regularity in repeated reasoning.

MP

Good math thinkers look for things that repeat, and they make generalizations.

I used reasoning to generalize about calculations.

Find the sum for each of these addends.

185 + 100 = ?

? = 292 + 100

100 + 321 = ?

Daniel's Work

185 + 100 = 285

392 = 292 + 100

100 + 321 = 421

100 is added in each problem.

Adding 100 makes the hundreds digit go up by 1.

Thinking Habits

Be a good thinker! These questions can help you.

- Are any calculations repeated?

- Can I generalize from examples?

- What shortcuts do I notice?

Problem Solving Guide

These questions can help you solve problems.

Make Sense of the Problem

Reason Abstractly and Quantitatively

- What do I need to find?
- What given information can I use?
- How are the quantities related?

Think About Similar Problems

- Have I solved problems like this before?

Persevere in Solving the Problem

Model with Math

- How can I use the math I know?
- How can I represent the problem?
- Is there a pattern or structure I can use?

Use Appropriate Tools Strategically

- What math tools could I use?
- How can I use those tools strategically?

Check the Answer

Make Sense of the Answer

- Is my answer reasonable?

Check for Precision

- Did I check my work?
- Is my answer clear?
- Did I construct a viable argument?
- Did I generalize correctly?

Some Ways to Represent Problems

- Draw a Picture
- Make a Bar Diagram
- Make a Table or Graph
- Write an Equation

Some Math Tools

- Objects
- Grid Paper
- Rulers
- Technology
- Paper and Pencil

Problem Solving Handbook

Problem Solving Recording Sheet

> This sheet helps you organize your work.

Name **Carlos**

Problem Solving Recording Sheet

Problem:

Cory wants to buy a video game that costs $60. He has $48 saved. On Monday he used part of his savings to buy a shirt for $15. How much more money does Cory need to save to buy the video game?

MAKE SENSE OF THE PROBLEM

Need to Find

Money needed to buy video game

Given

Video game costs $60
Saved $48
Used $15 of savings

PERSEVERE IN SOLVING THE PROBLEM

Some Ways to Represent Problems

☐ Draw a Picture
☑ Make a Bar Diagram
☐ Make a Table or Graph
☐ Write an Equation

Some Math Tools

☐ Objects
☐ Grid Paper
☐ Rulers
☐ Technology
☑ Paper and Pencil

Solution and Answer

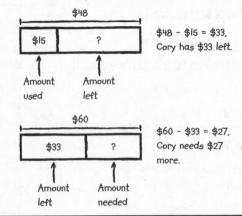

$48 − $15 = $33,
Cory has $33 left.

$60 − $33 = $27,
Cory needs $27 more.

CHECK THE ANSWER

Estimate
50 − 20 = 30   60 − 30 = 30
Check
33 + 15 = 48   27 + 33 = 60

My answer is reasonable and makes sense.
My answer is correct.

T1

Bar Diagrams

You can draw a **bar diagram** to show how the quantities in a problem are related. Then you can write an equation to solve the problem.

Add To

Draw this **bar diagram** for situations that involve *adding* to a quantity.

Result → | 82 |

| 15 | 67 |

↑ Start   ↑ Change

Result Unknown

Greg bought a baseball and a baseball glove. How much did he pay for both?

$30

$13

? dollars → spent on both

| ? |
| 13 | 30 |

↑ $13 for baseball   ↑ $30 for baseball glove

$13 + 30 = ?$

Greg spent $43 on both.

Start Unknown

Robin had some rings. Her sister gave her the rings shown below. After that, Robin had 90 rings. How many rings did Robin start with?

90 rings → | 90 |

| ? | 34 |

↑ ? rings to start   ↑ 34 rings added

$? + 34 = 90$

Robin started with 56 rings.

You can use bar diagrams to make sense of addition and subtraction problems.

Bar Diagrams

Take From

Draw this **bar diagram** for situations that involve *taking* from a quantity.

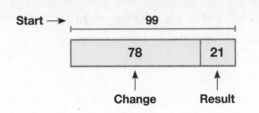

Start → 99

| 78 | 21 |

Change   Result

Result Unknown

Maurice had 78 e-mails. He deleted 49 of them. How many e-mails did Maurice keep?

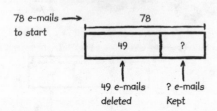

78 e-mails to start → 78

| 49 | ? |

49 e-mails deleted   ? e-mails Kept

$78 - 49 = ?$

Maurice kept 29 e-mails.

Start Unknown

Layla picked some apples at an orchard. She gave the apples below to her grandmother. Now Layla has 29 apples left. How many apples did Layla pick?

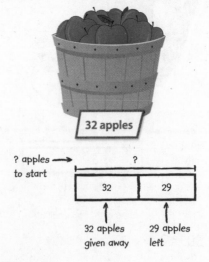

32 apples

? apples to start → ?

| 32 | 29 |

32 apples given away   29 apples left

$? - 32 = 29$

Layla had 61 apples before she gave some to her grandmother.

The **bar diagrams** on this page can help you make sense of more addition and subtraction situations.

Put Together/Take Apart

Draw this **bar diagram** for situations that involve *putting together* or *taking apart* quantities.

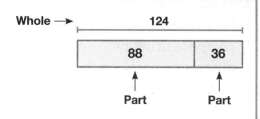

Whole Unknown

The bar graph shows how far Lana drove her car for 3 days. How many total miles did she drive?

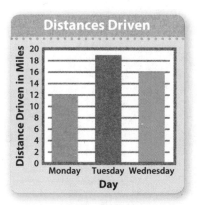

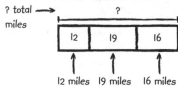

$12 + 19 + 16 = ?$

Lana drove a total of 47 miles.

Part Unknown

Pier school collected a total of 46 toys during two weeks of a toy drive for charity. How many toys were collected during the second week?

28 toys collected first week

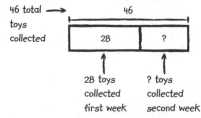

$28 + ? = 46$ or $46 - 28 = ?$

Pier school collected 18 toys during the second week.

Bar Diagrams

Compare: Addition and Subtraction

Draw this **bar diagram** for *compare* situations involving the difference between two quantities (how many more or fewer).

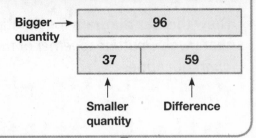

Bigger → quantity **96**

37 | **59**

↑ Smaller quantity   ↑ Difference

Difference Unknown

The larger dog weighs 82 pounds. The smaller dog weighs 6 pounds. How many more pounds does the larger dog weigh?

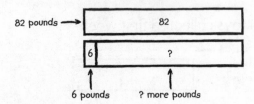

82 pounds → | 82 |

| 6 | ? |

↑ 6 pounds   ↑ ? more pounds

6 + ? = 82 or 82 − 6 = ?

The larger dog weighs 76 more pounds.

Smaller Unknown

Tim has 12 more postage stamps than Pedro. Tim has 30 postage stamps. How many postage stamps does Pedro have?

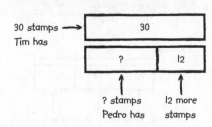

30 stamps → Tim has | 30 |

| ? | 12 |

↑ ? stamps Pedro has   ↑ 12 more stamps

30 − 12 = ? or ? + 12 = 30

Pedro has 18 postage stamps.

The **bar diagrams** on this page can help you solve problems involving multiplication and division.

Equal Groups: Multiplication and Division

Draw this **bar diagram** for situations that involve *equal groups*.

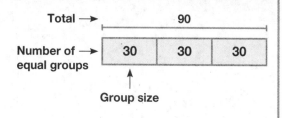

Total → 90

Number of → equal groups

| 30 | 30 | 30 |

Group size

Number of Groups Unknown

Josie spent $40 on tickets to a movie for herself and some friends on Saturday. How many tickets did Josie buy?

$40 → 40

? tickets → 8

$8 for each ticket

$? \times 8 = 40$ or $40 \div 8 = ?$

Josie bought 5 tickets.

Group Size Unknown

Marie placed an equal number of marbles in each bag below. She has 36 total marbles. How many marbles did Marie place in each bag?

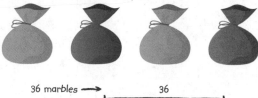

36 marbles → 36

4 bags → | ? | ? | ? | ? |

? marbles in each bag

$4 \times ? = 36$ or $36 \div 4 = ?$

Marie placed 9 marbles in each bag.

TOPIC 1

Understand Multiplication and Division of Whole Numbers

Essential Question: What are different meanings of multiplication and division?

Digital Resources

Solve   Learn   Glossary   Practice Buddy

Tools   Assessment   Help   Games

Math and Science Project: Forming Groups

Do Research Many kinds of animals form groups. Use the Internet or other sources to discover which animals form groups. When do they do this? What are the benefits for these animals of being in a group?

Journal: Write a Report Include what you found. Also include in your report:

- Draw pictures of animals in equal groups. Give a reason why those animals formed groups.

- Use a multiplication equation to show the total number of animals. Use a division equation to show the number in each group.

Name _____

Review What You Know

A-Z Vocabulary

Choose the best term from the box.
Write it on the blank.

• add	• subtract
• skip count	• ones

1. If you combine different sized groups to find how many in all, you _____.

2. _____ are groups of single objects.

3. When you say the numbers 5, 10, 15, 20, you _____.

Adding

Find each sum.

4. $5 + 5 + 5$

5. $7 + 7$

6. $3 + 3 + 3$

7. $2 + 2 + 2 + 2$

8. $6 + 6 + 6$

9. $9 + 9 + 9$

Subtracting

Find each difference.

10. $21 - 7$
$14 - 7$
$7 - 7$

11. $15 - 5$
$10 - 5$
$5 - 5$

12. $27 - 9$
$18 - 9$
$9 - 9$

Skip Counting on the Number Line

13. If you continue skip counting, what is the next number on the number line?

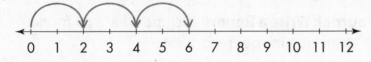

0 1 2 3 4 5 6 7 8 9 10 11 12

Ⓐ 8

Ⓑ 10

Ⓒ 12

Ⓓ 14

My Word Cards

Use the examples for each word on the front of the card to help complete the definitions on the back.

A-Z
Glossary

equal groups

multiplication

$4 \times 3 = 12$

factors

$7 \times 3 = 21$

factors

product

$7 \times 3 = 21$

product

equation

addition	subtraction
$2 + 5 = 7$	$7 - 5 = \square$
multiplication	division
$2 \times 5 = 10$	$10 \div \square = 2$

unknown

$\square \div 8 = 2 \quad 4 \times ? = 32 \quad 9 \times 8 = g$

unknown

number line

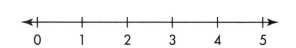

0   1   2   3   4   5

array

3 columns

2 rows

My Word Cards

_____ is an operation that gives the total number when you join equal groups.

_____ have the same number of items in each group.

The answer to a multiplication problem is called the _____.

The numbers that are multiplied together to give a product are called

_____.

A symbol or letter that stands for a number in an equation is called an

_____.

A number sentence that uses an equal sign (=) to show the value to its left is the same as the value to its right is

called an _____.

An _____ is a way of displaying objects in equal rows and columns.

A line divided into equal units and numbered in order is called a

_____.

My Word Cards

Use the examples for each word on the front of the card to help complete the definitions on the back.

row

2 rows

column

3 columns

Commutative (Order) Property of Multiplication

$5 \times 7 = 35$

division

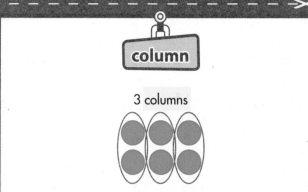

$12 \div 3 = 4$

Total   Number of equal groups   Number in each group

My Word Cards

Complete each definition. Extend learning by writing your own definitions.

Objects that are arranged in a line up and down are in a ________________.

Objects that are arranged in a line across are in a ____________.

____________ is an operation that tells how many equal groups there are or how many are in each group.

Numbers can be multiplied in any order and the product will be the same because of the ______________________ ______________________________ ______________________________.

Name _____

Solve & Share

Ms. Witt bought 3 boxes of paint with 5 jars of paint in each box. What is the total number of jars Ms. Witt bought? *Solve this problem any way you choose.*

I can ...
use addition or multiplication to join equal groups.

SOL 3.4a, 3.4b, 3.17

Make sense of this problem. Think about what you know and what you need to find.

Look Back! **Model with Math** How can you use a picture to show the math you did in the problem?

Essential Question

How Can You Find the Total Number of Objects in Equal Groups?

A

Jessie used 3 bags to bring home the goldfish she won at the Fun Fair. She put the same number of goldfish in each bag. How many goldfish did she win?

I can use counters to show the groups.

8 goldfish in each bag

B The counters show 3 groups of 8 goldfish.

You can use addition to join equal groups.

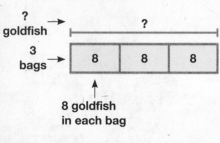

? goldfish

3 bags → | 8 | 8 | 8 |

8 goldfish in each bag

$8 + 8 + 8 = 24$

C Multiplication is an operation that gives the total number when you join equal groups.

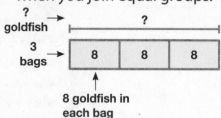

? goldfish | ? |

3 bags → | 8 | 8 | 8 |

8 goldfish in each bag

3 times 8 equals 24

$$3 \quad \times \quad 8 \quad = \quad 24$$

factor   factor   product

Factors are the numbers that are being multiplied. The **product** is the answer to a multiplication problem.

D You can write **equations**.

An **unknown** is a symbol that stands for a number in an equation.

Addition equation:
$8 + 8 + 8 = ?$
$8 + 8 + 8 = 24$

Multiplication equation:
$3 \times 8 = ?$
$3 \times 8 = 24$

Jessie won 24 goldfish.

Convince Me! **Model with Math** Suppose Jessie won 5 bags of 8 goldfish. Draw a bar diagram and write an addition equation and a multiplication equation to represent the problem.

Practice Buddy   Tools   Assessment

☆ Guided Practice*

Do You Understand?

1. **Reasoning** Can you write
   $5 + 5 + 5 + 5 = 20$ as a multiplication equation? Explain.

2. **Reasoning** Can you write
   $3 + 4 + 7 = 14$ as a multiplication equation? Explain.

3. Write an addition equation and a multiplication equation to solve this problem.
   Jessie buys 4 packages of stones. There are 6 stones in each package. How many stones does Jessie buy?

Do You Know How?

Complete **4** and **5**. Use the pictures to help.

4.

2 groups of ____

$4 + 4 =$ ____

$2 \times$ ____ $=$ ____

5.

____ groups of 6

$6 +$ ____ $+$ ____ $=$ ____

$3 \times$ ____ $=$ ____

☆ Independent Practice ☆

Leveled Practice Complete **6** and **7**. Use the pictures to help.

6.

2 groups of ____

$5 +$ ____ $=$ ____

$2 \times$ ____ $=$ ____

7.

5 groups of ____

$4 + 4 + 4 +$ ____ $+$ ____ $=$ ____

$5 \times$ ____ $=$ ____

In **8–11**, complete each equation. Use counters or draw a picture to help.

8. $8 + 8 + 8 + 8 = 4 \times$ ____

9. ____ $+$ ____ $+$ ____ $= 3 \times 7$

10. $9 +$ ____ $+$ ____ $= 3 \times$ ____

11. $6 + 6 + 6 + 6 + 6 =$ ____ $\times$ ____

12. Be Precise Debra draws this shape on the back of her notebook.

What is the name of the shape Debra draws? How do you know?

13. Model with Math Salvatore gets 50 trading cards for his birthday. He trades some cards with his friend Madison. Salvatore gives 22 cards to Madison, and Madison gives 18 cards to Salvatore. Then Salvatore's sister gives him 14 cards. How many trading cards does Salvatore have now? Use math to represent the problem.

14. Higher Order Thinking Luke says you can always add and you can always multiply to join groups. Is he correct? Explain why or why not.

15. Critique Reasoning Lois says any addition equation where the addends are all the same can be written as a multiplication equation. Is Lois correct? Explain why or why not.

✓ Assessment

16. Mark has 12 ears of field corn to make table decorations. He arranges them in 2 groups of 6. How can you represent this? Choose all that apply.

- ☐ 12 × 2
- ☐ 2 + 2 + 2 + 2 + 2 + 2
- ☐ 6 + 6
- ☐ 2 × 6
- ☐ 12 + 2 + 6

17. Jenna saves $5 each week. She wants to know how much money she has saved after 6 weeks. How can you represent this? Choose all that apply.

- ☐ 5 + 5 + 5 + 5 + 5 + 5
- ☐ 5 × 5
- ☐ 5 + 6
- ☐ 6 + 6 + 6 + 6 + 6
- ☐ 5 × 6

Help Practice Tools Games
      Buddy

**Homework
& Practice** 1-1
Multiplication as
Repeated Addition

Another Look!

Each group below has the same number of squares. There are 5 groups of 4 squares.

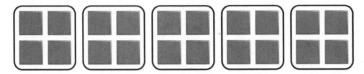

20 squares

4	4	4	4	4

There are 20 squares in all.

An addition equation or a multiplication equation can represent the total number of squares.

$4 + 4 + 4 + 4 + 4 = 20$

$5 \times 4 = 20$

Complete **1** and **2**. Use the pictures to help.

1.

4 groups of _____

$4 + 4 + 4 + 4 =$ _____

$4 \times$ _____ $=$ _____

2.

32			

8	8	8	8

_____ groups of 8

____ + ____ + ____ + ____ = 32

____ $\times$ 8 = ____

In **3** and **4**, write the addition equation as a multiplication equation.

3. $3 + 3 + 3 + 3 + 3 = 15$

4. $7 + 7 + 7 = 21$

In **5–8**, write the multiplication equation as an addition equation.

5. $5 \times 5 = 25$

6. $6 \times 2 = 12$

7. $3 \times 4 = 12$

8. $5 \times 6 = 30$

9. **Model with Math** Jan buys 3 bags of beads. Each bag contains 7 beads. Draw a bar diagram and write an addition equation and a multiplication equation to show how many beads Jan buys. How are the two equations related?

10. Misha buys 4 boxes of 6 markers each. He writes this addition equation to show how many markers he buys: $6 + 6 + 6 + 6 = 24$. What multiplication equation can Misha write to represent this situation?

11. **Math and Science** Some scientists think that geese fly in a V-shaped group to save energy, which helps them fly farther against the wind. Ellen sees 3 groups. Each group has 9 geese. How many geese does she see in all? Write an addition equation and a multiplication equation.

12. **Critique Reasoning** Carrie draws this picture to show 3 groups of 3.

Is Carrie's picture correct? Explain why or why not.

13. **Higher Order Thinking** Marion has 4 cards, Jake has 4 cards, and Sam has 3 cards. Can you write a multiplication equation to find how many cards they have in all? Explain why or why not.

✔ **Assessment**

14. Martin has 3 piles of coins. Each pile has 5 dimes. How can you represent this? Choose all that apply.

☐ $5 + 5 + 5$
☐ $3 + 3 + 3$
☐ 5×4
☐ 3×5
☐ 3×3

15. Snazzy Sneakers is having a shoe sale. Anthony buys 4 pairs of shoes. How can you represent this? Choose all that apply.

☐ $4 + 4$
☐ $2 + 2 + 2 + 2$
☐ 4×4
☐ 2×2
☐ 4×2

12   **Topic 1** | Lesson 1-1

Name _____

Solve & Share

Harvey the Hop Toad jumps 4 times in the same direction. He jumps 5 inches in each jump. How can you show how far he goes on a number line?

I can ...
use a number line to represent and solve multiplication facts.

SOL 3.4a, 3.4b

Model with math.
A number line can be used to record and count equal groups.

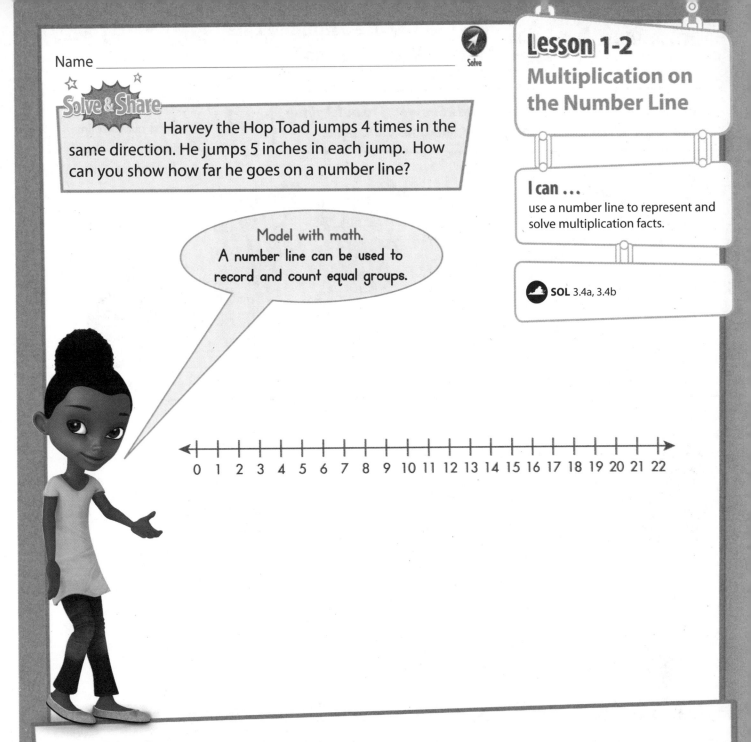

0 1 2 3 4 5 6 7 8 9 10 11 12 13 14 15 16 17 18 19 20 21 22

Look Back! **Generalize** How are Harvey's jumps on the number line like repeated addition? How are they like skip counting?

How Can You Use a Number Line to Show Multiplication?

A

Clara is making gift bags for her 5 friends. She wants to put 3 glitter pens in each gift bag. How many glitter pens does Clara need?

You can use a number line and skip counting to show multiplication.

B

Draw arrows on the number line to show the number of glitter pens for each gift bag.

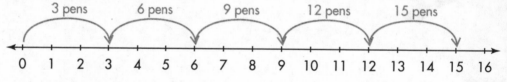

Skip counting: 3, 6, 9, 12, 15

Multiplication: $5 \times 3 = 15$

Clara needs 15 glitter pens.

Convince Me! **Reasoning** What would skip counting by 6 look like on the number line?

☆ Guided Practice *

Do You Understand?

1. On page 14, why do you skip count by 3s on the number line?

2. On page 14, why do you make five jumps on the number line?

3. **Reasoning** How would the jumps on the number line look different if there were 4 pens in each gift bag?

Do You Know How?

In **4**, complete the arrows on the number line to show the jumps and fill in the blanks.

4. Jim ran 3 miles a day for 4 days in a row. How many miles did he run?

0 1 2 3 4 5 6 7 8 9 10 11 12 13 14 15

Number of jumps: _____

I skip counted by _____.

Jim ran _____ miles.

_____ × _____ = _____

Independent Practice ☆

In **5**, show how you found the solution using the number line.

5. Judy has 6 fruit baskets. She wants to put 2 apples into each basket. How many apples will she need? Draw the remaining jumps on the number line with arrows to show how many apples Judy will need.

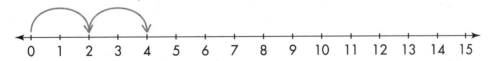

0 1 2 3 4 5 6 7 8 9 10 11 12 13 14 15

Judy will need _____ apples.

In **6** and **7**, show the multiplication fact with arrows on the number line. Write the product.

6. $7 \times 2 =$ _____

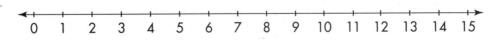

0 1 2 3 4 5 6 7 8 9 10 11 12 13 14 15

7. $3 \times 3 =$ _____

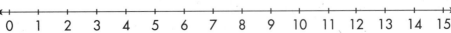

0 1 2 3 4 5 6 7 8 9 10 11 12 13 14 15

Problem Solving

8. Nikki wants to use 3 glass beads in a necklace she is making. She wants to make 6 necklaces. How many glass beads will Nikki need? Write an addition equation and a multiplication equation.

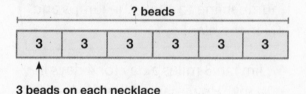

? beads

| 3 | 3 | 3 | 3 | 3 | 3 |

3 beads on each necklace

9. Math and Science Guinea pigs in the wild usually live in groups of between 5 and 10. The group members can warn each other of danger. If there are 2 groups of 7 guinea pigs, how many guinea pigs are there in all? Use the number line to solve.

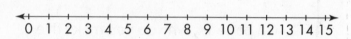

0 1 2 3 4 5 6 7 8 9 10 11 12 13 14 15

10. Make Sense and Persevere Tim drew this number line to show the multiplication fact $4 \times 2 = 8$.

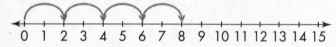

0 1 2 3 4 5 6 7 8 9 10 11 12 13 14 15

Which parts represent the factors? Which part shows the product?

11. Higher Order Thinking Draw a number line to compare skip counting by 3s four times and skip counting by 4s three times. How are they different? How are they alike?

 Assessment

12. Suki invites 5 friends to a party. She gives each friend 2 party favors. How many party favors does she give out? Show how to find the answer using the number line.

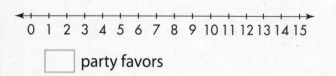

0 1 2 3 4 5 6 7 8 9 10 11 12 13 14 15

[ ] party favors

13. In the last 5 months Stan read 3 books each month. How many books has he read in all? Show how to find the answer using the number line.

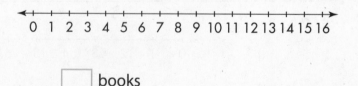

0 1 2 3 4 5 6 7 8 9 10 11 12 13 14 15 16

[ ] books

16 **Topic 1** | Lesson 1-2

Homework & Practice 1-2
Multiplication on the Number Line

Another Look!

There are 4 fruit bars in a package. Abby buys 5 packages. How many fruit bars does she buy?

Use a number line. Skip count by 4s, five times.

You can use a number line to show 5 × 4.

```
        4       8       12      16      20
   0 1 2 3 4 5 6 7 8 9 10 11 12 13 14 15 16 17 18 19 20 21 22 23 24 25
```

Number of jumps: 5   Number in each jump: 4

$5 \times 4 = 20$ Abby buys 20 fruit bars.

In **1–3**, use the number line.

1. Jack puts 2 photos on each of 7 pages of his photo album. How many photos does he use? Complete the jumps on the number line by adding arrows.

```
      2   4   6
   0 1 2 3 4 5 6 7 8 9 10 11 12 13 14 15 16 17 18 19 20
```

Number of jumps: _____   Number in each jump: _____

_____ × _____ = _____

Jack uses _____ photos.

2. Why do you skip count by 2s on the number line?

3. Why do you make 7 jumps on the number line?

---

4. Tony buys 7 packages of mini-muffins. There are 3 mini-muffins in each package. How many mini-muffins does Tony buy? Use the number line to help find the answer.

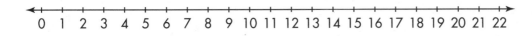

```
   0 1 2 3 4 5 6 7 8 9 10 11 12 13 14 15 16 17 18 19 20 21 22
```

5. Mrs. Calvino's classroom has 6 rows of desks. Each row has 4 desks. Explain how to use skip counting to find how many desks there are.

6. Alyssa has saved $77 from mowing lawns. She spends $34 on back-to-school shopping. How much of her savings does Alyssa have left?

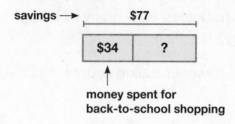

7. Critique Reasoning Tina drew this number line to show 5 × 3 = 15.

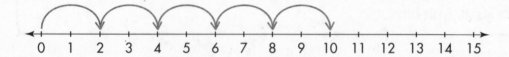

Is her number line correct? Why or why not?

8. Higher Order Thinking Draw a number line to compare skip counting by 4s four times to skip counting by 8s two times. How are they alike? How are they different? Explain.

✔ Assessment

9. Diane uses 2 feet of ribbon to decorate each gift she is wrapping. She wraps 7 gifts. How much ribbon does she need? Show how to find the answer using the number line.

▢ feet

10. Jerry has a bookshelf with 4 shelves. He places 4 books on each of the shelves. How many books are on the bookshelf? Show how to find the answer using the number line.

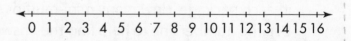

▢ books

Solve

Lesson 1-3
Arrays and Multiplication

Solve & Share

Mark put sports cards in an album. He put 4 rows of cards on each page. He put 3 cards in each row. How many cards are on each page? *Solve this problem any way you choose.*

I can ...
use arrays to show and solve multiplication problems.

SOL 3.4a, 3.4b, 3.17

You can use tools. Sometimes using objects can help you solve a problem. Show your work in the space below!

Look Back! **Make Sense and Persevere** Will your answer be the same if Mark puts 3 rows of 4 cards on each page? Explain.

Dana keeps her swimming medal collection in a display on the wall.

The display has 4 rows. Each row has 5 medals. How many medals are in Dana's collection?

The medals are in an array. An array shows objects in equal rows and columns.

B The counters show 4 rows and 5 columns.

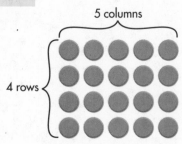

5 columns

4 rows

Each row is a group. You can use addition or skip counting to find the total.

Addition: $5 + 5 + 5 + 5 = 20$
Skip counting: 5, 10, 15, 20

C Multiplication can also be used to find the total in an array.

You say, "4 times 5 equals 20."

$$4 \times 5 = 20$$

number of rows   number in each row

There are 20 medals in Dana's collection.

Convince Me! **Construct Arguments** Jason also has a swimming medal collection. His display has 5 rows with 5 medals in each row. Who has more medals, Jason or Dana? Draw an array then write an addition equation and a multiplication equation to show your work.

Practice Buddy Tools Assessment

☆Guided Practice☆

Do You Understand?

1. Look at page 20. What does the first factor tell you about the array?

2. Mia puts muffins in 4 rows with 7 muffins in each row. Draw an array to find the total number of muffins.

Do You Know How?

In **3** and **4**, write a multiplication equation for each array.

3.

4.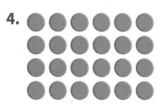

Independent Practice ☆

In **5–7**, fill in the blanks to show addition, skip counting, and multiplication for each array.

5.

6 + __ + __ = 18
6, __, __
3 × __ = 18

6.

4 + __ + __ + __ = 16
4, __, __, __
4 × __ = 16

7.

__ + __ + __ + __ + __ = 25
__, __, __, __, __
__ × __ = 25

In **8** and **9**, draw an array to show each equation. Write the product.

8. 5 × 6 = ____

9. 2 × 9 = ____

Problem Solving

10. Look for Relationships Liza draws these two arrays. How are the arrays alike? How are they different?

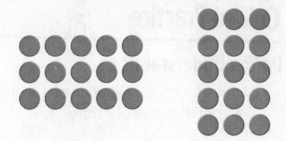

11. Construct Arguments How many more oak trees are there than birch and pine trees? Explain how you know.

DATA	Trees in the Park	
	Birch	⫶ 卌 卌 ///
	Oak	⫶ 卌 卌 卌 //
	Maple	⫶ 卌 卌
	Pine	⫶ //

12. Higher Order Thinking Margo has 23 pictures. Can she use all the pictures to make an array with exactly two equal rows? Why or why not?

13. Delbert puts 5 nickels in each of his 3 empty piggy banks. How many nickels did Delbert put in the banks? Write a multiplication equation to show how you solved the problem.

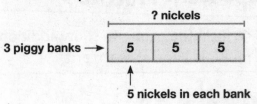

✓ **Assessment**

14. Mr. Lopez planted 8 rows of apple trees on his farm. The apple trees are in 5 columns. How many trees are there in all?

Ⓐ 5 trees

Ⓑ 8 trees

Ⓒ 13 trees

Ⓓ 40 trees

15. Dan bought the stickers shown below. Which of the following shows how many stickers Dan bought?

Ⓐ $5 + 5$

Ⓑ 5×4

Ⓒ $5 + 4$

Ⓓ $5 - 4$

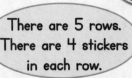

There are 5 rows. There are 4 stickers in each row.

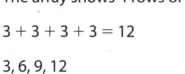

Homework & Practice 1-3
Arrays and Multiplication

Another Look!

Scott arranges some apples in an array. He makes 4 rows with 3 apples in each row. How many apples does Scott have?

The array shows 4 rows of 3 apples.

$3 + 3 + 3 + 3 = 12$

$3, 6, 9, 12$

Say, "4 times 3 equals 12."

Write: $4 \times 3 = 12$.

Multiplication can be used to find the total in an array.

In **1–3**, fill in the blanks to show addition, skip counting, and multiplication for each array.

1.
⬤ ⬤ ⬤
⬤ ⬤ ⬤
⬤ ⬤ ⬤

$3 + \underline{} + \underline{} = 9$

$3, \underline{}, \underline{}$

$3 \times \underline{} = 9$

2.
⬤ ⬤ ⬤ ⬤
⬤ ⬤ ⬤ ⬤

$4 + \underline{} = \underline{}$

$\underline{}, \underline{}$

$2 \times \underline{} = \underline{}$

3.
⬤ ⬤ ⬤ ⬤ ⬤
⬤ ⬤ ⬤ ⬤ ⬤
⬤ ⬤ ⬤ ⬤ ⬤

$\underline{} + \underline{} + \underline{} = 15$

$\underline{}, \underline{}, 15$

$\underline{} \times \underline{} = 15$

In **4–7**, draw an array. Write an addition equation and a multiplication equation for your array.

4. 3×4

5. 2×3

6. 2×5

7. 3×6

8. A-Z Vocabulary Paula says that she can draw an array with a total of 17 counters placed in 3 rows. Is she correct? If she is, draw the array. If she is not, explain why not.

9. Make Sense and Persevere Shelly wants to plant 6 rows of flowers, with 7 flowers in each row. What addition equation and what multiplication equation can she write to find how many flowers she needs to plant? Which equation do you find easier to use? Why?

10. Reasoning Marie has one of the solid figures shown below.

Cylinder   Sphere   Cone

Marie's solid figure has 2 flat surfaces, 0 edges, and 0 vertices. Which solid figure does Marie have?

11. Higher Order Thinking Vince has 16 beads. How many different arrays can Vince draw to represent the total number of beads he has? List the sizes of the arrays.

Assessment

12. Jana makes the array below to show how she wants to arrange some pictures. Which multiplication equation describes Jana's array?

     Ⓐ $3 \times 12 = 36$

     Ⓑ $2 \times 18 = 36$

     Ⓒ $6 \times 6 = 36$

     Ⓓ $4 \times 9 = 36$

13. Carole makes an array of magnets on her refrigerator. She makes 7 rows with 8 magnets in each row. Which of the following shows how to find the total number of magnets in Carole's array?

     Ⓐ   7, 14, 21, 28, 35, 42, 49

     Ⓑ 7×8

     Ⓒ $7 + 7 + 7 + 7 + 7 + 7 + 7$

     Ⓓ $8 + 7$

Name _____

Solve & Share

Cathy arranged seashells in two different arrays. One array has 2 rows with 6 shells in each row. The other array has 6 rows with 2 shells in each row. Do both arrays have the same number of shells? Draw the arrays, then write a multiplication equation for each.

You can use structure. What do you notice is the same in each array?

Lesson 1-4
The Commutative Property

I can ...
multiply factors in any order to solve multiplication problems.

SOL 3.4a, 3.4b, 3.17

Look Back! **Look for Relationships** Explain what happened to the product when you changed the order of the factors.

Essential Question: Does Order Matter When You Multiply?

A

Libby and Sydney each say her poster has more stickers. Which poster has more stickers?

Sydney's poster

Remember, an array shows objects in equal rows and columns.

Libby's poster

B Libby's Poster

On Libby's poster, there are 4 rows with 3 stickers in each row. Here are two ways to write this:

3 + 3 + 3 + 3 = 12

and

4 × 3 = 12

C Sydney's Poster

On Sydney's poster, there are 3 rows with 4 stickers in each row. Here are two ways to write this:

4 + 4 + 4 = 12

and

3 × 4 = 12

D Both posters have the same number of stickers.

The Commutative (Order) Property of Multiplication says you can multiply numbers in any order and the product is the same. So, 4 × 3 = 3 × 4.

Convince Me! **Look for Relationships** Circle the pair of equations that shows the Commutative Property of Multiplication. Explain your answer.

2 × 4 = 8   2 × 4 = 8   2 + 2 + 2 + 2 = 8

2 × 8 = 16   4 × 2 = 8   4 × 2 = 8

☆ Guided Practice *

Do You Understand?

1. Complete the following statement.

   $6 \times 4 = 24$, so $4 \times 6 =$ _____.

2. **Use Structure** What multiplication fact can be paired with $2 \times 8 = 16$ to make a pair of facts showing the Commutative Property of Multiplication?

3. Why is the Commutative Property of Multiplication sometimes called the *order* property?

Do You Know How?

In **4**, draw an array and give the product for each fact.

4. $5 \times 2 =$ _____ $2 \times 5 =$ _____

In **5** and **6**, complete the equation.

5. $5 \times 2 =$ _____ $\times 5$

6. $6 \times 1 = 1 \times$ _____

☆ Independent Practice ☆

In **7** and **8**, write a multiplication equation for each array in the pair.

7.

8.

In **9**, draw an array to show each equation. Write the products.

9. $5 \times 6 =$ _____ $6 \times 5 =$ _____

In **10–12**, fill in the missing number.

10. $5 \times 3 =$ _____ $\times 5$

11. $8 \times$ _____ $= 4 \times 8$

12. _____ $\times 6 = 6 \times 7$

Problem Solving

13. Effie earns $26 from babysitting and $45 from mowing lawns. She spends $12 on lunch. How much money does Effie have now?

Bar diagrams can show addition or subtraction.

14. Use Structure Chen arranged 32 berries in the array shown below.

What other array can he use to show the same number of berries?

---

15. Higher Order Thinking Ramón says he can use the Commutative Property of Multiplication to show the product of 4 × 6 is the same as the product of 3 × 8. Is he correct? Why or why not?

16. ⒶⓏ **Vocabulary** Fill in the blanks. You can show the Commutative Property of Multiplication using 2 arrays. The number of _____ in the first array is equal to the number of _____ in the second array. The number of _____ in the first array is equal to the number of _____ in the second array.

✓ **Assessment**

17. How do the arrays at the right show the Commutative Property of Multiplication?

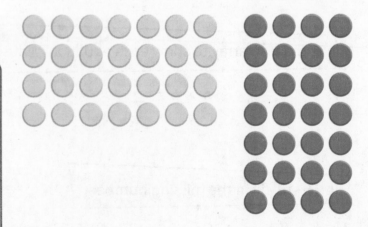

Help   Practice   Tools   Games
        Buddy

Another Look!

This array shows 2 rows of 3 pennies.

This array shows 3 rows of 2 pennies.

An array shows objects in equal rows.

$2 \times 3 = 6$ $3 \times 2 = 6$

You can use the **Commutative Property of Multiplication** to multiply the numbers in any order.

$2 \times 3 = 6$ so $3 \times 2 = 6$

In **1** and **2**, draw an array to show each equation. Write the products.

1. $2 \times 8 =$ ____ $8 \times 2 =$ ____

2. $4 \times 4 =$ ____

In **3–10**, complete each multiplication equation. You may use counters or draw pictures to help.

3. $3 \times 4 = 12$, so ____ $\times 3 = 12$.

4. $5 \times 6 = 30$, so ____ $\times 5 = 30$.

5. $5 \times 2 = 10$, so $2 \times$ ____ $= 10$.

6. $4 \times 8 = 32$, so ____ $\times 4 = 32$.

7. $7 \times 9 = 63$, so ____ $\times$ ____ $= 63$.

8. $7 \times 8 = 56$, so ____ $\times$ ____ $= 56$.

9. $3 \times 8 = 24$, so ____ $\times$ ____ $= 24$.

10. $5 \times 3 = 15$, so ____ $\times$ ____ $= 15$.

11. Use Structure Use the Commutative Property of Multiplication to draw the second array. Complete the multiplication equations.

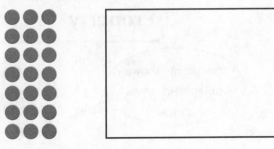

$7 \times 3 =$ _____ $3 \times$ _____ $=$ _____

12. Construct Arguments Scott puts some sports stickers in rows. He makes 6 rows with 5 stickers in each row. If he puts the same number of stickers in 5 equal rows, how many stickers would be in each row? How do you know?

A good math explanation can include words, numbers, and symbols.

---

13. Karen arranges 24 star stickers in the array shown below.

What other array could the same number of stickers be arranged in?

14. Higher Order Thinking Ed arranged some tiles in different arrays. One array has 3 rows with 6 tiles in each row. The other array has 2 rows with 9 tiles in each row. Ed says that he can use the Commutative Property to show that the arrays both have 18 tiles. Is he correct? Explain.

 Assessment

15. Taylor made these arrays to show the Commutative Property of Multiplication. Is that what the arrays show? Why or why not?

Name _____

Solve & Share

Four friends picked 20 apples. They want to share them equally. How many apples should each person get? *Solve this problem any way you choose.*

I can ...
use objects or pictures to show how objects can be divided into equal groups.

SOL 3.4b, 3.4a

Model with math. Drawing a picture that represents the problem can help you solve it. Show your work!

Look Back! **Use Appropriate Tools** Can you use counters to help you solve this problem? Explain.

A

Three friends have 12 toys to share equally.
How many toys will each friend get?

Think of arranging 12 toys into 3 equal groups.

Division is an operation that is used to find how many equal groups there are or how many are in each group.

B **What You Think**

Put one toy at a time in each group.

12 toys

4 toys for
each friend

When all the toys are grouped, there will
be 4 in each group.

C **What You Write**

You can write a division equation
to find the number in each group.

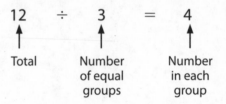

$$12 \div 3 = 4$$

Total   Number   Number
         of equal   in each
         groups   group

Each friend will get 4 toys.

Convince Me! **Be Precise** What would happen if 3 friends wanted to
share 13 toys equally?

Name _____

☆ Guided Practice *

Do You Understand?

1. 18 eggs are divided into 3 rows. How many eggs are in each row? Use the bar diagram to solve.

18		
?	?	?

18 ÷ 3 = _____ eggs

2. Be Precise Can 12 grapes be shared equally among 5 children with no grapes remaining? Explain.

Do You Know How?

In **3** and **4**, draw a picture to solve.

3. 15 bananas are shared equally by 3 monkeys. How many bananas does each monkey get?

4. 16 plants are divided equally into 4 pots. How many plants are in each pot?

Independent Practice ☆

In **5** and **6**, draw a picture to solve.

5. 18 marbles are divided equally into 6 sacks. How many marbles are in each sack?

6. 16 crayons are shared equally by 2 people. How many crayons does each person have?

In **7–10**, complete each equation.

7. 12 ÷ 2 = ☐

12	
?	?

8. 16 ÷ 8 = ☐

16							
?	?	?	?	?	?	?	?

9. 9 ÷ 3 = _____

10. 14 ÷ 7 = _____

Problem Solving

11. Critique Reasoning Jim is putting 18 pens into equal groups. He says if he puts them into 2 equal groups he will have more pens in each group than if he puts them in 3 equal groups. Is Jim correct? Explain.

12. Make Sense and Persevere Ms. Terry's class is hosting a fundraising challenge. The students in her class are divided into 4 teams. Each team has an equal number of students. Do you have enough information to find how many students are on each team? Explain.

13. Erika draws a hexagon. Maria draws a pentagon. Who draws the shape with more sides? How many more sides does that shape have?

14. Model with Math The flag bearers in a parade march in 9 rows with 5 flags in each row. Write an equation to show how many flags there are.

15. Number Sense Jenn equally shares 40 jellybeans with some friends. Is the number that each friend gets greater than 40 or less than 40? Explain.

16. Higher Order Thinking Joy has 12 shells. She gives 2 shells to her mom. Then she and her sister share the other shells equally. How many shells does Joy get? How many shells does her sister get? How do you know?

17. Max has the 14 stickers shown at the right. He wants to put an equal number of stickers on each of 2 posters. Draw circles in each box to represent the stickers Max puts on each poster.

Poster 1

Poster 2

Name _____

Another Look!

A.J. has 15 T-shirts. He sorted them equally into 5 laundry bins. How many T-shirts did A.J. put in each bin? You can use a bar diagram to solve.

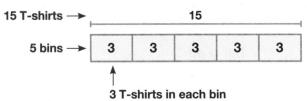

15 T-shirts →   15

5 bins → | 3 | 3 | 3 | 3 | 3 |

↑
3 T-shirts in each bin

There are 15 T-shirts. There are 5 groups.
There are 3 T-shirts in each group.
So, $15 \div 5 = 3$.

A.J. put 3 T-shirts in each laundry bin.

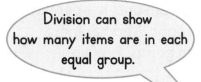
Division can show how many items are in each equal group.

In **1**, use the bar diagram to help divide.

1. There are 12 tennis balls that need to be packaged equally into 4 cans.

   How many tennis balls will be in each can?

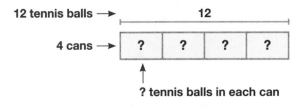

   12 tennis balls →   12

   4 cans → | ? | ? | ? | ? |

   ↑
   ? tennis balls in each can

    There are _____ tennis balls.

    There are _____ groups.

    There are _____ tennis balls in each group.

    $12 \div$ _____ = _____

In **2–7**, put an equal number of objects in each group. Use counters or draw a picture to solve. Write the unit for each answer.

2. Sort 16 apples equally into 2 baskets. How many apples are in each basket?

3. Arrange 20 chairs equally at 4 tables. How many chairs are at each table?

4. 7 rabbits share 21 carrots equally. How many carrots does each rabbit get?

5. 5 children share 25 dimes equally. How many dimes does each child get?

6. Divide 14 books equally on 2 shelves. How many books are on each shelf?

7. 24 people divide among 3 elevators equally. How many people are in each elevator?

8. **Construct Arguments** Can you divide 14 shirts into 2 equal piles? Why or why not?

9. In February 2015, there were 28 days, all in complete weeks. There are 7 days in a complete week. How many weeks were there in February 2015?

10. **Be Precise** Ron and Pam each have 20 pennies. Ron puts his pennies into 4 equal groups. Pam puts her pennies into 5 equal groups. Who has more pennies in each group? Explain.

11. Write the division equation that matches the bar diagram.

16			
?	?	?	?

12. **Algebra** There are 92 students in the third and fourth grades at Johnsonville Elementary. Of these, 47 are in fourth grade. Write an equation to find how many third graders there are. Use a question mark to represent the unknown number and solve.

13. **Higher Order Thinking** Kyra has a rock collection. When she puts her rocks into 2 equal piles, there are no rocks left over. When she puts her rocks into 3 equal piles, there are still no rocks left over. When she puts her rocks into 4 equal piles, there are still no rocks left over. How many rocks could Kyra have?

✔ **Assessment**

14. Sam, Clara, and Dylan are each making a necklace. They divide 26 beads equally. Draw pictures in the boxes to show how many beads each person will get. Draw any remaining beads in the Leftover box.

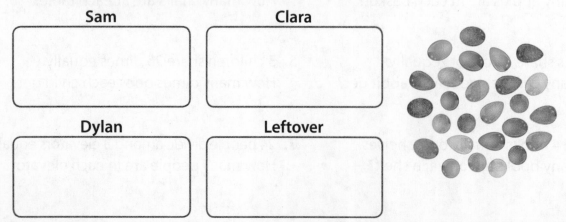

Sam

Clara

Dylan

Leftover

Name _____

☆ ☆
Solve & Share

Li made 12 tacos. He wants to give some of his friends 2 tacos each. If Li does not get any of the tacos, how many of his friends will get tacos? *Solve this problem any way you choose.*

I can ...
use repeated subtraction to understand and solve division problems.

 SOL 3.4b, 3.4a

You can use reasoning. How can what you know about sharing help you solve the problem? Show your work in the space below!

Look Back! **Use Appropriate Tools** How can counters or other objects help you show your work?

Essential Question **How Can You Divide Using Repeated Subtraction?**

A

June has 10 strawberries to serve to her guests. If each guest eats 2 strawberries, how many guests can June serve?

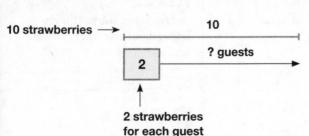

10 strawberries ⟶

10

? guests

2

2 strawberries for each guest

B

You can use repeated subtraction to find how many groups of 2 are in 10.

$10 - 2 = 8$
$8 - 2 = 6$
$6 - 2 = 4$
$4 - 2 = 2$
$2 - 2 = 0$

You can subtract 2 five times. There are five groups of 2 in 10.

There are no strawberries left.

June can serve 5 guests.

C

You can write a division equation to find the number of groups.

Write: $10 \div 2 = ?$

Read: Ten divided by 2 equals what number?

Solve: $10 \div 2 = 5$

June can serve 5 guests.

Convince Me! **Model with Math** In the example above, what if each guest ate 5 strawberries? Use the math you know to represent the problem and find how many guests June could serve.

38 **Topic 1** | Lesson 1-6

Name _____

☆ Guided Practice *

Do You Understand?

1. Show how you can use repeated subtraction to find how many groups of 4 there are in 20. Then write a division equation to solve the problem.

Do You Know How?

In **2** and **3**, use counters or draw a picture to solve.

2. The bell choir has 16 gloves. There are 2 gloves in each pair. How many pairs of gloves are there?

3. Ruth has 15 dog treats. She gives each of her dogs 3 treats. How many dogs does Ruth have?

☆ Independent Practice ☆

Leveled Practice In **4** and **5**, complete the equations.

4. Ruth picks 14 apples. She places 7 apples in each bag. How many bags does Ruth have?

$14 - 7 =$ ___

___ $- 7 =$ ___

___ $\div 7 =$ ___

Ruth has ___ bags.

5. The wagons on the farm have 4 wheels each. There are 12 wheels. How many wagons are on the farm?

$12 - 4 =$ ___

___ $- 4 =$ ___

___ $-$ ___ $=$ ___

___ $\div$ ___ $=$ ___

There are ___ wagons.

In **6** and **7**, use counters or draw a picture to solve.

6. Shirley bought 30 markers that came in packages of 5 markers each. How many packages did Shirley buy?

7. Marcus has 18 pencils. He places 2 pencils on each desk. How many desks are there?

Problem Solving

8. **Generalize** The chart shows the number of pennies each of three friends has in her pocket. Each friend divides her money into piles of 3 coins. Write division equations to show how many equal piles each friend can make. Explain what repeats in the equations and how it helps you solve.

Money in Pockets	
Claudia	18 cents
Zoe	12 cents
Jenna	15 cents

DATA

9. If Zoe makes columns of 6 pennies each, how many rows does she make?

10. **Model with Math** Bella has $52. She spends $21, then finds $12. How much money does she have now? Use math to represent the problem.

11. **Higher Order Thinking** An ice cream store plans to make 8 new flavors each year. How many years will it take for the store to make 80 flavors? Write and solve an equation.

 Assessment

12. Eric writes the following:

    20 – 5 = 15
    15 – 5 = 10
    10 – 5 = 5
    5 – 5 = 0

    What equation could Eric use to represent the same problem?

    Ⓐ $5 \times 5 = 25$

    Ⓑ $5 \div 5 = 1$

    Ⓒ $15 \div 5 = 3$

    Ⓓ $20 \div 5 = 4$

13. Jacqui writes the following:

    24 – 8 = 16
    16 – 8 = 8
    8 – 8 = 0

    Which problem is Jacqui trying to solve?

    Ⓐ $24 \div 8$

    Ⓑ $24 \div 6$

    Ⓒ $24 - 16$

    Ⓓ 24×3

Another Look!

Layla has 20 raffle tickets.
There are 5 tickets in each book.
How many books of raffle tickets
does Layla have? Find $20 \div 5 =$ ☐.

$$20 - 5 = 15$$
$$15 - 5 = 10$$
$$10 - 5 = 5$$
$$5 - 5 = 0$$

There are four groups of 5 in 20.

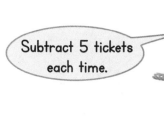

Subtract 5 tickets each time.

You subtracted 5 four times. So, $20 \div 5 = 4$.

Layla has 4 books of raffle tickets.

In **1**, use repeated subtraction to help you solve.

1. Ryan has 10 markers.
   There are 5 markers in each box.
   How many boxes of markers are there?
   Find $10 \div 5 =$ ☐.

   $10 - 5 =$ _____

   $5 -$ _____ $=$ _____

   I subtracted 5 two times.

   So, _____ $\div$ _____ $=$ _____.

   Ryan has _____ boxes of markers.

In **2** and **3**, use bar diagrams or counters or draw a picture to solve.

2. There are 16 books. The librarian arranged 4 books on each shelf. How many shelves are there?

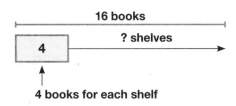

3. Joseph had 28 paintbrushes to give to 4 members of the Art Club. He wanted to give an equal number of brushes to each member. How many brushes did each member get?

4. Daniel has to carry 32 boxes to his room. He can carry 4 boxes on each trip. How many trips will Daniel take? Show your work.

You can use repeated subtraction or draw a picture to solve.

5. Model with Math The United States Mint released five state quarters every year. There are 50 states. How many years did it take for all 50 state quarters to be released? Write and solve an equation.

6. Write an equation that represents the bar diagram below.

40				
8	8	8	8	8

7. Number Sense Compare 249 and 271. Write the greater number in word form.

8. Higher Order Thinking A newspaper has more than 30 pages and fewer than 40 pages. The newspaper is divided into sections, and each section has exactly 8 pages. How many sections does the newspaper have?

9. The store clerk has 21 mugs to display on shelves. She wants to display an equal number of mugs on each shelf with no mugs left over. Which problem below shows a way she can do this?

    Ⓐ $21 \div 2$

    Ⓑ $21 \div 5$

    Ⓒ $21 \div 7$

    Ⓓ $21 \div 10$

10. Tamara has 20 dolls. She wants to store them in boxes with an equal number of dolls in each box. She does not want any dolls left over. How can she divide the dolls equally into boxes with none left over?

    Ⓐ Put 3 dolls in each box.

    Ⓑ Put 4 dolls in each box.

    Ⓒ Put 6 dolls in each box.

    Ⓓ Put 8 dolls in each box.

Name _____

Solve & Share

Carolyn earned $8 a week for 2 weeks. She wants to buy some books that cost $4 each. How many books can she buy?

Choose a tool to represent and solve the problem. Explain why you chose that tool.

I can ...
think strategically to determine which tool will be most useful.

SOL 3.4b, 3.4a

Thinking Habits

Be a good thinker! These questions can help you.

- Which tools can I use?

- Why should I use this tool to help me solve the problem?

- Is there a different tool I could use?

- Am I using the tool appropriately?

Look Back! **Use Appropriate Tools** Explain how you used the tool you chose.

How Can You Use Appropriate Tools to Represent and Solve Problems?

A

A hardware store has boxes of 18 light bulbs. 3 light bulbs cost $4. How much does it cost to buy a whole box of light bulbs? Choose a tool to represent and solve the problem.

Sometimes you can use more than one tool to help you solve problems.

What do I need to do?

I need to choose an appropriate tool to help me find how much it costs to buy a box of 18 light bulbs.

B ## Which tools can I use to help me solve this problem?

I can

- decide which tools are appropriate.

- use cubes and counters to solve this problem.

- use the tools correctly.

C

Here's my thinking...

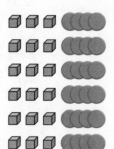

I will use two tools. Both counters and ones cubes are easy to count and move around.

Each cube is 1 light bulb.
I will separate 18 cubes into groups of 3.

Each counter is $1.
I will put 4 counters with each group of 3 light bulbs.

There are 24 counters.
A box of light bulbs costs $24.

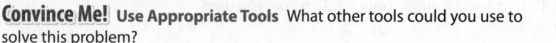

Convince Me! Use Appropriate Tools What other tools could you use to solve this problem?

Name _____

☆ Guided Practice *

Use Appropriate Tools

3 friends each have 8 books. They put their books into 4 equal piles. How many books are in each pile?

You can also use a digital tool. Technology can help you solve a problem.

1. Choose a tool to represent the problem. Explain why you chose that tool.

2. Solve the problem. Explain how you used the tool you chose.

Independent Practice ☆

Use Appropriate Tools

15 students are working in equal groups to make posters. There are 5 students in each group. For each group of students, there needs to be 2 adults helping. How many adults are needed?

3. Choose a tool to represent the problem. Explain why you chose that tool.

4. Solve the problem. Explain how you used the tool you chose.

5. The posters need to be 20 inches long. What tool could the students use to check the posters are the correct size? Explain how they could use this tool.

Bottle Cap Display
The soda bottle caps at the right are shared equally between Kerry and Nita. There are 4 orange bottle caps. Kerry wants to arrange her bottle caps into an array.

6. **Make Sense and Persevere** What do you need to find out before you make an array? Show a way to find this. You can use a tool to help.

7. **Use Appropriate Tools** Choose a tool to represent the array of soda bottle caps. Explain why you chose that tool.

8. **Model with Math** Draw a picture to show one way the array might look. Then write a multiplication equation for the array.

> Think about what you need to do in the problem. Then choose a tool that can help you solve it.

9. **Use Structure** Write a different multiplication equation with the same two factors you used in **8**. Has the product changed? Explain.

10. **Critique Reasoning** Kerry says she can use a tens rod to represent the array. Do you agree? Explain.

Name _____

Another Look!

Mal downloads 4 songs each week for 5 weeks. Then he sorts the songs into equal groups. There are 10 songs in each group. How many groups are there?

Tell how you can use tools to help solve the problem.

- I can decide which tool is appropriate.

- I can use a tool to represent the situation.

- I can use the tool correctly.

Solve the problem. Explain how you used the tool you chose.

I can use grid paper. Each shaded square represents 1 song.

I shade 4 squares for each week. There are 20 songs. Then I separate them into groups of 10. There are 2 groups.

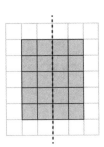

Grid paper, counters, cubes, or other objects can all be used as tools to help solve problems.

Use Appropriate Tools

Niko bought 4 stamps each week for 3 weeks. He wants to put 6 stamps on each page of his album. How many pages will Niko use?

1. Tell how you can use tools to help solve the problem.

2. Choose a tool to represent the problem. Explain why you chose that tool.

3. Solve the problem. Explain how you used the tool you chose.

Summer Jobs

The table at the right shows how much Tony earns per hour for his summer jobs. One day Tony spends 3 hours running errands. He wants to use the money from this job to buy two banners.

4. Use Appropriate Tools Choose a tool to represent the problem. Explain why you chose that tool.

Tony's Summer Jobs	
Job	**Hourly Pay**
Walking Dogs	$8
Mowing Lawns	$10
Running Errands	$6

DATA

5. Make Sense and Persevere What do you need to find out before you can solve the problem? Show a way to find this. You can use a tool to help.

6. Reasoning Does Tony have enough money? Use what you know to solve the problem.

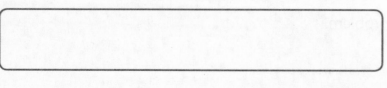

You can use tools to represent different parts of a problem.

7. Make Sense and Persevere Did you need all the information in the table to solve the problem? Explain.

8. Construct Arguments Tony decides not to buy the banners. Does he have enough money to buy one cap instead? Explain why or why not.

Find a Match

Work with a partner. Point to a clue. Read the clue.

Look below the clues to find a match. Write the clue letter in the box next to the match.

Find a match for every clue.

I can ...
add and subtract within 20.

Clues

A Is equal to 9 + 11

B Is equal to 13 − 6

C Is equal to 8 + 8

D Is equal to 12 − 8

E Is equal to 19 − 9

F Is equal to 9 + 6

G Is equal to 10 − 7

H Is equal to 8 + 9

I Is equal to 2 − 2

J Is equal to 9 + 10

K Is equal to 16 − 8

L Is equal to 6 + 7

☐ 3 + 0	☐ 10 + 6	☐ 9 − 9
☐ 15 − 8	☐ 13	☐ 4 + 4
☐ 17	☐ 13 − 9	☐ 12 + 8
☐ 5 + 5	☐ 8 + 7	☐ 19

Vocabulary Review

A-Z
Glossary

Word List

- array
- column
- Commutative Property of Multiplication
- division
- equal groups
- equation
- factors
- multiplication
- number line
- product
- row
- unknown

Understand Vocabulary

Choose the best term from the Word List. Write it on the blank.

1. Addition and _____ are operations you can use to join _____.

2. You solve an equation by finding the value that is _____.

3. You can use a(n) _____ to display objects in equal rows and columns.

4. A line marked in equal units and numbered in order is called a(n) _____.

For each of these terms, give an example and a non-example.

	Example	Non-example
5. division	_____	_____
6. equation	_____	_____
7. Commutative Property of Multiplication	_____	_____

Use Vocabulary in Writing

8. Explain how you can multiply 3 × 4. Use at least 2 terms from the Word List in your explanation.

Name _____

Set A | pages 7–12 _____

Reteaching

How many is 3 groups of 4?

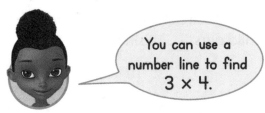

$4 + 4 + 4 = 12$

$3 \times 4 = 12$

$4 + 4 + 4 = 3 \times 4$

Remember that you can use addition or multiplication to join equal groups.

Complete each equation. Use counters or draw a picture to help.

1. $2 + 2 + 2 = 3 \times$ _____

2. _____ + _____ + _____ $= 3 \times 6$

3. $8 +$ _____ $+$ _____ $=$ _____ $\times 8$

Set B | pages 13–18 _____

Skip count by 4s three times.

You can use a number line to find 3×4.

Number of jumps: 3
Number in each jump: 4

$3 \times 4 = 12$

Remember that you can show skip counting on a number line.

Use the number line to complete each multiplication equation.

1. $2 \times 3 =$ _____

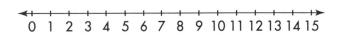

2. $4 \times 3 =$ _____

Set C | pages 19–24 _____

Find 4×6.
The array shows 4 rows of 6 counters.

Each row is an equal group. You can use addition, skip counting, or multiplication to find the total.

$6 + 6 + 6 + 6 = 24$

$6, 12, 18, 24$

$4 \times 6 = 24$

Remember that an array shows objects in equal rows.

Show how to use addition, skip counting, and multiplication for each array.

1.

2.

This array shows
3 rows of 4.

This array shows
4 rows of 3.

$3 \times 4 = 12$

$4 \times 3 = 12$

So, $3 \times 4 = 4 \times 3$.

Remember that the Commutative Property of Multiplication says you can multiply factors in any order and the product is the same.

Draw an array and write the products.

1. $2 \times 5 =$ _____ $5 \times 2 =$ _____

2 friends share 6 fruit snacks equally. How many fruit snacks does each friend get?

$6 \div 2 = 3$ fruit snacks

You can use repeated subtraction.

$6 - 2 = 4$ You subtract 2 from 6 three
$4 - 2 = 2$ times to reach zero.
$2 - 2 = 0$

$6 \div 2 = 3$

Remember that division is an operation to find the number of equal groups or the number in each equal group.

1. 9 raisin boxes are shared by 3 children. Each child gets ☐ raisin boxes.

2. $12 \div 2 =$ _____   **3.** $10 \div 5 =$ _____

4. $25 \div 5 =$ _____   **5.** $16 \div 4 =$ _____

Think about these questions to help you **use appropriate tools strategically**.

Thinking Habits

Which tools can I use?

Why should I use this tool to help me solve the problem?

Is there a different tool I could use?

Am I using the tool appropriately?

Remember that you can use digital tools.

Sam makes enough muffins to give 8 of her friends 3 muffins each. Each tray holds 6 muffins. How many trays does she need?

1. Choose a tool to represent the problem. Explain why you chose that tool.

2. Solve. Explain how the tool helped.

Name _____

1. Jace drew a picture. Choose all of the equations that go with Jace's picture.

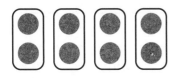

- ☐ $1 + 2 + 1 + 3 = 8$
- ☐ $2 + 2 + 8 = 12$
- ☐ $2 + 2 + 2 + 2 = 8$
- ☐ $4 + 2 + 2 = 8$
- ☐ $4 \times 2 = 8$

2. Aidan puts 2 turtles in each of 4 aquariums. What is the total number of turtles? Show the multiplication problem on a number line. Then write the answer.

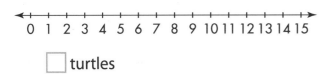

☐ turtles

3. Minh paints 12 rooms. To paint 3 rooms, he needs 2 cans of paint. He wants to know how many cans he needs in all. Which tools would be appropriate for Minh to use to solve the problem? Choose all that apply.

- ☐ Counters
- ☐ Ruler
- ☐ Pencil and paper
- ☐ Tiles
- ☐ Money

4. Megan organized her photos in this array. Draw a different array that has the same factors. Then write multiplication equations for each array.

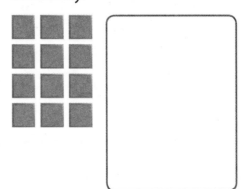

5. Josiah makes six 3-point baskets in his basketball game. For questions 5a–5d, choose *Yes* or *No* to tell if the equation shows a way to find the number of points that Josiah scores.

5a. $6 \times 3 = 18$ ○ Yes   ○ No

5b. $2 \times 6 = 12$ ○ Yes   ○ No

5c. $3 + 3 + 3 +$
    $3 + 3 + 3 = 18$ ○ Yes   ○ No

5d. $6 + 6 = 12$ ○ Yes   ○ No

6. Teresa is growing 2 rows of tomato plants, with 4 plants in each row. Draw an array to show the plants. Find the total number of plants.

7. Ann has 25 tennis balls. She wants to put them into cans that hold 3 balls each. Can there be equal shares of balls with no balls remaining? Why or why not?

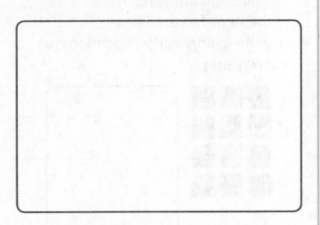

8. Crystal draws jumps on a number line to solve a multiplication problem. Which multiplication equation does her number line show?

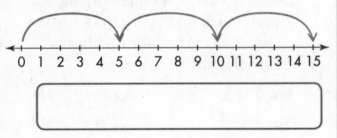

9. Al needs to put 9 basketballs in each bin. He has 45 basketballs. Which equation can help you find how many bins Al can fill?

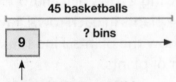

45 basketballs

? bins

9

9 basketballs in each bin

Ⓐ $9 \div 45 = \square$

Ⓑ $45 \times 5 = \square$

Ⓒ $45 \div \square = 8$

Ⓓ $45 \div \square = 9$

10. Zak uses repeated subtraction to find $48 \div 8$. How many groups of 8 does Zak subtract?

11. Saima makes 14 muffins to give to her friends. She wants to give 2 muffins to each friend at her party.

Part A

Explain how Saima can figure out how many friends to invite.

Part B

Explain a different way that Saima can figure out how many friends to invite.

Sticker Collection
Jamie saved money to buy a sticker album.
The money he has saved each week is shown in the table.

Sticker Prices
• Green sticker albums cost $6.
• Blue sticker albums cost $9.
• Yellow sticker albums cost $12.
• Stickers cost $1 for 3 stickers.

Use the **Money Saved Each Week** table to answer
Question 1.

1. How much money has Jamie saved after 4 weeks?
   Write an addition equation to solve.

Money Saved Each Week	
Week	**Dollars Saved per Week**
1	$3
2	$3
3	$3
4	$3

Use the **Sticker Prices** list to answer Questions 2–4.

2. Jamie divides his money into two equal parts. Jamie spends 1 part on a
   sticker album. Which of the albums can Jamie buy?

3. Jamie spends the other part of his money on stickers.
   How many stickers can Jamie buy?

4. After spending his money, Jamie decides that he wants a second album.
   He plans to save $3 per week until he can also buy a blue sticker album.
   How many weeks does Jamie need to save money?

Use the **Sticker Arrays** table to answer Question 5.

5. Jamie wants to organize his stickers into arrays on a page of the album. Jamie started to make a table to show three ways he could do this.

Sticker Arrays

Array	Number of Rows	Stickers in Each Row
Way 1	6	3
Way 2	2	9
Way 3	_____	_____

Part A

Draw arrays to show the two ways Jamie planned to organize his stickers.

Way 1

Way 2

Part B

Draw an array to show another way Jamie could organize his stickers. Complete the Sticker Arrays table for Way 3.

Way 3

6. Write multiplication equations for each array to check that Jamie uses all of his stickers in each plan. Do two ways show the same factors? Explain.

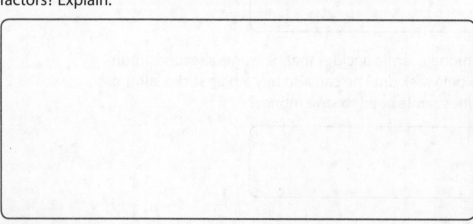

Multiplication Facts : Use Patterns

Essential Question: How can unknown multiplication facts be found using patterns and properties?

Digital Resources

Solve Learn Glossary Practice Buddy

Tools Assessment Help Games

Force makes objects move.

You can use patterns to predict how objects will move!

Let's move some numbers! Here's a project on motion and patterns.

Math and Science Project: Motion Patterns

Do Research Swings, see-saws, and some other playground objects move with force. Use the Internet or other sources to see what happens when these objects move. Record the number of times that someone pushes or pulls to make the object move. Record the number of times that the object moves.

Journal: Write a Report Include what you found. Also in your report:

- Explain any patterns you found. Tell how you can use your patterns to predict how the objects will move in the future.

- Write an equation for one of the patterns.

- Explain what the numbers in your equation represent.

Name _____

Review What You Know

A-Z Vocabulary

Choose the best term from the box.
Write it on the blank.

| • multiplication | • factors |
| • array | • product |

1. The _____ is the answer to a multiplication problem.

2. Numbers that are being multiplied are _____.

3. An operation that gives the total when you join equal groups is _____.

Multiplication as Repeated Addition

Complete each equation.

4. $2 + 2 + 2 + 2 = 4 \times$ ____

5. $9 +$ ____ $+$ ____ $=$ ____ $\times 9$

6. ____ $+$ ____ $+$ ____ $+ 5 =$ ____ $\times 5$

7. $2 \times 6 =$ ____ $+$ ____

Multiplication on the Number Line

8. Marty drew this number line.

   Which multiplication fact does the number line show?

   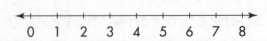

   0 1 2 3 4 5 6 7 8 9 10 11 12

   Ⓐ $3 \times 5 = 15$ Ⓑ $3 \times 4 = 12$ Ⓒ $3 \times 3 = 9$ Ⓓ $3 \times 6 = 18$

9. Show the multiplication fact on the number line. Write the product.

   $3 \times 2 =$ ____

   0 1 2 3 4 5 6 7 8

The Commutative Property

10. How do the arrays represent the Commutative Property of Multiplication?

My Word Cards

Use the examples for each word on the front of the card to help complete the definitions on the back.

multiple

0, 5, 10, 15, and 20 are multiples of 5.

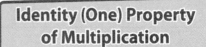

Identity (One) Property of Multiplication

$4 \times 1 = 4$

$5 \times 1 = 5$

Zero Property of Multiplication

$4 \times 0 = 0$

$5 \times 0 = 0$

My Word Cards

Complete each definition. Extend learning by writing your own definitions.

The _____

_____

_____ states that the product of any number and 1 is that number.

The product of a given number and any other whole number is called a

_____.

The _____

_____ states that the product of any number and zero is zero.

Name _____

Solve & Share

Each chicken has 2 legs. How many legs are there in a group of 9 chickens? Show how you decided.

Solve

You can make sense of the problem by using a number line or a table to record and analyze information.

Number of Chickens									
Number of Legs									

Look Back! **Use Structure** Explain another way you could solve this problem.

Essential Question: How Can You Use Patterns to Multiply by 2 and 5?

A

How many socks are in 7 pairs of socks? Find 7 × 2.

1 pair	2 pairs	3 pairs	4 pairs	5 pairs	6 pairs	7 pairs
1 × 2	2 × 2	3 × 2	4 × 2	5 × 2	6 × 2	7 × 2
2	4	6	8	10	12	14

There are 14 socks in 7 pairs.

B

How many fingers are on 7 gloves?

Find 7 × 5.

C

1 × 5 = 5
2 × 5 = 10
3 × 5 = 15
4 × 5 = 20
5 × 5 = 25
6 × 5 = 30
7 × 5 = 35

You can use skip counting or patterns to find the number of fingers on 7 gloves.

There are 35 fingers on 7 gloves.

Convince Me! **Use Structure** Use skip counting or patterns to answer these questions:

How many socks are in 9 pairs? 10 pairs?

How many fingers are on 9 gloves? 10 gloves?

Another Example!

Multiples are the products of a number and other whole numbers.

2s Facts	
$0 \times 2 = 0$	$5 \times 2 = 10$
$1 \times 2 = 2$	$6 \times 2 = 12$
$2 \times 2 = 4$	$7 \times 2 = 14$
$3 \times 2 = 6$	$8 \times 2 = 16$
$4 \times 2 = 8$	$9 \times 2 = 18$

5s Facts	
$0 \times 5 = 0$	$5 \times 5 = 25$
$1 \times 5 = 5$	$6 \times 5 = 30$
$2 \times 5 = 10$	$7 \times 5 = 35$
$3 \times 5 = 15$	$8 \times 5 = 40$
$4 \times 5 = 20$	$9 \times 5 = 45$

The products for the 2s facts are multiples of 2. Multiples of 2 end in 0, 2, 4, 6, or 8.

The products for the 5s facts are multiples of 5. Multiples of 5 end in 0 or 5.

☆ Guided Practice *

Do You Understand?

1. Is 25 a multiple of 2 or 5? How do you know?

2. **Use Structure** Bert says 2×9 is 19. How can you use patterns to show Bert's answer is wrong?

Do You Know How?

In **3–5**, find each product.

3. $2 \times 4 =$ _____ $2 \times 1 = 2$
$2 \times 2 = 4$
$2 \times 3 =$ _____
$2 \times 4 =$ _____

4.   8
   $\times\ 2$

5.   5
   $\times\ 8$

Independent Practice ☆

In **6–12**, find the missing product or factor.

6. $2 \times 2 =$ _____

7. $3 \times$ _____ $= 15$

8. _____ $\times 2 = 14$

9.   6
   $\times\ 5$

10.   4
    $\times\ 2$

11.   9
    $\times\ 2$

12.   5
    $\times\ 7$

Problem Solving

13. Make Sense and Persevere
Eric has some nickels. He says they are worth exactly 34 cents. Can you tell if Eric is correct or not? Why or why not?

14. Critique Reasoning Brian said 78 + 92 + 85 is greater than 300. Explain why Brian's answer is not reasonable.

15. Shannon traded 6 nickels in for dimes. How many dimes did Shannon receive?

16. Math and Science Mike watches how the pendulum swings in his clock. He notices that it swings 1 time every 2 seconds. How long will it take to swing 5 times?

17. April has the coins shown below.

April counted the value of her coins in cents. List the numbers April would have named.

18. Higher Order Thinking Jake went bowling. On his first turn, he knocked down 2 pins. On his second turn, he knocked down twice as many pins. So far, how many pins has Jake knocked down? How do you know?

Assessment

19. Write each number in the correct column to show if it is a multiple of 2 or 5.

Multiple of 2	Multiple of 5

5   6   10   14   18   25

Homework & Practice 2-1
2 and 5 as Factors

Another Look!

When you multiply by 2, you can use a doubles fact. For example, 2 × 6 is the same as adding 6 + 6. Both equal 12.

When you multiply by 5, you can use a pattern to find the product.

2s Facts	
2 × 0 = 0	2 × 5 = 10
2 × 1 = 2	2 × 6 = 12
2 × 2 = 4	2 × 7 = 14
2 × 3 = 6	2 × 8 = 16
2 × 4 = 8	2 × 9 = 18

5s Facts	
5 × 0 = 0	5 × 5 = 25
5 × 1 = 5	5 × 6 = 30
5 × 2 = 10	5 × 7 = 35
5 × 3 = 15	5 × 8 = 40
5 × 4 = 20	5 × 9 = 45

Each multiple of 2 ends in 0, 2, 4, 6, or 8.   Each multiple of 5 ends in 0 or 5.

In **1–17**, solve each equation.

1. 2 × 5 = ?

5 + 5 = ____

2 × 5 = ____

2. 2 × 4 = ?

4 + 4 = ____

2 × 4 = ____

3. 1 × 2 = ?

1 + 1 = ____

2 × 1 = ____

4. 5 × ____ = 25

5. 3 × 5 = ____

6. 35 = 7 × ____

7. ____ × 8 = 16

8. 5 × 9 = ____

9. 2 × 7 = ____

10.   5
       × 4

11.   1
       × 5

12.   2
       × 0

13.   8
       × 2

14. What is 9 times 2? ____

15. What is 5 times 8? ____

16. What is 6 times 2? ____

17. What is 5 times 0? ____

18. Georgia is making sock puppets. Each pair of socks costs $2. Georgia bought 6 pairs of socks. How much did she spend? Draw a number line to solve.

19. 🔤 **Vocabulary** Write an equation where 45 is the product.

20. Reasoning There are 5 school days in each week. How many school days are in 9 weeks? Explain.

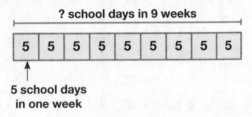

? school days in 9 weeks

5	5	5	5	5	5	5	5	5

↑
5 school days
in one week

21. Make Sense and Persevere Tara walks 2 miles each day. How many miles does Tara walk in a week? How did you find the answer?

22. Mika drew this shape. What is the name of the shape Mika drew? Mika then drew a shape that has 2 fewer sides. What is the name of that shape?

23. Higher Order Thinking How can adding doubles help you multiply by 2? Give an example.

✔ **Assessment**

24. Write the expressions in the correct column.

Product is 10	Product is 12	Product is 35

2×5 7×5 6×2 2×6 5×2 5×7

Name _____

Solve & Share

Maria bought 4 packages of bottled water. There are 9 bottles in each package. How many bottles did Maria buy? Explain how you solved this problem.

I can ...
use patterns to multiply by 9.

SOL 3.4a; 3.4b

An array or a data table can help you construct arguments.

● ● ● ● ● ● ● ● ●

Look Back! **Make Sense and Persevere** If Maria bought 9 packages of bottled water and there were 4 bottles in each package, would the number of bottles she bought be the same or different? Explain.

Essential Question   How Can Patterns Be Used to Find 9s Facts?

A

The owner of a flower shop puts 9 roses in each package. How many roses are in 8 packages?

You can use patterns to find 8 × 9.

9s Facts
0 × 9 = 0
1 × 9 = 9
2 × 9 = 18
3 × 9 = 27
4 × 9 = 36
5 × 9 = 45
6 × 9 = 54
7 × 9 = 63
8 × 9 = ▪
9 × 9 = ▪

DATA

B **One Way**

Use these patterns. Start with 1 × 9 = 9.

The ones digit decreases by 1 each time. So, the ones digit in the product after 63 in the facts table above is 2.

The tens digit increases by 1 each time.

So, the tens digit in the product after 63 in the facts table above is 7.

8 × 9 = 72

There are 72 roses in 8 packages.

C **Another Way**

Use these patterns to find the product.

The tens digit is 1 less than the factor being multiplied by 9.

$$8 - 1 = 7$$
$$8 \times 9 = 72$$
$$7 + 2 = 9$$

The digits of the product have a sum of 9 or a multiple of 9.

Convince Me! **Use Structure** Use the patterns above to find 9 × 9. Explain how you found the product.

Name _____

☆ Guided Practice ☆

Do You Understand?

1. Critique Reasoning Paul thinks 3 × 9 is 24. Use a 9s pattern to show Paul is wrong.

2. Look for Relationships Look at the table of 9s facts on page 68. Describe a number pattern in the multiples of 9.

Do You Know How?

In **3–10**, find each product.

3. $9 \times 2 =$ _____

4. $5 \times 9 =$ _____

5. $7 \times 9 =$ _____

6. $4 \times 9 =$ _____

7. $2 \times 9 =$ _____

8. $6 \times 9 =$ _____

You can use patterns to solve multiplication facts with 9s.

9.   3
    × 9
    ____

10.   8
    × 9
    ____

☆ Independent Practice ☆

In **11–22**, find the missing product or factor.

11. $9 \times 0 =$ _____   **12.** $2 \times$ _____ $= 18$ **13.** _____ $\times 9 = 72$ **14.** $9 \times 9 =$ _____

15.   4   **16.**   9   **17.**   9   **18.**   9
    × 9   × 5   × 7   × 1
    ____   ____   ____   ____

19. What is $9 \times 3?$ _____   **20.** What is $9 \times 6?$ _____

21. What is $0 \times 9?$ _____   **22.** What is $9 \times 8?$ _____

For another example, see Set B on page 99.   **Topic 2** | Lesson 2-2   **69**

Problem Solving

In **23–25**, use the table to the right.

23. Reasoning The library is having a used book sale. How much do 4 hardcover books cost? Draw a number line to show the answer.

Library Book Sale	
Paperback Books	$5
Hardcover Books	$9
Magazines	$2

DATA

24. Higher Order Thinking How much more would Chico spend if he bought 3 hardcover books rather than 3 paperback books? Show how you found the answer.

25. Make Sense and Persevere Maggie bought only magazines. The clerk told her she owed $15. How does Maggie know the clerk made a mistake?

26. The owner of a flower shop put 9 sunflowers in each of 6 vases. Then he counted the flowers by 9s. List the numbers he named.

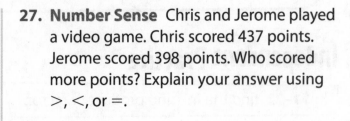

27. Number Sense Chris and Jerome played a video game. Chris scored 437 points. Jerome scored 398 points. Who scored more points? Explain your answer using >, <, or =.

28. Which numbers are **NOT** multiples of 9? Choose all that apply.

- ☐ 9
- ☐ 16
- ☐ 18
- ☐ 21
- ☐ 23

29. Which numbers are multiples of 9? Choose all that apply.

- ☐ 18
- ☐ 36
- ☐ 42
- ☐ 54
- ☐ 69

Name _____

Homework & Practice 2-2

9 as a Factor

Another Look!

9s Facts
$0 \times 9 = 0$
$1 \times 9 = 9$
$2 \times 9 = 18$
$3 \times 9 = 27$
$4 \times 9 = 36$
$5 \times 9 = 45$
$6 \times 9 = 54$
$7 \times 9 = $
$8 \times 9 = $
$9 \times 9 = $

The table shows patterns in the 9s facts.

- The tens digit in a product will be 1 less than the factor being multiplied by 9.
- The sum of the digits of the product will always be 9 or a multiple of 9, unless the other factor is 0.

Find 9×7.

The tens digit must be 1 less than 7.
The tens digit is 6.

The sum of the digits is 9.
$6 + 3 = 9$, so the ones digit is 3.

The product is 63.

You can use patterns to help remember 9s facts.

In **1–13**, solve each equation.

1. $3 \times 9 = ?$

Tens digit: $3 - 1 = $ _____

Sum of digits:
_____ + _____ = 9

$3 \times 9 = $ _____

2. $2 \times 9 = ?$

Tens digit: $2 - 1 = $ _____

Sum of digits:
_____ + _____ = 9

$2 \times 9 = $ _____

3. $1 \times 9 = ?$

Tens digit: $1 - 1 = $ _____

Sum of digits:
_____ + _____ = 9

$1 \times 9 = $ _____

4. $9 \times 0 = $ _____

5. $9 \times$ _____ $= 54$

6. $81 = 9 \times$ _____

7.
$$\begin{array}{r} 9 \\ \times\ 8 \\ \hline \end{array}$$

8.
$$\begin{array}{r} 7 \\ \times\ 9 \\ \hline \end{array}$$

9.
$$\begin{array}{r} 4 \\ \times\ 9 \\ \hline \end{array}$$

10.
$$\begin{array}{r} 2 \\ \times\ 9 \\ \hline \end{array}$$

11. Find 6 times 9.

12. Find 5 times 9.

13. Find 0 times 9.

14. Reasoning Paula's hair was put into 9 braids. Each braid used 4 beads. How many beads were used? Explain how you found the product.

15. Algebra Tony has 9 sets of baseball cards. Each set contains 6 cards. Write 2 equations that Tony could use to find how many cards he has.

16. Critique Reasoning Sasha says if she knows the product of 9 × 8, she also knows the product of 8 × 9. Is Sasha correct? Why or why not?

17. Make Sense and Persevere Dustin had $52. He got $49 more and then he spent some money. Dustin has $35 left. How much money did Dustin spend?

18. Higher Order Thinking Jordan received 9 text messages last week. She received 3 times more text messages this week than last week. How many text messages did Jordan receive this week?

19. Construct Arguments Rita bought 5 pairs of socks. Each pair cost $4. How much did Rita spend on socks? Explain how you know.

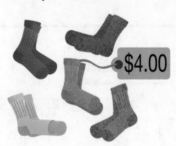
$4.00

✔ **Assessment**

20. Which numbers are factors of 45? Choose all that apply.

_____ × _____ = 45

☐ 4
☐ 5
☐ 6
☐ 8
☐ 9

21. Which numbers are factors of 18? Choose all that apply.

_____ × _____ = 18

☐ 2
☐ 3
☐ 6
☐ 8
☐ 9

Name _____

Solve & Share

Carlos said that 6 times 0 equals 6. Do you agree? Explain your thinking.

I can ...
use patterns and properties to multiply by 0 and 1.

SOL 3.4a; 3.4b; 3.4c; 3.17

Be precise.
What does it mean to multiply something by zero?

Look Back! **Make Sense and Persevere** Draw a picture to show $5 \times 0 = 0$.

Essential Question

What Are the Patterns in Multiples of 1 and 0?

A

Kira has 8 plates with 1 orange on each plate. How many oranges does Kira have?

You can use patterns to find 8 × 1.

B 8 groups with 1 in each group equals 8 in all.

$$8 \times 1 = 8$$

Kira has 8 oranges.

1 plate with 8 oranges also equals 8 oranges.

$$1 \times 8 = 8$$

The Identity (One) Property of Multiplication: When you multiply a number by 1, the product is that number.

C If Kira has 4 plates with 0 oranges on each plate, she has 0 oranges.

$$4 \times 0 = 0$$

If $4 \times 0 = 0$, then $0 \times 4 = 0$.

The Zero Property of Multiplication: When you multiply a number by 0, the product is 0.

Convince Me! **Use Appropriate Tools** How would you use counters to show 7 × 1? How many counters would you have in all?

Name _____

☆ Guided Practice ☆

Do You Understand?

1. **Make Sense and Persevere** Draw a number line to show $8 \times 1 = 8$.

2. Chad has 6 plates. There is 1 apple and 0 grapes on each plate. How many apples are there? How many grapes are there?

Do You Know How?

In **3–8**, find each product.

3.

$3 \times 1 =$ _____

4.

$3 \times 0 =$ _____

5. $1 \times 7 =$ _____

6. $5 \times 0 =$ _____

7. $\begin{array}{r} 4 \\ \times\, 0 \\ \hline \end{array}$

8. $\begin{array}{r} 2 \\ \times\, 1 \\ \hline \end{array}$

You can use the Identity and Zero Properties of Multiplication to find these products.

Independent Practice ☆

In **9–15**, find each product.

9. $0 \times 4 =$ _____

10. $1 \times 6 =$ _____

11. $4 \times 1 =$ _____

12. $\begin{array}{r} 9 \\ \times\, 1 \\ \hline \end{array}$

13. $\begin{array}{r} 0 \\ \times\, 2 \\ \hline \end{array}$

14. $\begin{array}{r} 1 \\ \times\, 1 \\ \hline \end{array}$

15. $\begin{array}{r} 6 \\ \times\, 0 \\ \hline \end{array}$

In **16–21**, write $<$, $>$, or $=$ in each $\bigcirc$ to compare.

16. $1 \times 6 \bigcirc 8 \times 0$

17. $0 \times 6 \bigcirc 6 \times 0$

18. $0 \times 7 \bigcirc 5 \times 1$

19. $0 \times 0 \bigcirc 0 \times 9$

20. $1 \times 7 \bigcirc 5 \times 1$

21. $1 \times 4 \bigcirc 4 \times 1$

Problem Solving

22. Critique Reasoning Brent drew this model to show 5 groups of 1 is the same as 1 group of 5. Is Brent correct? Explain how you know.

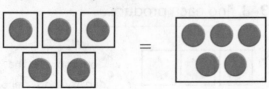

23. Make Sense and Persevere A unicycle relay team has 4 riders. Each rider has one unicycle. If each unicycle has 1 wheel, how many wheels does the team have? What property of multiplication can you use to find the answer?

24. Tickets for a school concert are free to students. The cost is $1 for each adult. What is the total cost of tickets for 5 students?

25. Higher Order Thinking The product of two factors is 0. One of the factors is 0. Can you tell what the other factor is? Explain your answer.

26. Reasoning The children in the third-grade classes are having a bike parade. Barb's class has 18 bikes. Tim's class has some rows of bikes with 5 bikes in each row. Tim's class has more bikes than Barb's class. How many rows of bikes could Tim's class have? Explain.

✓ **Assessment**

27. Is the equation correct? Choose *Yes* or *No*.

27a. $1 \times 4 = 1$ ○ Yes   ○ No

27b. $4 \times 4 = 0$ ○ Yes   ○ No

27c. $7 \times 1 = 7$ ○ Yes   ○ No

27d. $0 \times 9 = 9$ ○ Yes   ○ No

Another Look!

Zero and one have special multiplication properties.

The Identity (One) Property of Multiplication

When you multiply a number by 1, the product is that number.

Examples:
$4 \times 1 = 4$ $16 \times 1 = 16$
$1 \times 9 = 9$ $13 \times 1 = 13$
$51 \times 1 = 51$ $1 \times 48 = 48$

The Zero Property of Multiplication

When you multiply a number by 0, the product is 0.

Examples:
$5 \times 0 = 0$ $123 \times 0 = 0$
$17 \times 0 = 0$ $0 \times 58 = 0$
$0 \times 51 = 0$ $74 \times 0 = 0$

In **1–6**, draw a picture to represent the multiplication fact and then solve.

1. $1 \times 3 =$ _____

2. $0 \times 6 =$ _____

3. $9 \times 0 =$ _____

4. $5 \times 0 =$ _____

5. $1 \times 7 =$ _____

6. $0 \times 4 =$ _____

In **7–10**, find each product.

7. $\begin{array}{r} 7 \\ \times\, 1 \\ \hline \end{array}$

8. $\begin{array}{r} 8 \\ \times\, 0 \\ \hline \end{array}$

9. $\begin{array}{r} 8 \\ \times\, 1 \\ \hline \end{array}$

10. $\begin{array}{r} 10 \\ \times\, 0 \\ \hline \end{array}$

In **11–13**, write $<$, $>$, or $=$ in each ◯ to compare.

11. $0 \times 4 \bigcirc 0 \times 4$

12. $1 \times 8 \bigcirc 6 \times 1$

13. $1 \times 5 \bigcirc 5 \times 1$

14. Number Sense Chen says the product of 4×0 is the same as the sum of $4 + 0$. Is Chen correct? Explain.

15. Model with Math Sara put 7 boxes in her closet. Each box is for holding a different type of seashell. So far, there are 0 shells in each box. How many shells does Sara have? Tell what math you used to find the answer.

16. Bob made a picture graph of the marbles he and his friends have. How many more marbles does Bob have than Kayla? Explain how you found the answer.

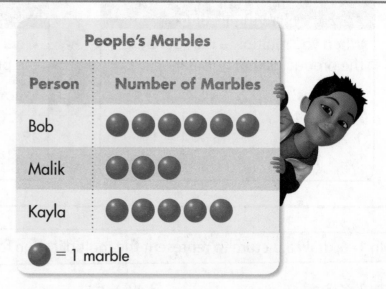

People's Marbles

Person	Number of Marbles
Bob	● ● ● ● ● ●
Malik	● ● ●
Kayla	● ● ● ● ●

● = 1 marble

17. Reasoning Kirsten has 6 coins. She puts the same number of coins in each of 3 envelopes. How many coins did Kirsten put in each envelope?

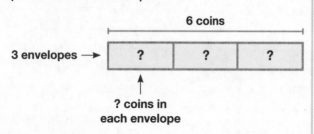

6 coins

3 envelopes → | ? | ? | ? |

? coins in each envelope

18. Higher Order Thinking Chef Morgan's restaurant has 24 tables. Fifteen of the tables each have one flower in a vase. The remaining tables have 5 flowers in each vase. How many flowers are there? Show how you found the answer.

✓ **Assessment**

19. Can you multiply the numbers on the left side of the equal sign to get the number on the right side of the equal sign? Choose *Yes* or *No*.

19a. $0 \times 2 = 0$ ○ Yes ○ No   **19b.** $1 \times 1 = 1$ ○ Yes ○ No

19c. $1 \times 4 = 5$ ○ Yes ○ No   **19d.** $5 \times 0 = 5$ ○ Yes ○ No

Name _____

Solve & Share

Duke runs 10 miles each week. How many miles will he run in 6 weeks? 7 weeks? 8 weeks? Describe patterns you find. *Solve these problems any way you choose.*

Solve

I can ...
use patterns to multiply by 10.

SOL 3.4a; 3.4b; 3.4c

You can generalize. What repeats in this problem?

Look Back! **Look for Relationships** How are the patterns when multiplying by 10 related to the patterns when multiplying by 5?

Essential Question: What Are the Patterns in Multiples of 10?

A

Greg wants to train for a race that is 10 weeks away. The chart shows his training schedule. How many miles will Greg run to train for the race?

You can use patterns to find 10×10.

Weekly Training Schedule	
Activity	**Miles**
Swimming	4 miles
Running	10 miles
Biking	9 miles

DATA

B

10s Facts	
$0 \times 10 = 0$	$5 \times 10 = 50$
$1 \times 10 = 10$	$6 \times 10 = 60$
$2 \times 10 = 20$	$7 \times 10 = 70$
$3 \times 10 = 30$	$8 \times 10 = 80$
$4 \times 10 = 40$	$9 \times 10 = 90$
	$10 \times 10 = ?$

DATA

Use patterns to find the product.

• Write the factor you are multiplying by 10.

• Write a zero to the right of that factor. A multiple of 10 will always have a 0 in the ones place.

$$10 \times 10 = 100$$

Greg will run 100 miles.

Convince Me! **Use Structure** How many miles will Greg swim in 10 weeks? Write an equation, and explain how to use a pattern to find the product.

Practice Buddy   Tools   Assessment

Another Example!

You can use a number line to find 3×10.

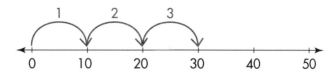

$$3 \times 10 = 30$$

☆ Guided Practice *

Do You Understand?

1. **Reasoning** Is 91 a multiple of 10? Explain.

2. **Generalize** If you multiply any one-digit number by 10, what do you write in the tens digit of the product?

Do You Know How?

In **3–6**, find each product.

3. $2 \times 10 = $ ____ 0

4. $6 \times 10 = $ ____ 0

5. $8 \times 10 = $ ____

6. $9 \times 10 = $ ____

☆ Independent Practice ☆

In **7** and **8**, use the number lines to help find the product.

7. $1 \times 10 = $ ____

8. $5 \times 10 = $ ____

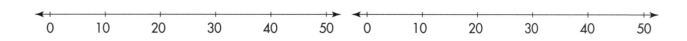

In **9–14**, find the missing product or factor.

9. $10 \times 2 = $ ____ 0

10. $9 \times 10 = $ ____ 0

11. $7 \times 10 = $ ____ 0

12. $3 \times 10 = $ ____

13. $5 \times $ ____ $ = 50$

14. $80 = 10 \times $ ____

Problem Solving

15. Reasoning Eddie borrowed $65 from his dad. Every month, he pays back $12. Complete the table to find how much money Eddie still owes his dad after 4 months.

Month	Amount Eddie Owes
April	$65 − $12 = _____
May	_____ − $12 = _____
June	_____ − _____ = _____
July	_____ − _____ = _____

16. Model with Math Kimmy bought 7 tickets to a concert. Each ticket costs $10. She also paid $5 to have the tickets delivered. Write equations to show how much money Kimmy spent in all.

17. Use Structure Write an addition equation and a multiplication equation for the array below.

18. Use the table to find the total number of juice boxes bought for a school picnic.

DATA	Food Item	Number of Packages	Number in Each Package
	Hot dogs	8	10
	Rolls	10	9
	Juice boxes	7	10

Juice boxes: _____

19. Higher Order Thinking Look at the table at the top of page 80. Greg multiplied 5 × 10 to find how many more miles he biked than swam in the 10 weeks. Does that make sense? Why or why not?

✓ **Assessment**

20. Mai had 8 packs of pens. Each pack had 10 pens. She gave 5 packs to Ervin and 3 packs to Sara.

Part A

How many pens did Mai start with?

Part B

Did Mai give more pens to Ervin or to Sara? Explain how you know.

Name _____

Another Look!

The table shows multiplication facts for 10.

10s Facts	
$10 \times 0 = 0$	$10 \times 5 = 50$
$10 \times 1 = 10$	$10 \times 6 = 60$
$10 \times 2 = 20$	$10 \times 7 = 70$
$10 \times 3 = 30$	$10 \times 8 = 80$
$10 \times 4 = 40$	$10 \times 9 = 90$
	$10 \times 10 = 100$

DATA

Find 5×10.

To find the answer, you can use a number line, or you can write a zero after the 5.

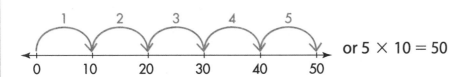

or $5 \times 10 = 50$

All multiples of 10 end with zero.

In **1** and **2**, use the number lines to help find the product.

1. $2 \times 10 =$ _____

2. $4 \times 10 =$ _____

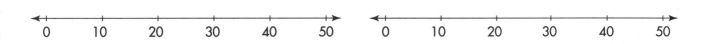

In **3–12**, find the product.

3. $10 \times 6 =$ _____

4. $10 \times 10 =$ _____

5. $0 \times 10 =$ _____

6. $1 \times 10 =$ _____

7. $10 \times 3 =$ _____

8. $9 \times 10 =$ _____

9. $\begin{array}{r} 10 \\ \times\ 1 \\ \hline \end{array}$

10. $\begin{array}{r} 10 \\ \times\ 3 \\ \hline \end{array}$

11. $\begin{array}{r} 10 \\ \times\ 8 \\ \hline \end{array}$

12. $\begin{array}{r} 10 \\ \times\ 7 \\ \hline \end{array}$

13. Reasoning Joey made this graph to show how many incorrect answers students got on a test. How many students got 3 answers incorrect? How do you know?

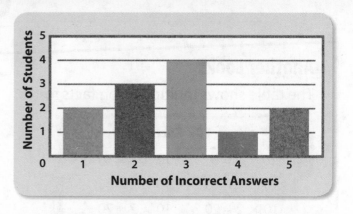

Number of Students

Number of Incorrect Answers

14. Math and Science Julie sees a ride that spins 10 turns each minute. She says it will spin 40 turns in 4 minutes. Is Julie correct? Explain.

15. Vocabulary Define *multiple of 10*. Give an example of a multiple of 10.

16. Critique Reasoning Greg has 3 rows of stamps with 10 stamps in each row. Greg says there are a total of 35 stamps. Use what you've learned about multiples of 10 to explain why Greg is incorrect.

17. Higher Order Thinking Junior says the product of 25 × 10 is 250. How can you use patterns to check Junior's answer?

 Assessment

18. Benjamin has 5 baskets. Each basket has 10 berries in it.

Part A

Explain how you could find how many berries Benjamin has.

Part B

If Benjamin instead had 10 baskets with 5 berries in each basket, explain how you could find how many berries he has.

Name _____

☆ ☆
Solve & Share

A company sells boxes of colored pencils. Each box contains 5 pencils. How many pencils are in 5 boxes? 9 boxes? 10 boxes? Explain how you found your answers.

I can ...
use basic multiplication facts to solve problems.

● **SOL** 3.4a; 3.4b; 3.4c

Number of Boxes	1	5	9	10
Number of Colored Pencils	5			

You can use appropriate tools to make an array to show the multiplication.

Look Back! **Model with Math** A different company sells boxes that have 9 colored pencils in each box. If the boxes had 9 pencils each, how would the way you solve the problem change? How would your answer change?

Essential Question

How Do You Use Multiplication Facts to Solve Problems?

A

Brendan has archery practice. The target shows the points he gets for hitting a section. How many points did Brendan get from his arrows that hit the black ring? How many points did he get from the red ring?

Section of Target	Number of Arrows
10	3
9	4
5	9
2	8
1	7

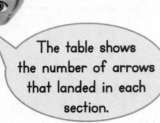 *The table shows the number of arrows that landed in each section.*

B **8 arrows hit the black ring.**

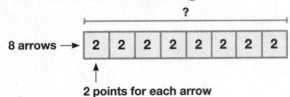

8 arrows → | 2 | 2 | 2 | 2 | 2 | 2 | 2 | 2 |

2 points for each arrow

The bar diagram shows 8 equal groups of 2.
$8 \times 2 = 16$

Brendan got 16 points from the 8 arrows.

C **4 arrows hit the red ring.**

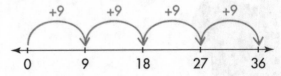

+9 +9 +9 +9

0   9   18   27   36

Skip count and record your counts.
9, 18, 27, 36
$4 \times 9 = 36$

Brendan got 36 points from the 4 arrows.

Convince Me! **Be Precise** How many points did Brendan get from the arrows that hit the yellow ring? Explain how you know.

86 **Topic 2** | Lesson 2-5

☆ Guided Practice*

Do You Understand?

1. To find 6×5, how does knowing $5 \times 6 = 30$ help you?

2. How can you find $8 + 8 + 8 + 8 + 8$ without adding?

Do You Know How?

In **3–9**, find each product.

3. $5 \times 9 =$ _____

4. $2 \times 1 =$ _____

5. $0 \times 10 =$ _____

6. $5 \times 4 =$ _____

7.   1
   $\times\ 2$

8.   2
   $\times\ 7$

9. What is 4×9?

☆ Independent Practice ☆

In **10–26**, find each product.

10. $2 \times 5 =$ _____

11. $9 \times 0 =$ _____

12. $1 \times 4 =$ _____

13. _____ $= 6 \times 2$

14. $10 \times 6 =$ _____

15. _____ $= 7 \times 1$

16.   2
   $\times\ 10$

17.   2
   $\times\ 1$

18.   9
   $\times\ 9$

19.   7
   $\times\ 2$

20.   9
   $\times\ 3$

21.   0
   $\times\ 7$

22.   4
   $\times\ 5$

23.   5
   $\times\ 7$

24. What is 1×1?

25. What is 10×10?

26. What is 3×9?

*For another example, see Set E on page 100.

Topic 2 | Lesson 2-5

87

27. **Critique Reasoning** Abdi says that 9 × 6 is less than 10 × 4 because 9 is less than 10. Do you agree with Abdi's reasoning? Explain why or why not.

28. **Model with Math** Victoria has 5 pairs of shoes. What equation could Victoria write to find out how many shoes she has?

29. Show 7:50 on the clock.

30. Robb has 35 red counters and 39 yellow counters. He gives his sister 18 red counters. How many counters does Robb have left?

31. **Use Structure** Kim makes an array with 4 rows and 9 columns. Rashida makes an array with 9 rows and 4 columns. Whose array has more items? Explain.

32. **Higher Order Thinking** Look at the table on page 86. Think about what you know about Brendan's points. What is the total number of points Brendan scored for all his arrows?

Assessment

33. Draw lines to match each pair of factors on the left with its product on the right.

2 × 8		4
10 × 9		16
5 × 5		25
4 × 1		70
7 × 10		90

Think about the different ways you know to find multiplication facts.

Help Practice Tools Games
Buddy

Another Look!

How many apples are in 5 baskets with 3 apples each?

5 groups of 3 and 3 groups of 5 both have the same number of items. $5 \times 3 = 3 \times 5$

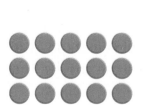 

You can multiply numbers in any order and the product is the same.

Use a pattern to multiply by 5.

5, 10, 15
$3 \times 5 = 15$
Also, $5 \times 3 = 15$.

In **1–3**, use a pattern to find each product.

1. 7×2 2, 4, ____, ____, ____, ____, ____

     $7 \times 2 =$ ____

2. 10×5 ____, ____, ____, ____, ____, ____, ____, ____, ____

     $10 \times 5 =$ ____

3. 5×10 ____, ____, ____, ____, ____

     $5 \times 10 =$ ____

You can use a pattern to multiply.

In **4–9**, find each product.

4. $2 \times 9 =$ ____   **5.** $5 \times 8 =$ ____   **6.** ____ $= 3 \times 2$

7. $9 \times 1 =$ ____   **8.** ____ $= 10 \times 10$ **9.** $0 \times 0 =$ ____

10. **Model with Math** Cassy has 9 books on her bookshelf and 3 books on her desk. She wants to know how many books she has in all. What operation should she use? Explain.

11. Ginger found 3 quarters, 2 dimes, and 3 pennies. How much money did she find?

12. **Be Precise** Norris wrote the equation $7 \times 9 = 63$. Blake wrote the equation $7 \times 9 = 9 \times 7$. Who wrote a correct equation? Explain.

13. **Use Appropriate Tools** Jana wants to multiply 8×5. Explain what tool she could use to help find the answer. Then solve the problem.

14. **Higher Order Thinking** Mrs. O'Malley is setting up for a party. Each adult will get 2 glasses, and each child will get 1 glass. How many glasses does Mrs. O'Malley need? Show your work.

Party Guests

DATA		
Adults	:	8
Children	:	5

 Assessment

15. Each ? below represents a factor between 1 and 9. Draw lines to match each fact on the left with a pattern for its products on the right.

? × 0		0 in the ones place
? × 1		0 or 5 in the ones place
? × 2		0, 2, 4, 6, or 8 in the ones place
? × 5		The other factor in the ones place
? × 9		1 less than the unknown factor in the tens place

Name _____

Solve & Share

At the pet store, Sam bought a hamster that cost $10. He also bought 5 mice at $4 each. How much did Sam spend in all? *Write to explain the math you used to solve this problem.*

I can ...
use math I know to solve problems.

 SOL 3.4a, 3.17, prepares for 4.4d

Thinking Habits
Be a good thinker!
These questions can help you.

- How can I use math I know to help solve this problem?

- How can I use pictures, objects, or an equation to represent the problem?

- How can I use numbers, words, and symbols to solve the problem?

Look Back! **Model with Math** How would your answer above change if Sam only bought 4 mice?

Essential Question **How Can You Model with Math?**

A

Keisha bought 2 yards of felt to make some puppets. Tanya bought 6 yards of felt. Each yard of felt costs the same amount. How much did the girls spend on felt in all?

$2
per yard

What math do I need to use to solve this problem?

I need to show what I know and then choose the needed operations.

B **How can I model with math?**

I can

- use the math I know to solve the problem.

- find and answer any hidden questions.

- use diagrams and equations to represent and solve this problem.

C

Here's my thinking...

I will use bar diagrams and equations.

The hidden question is: How many yards of felt did the girls buy?

? yards	
2 yards	6 yards

$2 + 6 = ?$

$2 + 6 = 8$. The girls bought 8 yards of felt.

So, I need to find the cost of 8 yards at $2 per yard.

? total cost

$2	$2	$2	$2	$2	$2	$2	$2

$8 \times \$2 = ?$

$8 \times \$2 = \$16$. The girls spent $16.

Convince Me! **Model with Math**   Use these number lines to show another way to represent the problem above.

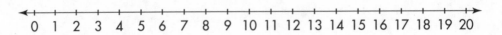

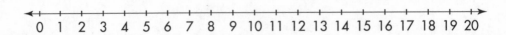

Name _____

☆ Guided Practice *

Practice Buddy · Tools · Assessment

Model with Math

A pack of gum contains 5 pieces. Phil had 7 packs of gum before he lost 2 pieces. How many pieces of gum does Phil have now?

Model with math. You can represent and solve each step in a two-step problem.

1. What is the hidden question you need to answer before you can solve the problem?

2. Solve the problem. Complete the bar diagrams. Show the equations you used.

One Pack [___]

Phil's Packs [___ | ___ | ___ | ___ | ___ | ___]

? pieces of gum

_____ pieces of gum

[? | ___]

Independent Practice ☆

Model with Math

Jen bought 4 tickets. Amber bought 5 tickets. The tickets cost $2 each. How much did the girls spend on tickets in all?

3. What is the hidden question you need to answer before you can solve the problem?

4. Solve the problem. Complete the bar diagrams. Show the equations you used.

5. How would your equations change if Amber bought only 3 tickets? Explain.

Problem Solving

✓ Performance Assessment

Coffee Shop
David and Jon are placing coffee orders for their friends.
David orders 10 large cups of coffee.
Jon orders 4 fewer large cups than David.
Jon pays for his orders with a $50 bill.
Jon wants to know how much he spent on coffee.

DATA	Coffee Shop Prices	
	Cup	**Cost**
	Small	$2
	Regular	$4
	Large	$5

6. **Make Sense and Persevere** What is a good plan to find the amount Jon spent on coffee?

7. **Model with Math** Find how much Jon spent on coffee. Complete the bar diagrams. Show the equations you used.

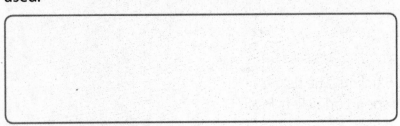

8. **Critique Reasoning** Jamie says the equation $0 \times \$2 = \$0$ shows the amount Jon spent on small cups of coffee. Is he correct? Explain.

Model with math. Think about the math you know to solve the problem.

9. **Reasoning** Would David have enough money if he paid for his order with a $20 bill? Explain.

Name _____

Homework & Practice 2-6
Model with Math

Another Look!

Ron has 6 bags. He puts 2 red, 3 yellow, and 4 blue marbles in each bag. How many marbles does Ron have in all?

Explain how you can use the math you know to solve the problem.

- I can find and answer any hidden questions.

- I can use bar diagrams and equations to represent and solve the problem.

You can model with math by using bar diagrams to show the whole and the parts.

Solve the problem.

Find the hidden question:
How many marbles are in each bag?

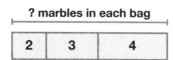
? marbles in each bag

| 2 | 3 | 4 |

$2 + 3 + 4 = 9$ marbles in each bag

Use the answer to solve the problem.

? marbles

| 9 | 9 | 9 | 9 | 9 | 9 |

$6 \times 9 = 54$ marbles in all

Model with Math

Paul has 7 piles of sports cards. There are 3 basketball, 3 football, and 4 baseball cards in each pile. How many total sports cards does Paul have?

1. Explain how you can use the math you know to solve the problem.

2. What is the hidden question you need to answer before you can solve the problem?

3. Solve the problem. Complete the bar diagrams. Show the equations you used.

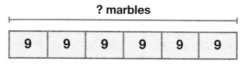
? sports cards in each pile

| ___ | ___ | ___ |

? sports cards

| | | | | | |

Jase's Farm

Jase's farm has 9 chickens, each of which laid 3 eggs. Jase's farm has 4 horses. Edna's farm has chickens which laid a total of 23 eggs. Jase wonders whose chickens laid more eggs.

? total chicken eggs

Jase's farm	3	3	3	3	3	3	3	3	3

4. **Make Sense and Persevere** What is a good plan to find whose chickens laid more eggs?

5. **Reasoning** What do you notice in the numbers shown in the bar diagram above? How can this help you solve the problem?

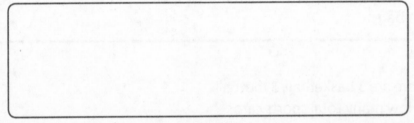

Model with math. When you write equations, think about which operations you can use.

6. **Model with Math** Use equations to show if Jase's or Edna's chickens laid more eggs. How many more eggs did those chickens lay?

7. **Use Appropriate Tools** Lucio says he can use counters to represent the number of eggs laid. Explain how he could do this to find out whose chickens laid more eggs.

Name _____

Fluency Practice Activity

Find a partner. Get paper and a pencil. Each partner chooses a different color: light blue or dark blue.

Partner 1 and Partner 2 each point to a black number at the same time. Both partners add those numbers.

If the answer is on your color, you get a tally mark. Work until one partner has seven tally marks.

I can ...
add within 100.

Point & Tally

Partner 1					Partner 2
55	80	54	94	36	13
23	62	25	41	57	45
37	76	30	100	82	39
12	86	50	73	68	26
41	49	67	38	63	18
	59	81	55	51	

Tally Marks for Partner 1

Tally Marks for Partner 2

Word List

- bar diagram
- factor
- Identity (One) Property of Multiplication
- multiplication
- multiples
- product
- Zero Property of Multiplication

Understand Vocabulary

Circle all correct responses.

1. Circle each number that is a *product*.

$4 \times 6 = 24$ $7 \times 3 = 21$ $8 \div 4 = 2$

2. Circle each example of the *Identity Property*.

$2 \times 2 = 4$ $5 \times 0 = 0$ $1 \times 6 = 6$

3. Circle each example of the *Zero Property*.

$1 \times 0 = 0$ $0 \times 9 = 0$ $2 \times 5 = 10$

4. Circle each equation that shows *multiplication*.

$5 + 6 = 11$ $4 \times 4 = 16$ $17 - 12 = 5$ $16 \div 2 = 8$

5. Circle each number that is a *multiple* of 9.

16   9   28   27   19   36   18   39

Write T for *true* or F for *false*.

_____ **6.** The number 14 is a *multiple* of 4.

_____ **7.** The *Identity Property* says that any number times 1 equals the number itself.

_____ **8.** A *bar diagram* can be used to show 3×6.

Use Vocabulary in Writing

9. Explain how you can find the product 4×2 and the product 8×2. Use at least 3 terms from the Word List in your explanation.

Name _____

Set A pages 61–66

Reteaching

Find 6 × 2.

Use skip counting. Draw 6 curved arrows on a number line. Each arrow should be 2 units wide.

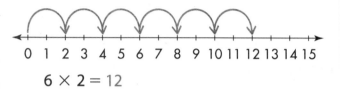

0 1 2 3 4 5 6 7 8 9 10 11 12 13 14 15

6 × 2 = 12

Find 6 × 5.

Use a pattern. Count by 5s. The 6th number in the pattern is the product.

5, 10, 15, 20, 25, 30

6 × 5 = 30

Remember that mutiples of 2 end in 0, 2, 4, 6, or 8. Multiples of 5 end in 0 or 5.

1. 2 × 3 = ____   **2.** 5 × 3 = ____

3. 5 × 5 = ____   **4.** 2 × 6 = ____

5. 8 × 2 = ____   **6.** 7 × 5 = ____

7.   2   **8.**   7
       × 2   × 2

9.   8   **10.**   9
       × 5   × 5

Set B pages 67–72

Find 9 × 4.

List 9s facts.

9 × 1 = 9
9 × 2 = 18
9 × 3 = 27
9 × 4 = 36

Remember that the digits in the multiples of 9 form a pattern.

1. 9 × 5 = ____   **2.** 9 × 7 = ____

3. 6 × 9 = ____   **4.** 8 × 9 = ____

5. 9 × 9 = ____   **6.** 9 × 0 = ____

Set C pages 73–78

Find 0 × 7.

Zero Property of Multiplication: When you multiply a number by 0, the product is 0.

0 × 7 = 0

Find 1 × 7.

Identity (One) Property of Multiplication: When you multiply a number by 1, the product is that number.

1 × 7 = 7

Remember that the product of 0 and any other number is 0. When you multiply a number by 1, the product is that same number.

1. 0 × 4 = ____   **2.** 1 × 9 = ____

3. 0 × 9 = ____   **4.** 1 × 6 = ____

5. 10 × 0 = ____   **6.** 9 × 0 = ____

7. 3 × 1 = ____   **8.** 8 × 1 = ____

9. 0 × 2 = ____   **10.** 1 × 0 = ____

Set D pages 79–84

Find 10 × 6.

When multiplying a number by 10, write a zero to the right of the number.

$10 \times 6 = 60$

Remember that when a number is multiplied by 10, the product has a zero in the ones place.

1. $10 \times 7 =$ _____ **2.** $10 \times 10 =$ _____

3. $3 \times 10 =$ _____ **4.** $9 \times 10 =$ _____

5. $10 \times 0 =$ _____ **6.** $1 \times 10 =$ _____

Set E pages 85–90

Find 5 × 10.

There are many patterns and properties you can use to multiply.

Use skip counting with 5 facts:
5, 10, 15, 20, 25, 30, 35, 40, 45, 50

Use a pattern for 10 facts:
Write a 0 after the 5: 50

The product is the same.
$5 \times 10 = 50$

Remember that you can use the Commutative Property of Multiplication to multiply 2 factors in any order.

1. $5 \times 9 =$ _____ **2.** $0 \times 6 =$ _____

3. $10 \times 3 =$ _____ **4.** $8 \times 1 =$ _____

5. $7 \times 2 =$ _____ **6.** $9 \times 6 =$ _____

Set F pages 91–96

Think about these questions to help you **model with math**.

Thinking Habits

- How can I use math I know to help solve the problem?

- How can I use pictures, objects, or an equation to represent the problem?

- How can I use numbers, words, and symbols to solve the problem?

Remember that representations can help you apply math that you know.

Umar has 5 dimes in his left pocket. He has 3 dimes in his right pocket. A dime is worth 10 cents. How much money does Umar have?

1. Draw a bar diagram to help answer the hidden question.

2. Draw a bar diagram to help answer the main question.

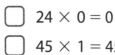

1. A building has 9 rows of mailboxes. There are 6 mailboxes in each row. How many mailboxes are there?

2. Tickets to a juggling show cost $5 for each adult and $2 for each child. 4 adults and 3 children go to see the show. What is the total cost of their tickets?

Part A

Identify any hidden questions.

Part B

Draw bar diagrams for this problem. Show the equations that you used.

3. Mr. Blonski wrote five equations on the board. Which of the equations did he write correctly? Choose all that apply.

☐ $24 \times 0 = 0$

☐ $45 \times 1 = 45$

☐ $67 \times 1 = 1 \times 67$

☐ $38 \times 0 = 38$

☐ $77 + 1 = 77$

4. Mark is thinking of a number that is a multiple of 9. Which of the following could be Mark's number? Choose all that apply.

☐ 27

☐ 45

☐ 48

☐ 67

☐ 81

5. Alex has 5 dimes in his pocket. How much money does Alex have?

6. Choose the greatest product.

Ⓐ 9×1

Ⓑ 10×0

Ⓒ 2×3

Ⓓ 5×2

7. Ben says that an array with 2 rows and 5 columns has 8 items. Is this reasonable? Explain why or why not.

8. Gabe has 4 birdcages. He keeps 5 birds in each cage. Then Gabe buys another birdcage. The new birdcage has the same number of birds. How many birds does Gabe have now? Use a bar diagram to represent the problem.

9. A set of blocks has 4 different types of blocks. There are 10 of each type of block. How many blocks are in the set?

Ⓐ 14 blocks

Ⓑ 30 blocks

Ⓒ 40 blocks

Ⓓ 44 blocks

10. Draw lines to connect equal expressions.

2 × 0		2
2 × 1		3 × 0
2 × 3		3 × 2

11. Ed is thinking of a number that is a multiple of both 2 and 5. For questions 11a–11d, choose Yes or No to tell if it could be Ed's number.

11a. 15   ○ Yes   ○ No

11b. 20   ○ Yes   ○ No

11c. 25   ○ Yes   ○ No

11d. 30   ○ Yes   ○ No

12. Dawn has 2 bananas. She cuts each banana into 8 slices. How many slices of banana does Dawn have?

13. Isabella has $45 to spend on shirts. All shirts in the store are on sale for $10 each. How many shirts can Isabella buy? Explain the math that you used.

Name _____

Selling Cards
A soccer team is selling boxes of cards to raise money.
There are boxes of small, medium, and large cards.
The team earns a different amount for each card type.

Boxes Sold
• On Monday, Will sold 4 boxes of large cards.
• On Wednesday, Mia sold 6 boxes of small cards
  and 3 boxes of large cards.

Use the **Selling Boxes of Cards** table and **Boxes Sold** list to answer Questions 1 and 2.

Selling Boxes of Cards	
Card Type	**Amount Earned per Box**
Box of small cards	$1
Box of medium cards	$2
Box of large cards	$5

1. How much money did Will earn? Write a multiplication equation to solve.

2. Complete the chart to find the amount that Mia earned for each card type.

Card Type	Number Sold	Amount Earned per Box	Total Earned
small			
medium			
large			

Use the **Selling Boxes of Cards** table to answer Question 3.

3. For 7 days, Logan sold a box of medium cards every day. How much did Logan earn? Create a representation for the problem.

Boxes Bought

• Mrs. Carlson buys 1 box of medium cards.

• Mr. Choi buys 6 boxes of small cards.

• Mrs. Willis buys 7 boxes of medium cards and 9 boxes of large cards.

Use the **Cards in Each Box** table and **Boxes Bought** list to answer Questions 4–6.

4. Part A

How many cards does Mr. Choi buy?

Cards in Each Box	
Card Type	**Number of Cards**
Box of small cards	5
Box of medium cards	9
Box of large cards	10

Part B

What is another way that Mr. Choi can buy the same number of cards?

5. Is there another way that Mrs. Carlson can buy the same amount of cards? Explain.

6. Complete the chart to find the number of cards Mrs. Willis buys of each card type.

Card Type	Number of Boxes Bought	Number of Cards in a Box	Total Cards
small			
medium			
large			

Apply Properties: Multiplication Facts for 3, 4, 6, 7, 8

Essential Question: How can unknown multiplication facts be found using known facts?

> Some roses are red and some violets are blue, but do you know why?

> Flowers inherit their color. They get their color from parent plants.

> My mom's roses are yellow! Here's a project on traits of organisms, multiplication, and equations.

Math and Science Project: Inherited Traits

Do Research Some characteristics of organisms are inherited. The traits are passed from generation to generation. In flowers, one of the inherited traits is color. Use the Internet or other sources to make a list of other traits that flowers inherit from their parent plants.

Journal: Write a Report Include what you found. Also in your report:

- Compare your list of traits with lists of traits other students have made. If there is a trait you don't have, add it to your list.

- Draw flowers or animals with similar traits in an array. Show how to break apart the array and use multiplication facts to find the total number.

Review What You Know

A-Z Vocabulary

Choose the best term from the box. Write it on the blank.

- skip counting
- The Commutative (Order) Property of Multiplication
- The Identity (One) Property of Multiplication
- The Zero Property of Multiplication

1. _____ says that the product of any number and zero is zero.

2. _____ says that 1 times any number is that number.

3. _____ says that you can multiply factors in any order, and the product stays the same.

Multiplying

Use multiplication to solve.

4. $10 \times 1 =$ _____   **5.** $2 \times 10 =$ _____   **6.** $0 \times 5 =$ _____

7. $9 \times 5 =$ _____   **8.** $2 \times 7 =$ _____   **9.** $1 \times 8 =$ _____

10. $5 \times 7 = ?$

Ⓐ $7 + 5$ Ⓑ $5 + 7$ Ⓒ 7×5 Ⓓ $7 \div 5$

Adding 2-Digit Numbers

Find the sum.

11. $16 + 12 =$ _____   **12.** $21 + 14 =$ _____   **13.** $24 + 12 =$ _____

Arrays

14. How can you represent 6×3 using an array? Draw an array, and explain how to use it to find the product.

My Word Cards

Use the examples for each word on the front of the card to help complete the definitions on the back.

Distributive Property

$7 \times 4 = (5 \times 4) + (2 \times 4)$

$7 \begin{cases} 5 \\ 2 \end{cases}$ 5×4 2×4

Associative (Grouping) Property of Multiplication

$(3 \times 2) \times 4 = 24$

$3 \times (2 \times 4) = 24$

$(3 \times 2) \times 4 = 3 \times (2 \times 4)$

My Word Cards

Complete each definition. Extend learning by writing your own definitions.

The _____
_____
_____ says that you can change the grouping of the factors and the product will be the same.

The _____ says that a multiplication fact can be broken apart into the sum of two other multiplication facts.

Name _____

Solve & Share

Find two ways to break the array below into two smaller arrays. What multiplication equation can you write for each array? What is the total? Tell how you decided.

I can ...
break apart unknown facts into known facts and solve multiplication problems.

SOL 3.4a; 3.4b, 3.17

You can be precise. You can explain what your equations mean.

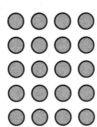

Look Back! Reasoning Find the total number of items in both of the smaller arrays. Compare their combined total to the total number of items in the one large array. Why are the totals the same even though the arrays are different?

Essential Question: How Can You Break Up a Multiplication Fact?

A

Maria wants to set up 7 rows of 4 chairs for a meeting. She wants to know how many chairs she needs but does not know the product of 7 × 4.

You can use known facts to help find the product of unknown facts.

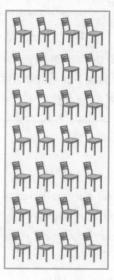

B **What You Think**

Maria thinks of **7** rows of 4 chairs as **5** rows of 4 chairs and another **2** rows of 4 chairs.

4

7 {
5   5 × 4
2   2 × 4
}

C **What You Write**

The Distributive Property says that a multiplication fact can be broken apart into the sum of two other multiplication facts.

Maria knows the two new facts.

7 × 4 = (5 × 4) + (2 × 4)
7 × 4 = 20 + 8
7 × 4 = 28

So, 7 × 4 = 28.

Maria needs 28 chairs.

Convince Me! **Use Structure** What are two ways that Maria could break up the array for 7 × 4? Draw a picture of the two new arrays and write the new facts.

☆ Guided Practice *

Do You Understand?

1. Rafael broke up an array for 6×3 into two new arrays. Both of his new arrays are the same. What were the two arrays?

2. **Use Structure** Ann broke up a large array into two smaller arrays. The two smaller arrays show 1×8 and 4×8. What was the large array that Ann started with?

Do You Know How?

In **3** and **4**, use the smaller arrays and the Distributive Property to find each missing factor. You may use counters to help.

3.
4×8

___ $\times$ 8 = (___ $\times$ 8) + (2 $\times$ 8)

4.
3×5

___ $\times$ ___ = (___ $\times$ 5) + (1 $\times$ ___)

☆ Independent Practice ☆

In **5** and **6**, separate the rows in the large array into two smaller arrays. Write the new facts.

5.

$4 \times 5 = ($___ $\times$ ___$) + ($___ $\times$ ___$)$

6.

$5 \times 6 = ($___ $\times$ ___$) + ($___ $\times$ ___$)$

In **7–10**, use the Distributive Property to find each missing factor. Use counters and arrays to help.

7. $6 \times 8 = (4 \times$ ___$) + (2 \times 8)$

8. $10 \times 3 = ($___ $\times 3) + (2 \times 3)$

9. $($___ $\times 7) = (3 \times 7) + (2 \times$ ___$)$

10. $(8 \times$ ___$) = ($___ $\times 8) + (4 \times 8)$

Problem Solving

11. Model with Math Paige bakes 5 cupcakes. She puts 7 jellybeans on each cupcake. How many jellybeans does Paige need? Use the bar diagram to help write an equation.

? jellybeans

7	7	7	7	7

12. Critique Reasoning Fred wants to separate the rows of the array below into a 2 × 4 array and a 3 × 4 array. Can Fred do this? Explain.

13. Lane uses counters to make a 4 × 7 array and a 1 × 7 array. What size array can he make using all of these counters?

14. Gavin had $75 on Monday. On Tuesday he spent $23. Then he spent $14 on Wednesday. How much money does he have left?

15. 🄰🄯 **Vocabulary** Explain how you can use the *Distributive Property* to solve 9 × 6.

16. Higher Order Thinking How can you use 3 × 5 = 15 to help you find 6 × 5?

✓ **Assessment**

17. Choose all of the ways you can separate the rows of the array at the right.

- ☐ (2 × 7) + (5 × 7)
- ☐ (4 × 7) + (1 × 7)
- ☐ (2 × 7) + (3 × 7)
- ☐ (2 × 5) + (5 × 7)
- ☐ (3 × 7) + (2 × 7)

Help Practice Tools Games
      Buddy

Another Look!

The array below shows
6 × 4 or 6 rows of 4 circles.

You can draw a line to break
6 rows of 4 circles into **2** rows
of 4 circles and **4** rows of
4 circles.

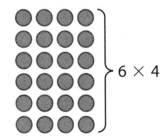

6 × 4

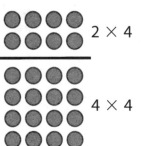

2 × 4

4 × 4

With the Distributive Property,
you can break apart a multiplication fact
into the sum of two other facts.

In **1** and **2**, draw a line to separate each array into two smaller arrays.
Write the new facts.

1. ○ ○ ○
   ○ ○ ○
   ○ ○ ○
   ○ ○ ○

   4 × 3 = (___ × ___) + (___ × ___)

2. ○ ○ ○ ○ ○ ○
   ○ ○ ○ ○ ○ ○
   ○ ○ ○ ○ ○ ○
   ○ ○ ○ ○ ○ ○
   ○ ○ ○ ○ ○ ○

   5 × 6 = (___ × ___) + (___ × ___)

In **3–10**, use the Distributive Property to find each missing factor.

3. 4 × 6 = (1 × 6) + (___ × 6)

4. 5 × 8 = (___ × 8) + (2 × 8)

5. 4 × 5 = (___ × 5) + (2 × ___)

6. 7 × 6 = (3 × ___) + (___ × ___)

7. 3 × 8 = (___ × 8) + (2 × ___)

8. 5 × 7 = (2 × ___) + (3 × ___)

9. 4 × 7 = (___ × ___) + (2 × ___)

10. 5 × 5 = (___ × 5) + (4 × ___)

11. **Use Structure** Tony broke a larger array into a 2 × 3 array and a 4 × 3 array. What did the larger array look like? Draw a picture. Write an equation to show the relationship between the larger array and the two smaller arrays.

12. **Higher Order Thinking** Rosa says she can break this array into 3 different sets of two smaller arrays. Is Rosa correct? Explain.

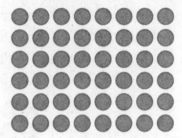

13. **Algebra** Marcus passed for 16 yards in the first half of a football game. He passed for a total of 49 yards in the entire game. What was Marcus's total passing yardage in the second half?

Write equations to represent and solve the problem. Use ? for the unknown number.

49	
16	?

14. Lulu buys a dress for $67, a hat for $35, and shoes for $49. How much did Lulu spend?

?		
$67	$35	$49

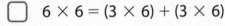

15. Akela drew these smaller arrays to find the product of a larger array. Which of the following equations show the relationship between the larger array and these two smaller arrays? Choose all that apply.

☐ 6 × 6 = (3 × 6) + (3 × 6)

☐ 7 × 6 = (3 × 6) + (4 × 6)

☐ 8 × 7 = (4 × 7) + (4 × 7)

☐ 7 × 6 = (4 × 6) + (3 × 6)

☐ 7 × 7 = (3 × 7) + (4 × 7)

Name _____

Solve & Share

There are 3 rows of pictures on a wall. Each row has 6 pictures. How many pictures are on the wall? *Solve this problem any way you choose.*

I can ...
use tools and properties strategically to solve problems when I multiply by 3.

SOL 3.4a; 3.4b; 3.17

You can use tools. You can draw arrays or make arrays with counters to help you solve the problem. *Show your work!*

Look Back! **Generalize** How can you use what you know about multiplication facts for the 1s and 2s to solve multiplication facts for the 3s?

Essential Question

How Can You Break Apart Arrays to Multiply with 3?

A

The Park District has canoes stored in 3 rows. There are 6 canoes in each row. What is the total number of canoes stored?

You can multiply to find the total for an array.

B ## What You Show

Find 3×6.

Use 1s facts and 2s facts to help you multiply with 3.

Make an array for each multiplication sentence.

$2 \times 6 = 12$

$12 + 6 = 18$

$1 \times 6 = 6$

C ## What You Think

3×6 is 3 rows of 6. That is 2 sixes plus 1 more six.

2 sixes are 12.
1 six is 6.

$12 + 6 = 18$

$3 \times 6 = 18$

There are 18 canoes.

Convince Me! **Use Structure** Suppose there were 7 canoes in each of 3 rows. How can $2 \times 7 = 14$ help you find the total number of canoes?

116   **Topic 3** | Lesson 3-2

Practice Buddy Tools Assessment

☆Guided Practice*

Do You Understand?

1. Selena arranged plants in 3 rows in her garden. She put 6 plants in each row. How many plants did Selena arrange?

2. **Use Structure** Alicia has 3 vases. She wants 9 flowers in each vase. She buys enough flowers for 2 vases. For the third vase, she cuts 9 flowers from her garden. How can Alicia use $2 \times 9 = 18$ to find how many flowers she needs?

Do You Know How?

In **3–8**, multiply. You may use counters or pictures to help.

3. $3 \times 10 =$ _____

4. $3 \times 6 =$ _____

5. $\begin{array}{r} 3 \\ \times\ 8 \\ \hline \end{array}$

6. $\begin{array}{r} 3 \\ \times\ 2 \\ \hline \end{array}$

7. $\begin{array}{r} 3 \\ \times\ 7 \\ \hline \end{array}$

8. $\begin{array}{r} 3 \\ \times\ 3 \\ \hline \end{array}$

☆Independent Practice ☆

Leveled Practice In **9–20**, multiply. You may use counters or pictures to help.

9. 3×4

$2 \times 4 =$ _____

$1 \times 4 =$ _____

$8 + 4 =$ _____

10. 3×5

$2 \times 5 =$ _____

$1 \times 5 =$ _____

$10 + 5 =$ _____

11. $2 \times 3 =$ _____

12. $9 \times 3 =$ _____

13. $10 \times 3 =$ _____

14. $8 \times 3 =$ _____

15. $5 \times 3 =$ _____

16. $0 \times 3 =$ _____

17. $\begin{array}{r} 7 \\ \times\ 3 \\ \hline \end{array}$

18. $\begin{array}{r} 3 \\ \times\ 1 \\ \hline \end{array}$

19. $\begin{array}{r} 3 \\ \times\ 3 \\ \hline \end{array}$

20. $\begin{array}{r} 4 \\ \times\ 3 \\ \hline \end{array}$

Problem Solving ☆

21. What is the total number of stamps in a package of car stamps and a package of outer space stamps? Show how you found the answer.

DATA

Number of Stamps in Different Packages		
Kind of Stamp	**Number of Rows**	**Number in Each Row**
Dinosaur	3	7
Car	3	9
Outer Space	3	8
Reptile	5	6

22. Use Appropriate Tools Cara bought 1 package of reptile stamps. What tool could you use to find the total number of stamps that Cara bought?

23. Critique Reasoning Allison bought 10 packages of energy bars. Each package contains 6 bars. Allison says she has a total of 65 energy bars. Is her answer reasonable? Why or why not?

24. Higher Order Thinking What two multiplication facts can help you find 3×9? How could you use 3×9 to find 9×3?

✓ **Assessment**

25. Mr. Torres has some tomatoes. He arranges them in 3 rows and 8 columns.

Part A

Complete the equation and find the total number of tomatoes.

$(3 \times \underline{\quad}) + (3 \times \underline{\quad}) = \underline{\quad}$ tomatoes

Part B

Draw a picture to represent this problem.

Help Practice Tools Games
      Buddy

Another Look!

You can use arrays to show 3s facts.

Find 2 × 3.

2 × 3 = 6

You can also use a 2s and a 1s fact to find a 3s fact.

Find 7 × 3.
7 × 3 = (7 × 2) + (7 × 1)
7 × 3 = 14 + 7
7 × 3 = 21

In **1–4**, use arrays or the Distributive Property to find each product.

1.

3 × 4 = ____

2. Find 3 × 5.

3 × 5 = (____ × 5) + (1 × ____)

3 × 5 = ____ + ____

3 × 5 = ____

3. Find 4 × 3.

4 × 3 = (4 × ____) + (____ × 1)

4 × 3 = ____ + ____

4 × 3 = ____

4. Find 3 × 6.

3 × 6 = (2 × 6) + (____ × ____)

3 × 6 = ____ + ____

3 × 6 = ____

In **5–14**, find each product.

5. 6 × 3 = ____

6. 3 × 7 = ____

7. 3 × 3 = ____

8. 1 × 3 = ____

9. 3 × 9 = ____

10. 5 × 3 = ____

11. 3
      × 8
      ____

12. 3
      × 0
      ____

13. 3
      × 2
      ____

14. 9
      × 3
      ____

15. Generalize How can you use a 2s fact and a 1s fact to find 3 × 8?

16. Construct Arguments Maria said 7 × 3 = 21. Connie said 3 × 7 = 21. Who is correct? Explain.

17. Five people bought tickets to a football game. They bought 3 tickets each. How many tickets were bought? Draw an array.

18. Higher Order Thinking Sid says 26 is a multiple of 3. Is Sid correct? Why or why not?

19. Barney divides a rectangle into fourths. Show two ways he could do this.

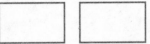

20. Kenichi's jump rope team is competing in a tournament. There are 10 teams in the tournament.

Jump Rope
Tournament
Teams of 3 Only

Part A

Use the numbers to complete the equation and find the total number of players in the tournament.

3 × 10 = (3 × ____) + (3 × ____) = ____ players

Part B

Draw a picture to represent the problem.

Name _____

Solve & Share

Ed made 8 key chains each week for 4 weeks. How many key chains did Ed make? *Solve this problem any way you choose.*

I can ...
use what I know about multiplying by 2s and properties to multiply by 4.

SOL 3.4a; 3.4b, 3.17

You can use structure. What number relationships do you see when when you multiply by 4? *Show your work in the space below!*

Look Back! **Look for Relationships** How can you use multiplication facts for 2s to solve multiplication facts for 4s?

Essential Question **How Can You Use Doubles to Multiply with 4?**

A

Anna painted piggy banks to sell at the student art show. She painted one bank on each of the 7 days of the week for 4 weeks. How many piggy banks did Anna paint?

Four is a double of 2. So, 4 × 7 is double 2 × 7.

B

What You Show

Find 4 × 7.

To multiply with 4, think of a 2s fact and then double it.

You can make arrays.

$2 \times 7 = 14$

$2 \times 7 = 14$
$14 + 14 = 28$

C

What You Think

4 × 7 is 4 rows of 7. That is 2 sevens plus 2 sevens.

2 sevens are 14.

$14 + 14 = 28$

So, $4 \times 7 = 28$.

Anna painted 28 piggy banks.

Convince Me! **Construct Arguments** Zach knows $2 \times 8 = 16$. Explain how he can find 4×8.

Practice Buddy · Tools · Assessment

☆ Guided Practice ☆

Do You Understand?

1. Besides using a 2s fact and doubling it, what is another way to break apart 4×7 using facts you already know?

2. Nolan made lamps to sell at the school art show. He made 9 lamps each week for 4 weeks. How many lamps did Nolan make?

Do You Know How?

In **3–8**, multiply. You may use counters or pictures to help.

3. $3 \times 4 =$ ____   **4.** $5 \times 4 =$ ____

5. $4 \times 9 =$ ____   **6.** $1 \times 4 =$ ____

7. $\begin{array}{r} 2 \\ \times\,4 \\ \hline \end{array}$ **8.** $\begin{array}{r} 10 \\ \times\,4 \\ \hline \end{array}$

☆ Independent Practice ☆

Leveled Practice In **9–17**, multiply. You may use counters or pictures to help.

9. Find 4×6.

 } $2 \times 6 =$ ____

} $2 \times 6 =$ ____

$12 + 12 =$ ____

So, $4 \times 6 =$ ____.

10. Find 4×9.

} $2 \times 9 =$ ____

} $2 \times 9 =$ ____

$18 + 18 =$ ____

So, $4 \times 9 =$ ____.

11. $4 \times 8 =$ ____   **12.** $4 \times 3 =$ ____   **13.** $6 \times 4 =$ ____

14. $\begin{array}{r} 7 \\ \times\,4 \\ \hline \end{array}$ **15.** $\begin{array}{r} 9 \\ \times\,4 \\ \hline \end{array}$ **16.** $\begin{array}{r} 4 \\ \times\,5 \\ \hline \end{array}$ **17.** $\begin{array}{r} 4 \\ \times\,2 \\ \hline \end{array}$

Problem Solving

18. Make Sense and Persevere James needs to buy supplies for his trail walk. What is the total number of cereal bars James needs to buy? Explain how you used the table to find the answer.

19. Reasoning How many more apples than juice drinks does James need? Show how you found the answer.

Trail Walk Supplies

DATA

Item	Number of Packages Needed	Number of Items in Each Package
Apples	2	8
Cereal Bars	4	6
Juice Drinks	4	3

20. Math and Science Martin studied slugs in science class. He learned each slug has 4 feelers. That evening, he saw 7 slugs. How many feelers did all the slugs have? What are two strategies you can use to find the answer?

21. Higher Order Thinking Lila makes a chart that has 9 rows and 4 columns. How many spaces are in her chart? Explain why Lila can use 9s facts or 4s facts to solve.

✔ **Assessment**

22. Bess has boxes of candles on the table. Each box has 4 candles. If Bess skip counts the candles in groups of 4, which list shows numbers she names?

Ⓐ 8, 12, 16, 20   Ⓒ 4, 6, 12, 14

Ⓑ 8, 12, 14, 18   Ⓓ 4, 8, 10, 14

23. Ramona has 9 candy boxes with 4 chocolate-covered cherries in each. Which of the following shows a way she can find how many candies there are in all?

Ⓐ $(4 \times 2) + (4 \times 2)$

Ⓑ $(9 \times 2) + (9 \times 2)$

Ⓒ $(9 \times 2) + (4 \times 2)$

Ⓓ $(9 + 2) \times (4 + 2)$

124   **Topic 3** | Lesson 3-3

Another Look!

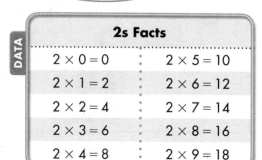

If you know a 2s multiplication fact, you can find a 4s multiplication fact.

2s Facts	
$2 \times 0 = 0$	$2 \times 5 = 10$
$2 \times 1 = 2$	$2 \times 6 = 12$
$2 \times 2 = 4$	$2 \times 7 = 14$
$2 \times 3 = 6$	$2 \times 8 = 16$
$2 \times 4 = 8$	$2 \times 9 = 18$

Find 4×3. Draw an array.

$2 \times 3 = 6$

$2 \times 3 = 6$

$6 + 6 = 12$

So, $4 \times 3 = 12$.

In **1** and **2**, use a 2s fact to find the product of the 4s fact.

1. Find 4×9.

_____ $\times 9 =$ _____

$2 \times$ _____ $=$ _____

_____ $+ 18 =$ _____

So, $4 \times 9 =$ _____.

2. Find 4×2.

_____ $\times 2 =$ _____

$2 \times$ _____ $=$ _____

_____ $+ 4 =$ _____

So, $4 \times 2 =$ _____.

In **3–14**, find the product.

3. $4 \times 6 =$ _____

4. $8 \times 4 =$ _____

5. $4 \times 9 =$ _____

6. $2 \times 4 =$ _____

7. $4 \times 1 =$ _____

8. $4 \times 7 =$ _____

9. $0 \times 4 =$ _____

10. $4 \times 4 =$ _____

11. $4 \times 10 =$ _____

12. $3 \times 4 =$ _____

13. $5 \times 4 =$ _____

14. $4 \times 0 =$ _____

15. Make Sense and Persevere Jero and Max rented a canoe for 4 hours. They each rented a life jacket. How much money did they spend? How did you find the answer?

DATA

Canoeing	
Cost per hour	$4
Life jacket rental	$6

16. Tina paid for 6 hours of canoeing and 1 life jacket rental with two twenty-dollar bills. How much change did Tina get back? Show your work.

---

17. Critique Reasoning Rob says he can use 2 × 5 to find 4 × 5. Is he correct? Explain.

18. Higher Order Thinking Mark is having a party. He invited 35 people. Mark set up 8 tables with 4 chairs at each table. Does Mark have enough tables and chairs for all his guests? Explain.

✓ **Assessment**

19. Emmitt is grilling hot dogs for a cookout. He has 7 plates and put 4 hot dogs on each plate. Which of the following is **NOT** a way to find how many hot dogs Emmitt grilled?

Ⓐ Make two 4 × 3 arrays

Ⓑ Multiply 7 × 4

Ⓒ Add 2 × 7 and 2 × 7

Ⓓ Multiply 4 × 7

20. Jillian bought 3 boxes of crayons. Each box had the same number of crayons. How many crayons did Jillian buy?

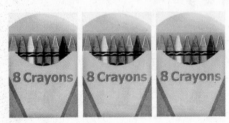

Ⓐ 16 crayons

Ⓑ 24 crayons

Ⓒ 32 crayons

Ⓓ 36 crayons

Name _____

Solve & Share

Students set up 6 rows of seats for a music concert. They put 6 seats in each row. What is the total number of seats? *Solve this problem any way you choose.*

I can ...
make and use models to solve multiplication problems that have 6 and 7 as factors.

SOL 3.4a; 3.4b, 3.17

You can model with math. Pictures, numbers, symbols, and words can be used to represent and solve multiplication problems. *Show your work in the space below!*

Look Back! **Look for Relationships** How can 3s facts help you solve 6s facts?

How Can You Break Apart Arrays to Multiply?

A

The members of the band march in 6 equal rows. There are 8 band members in each row. How many are in the band?

You can multiply to find the total for an array.

B ## What You Show

Find 6 × 8.

Use 5s facts and 1s facts.

Make an array for each multiplication sentence.

$5 \times 8 = 40$

$1 \times 8 = 8$

C ## What You Think

6 × 8 is 6 rows of 8. That is 5 eights plus 1 more eight.

5 eights are 40.
8 more is 48.
$40 + 8 = 48$

So, $6 \times 8 = 48$.

The band has 48 members.

Convince Me! Use Structure Use a 5s fact and a 1s fact to find 6 × 9. Draw two arrays. Explain your drawings.

Another Example !

Find 7×8. Use 5s facts and 2s facts to help you multiply by 7.

$5 \times 8 = 40$

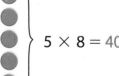

$2 \times 8 = 16$

7×8 equals 7 rows of 8.
That is 5 eights plus 2 eights.

5 eights are 40.
2 eights are 16.

$40 + 16 = 56$

So, $7 \times 8 = 56$.

☆ Guided Practice *

Do You Understand?

1. **Model with Math** The students who are graduating are standing in 7 equal rows. There are 9 students in each row. How many students are graduating? Use a 5s fact and a 2s fact.

2. Chrissy bakes 3 cherry pies. She cuts each pie into 6 slices. How many slices does Chrissy have?

Do You Know How?

In **3–8**, multiply. You may draw pictures or use counters to help.

3. $6 \times 10 =$ _____

4. $7 \times 6 =$ _____

5. $\begin{array}{r} 7 \\ \times\ 7 \\ \hline \end{array}$

6. $\begin{array}{r} 9 \\ \times\ 7 \\ \hline \end{array}$

7. Find 4 times 7. _____

8. Multiply 6 times 5. _____

Independent Practice ☆

In **9–16**, find the product. You may draw pictures to help.

9. $\begin{array}{r} 5 \\ \times\ 7 \\ \hline \end{array}$

10. $\begin{array}{r} 3 \\ \times\ 6 \\ \hline \end{array}$

11. $\begin{array}{r} 7 \\ \times\ 8 \\ \hline \end{array}$

12. $\begin{array}{r} 1 \\ \times\ 7 \\ \hline \end{array}$

13. $\begin{array}{r} 10 \\ \times\ 6 \\ \hline \end{array}$

14. $\begin{array}{r} 4 \\ \times\ 7 \\ \hline \end{array}$

15. $\begin{array}{r} 7 \\ \times\ 3 \\ \hline \end{array}$

16. $\begin{array}{r} 8 \\ \times\ 6 \\ \hline \end{array}$

Problem Solving

17. Model with Math The National Toy Train Museum has 5 exhibits for trains. In one of the exhibits, the trains are on 5 tracks. How many trains are on display at that exhibit? Write an equation to solve the problem.

Equations can help you describe a situation.

6 trains on each track

---

18. Tracy used the flat surface of a cube to draw a plane shape. What plane shape did Tracy draw? How do you know?

19. The dance team lines up in 4 rows of 6 dancers each. How many dancers are on the dance team?

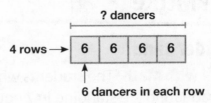

? dancers

4 rows → | 6 | 6 | 6 | 6 |

6 dancers in each row

---

20. Higher Order Thinking Marge says 7×0 is equal to $7 + 0$. Is Marge correct? Why or why not?

21. One train has 77 seats. Another train has 32 fewer seats. How many seats are on both trains?

✓ Assessment

22. Miguel has the baskets of oranges shown at the right. Each basket holds 6 oranges. How many oranges does Miguel have? Explain how to use 2 other known facts to solve this problem.

Name _____

Another Look!

You can use multiplication facts you already know to find other multiplication facts.

Find 6 × 9. Use a 3s fact.

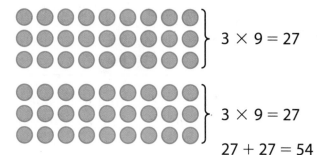

$3 \times 9 = 27$

$3 \times 9 = 27$

$27 + 27 = 54$

So, 6 × 9 = 54.

Find 7 × 5. Use a 2s fact.

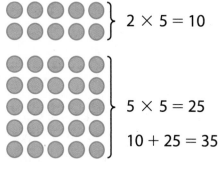

$2 \times 5 = 10$

$5 \times 5 = 25$

$10 + 25 = 35$

So, 7 × 5 = 35.

In **1** and **2**, use known facts to find each product.

1. 6 × 4 = ?

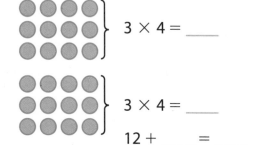

$3 \times 4 =$ _____

$3 \times 4 =$ _____

$12 +$ _____ = _____

So, 6 × 4 = _____.

2. 7 × 4 = ?

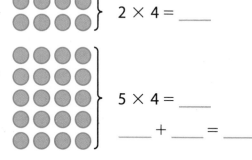

$2 \times 4 =$ _____

$5 \times 4 =$ _____

_____ + _____ = _____

So, 7 × 4 = _____.

In **3–11**, find each product.

3. 2 × 7 = _____

4. 6 × 7 = _____

5. 7 × 9 = _____

6. 6 × 4 = _____

7. 6 × 8 = _____

8. 7 × 7 = _____

9. 6 × 2 = _____

10. 8 × 7 = _____

11. 3 × 7 = _____

12. Emmet buys 7 egg salad sandwiches at Sam's Café. How much money does Emmet spend?

13. Make Sense and Persevere Al buys 4 chicken salad sandwiches and 3 tuna salad sandwiches. How much money does Al spend? How did you find the answer?

Sandwiches	
Tuna Salad	$6
Egg Salad	$4
Chicken Salad	$7

14. Math and Science Raul's science class is studying chicken eggs. The eggs take 3 weeks to hatch. There are 7 days in each week. How many days does it take for the eggs to hatch?

15. Number Sense What multiplication fact can be found by using the arrays for 2×9 and 5×9?

16. Use Appropriate Tools Nan made an array to find $5 \times 3 = 15$. How can she use a tool to show 6×3?

17. Higher Order Thinking Harold says, "To find 6×8, I can use the facts for 5×4 and 1×4." Do you agree? Explain.

✓ **Assessment**

18. Emily has 7 apples. She cuts each apple into 6 slices. How many slices does Emily have? Write an equation to show how you solved the problem.

Solve

Solve & Share

There are 8 rows of prizes. There are 6 prizes in each row. How many prizes are there? **Solve this problem any way you choose.**

Lesson 3-5
Apply Properties: 8 as a Factor

I can ...
use known facts and properties to multiply by 8.

SOL 3.4a; 3.4b, 3.17

You can make sense of problems by using known facts to solve unknown facts. *Show your work!*

Look Back! **Generalize** Tell how you can use 2s, 3s, or 4s facts to solve the problem.

Essential Question **How Can You Use Doubles to Multiply with 8?**

At a school fun fair, students try to toss a table tennis ball into a bowl. There are 8 rows of bowls. There are 8 bowls in each row. How many bowls are there?

What 2s and 4s facts can you find in the bowl array?

B One Way

Use 2s facts to find 8×8.

8×8 equals 4 groups of 2 eights.

$\left.\right\}$ $2 \times 8 = 16$

$\left.\right\}$ $2 \times 8 = 16$

$\left.\right\}$ $2 \times 8 = 16$

$\left.\right\}$ $2 \times 8 = 16$

$16 + 16 + 16 + 16 = 64$

So, $8 \times 8 = 64$.

C Another Way

Double a 4s fact to find 8×8.

8×8 equals 4 eights plus 4 eights.

$\left.\right\}$ $4 \times 8 = 32$

$\left.\right\}$ $4 \times 8 = 32$

$32 + 32 = 64$

So, $8 \times 8 = 64$.

Convince Me! **Use Structure** How does knowing $5 \times 8 = 40$ help you find 8×8?

☆ Guided Practice *

Do You Understand?

1. Multiply 8 times 3. Write and solve a multiplication equation.

2. Multiply 5 times 8. Write and solve a multiplication equation.

3. Multiply 8 times 1. Write and solve a multiplication equation.

Do You Know How?

In **4–9**, multiply. You may draw pictures or use counters to help.

4. $8 \times 7 =$ _____

5. $8 \times 4 =$ _____

6. $6 \times 8 =$ _____

7. $10 \times 8 =$ _____

8. $\begin{array}{r} 9 \\ \times\ 8 \\ \hline \end{array}$

9. $\begin{array}{r} 8 \\ \times\ 3 \\ \hline \end{array}$

☆ Independent Practice ☆

In **10–23**, find the product. You may draw pictures to help.

10. $8 \times 4 =$ _____

11. $1 \times 8 =$ _____

12. $2 \times 8 =$ _____

13. $5 \times 8 =$ _____

14. $8 \times 2 =$ _____

15. $8 \times 6 =$ _____

16. $\begin{array}{r} 8 \\ \times\ 8 \\ \hline \end{array}$

17. $\begin{array}{r} 8 \\ \times\ 5 \\ \hline \end{array}$

18. $\begin{array}{r} 0 \\ \times\ 8 \\ \hline \end{array}$

19. $\begin{array}{r} 4 \\ \times\ 8 \\ \hline \end{array}$

20. $\begin{array}{r} 10 \\ \times\ 8 \\ \hline \end{array}$

21. $\begin{array}{r} 8 \\ \times\ 1 \\ \hline \end{array}$

22. $\begin{array}{r} 3 \\ \times\ 8 \\ \hline \end{array}$

23. $\begin{array}{r} 7 \\ \times\ 8 \\ \hline \end{array}$

Problem Solving

24. **Use Structure** Ming bought 8 belts for gifts. How much money did Ming spend? Show how you can use a 4s fact to find the answer.

25. **Make Sense and Persevere** Willa bought a shirt and a sweater. She had $14 left. How much money did Willa start with? How do you know?

DATA	Clothing Sale	
	Shirt	$23
	Belt	$9
	Sweater	$38
	Pair of jeans	$42

26. **Model with Math** Mr. Garner spends $52 on groceries and $24 on gas. How much did Mr. Garner spend? Write an equation and solve.

?	
$52	$24

27. **Algebra** Mischa bought 7 boxes of orange tiles. There are 8 tiles in each box. How many tiles did Mischa buy? Write an equation and solve. Use ? to represent the unknown quantity of tiles.

28. Aaron bought 6 packs of sports cards. There are 7 cards in each pack. How many sports cards did Aaron buy in all? Use properties to solve the problem.

29. **Higher Order Thinking** Sophi says, "To find 8 × 8, I can find 8 × (4 + 4)." Do you agree? Explain.

✓ **Assessment**

30. Ms. Vero has boxes of crayons in her classroom closet. Each box has 8 crayons in it. Draw lines to show how many total crayons are found in each group of crayon boxes.

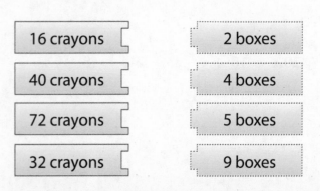

16 crayons	2 boxes
40 crayons	4 boxes
72 crayons	5 boxes
32 crayons	9 boxes

Name _____

Another Look!

You can double a 4s fact to multiply with 8.

Find 8 × 6. Double a 4s fact.

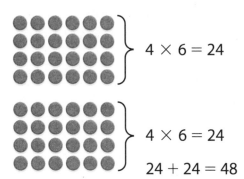

$4 \times 6 = 24$

$4 \times 6 = 24$

$24 + 24 = 48$

So, $8 \times 6 = 48$.

4s Facts	
$4 \times 0 = 0$	$4 \times 5 = 20$
$4 \times 1 = 4$	$4 \times 6 = 24$
$4 \times 2 = 8$	$4 \times 7 = 28$
$4 \times 3 = 12$	$4 \times 8 = 32$
$4 \times 4 = 16$	$4 \times 9 = 36$

DATA

In **1** and **2**, double a 4s fact to find the product.

1. $8 \times 5 = ?$

$4 \times 5 =$ _____

$4 \times 5 =$ _____

$20 +$ _____ $=$ _____

So, $8 \times 5 =$ _____.

2. $8 \times 3 = ?$

$4 \times 3 =$ _____

$4 \times 3 =$ _____

_____ $+$ _____ $=$ _____

So, $8 \times 3 =$ _____.

In **3–9**, find the products.

3. $2 \times 8 =$ _____

4. $4 \times 8 =$ _____

5. $8 \times 5 =$ _____

6. $\begin{array}{r} 7 \\ \times\ 8 \\ \hline \end{array}$

7. $\begin{array}{r} 8 \\ \times\ 9 \\ \hline \end{array}$

8. $\begin{array}{r} 1 \\ \times\ 8 \\ \hline \end{array}$

9. $\begin{array}{r} 8 \\ \times\ 6 \\ \hline \end{array}$

10. Luis made the arrays shown at the right to find 5 × 8. Explain how he could change the arrays to find 7 × 8. Add to Luis's drawing to show your solution.

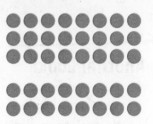

11. **Math and Science** An octopus has 8 arms. At the aquarium there are 3 octopuses in one tank. How many arms do the octopuses have all together? What are two strategies you can use to find the answer?

12. **Use Structure** During the California Gold Rush, miners sometimes paid $10 for a glass of water. What was the total cost if 8 miners each bought one glass of water? How can you use a 4s fact to find the answer?

13. How many pints are in 5 gallons?

1 gallon = 8 pints

14. **Higher Order Thinking** Lani said all of the multiples of 8 are also multiples of 2. Jamila said all of the multiples of 8 are also multiples of 4. Who is correct? Explain.

<image src="assessment-check" /> **Assessment**

15. Ted works in a store where rolls are sold in packages of 8. Customers came in asking Ted for 16, 48, 8, and 40 rolls. Draw lines to connect each quantity of rolls to the number of packages Ted should tell the customers to buy.

16 rolls		1 package
48 rolls		2 packages
8 rolls		5 packages
40 rolls		6 packages

Name _____

Solve & Share

Jermaine has 7 coolers. Each cooler contains 8 bottles of sports drink. How many bottles of sports drink does Jermaine have in all? *Solve this problem any way you choose.*

You can model with math. Pictures, objects, words, numbers, and symbols can be used to represent and solve the problem. *Show your work in the space below!*

I can ...
use strategies and tools to represent and solve multiplication facts.

🔺 **SOL** 3.4a; 3.4b; 3,4c, 3.17

Look Back! **Construct Arguments** Jermaine instead has 8 coolers with 7 bottles of sports drink in each cooler. Does that change the total number of bottles of sports drinks that he has? Explain why or why not.

Essential Question **How Do You Use Strategies to Multiply?**

A

Justin and Dolores made a dragon float for a parade. They connected 9 equal sections to make the dragon's body. What is the total length of the dragon's body in feet?

The dragon's body is made of equal sections, so you can multiply to find its length.

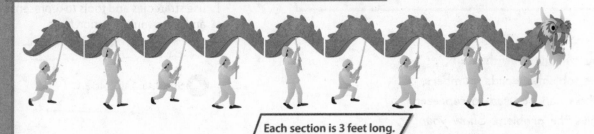

Each section is 3 feet long.

B **One Way**

Draw a picture to find 9 × 3.

9 × 3 means 9 groups of 3. Combine the groups to find the product.

Dragon's body length
?

| 3 | 3 | 3 | 3 | 3 | 3 | 3 | 3 | 3 |

↑
3 feet each section
9 × 3 = 27.

The dragon's body is 27 feet long.

C **Another Way**

Use known facts to find 9 × 3.

Use 4s facts and 5s facts to help.

4 × 3 = 12

5 × 3 = 15

12 + 15 = 27

The dragon's body is 27 feet long.

Convince Me! **Make Sense and Persevere** What two other facts can you use to find 9 × 3? Explain.

Practice Buddy   Tools   Assessment

☆Guided Practice*

Do You Understand?

1. What known facts can you use to find 7 × 5?

2. To find 8 × 6, how does knowing 6 × 6 = 36 help you?

Do You Know How?

In **3–8**, multiply.

3. 3 × 7 = _____   **4.** 6 × 5 = _____

5. 9 × 4 = _____   **6.** 3 × 0 = _____

7.   1
       × 7
       ____

8.   10
       × 8
       ____

Independent Practice ☆

In **9–25**, use known facts and strategies to find the product.

9. 7 × 7 = _____

10. 8 × 2 = _____

11. 3 × 10 = _____

12. _____ = 8 × 9

13. _____ = 4 × 6

14. _____ = 4 × 4

15.   10
        × 7
        ____

16.   2
        × 6
        ____

17.   1
        × 3
        ____

18.   2
        × 7
        ____

19.   8
        × 0
        ____

20.   10
        × 6
        ____

21.   4
        × 7
        ____

22.   8
        × 9
        ____

23. What is 6 × 9? _____

24. What is 7 × 2? _____

25. What is 8 × 1? _____

*For another example, see Set D on page 160.   **Topic 3** | Lesson 3-6   **141**

Problem Solving

26. Reasoning Mr. Ling walks 5 miles each day. How many total miles does he walk in one week? Explain.

Remember, there are 7 days in a week.

27. David wants to buy new shoes and a jersey. The shoes cost $56. The jersey costs $42. How much money does David need to buy both items?

?	
$56	$42

28. Model with Math Ms. Wilson drank three 8-ounce glasses of tea before lunch. Then she drank three 8-ounce glasses of water before dinner. How many ounces of liquid did she drink in all? Write an equation to help solve.

29. Higher Order Thinking Show how you can use known facts to find 4×11. Explain how you chose the known facts.

30. Critique Reasoning Mr. Evans needs to assign 32 students into 8 equal groups. He says, "I can use repeated subtraction. Since I subtract 3 times, each group has 3 students." Do you agree with Mr. Evans? Explain why or why not.

$32 - 16 = 16$
$16 - 8 = 8$
$8 - 8 = 0.$

31. Rory played 9 holes of golf. On each hole it took him 4 strokes to get his ball in the hole. Choose *Yes* or *No* to tell if each equation can be used to find the total number of strokes it took Rory to complete 9 holes.

$(8 \times 4) + (1 \times 4) = ?$ ◯ Yes ◯ No

$9 \times 4 = ?$ ◯ Yes ◯ No

$(3 \times 3) + (1 \times 4) = ?$ ◯ Yes ◯ No

$9 \times (2 \times 2) = ?$ ◯ Yes ◯ No

32. Rachel has a collection of 24 ceramic figures. She displays them in equal groups in her room. Choose *Yes* or *No* to tell if each example is a possible way to display all of Rachel's figures.

8 groups of 4	◯ Yes	◯ No
3 groups of 6	◯ Yes	◯ No
6 groups of 4	◯ Yes	◯ No
3 groups of 8	◯ Yes	◯ No

Help Practice Tools Games
Buddy

Another Look!

Find 8 × 4.

You can use a picture or known facts to find 8 × 4.

Picture
8 × 4 means 8 groups of 4.

?

4	4	4	4	4	4	4	4

Combine equal groups to find the product.

So, 8 × 4 = 32.

Known Facts
Use 4s facts to help.

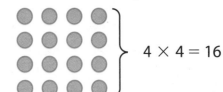

4 × 4 = 16

4 × 4 = 16
16 + 16 = 32

So, 8 × 4 = 32.

In **1** and **2**, use a picture and known facts to find the product.

1. 3 × 6 = ?

?

6	6	

6   12

2 × 6 = _____

1 × 6 = _____

3 × 6 = _____

12 + _____ = _____

2. 3 × 3 = ?

?

3	3	

3   6

2 × 3 = _____

1 × 3 = _____

3 × 3 = _____

6 + _____ = _____

In **3–8**, multiply.

3. 3 × 2 = _____

4. 8 × 3 = _____

5. 6 × 7 = _____

6. 10 × 7 = _____

7. 4 × 0 = _____

8. 7 × 2 = _____

9. **Make Sense and Persevere** The home team had 4 three-pointers, 10 two-pointers, and 6 free throws. The visiting team scored 5 three-pointers, 8 two-pointers, and 5 free throws. Which team scored more points? Explain.

Think about what you know, and what you need to find.

Basketball Points

Type	Points
Three-Pointer	3 points
Two-Pointer	2 points
Free Throw	1 point

10. **Higher Order Thinking** Martina has 3 bags of tennis balls. There are 6 pink, 5 yellow, and 2 white balls in each bag. How many tennis balls does Martina have in all? Show how you found the answer.

11. **Number Sense** Without multiplying, how can you tell which product will be greater, 4×3 or 4×5? Explain.

✔ **Assessment**

12. A park ranger is counting visitors who drive into a national park. In 30 minutes, she counts 7 cars with 4 passengers in each. Choose *Yes* or *No* to tell if each equation shows a way to find how many visitors the park ranger counted.

$4 \times 7 = ?$ ◯ Yes ◯ No
$4 \times 7 + 30 = ?$ ◯ Yes ◯ No
$(2 \times 7) + (2 \times 7) = ?$ ◯ Yes ◯ No
$(4 \times 3) + (4 \times 4) = ?$ ◯ Yes ◯ No

13. Harris buys one cap for every city he has visited in the United States. The number of caps he has is shown below. Choose *Yes* or *No* to tell if each equation shows a way to find how many cities Harris has visited.

$3 \times 6 = ?$ ◯ Yes ◯ No
$(2 \times 5) + (1 \times 5) = ?$ ◯ Yes ◯ No
$(3 + 5) \times 3 = ?$ ◯ Yes ◯ No
$3 \times 5 = ?$ ◯ Yes ◯ No

144 **Topic 3** | Lesson 3-6

Name _____

Solve & Share

Gina has 2 quilts. Each quilt has 5 rows with 3 squares in each row. How many squares are in both quilts? *Solve this problem any way you choose.* Then find another way to solve the problem.

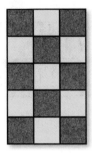

I can ...
multiply 3 factors in any order to find a product.

 SOL 3.4a; 3.4b, 3.17

You can make sense of problems and persevere in solving them. You can solve this problem in more than one way. *Show your work!*

Look Back! **Construct Arguments** Did you get a different answer when you solved the problem a different way? Explain why or why not.

Essential Question **How Can You Multiply 3 Numbers?**

A

Drew is joining 3 sections of a quilt. Each section has 2 rows with 4 squares in each row. How many squares are in these 3 sections? Find 3 × 2 × 4.

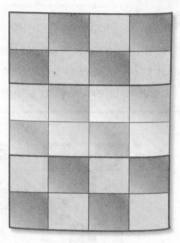

You can multiply to find the total for an array.

B **One Way**

Find 3 × 2 first.

(3 × 2) × 4

6 × 4 = 24

6 rows, 4 squares in each row

There are 24 squares in all.

C **Another Way**

Find 2 × 4 first.

3 × (2 × 4)

3 × 8 = 24

3 sections, 8 squares in each section

There are 24 squares in Drew's quilt.

The Associative (Grouping) Property of Multiplication says that you can change the grouping of the factors and the product will be the same.

Convince Me! **Generalize** Use the Associative Property of Multiplication to show two different ways to find 5 × 2 × 3. Did you get the same answer both ways? What can you generalize?

☆ Guided Practice*

Do You Understand?

1. Sarah has 4 pages of stickers in an album. Each page has 3 rows with 2 stickers in each row. How many stickers are in Sarah's album? You may use objects to help.

2. **Critique Reasoning** Billy concludes the product of $(2 \times 3) \times 5$ is not equal to the product of $2 \times (3 \times 5)$. Is Billy correct? Explain.

Do You Know How?

In **3–6**, use the Associative Property of Multiplication to find the missing number. You may use objects or draw a picture to help.

3. $2 \times (4 \times 2) = (2 \times 4) \times$ _____

4. $(3 \times 4) \times 3 = 3 \times ($ _____ $\times 3)$

5. $2 \times (2 \times 3) = (2 \times 2) \times$ _____

6. $(3 \times 2) \times 4 =$ _____ $\times (2 \times 4)$

Independent Practice ☆

In **7–12**, use the Associative Property of Multiplication to find the missing number. You may use objects or draw a picture to help.

7. $8 \times (3 \times 6) = (8 \times 3) \times$ _____

8. $5 \times (6 \times 9) = (5 \times 6) \times$ _____

9. $5 \times (7 \times 2) = (5 \times 7) \times$ _____

10. $5 \times (2 \times 9) = (5 \times$ _____ $) \times 9$

11. $3 \times (2 \times 5) = (3 \times 2) \times$ _____

12. $4 \times (2 \times 2) = (4 \times$ _____ $) \times 2$

In **13–18**, use the Associative Property of Multiplication to find the product. You may use objects or draw a picture to help.

13. $2 \times 3 \times 2 =$ _____

14. $3 \times 6 \times 2 =$ _____

15. $2 \times 6 \times 2 =$ _____

16. $5 \times 2 \times 4 =$ _____

17. $5 \times 2 \times 2 =$ _____

18. $3 \times 3 \times 2 =$ _____

Problem Solving

19. **Reasoning** There are 7 mockingbird nests at a park. What is the greatest number of eggs there could be at this park? What is the least number of eggs there could be?

Mockingbirds lay 3 to 5 eggs.

20. At another park, there are 3 mockingbird nests with 4 eggs in each nest and 1 more nest with 3 eggs. How many eggs are there at this park?

---

21. **Critique Reasoning** Maria says she can find the product for $2 \times 3 \times 4$ by solving $3 \times 2 \times 4$. Is Maria correct? Explain.

22. **Number Sense** Anita says the product of $5 \times 2 \times 3$ is less than 20. Do you agree? Explain.

---

23. **Algebra** Which number makes both equations true?

$4 \times (3 \times 2) = (4 \times ?) \times 2$

$3 \times (5 \times 2) = (? \times 5) \times 2$

24. **Higher Order Thinking** How do you know that $4 \times 2 \times 2$ is the same as 4×4? Explain.

Assessment

Fill in the blanks to make the equations correct.

25. $(7 \times 2) \times 3 = \underline{\quad} \times (\underline{\quad} \times 3)$

$(7 \times 2) \times 3 = \underline{\quad}$

26. $(9 \times 3) \times 3 = \underline{\quad} \times (\underline{\quad} \times 3)$

$(9 \times 3) \times 3 = \underline{\quad}$

Use properties to help multiply.

Another Look!

Use the Associative Property of Multiplication to find the product of $4 \times 2 \times 5$.

> The Associative Property of Multiplication states that the way the factors are grouped does not change the product.

One Way
$4 \times 2 \times 5$
$(4 \times 2) \times 5$
$8 \times 5 = 40$

Another Way
$4 \times 2 \times 5$
$4 \times (2 \times 5)$
$4 \times 10 = 40$

1. Find the product of $4 \times 2 \times 3$ two different ways.

$4 \times 2 \times 3$
$(4 \times 2) \times 3$

_____ $\times 3 =$ _____

$4 \times 2 \times 3$
$4 \times (2 \times 3)$

$4 \times$ _____ $=$ _____

In **2–16**, find each product. You may draw a picture to help.

2. $3 \times 2 \times 1 =$ _____

3. $2 \times 3 \times 5 =$ _____

4. $4 \times 3 \times 2 =$ _____

5. $4 \times 2 \times 7 =$ _____

6. $3 \times 3 \times 2 =$ _____

7. $2 \times 4 \times 5 =$ _____

8. $2 \times 2 \times 6 =$ _____

9. $4 \times 1 \times 5 =$ _____

10. $5 \times 1 \times 3 =$ _____

11. $6 \times 1 \times 5 =$ _____

12. $3 \times 3 \times 4 =$ _____

13. $4 \times 2 \times 6 =$ _____

14. $5 \times 5 \times 2 =$ _____

15. $2 \times 2 \times 5 =$ _____

16. $3 \times 2 \times 2 =$ _____

17. Model with Math Mrs. Stokes bought 3 packages of fruit juice. Each package has 2 rows with 6 boxes in each row. How many boxes of fruit juice did Mrs. Stokes buy? Use equations to solve.

18. Higher Order Thinking Write two different multiplication equations for the arrays shown and find the product.

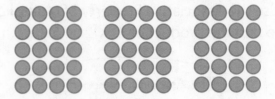

19. Matt has a block. He uses one of the flat surfaces of the block to trace a triangle. What type of solid figure is Matt's block?

20. **Vocabulary** Write an equation that has 20 as the *product* and 4 as a *factor*.

21. Reasoning Amy has 3 bags of marbles, and Ron has 2 bags of marbles. There are 6 marbles in each of their bags. How many marbles do they have in all? Show how you know.

22. Make Sense and Persevere Marco bought 6 sheets of stamps. On each sheet there are 3 rows of stamps with 3 stamps in each row. How many stamps did Marco buy?

✓ **Assessment**

Write numbers to make the equations correct.

23. $(8 \times 2) \times 4 = \underline{\quad} \times (\underline{\quad} \times 4)$

$(8 \times 2) \times 4 = \underline{\quad}$

24. $(6 \times 5) \times 2 = \underline{\quad} \times (\underline{\quad} \times 2)$

$(6 \times 5) \times 2 = \underline{\quad}$

You can solve problems different ways using properties.

Name _____

Solve & Share

You have learned that you can use known facts to find unknown facts. For each of the 4 multiplication facts below, list two multiplication facts from the box that can be added to find the given product. The first solution is completed for you.

What do you notice about the facts you used to find the products when 6 or 7 is a factor?

I can ...
use reasoning to look for and describe general strategies for finding products.

 SOL 3.4a; 3.17

6×7

$5 \times 7 + 1 \times 7 = 42$

6×9

_____ + _____ = 54

7×8

_____ + _____ = 56

7×9

_____ + _____ = 63

1×9	2×8	1×7
5×8	5×9	1×8
5×7	2×7	2×9

Thinking Habits
Be a good thinker!
These questions can help you.

- Are any calculations repeated?

- Can I generalize from examples?

- What shortcuts do I notice?

Look Back! **Generalize** Use your observations from your work above to complete these facts.

$(\underline{\quad} \times 6) + (\underline{\quad} \times 6) = 36$

$(\underline{\quad} \times 7) + (\underline{\quad} \times 7) = 49$

How Can You Use Repeated Reasoning When Multiplying?

A

Ellie wrote the equations below to find the total number of squares in each of these rectangles. Look at the equations. Known facts with which factors are used repeatedly to find the products?

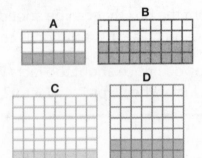

A $3 \times 6 = (2 \times 6) + (1 \times 6) = 12 + 6 = 18$

B $4 \times 9 = (2 \times 9) + (2 \times 9) = 18 + 18 = 36$

C $6 \times 8 = (5 \times 8) + (1 \times 8) = 40 + 8 = 48$

D $7 \times 7 = (5 \times 7) + (2 \times 7) = 35 + 14 = 49$

What do I need to do to complete the task?

I need to see if there are known facts that can be used repeatedly to find other facts.

B **How can I make a generalization from repeated reasoning?**

I can

- look for repeated calculations.

- make generalizations about the repeated calculations.

- test whether my generalizations work for other numbers.

C I see that the factors 1, 2, and 5 are used repeatedly. I see two generalizations.

Here's my thinking...

I can break facts with 3 or 4 into 2s and 1s facts.
$3 \times 6 = (2 \times 6) + (1 \times 6)$
$4 \times 9 = (2 \times 9) + (2 \times 9)$

I can break facts with 6 or 7 into 5s, 2s, and 1s facts.
$6 \times 8 = (5 \times 8) + (1 \times 8)$
$7 \times 7 = (5 \times 7) + (2 \times 7)$

I can test this with other facts.
$3 \times 5 = (2 \times 5) + (1 \times 5)$
$6 \times 7 = (5 \times 7) + (1 \times 7)$

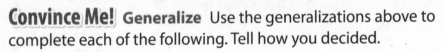

Convince Me! **Generalize** Use the generalizations above to complete each of the following. Tell how you decided.

$7 \times 5 = (\underline{\hspace{1cm}}) + (\underline{\hspace{1cm}})$

$7 \times 6 = (\underline{\hspace{1cm}}) + (\underline{\hspace{1cm}})$

☆ Guided Practice *

Generalize

Ricardo wrote the equations below.

> When you generalize, you make a statement about a larger group based on examples that are true.

1. Which factors did Ricardo use repeatedly to find the products? Make a generalization.

$3 \times 8 = (2 \times 8) + (1 \times 8) = 24$

$3 \times 7 = (2 \times 7) + (1 \times 7) = 21$

$6 \times 3 = (6 \times 1) + (6 \times 2) = 18$

2. Complete this equation to test whether your generalization is true for other facts. Explain.

$3 \times 9 = (\underline{} \times \underline{}) + (\underline{} \times \underline{}) = \underline{}$

Independent Practice ☆

Generalize

Mary wrote the equations at the right.

$8 \times 7 = (5 \times 7) + (3 \times 7) = 56$

3. Which factors did Mary use repeatedly to find the products? Make a generalization.

$6 \times 8 = (6 \times 5) + (6 \times 3) = 48$

$8 \times 9 = (3 \times 9) + (5 \times 9) = 72$

4. Complete this equation to test whether your generalization is true for other facts. Explain.

$8 \times 3 = (\underline{} \times \underline{}) + (\underline{} \times \underline{}) = \underline{}$

5. What is another way you can use known facts to solve 8×3? What generalization can you make from this way?

*For another example, see Set F on page 160.

Problem Solving

Baking Pizzas

Adam is baking 4 pizzas. Each pizza is a rectangle. It takes Adam 35 minutes to bake the pizzas. He divides each pizza into the equal-size square slices shown.

Pizza 1 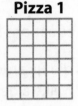 **Pizza 2**

6. Make Sense and Persevere Adam multiplies to find the total number of square slices for each pizza. For each pizza, tell the factors Adam multiplies.

Pizza 3 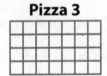 **Pizza 4**

7. Use Structure Look at the facts you wrote in **6**. Break apart these facts into 1s, 2s, or 5s facts to find the total number of slices for each pizza.

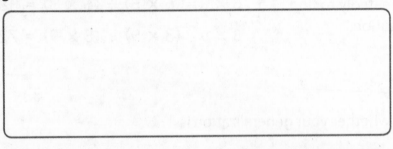

Pizza 1

(__ × __) = (__ × __) + (__ × __) = ____

Pizza 2

(__ × __) = (__ × __) + (__ × __) = ____

Pizza 3

(__ × __) = (__ × __) + (__ × __) = ____

Pizza 4

(__ × __) = (__ × __) + (__ × __) = ____

8. Generalize Look at how you used the 1s, 2s, and 5s facts above. What generalizations can you make? Test your generalizations with another fact.

You can test your generalization by checking to see if it is true for other facts.

9. Critique Reasoning Look at the model for Pizza 3. Adam says he can use 2s facts to solve 4 × 7 or 7 × 4. Is he correct? Explain.

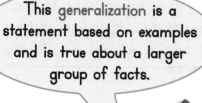

Homework & Practice 3-8
Repeated Reasoning

Another Look!

John used facts he knows to solve 6×7 and 6×5.
He wrote these equations.

$6 \times 7 = (5 \times 7) + (1 \times 7) = 42$

$6 \times 5 = (5 \times 5) + (1 \times 5) = 30$

Tell how you can use repeated reasoning to find multiplication facts.

- I can look for repeated calculations.

- I can make generalizations about the repeated calculations.

Make a generalization.
Test whether this is true for other facts.

I can break facts with 6 into 5s and 1s facts.

This is true for other facts with 6: $6 \times 9 = (5 \times 9) + (1 \times 9) = 54$

This generalization is a statement based on examples and is true about a larger group of facts.

Generalize

Pam wrote the equations below.

1. Tell how you can use repeated reasoning to find multiplication facts.

2. Which factors did Pam use repeatedly?
   Make a generalization.

   $7 \times 6 = (5 \times 6) + (2 \times 6) = 42$

   $7 \times 9 = (5 \times 9) + (2 \times 9) = 63$

   $7 \times 7 = (5 \times 7) + (2 \times 7) = 49$

3. Complete this equation to test whether your generalization is
   true for other facts. Explain.

   $7 \times 8 = (\_\_ \times \_\_) + (\_\_ \times \_\_) = \_\_\_$

Julia puts her stickers into arrays in an album. Some of her stickers are animal stickers. There are a different number of stickers on each page. The table at the right shows information about the stickers in Julia's album.

DATA

Julia's Stickers

Page Number	Animal Stickers	Rows of Stickers	Columns of Stickers
1	7	4	7
2	4	4	6
3	9	8	9
4	9	8	6

4. **Use Appropriate Tools** Explain how you can use one of these tools to find the number of stickers on each page: a number line, counters, a hundreds chart.

5. **Make Sense and Persevere** Julia multiplies to find the total number of stickers on each page. For each page, tell the factors that she multiplies.

> You can generalize by thinking about the factors that you use repeatedly to solve problems.

6. **Use Structure** Look at the facts you wrote for **5**. Break these facts into 1s, 2s, 3s, and 5s facts to find the total number of stickers on each page.

Page 1
$(\_ \times \_) = (\_ \times \_) + (\_ \times \_) = \_\_$
Page 2
$(\_ \times \_) = (\_ \times \_) + (\_ \times \_) = \_\_$
Page 3
$(\_ \times \_) = (\_ \times \_) + (\_ \times \_) = \_\_$
Page 4
$(\_ \times \_) = (\_ \times \_) + (\_ \times \_) = \_\_$

7. **Generalize** Look at the 1s, 2s, 3s, and 5s facts above. What generalizations can you make? Test each generalization with another fact.

Name _____

Shade a path from **START** to **FINISH**. Follow the differences that are correct. You can only move up, down, right, or left.

I can ...
subtract within 100.

Start				
75 − 13 **62**	99 − 63 **36**	85 − 39 **46**	70 − 48 **32**	41 − 31 **11**
39 − 21 **12**	24 − 16 **10**	59 − 37 **22**	55 − 32 **67**	91 − 65 **47**
77 − 38 **45**	47 − 40 **87**	46 − 27 **19**	100 − 62 **58**	45 − 27 **17**
69 − 21 **47**	34 − 29 **15**	65 − 59 **6**	81 − 29 **52**	67 − 19 **48**
82 − 46 **58**	38 − 12 **23**	93 − 34 **69**	24 − 18 **9**	78 − 35 **43**

Finish

Vocabulary Review

A-Z
Glossary

Word List

- Associative (Grouping) Property of Multiplication
- Commutative (Order) Property of Multiplication
- Distributive Property
- Identity (One) Property of Multiplication
- factor
- multiple
- product
- Zero Property of Multiplication

Understand Vocabulary

Match the example to the term.

1. $5 \times 0 = 0 \times 5$

2. $(3 \times 8) + (1 \times 8) = 4 \times 8$

3. $(6 \times 2) \times 2 = 6 \times (2 \times 2)$

4. $7 \times 1 = 7$

Associative (Grouping) Property of Multiplication

Commutative (Order) Property of Multiplication

Distributive Property

Identity (One) Property of Multiplication

Write T for *true* or F for *false*.

_____ **5.** 3 and 8 are *multiples* of 24.

_____ **6.** You can multiply *factors* in any order.

_____ **7.** The *product* of zero and any number is that number.

_____ **8.** There are 3 *factors* in the equation $5 \times 3 \times 2 = 30$.

Use Vocabulary in Writing

9. Explain how to use $8 \times 5 = 40$ to find 8×6. Use at least 2 terms from the Word List in your explanation.

Name _____

Set A pages 109–114 _____

You can break an array into 2 smaller arrays.

You can write an unknown fact as the sum of 2 known facts.

$8 \times 4 = (8 \times 3) + (8 \times 1)$

Remember that the Distributive Property says that a multiplication fact can be broken apart into the sum of two other multiplication facts.

In **1** and **2**, find the missing value.

1. _____ $\times 4 = (2 \times 4) + (2 \times 4)$

2. $6 \times 5 = (4 \times 5) + ($ _____ $\times 5)$

Set B pages 115–126 _____

Find 3×4.

You can use a 2s fact to help multiply by 3.

3×4
$\left. \begin{array}{l} \bigcirc \bigcirc \bigcirc \bigcirc \\ \bigcirc \bigcirc \bigcirc \bigcirc \end{array} \right\} 2 \times 4 = 8$
$\left. \begin{array}{l} \bigcirc \bigcirc \bigcirc \bigcirc \end{array} \right\} 1 \times 4 = 4$

$8 + 4 = 12$

You can also find 4s facts.
$3 \times 4 = (3 \times 2) + (3 \times 2) = 6 + 6 = 12$

Remember that to find a 3s fact, add a 2s fact and a 1s fact. To find a 4s fact, double the product of a 2s fact.

1. $3 \times 7 =$ _____   2. $4 \times 9 =$ _____

3. $4 \times 10 =$ _____   4. $3 \times 10 =$ _____

5. $3 \times 8 =$ _____   6. $8 \times 4 =$ _____

7. $9 \times 3 =$ _____   8. $10 \times 4 =$ _____

Set C pages 127–132 _____

You can use known facts to help multiply.
Find 6×9.

$6 \times 9 = (5 \times 9) + (1 \times 9)$

$6 \times 9 = 45 + 9$

$6 \times 9 = 54$

Find 7×4.

$7 \times 4 = (5 \times 4) + (2 \times 4)$

$7 \times 4 = 20 + 8$

$7 \times 4 = 28$

Remember that you can break a multiplication problem into two smaller problems.

1. $6 \times 6 =$ _____   2. $7 \times 9 =$ _____

3. $7 \times 7 =$ _____   4. $6 \times 8 =$ _____

5. $\begin{array}{r} 6 \\ \times 5 \\ \hline \end{array}$ 6. $\begin{array}{r} 6 \\ \times 3 \\ \hline \end{array}$ 7. $\begin{array}{r} 10 \\ \times 7 \\ \hline \end{array}$

Set D pages 133–144

Find 8×9.

You can use 2s facts.

$8 \times 9 = (2 \times 9) + (2 \times 9) + (2 \times 9) + (2 \times 9)$

$8 \times 9 = 18 + 18 + 18 + 18$

$8 \times 9 = 72$

You can use skip counting.

8, 16, 24, 32, 40, 48, 56, 64, 72

Remember to use patterns, known facts, or skip counting to find products.

1. $8 \times 6 =$ _____   **2.** $8 \times 8 =$ _____

3. $8 \times 7 =$ _____   **4.** $8 \times 10 =$ _____

5. $1 \times 8 =$ _____   **6.** $0 \times 8 =$ _____

7.   8   **8.**   8   **9.**   8
    $\times 5$ $\times 3$ $\times 2$

Set E pages 145–150

You can use the Associative Property to group the factors. The product does not change.

Find $4 \times 2 \times 2$.

One Way	Another Way
$4 \times (2 \times 2)$	$(4 \times 2) \times 2$
$4 \times 4 = 16$	$8 \times 2 = 16$

Remember that you can use properties to write unknown facts as known facts.

In **1–3**, find the product. Show how you grouped the factors.

1. $4 \times 5 \times 2 =$ _____ $\times$ _____ $=$ _____

2. $3 \times 7 \times 3 =$ _____ $\times$ _____ $=$ _____

3. $5 \times 5 \times 2 =$ _____ $\times$ _____ $=$ _____

Set F pages 151–156

Think about these questions to help you use **repeated reasoning**.

Thinking Habits

- Are any calculations repeated?
- Can I generalize from examples?
- What shortcuts do I notice?

Remember that patterns can help you make a generalization.

1. What is repeated in these equations? Use what you see to make a generalization.

$6 \times 6 = (6 \times 3) + (6 \times 3) = 18 + 18 = 36$

$7 \times 6 = (7 \times 3) + (7 \times 3) = 21 + 21 = 42$

$8 \times 6 = (8 \times 3) + (8 \times 3) = 24 + 24 = 48$

2. Solve this equation to test whether your generalization is true.

$10 \times 6 = ?$

___ $\times$ ___ $= ($ ___ $\times$ ___ $) + ($ ___ $\times$ ___ $)$

$=$ ___ $+$ ___ $=$ ___

1. Krista arranged her buttons in an array. Which shows a way to break Krista's array into two smaller arrays?

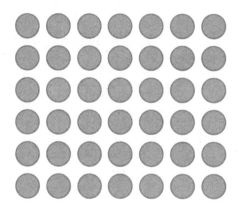

Ⓐ (3 × 6) + (3 × 1)

Ⓑ (3 × 7) + (3 × 7)

Ⓒ (3 × 6) + (3 × 6)

Ⓓ (3 × 7) + (4 × 7)

2. Choose *Yes* or *No* to tell if 16 is the missing product.

2a. 4 × 4 = ?   ○ Yes   ○ No

2b. 2 × 8 = ?   ○ Yes   ○ No

2c. 2 × 4 = ?   ○ Yes   ○ No

2d. 8 × 2 = ?   ○ Yes   ○ No

3. Jeff makes the generalization that a 10s fact can be broken into two 5s facts. Write an equation to test his generalization.

4. June broke up a large array into a 3 × 4 array and a 5 × 4 array. What was the large array that June started with?

5. Which facts can you use to find 4 × 8? Choose all that apply.

☐ 2 × 8 and 2 × 9

☐ 2 × 8 and 2 × 8

☐ 2 × 4 and 1 × 8

☐ 4 × 5 and 4 × 3

☐ 3 × 8 and 1 × 8

6. A bakery uses 3 cups of flour to make each loaf of bread. There are 3 loaves of bread on a tray. There are 6 trays on a cart. How many cups of flour are used to make a full cart of bread? Show your work.

7. What number makes this equation correct?

(3 × 4) + (3 × 4) = _____

8. Casey has 3 bags of baseballs. There are 6 baseballs in each bag. How many baseballs does Casey have?

Ⓐ 9

Ⓑ 12

Ⓒ 15

Ⓓ 18

9. Jonathan organizes his pictures into a 6 × 4 array. Kim organizes her pictures into a 7 × 5 array. How can Kim and Jonathan break apart their arrays? Write each pair of facts in the correct space.

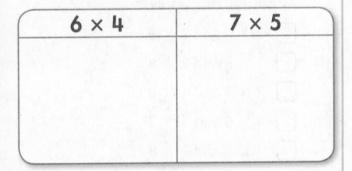

6 × 4	7 × 5

5 × 5 and 2 × 5

1 × 4 and 5 × 4

4 × 5 and 3 × 5

1 × 5 and 6 × 5

3 × 4 and 3 × 4

10. Which of the expressions below can you use to solve 3 × 2 × 4? Choose all that apply.

☐ 3 × 4 × 2

☐ 3 × 3 × 3

☐ 4 × 3 × 1

☐ 4 × 2 × 3

☐ 4 × 2 × 4

11. Amy arranged her counters into this array.

Part A

What two facts could Amy use to write an equation for the array?

Part B

If Amy adds one more row of 9 counters to her array, can she still use the facts you wrote in Part A to find the total number? Explain why or why not.

12. Tim's family rented a canoe for 6 hours on Monday and 2 hours on Tuesday. How much did they spend? Show any equations you used.

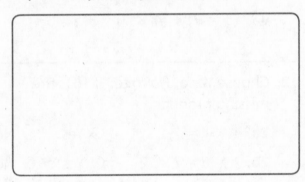

Rentals

Canoe $7 each hour

Kayak $6 each hour

Name _____

School Fair

Kay and Ben are helping to organize the School Fair.
Kay is organizing the school band.
Ben is organizing the bake sale.

The 3 × 7 array at the right shows how chairs
have been set up for the school band.
Use the array to answer Questions 1 and 2.

1. Kay wants to have chairs in a 6 × 7 array.
   Add to the array to show how the new array
   will look.

2. Kay needs a path between two of
   the rows, so she separates the chairs
   into two smaller arrays.

   Part A

   Draw a line to show one way Kay
   can separate the chairs into two
   smaller arrays.

   Part B

   Kay wants to know the number of chairs in each new
   array. Write a multiplication fact for each of the new
   arrays to show how she can find this.

   Part C

   Kay wants to find the total number of chairs that are
   being used. Show how to use the facts in Part B to find
   the total number of chairs.

The **Bake Sale** table shows the baked goods Ben has for sale at the School Fair. Use the **Bake Sale** table to answer Questions 3, 4, and 5.

Bake Sale			
Baked Goods	Number of Trays	Number on Each Tray	Cost per Tray
Blueberry Muffins	4	7	$6
Strawberry Tarts	7	8	$4
Granola Bars	8	6	$3

3. Ben sells 4 trays of granola bars in the morning and 4 trays of granola bars in the afternoon. How much money does this raise? Show your work.

4. Ben organizes the blueberry muffins into a 4 × 7 array.

   Part A

   Ben breaks up the array of blueberry muffins into 2 arrays that look the same. At the right draw the 2 arrays of blueberry muffins.

   Part B

   Ben wants to check the total number of blueberry muffins. He knows 2 × 7 = 14. How can he use this to find the total number of blueberry muffins?

5. 2 friends each bought 3 trays of strawberry tarts. Ben says they spent more than $20 in total. Do you agree? Explain.

Use Multiplication to Divide: Division Facts

Essential Question: How can unknown division facts be found using known multiplication facts?

Digital Resources

Solve   Learn   Glossary   Practice Buddy

Tools   Assessment   Help   Games

It takes a lot of testing to make a new car.

To build a better car, people make models or prototypes and then test them.

Let's see how numbers are used in testing. Here's a project on using tests to review models.

Math and Science Project: Testing Models

Do Research Tests can be done to see if a model works or if a change makes it better. Use the Internet or other sources to find information about a model or prototype that was tested. Identify how the testing was done.

Journal: Write a Report Include what you found. Also in your report:

- Make a chart that includes the model, what changed in the test, and what stayed the same.

- Explain the results of the test.

- Write an equation to show one of the relationships in the test. Explain what the numbers represent.

Name _____

Review What You Know

A-Z Vocabulary

Choose the best term from the box.
Write it on the blank.

• division	• factors
• equation	• multiplication

1. _____ are multiplied together to give a product.

2. Use _____ to find how many equal groups or how many are in each group.

3. _____ is an operation that gives the total number when you put together equal groups.

Division

Solve each problem. You can use bar diagrams or counters or draw a picture to help.

4. Stuart has 15 stickers to give to his 3 friends.
   How many stickers can each friend have?

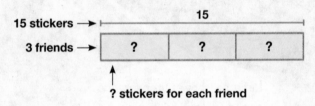

15 stickers → | 15 |
3 friends → | ? | ? | ? |
↑
? stickers for each friend

5. There are 32 muffins. Eight people share them equally.
   How many muffins does each person get?

6. Suzy has 12 granola bars. There are 2 granola bars in each package.
   How many packages of granola bars are there?

Equations

7. Brian has 5 boxes. He puts 8 markers in each box. Which equation shows the total number of markers?

   (A) $5 + 8 = 13$ (B) $5 \times 8 = 40$ (C) $40 \div 5 = 8$ (D) $40 \div 8 = 5$

My Word Cards

Use the examples for each word on the front of the card to help complete the definitions on the back.

fact family

$2 \times 3 = 6$

$3 \times 2 = 6$

$6 \div 2 = 3$

$6 \div 3 = 2$

dividend

$63 \div 9 = 7$

dividend

divisor

$63 \div 9 = 7$

divisor

quotient

$63 \div 9 = 7$

quotient

even number

Even numbers have a 0, 2, 4, 6, or 8 in the ones place.

odd number

Odd numbers have a 1, 3, 5, 7, or 9 in the ones place.

My Word Cards

The _____ is the number to be divided.

A _____ is a group of related facts using the same numbers.

The _____ is the answer to a division problem.

The number by which another number is divided is called the _____.

A number that is not divisible by 2 is an _____.

A number that is divisible by 2 is an _____.

Name _____

Solve

Lesson 4-1
Relate Multiplication and Division

I can ...
use fact families to see how
multiplication and division are related.

SOL 3.4a; 3.4b, 3.17

Solve & Share

Use 24 counters to make an array with
3 equal rows. Write a multiplication equation and a
division equation to describe the array.

You can use tools
to help you see the relationship
between multiplication
and division.

Look Back! Generalize Marisol arranged the same 24 counters
into an array with 6 counters in each row. Can you still write
a multiplication equation and a division equation to describe
Marisol's array? Explain why or why not.

Essential Question **How Can Multiplication Facts Help You Divide?**

A

This array can show the relationship between multiplication and division.

Multiplication
3 rows of 10 drums
3 × 10 = 30
30 drums

Division
30 drums in 3 equal rows
30 ÷ 3 = 10
10 drums in each row

B A fact family shows how multiplication and division are related.

Fact family for 3, 10, and 30:

3 × 10 = 30   30 ÷ 3 = 10

10 × 3 = 30   30 ÷ 10 = 3

dividend   divisor   quotient

A fact family is a group of related facts using the same numbers.

C The **dividend** is the number of objects to be divided.

The **divisor** is the number by which another number is divided.

The **quotient** is the answer to a division problem.

Remember, a product is the answer to a multiplication problem.

Convince Me! **Reasoning** 4 × 7 = 28 is one fact in a fact family. Draw an array for this fact. Write the other three facts in the fact family.

Name _____

☆ Guided Practice

Do You Understand?

1. Look at the fact family for 3, 10, and 30 on page 170. What do you notice about the products and the dividends?

2. **Generalize** Is $4 \times 6 = 24$ part of the fact family for 3, 8, and 24? Explain.

Do You Know How?

In **3–5**, complete each fact family.

3. $3 \times \underline{\hspace{1cm}} = 21$ $7 \times \underline{\hspace{1cm}} = 21$

   $21 \div 3 = \underline{\hspace{1cm}}$ $21 \div 7 = \underline{\hspace{1cm}}$

4. $2 \times \underline{\hspace{1cm}} = 18$ $9 \times \underline{\hspace{1cm}} = 18$

   $18 \div 2 = \underline{\hspace{1cm}}$ $18 \div 9 = \underline{\hspace{1cm}}$

5. $2 \times \underline{\hspace{1cm}} = 20$ $10 \times \underline{\hspace{1cm}} = 20$

   $20 \div 2 = \underline{\hspace{1cm}}$ $20 \div 10 = \underline{\hspace{1cm}}$

Independent Practice

In **6** and **7**, complete each fact family.

6. $2 \times \underline{\hspace{1cm}} = 16$

   $16 \div 2 = \underline{\hspace{1cm}}$

   $8 \times \underline{\hspace{1cm}} = 16$

   $16 \div 8 = \underline{\hspace{1cm}}$

7. $8 \times \underline{\hspace{1cm}} = 56$

   $56 \div 8 = \underline{\hspace{1cm}}$

   $7 \times \underline{\hspace{1cm}} = 56$

   $56 \div 7 = \underline{\hspace{1cm}}$

Some fact families have only 2 facts. The fact family for 2, 2, and 4 has $2 \times 2 = 4$ and $4 \div 2 = 2$.

In **8–13**, write the fact family.

8. Write the fact family for 6, 7, and 42.

9. Write the fact family for 9, 10, and 90.

10. Write the fact family for 2, 3, and 6.

11. Write the fact family for 1, 5, and 5.

12. Write the fact family for 3, 8, and 24.

13. Write the fact family for 5, 6, and 30.

For another example, see Set A on page 225.   **Topic 4** | Lesson 4-1   **171**

Problem Solving

14. Write a multiplication equation and division equation for the array.

$4 \times \underline{\hspace{0.6cm}} = 20$

$20 \div \underline{\hspace{0.6cm}} = 5$

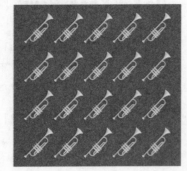

15. Make Sense and Persevere How many inches shorter is the red fabric than the green and yellow fabrics combined?

| Sophia's Fabrics | |
Color	Length in Inches
Red	72
Blue	18
Green	36
Yellow	54

16. Higher Order Thinking Anya says that with 24 counters she can make only 6 possible arrays. Todd says he can make 8 arrays. Who is correct? Explain.

17. Algebra Carla picked 9 apples a day for three days. Which number tells you how many apples she picked in three days and makes this equation true?

$\boxed{} \div 3 = 9$

18.  **Vocabulary** Can you write a *fact family* for 3, 5, and 7? Explain.

19. Use Structure Lisa, Bret, and Gary harvested apples. Lisa filled 3 carts with apples. Bret also filled 3 carts with apples. Gary filled another 3 carts with apples. Write a multiplication equation and a division equation for this story.

✔ Assessment

20. Nick made an array that has 10 counters. Draw 4 arrays that he might have made.

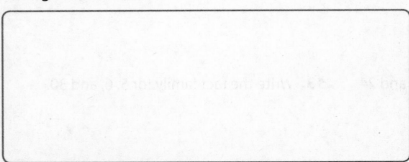

Name _____

Another Look!

Multiplication

6 rows of 4 glue sticks

$6 \times 4 = 24$

24 glue sticks

Division

24 glue sticks in 6 equal rows

$24 \div 6 = 4$

4 glue sticks in each row

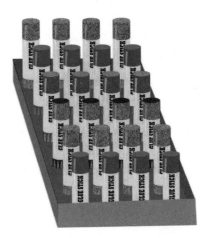

Look for relationships. Multiplication facts can help you learn division facts!

Here is the fact family for 4, 6, and 24:

$4 \times 6 = 24$ $24 \div 4 = 6$

$6 \times 4 = 24$ $24 \div 6 = 4$

In **1** and **2**, complete each fact family.

1. $2 \times$ _____ $= 14$ $7 \times$ _____ $= 14$

$14 \div 2 =$ _____ $14 \div 7 =$ _____

2. $9 \times$ _____ $= 81$

$81 \div 9 =$ _____

In **3** and **4**, write the fact family.

3. Write the fact family for 4, 7, and 28.

4. Write the fact family for 2, 10, and 20.

5. Model with Math Use the array to write a multiplication equation and a division equation.

6. Higher Order Thinking For every row of objects in an array there are 2 columns. The total number of objects in the array is 18. How many rows and columns does the array have?

7. Math and Science Julio's class was making bridges out of balsa wood to see which bridge could hold the most weight. Each person in Julio's group made 2 bridges. What fact family represents the total bridges made by the group?

DATA	Name	Bridges Made
	Julio	2
	Rosa	2
	Miguel	2
	Clara	2

8. Reasoning There are 5 pairs of scissors in one package. Mrs. Hill bought 35 scissors for students in her art classes. How many packages did she buy?

9. Serena has a set of toy trains. She has 3 passenger cars. What is the total length of her passenger cars?

DATA	Serena's Train Cars	
	Type	**Length in Inches**
	Engine	4
	Tender	3
	Passenger Car	9
	Caboose	7

✓ **Assessment**

10. Esther has 15 dimes. She wants to put them in stacks that are the same height. She has already made one stack. Draw the rest of the stacks to show all of Esther's dimes.

Esther has ____ stacks of ____ dimes.

Name _____

Solve & Share

Kara puts 30 toys into 5 party bags. She puts the same number of toys into each bag. How many toys are in each bag? *Solve this problem any way you choose.*

I can ...

divide by 2, 3, 4, and 5 by thinking about how I multiply with those numbers.

SOL 3.4a; 3.4b

You can use structure. How can a fact family that uses 30 and 5 help you solve the problem?

Look Back! **Reasoning** Show two pictures you might draw to represent 30 ÷ 5.

What Multiplication Fact Can You Use?

A

Dee has 14 noisemakers. She puts the same number on each of 2 tables. How many noisemakers are on each table?

Find 14 ÷ 2.

What You Think	What You Write
2 times what number is 14? 2 × 7 = 14	14 ÷ 2 = 7 7 noisemakers are on each table.

B Dee has 40 stickers. If she puts 5 stickers on each bag, how many bags can Dee decorate?

Find 40 ÷ 5.

What You Think	What You Write
What number times 5 is 40? 8 × 5 = 40	40 ÷ 5 = 8 Dee can decorate 8 bags.

C Dee wants to put 15 cups in 3 equal stacks on the table. How many cups will Dee put in each stack?

Find 15 ÷ 3.

What You Think	What You Write
3 times what number is 15? 3 × 5 = 15	15 ÷ 3 = 5 Dee will put 5 cups in each stack.

You can use multiplication to help divide.

Multiplication and division facts form relationships.

Convince Me! **Construct Arguments** How can you use multiplication to help solve 20 ÷ 4? Write the related multiplication fact you use to help solve the problem.

Practice Buddy   Tools   Assessment

Another Example!

Here are two ways to write a division problem.

$$24 \div 4 = 6$$

↑ dividend   ↑ divisor   ↑ quotient

$$\begin{array}{r} 6 \leftarrow \text{quotient} \\ \text{divisor} \longrightarrow 4\overline{)24} \leftarrow \text{dividend} \end{array}$$

☆ Guided Practice*

Do You Understand?

1. How can $5 \times 3 = 15$ help you divide 15 by 3?

2. **Reasoning** Dena has 3 children. She buys 30 pencils to share equally among her children for the school year. How many pencils will each of her children get? Write the answer and the fact family you used.

Do You Know How?

In **3** and **4**, complete each fact family.

3. $3 \times 6 = 18$ _____

   $18 \div 3 = 6$ _____

4. $9 \times 4 = 36$ _____

   $36 \div 4 = 9$ _____

In **5–8**, find each quotient.

5. $36 \div 4 =$ ____   6. $15 \div 5 =$ ____

7. $2\overline{)18}$ 8. $5\overline{)50}$

☆ Independent Practice*

In **9–20**, find each quotient.

9. $12 \div 2 =$ ____   10. $12 \div 3 =$ ____   11. $16 \div 4 =$ ____   12. $35 \div 5 =$ ____

13. $14 \div 2 =$ ____   14. $20 \div 4 =$ ____   15. $24 \div 4 =$ ____   16. $45 \div 5 =$ ____

17. $3\overline{)27}$ 18. $4\overline{)40}$ 19. $5\overline{)40}$ 20. $3\overline{)21}$

*For another example, see Set B on page 225.

Topic 4 | Lesson 4-2   **177**

Problem Solving

In **21** and **22**, use the rectangle at the right.

21. **Reasoning** How many individual squares are inside the rectangle? Write a division equation in which the quotient represents the number of rows.

22. **Make Sense and Persevere** If Anna arranges the squares into an array with 2 columns, how many rows will there be?

23. **Number Sense** Joey says, "I can't solve $8 \div 2$ by using the fact $2 \times 8 = 16$." Do you agree or disagree? Explain.

24. Miko and Bob want to buy a tablet that is on sale for $99. Miko has $45 and Bob has $52. Do they have enough to buy the tablet? If not, how much more do they need?

25. **A-Z Vocabulary** Write a division equation. Tell which is the *quotient*, the *dividend*, and the *divisor*.

26. **Higher Order Thinking** Chris gives 18 pretzels equally to 3 friends. Martha gives 20 pretzels equally to 4 friends. Whose friends got more pretzels? Use equations to justify your answer.

✓ Assessment

27. Which expression can help you divide $12 \div 3$?

   Ⓐ 2×3

   Ⓑ 3×3

   Ⓒ 4×3

   Ⓓ 5×3

28. Mike bought 28 marbles in bags that hold 4 marbles each. How many bags did he buy?

   Ⓐ 7 bags

   Ⓑ 5 bags

   Ⓒ 4 bags

   Ⓓ 3 bags

Name _____

Help Practice Buddy Tools Games

Another Look!

You can think multiplication to find division facts.

Example 1

Darren and Molly have 16 sheets of paper to share. Each will get the same number of sheets of paper. How many sheets will Darren and Molly each get?

 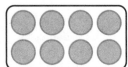

Find 16 ÷ 2.

What You Think	What You Write
2 times what number equals 16? 2 × 8 = 16	16 ÷ 2 = 8 Darren and Molly will each get 8 sheets of paper.

Example 2

Peter has 24 pennies. He puts the pennies into 4 equal rows. How many pennies are in each row?

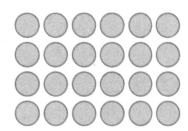

Find 24 ÷ 4.

What You Think	What You Write
4 times what number equals 24? 4 × 6 = 24	24 ÷ 4 = 6 Peter has 6 pennies in each row.

In **1–16**, find each quotient.

1. 14 ÷ 2 = _____   **2.** 35 ÷ 5 = _____   **3.** 15 ÷ 3 = _____   **4.** 32 ÷ 4 = _____

5. 9 ÷ 3 = _____   **6.** 18 ÷ 2 = _____   **7.** 16 ÷ 2 = _____   **8.** 21 ÷ 3 = _____

9. 2)‾12   **10.** 3)‾27   **11.** 5)‾25   **12.** 4)‾20

13. 5)‾30   **14.** 5)‾45   **15.** 2)‾10   **16.** 4)‾28

17. Be Precise You have 18 erasers and use 3 erasers each month. How many months will your erasers last? Identify the quotient, dividend, and divisor.

18. Use Structure Write a fact family using the numbers 5, 6, and 30.

19. Paul drew two different polygons. One shape has 4 sides. The other shape has fewer than 4 sides. What could be the two shapes Paul drew?

20. Model with Math Megan arranges 25 chairs into 5 equal rows. Write and solve an equation to find how many chairs are in each row.

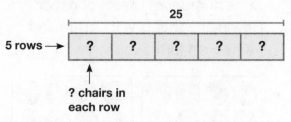

5 rows →

? chairs in each row

21. Higher Order Thinking Carl has 16 rubber balls to share with his 2 brothers and 1 sister. If Carl and his brothers and sister each get the same number of rubber balls, how many rubber balls will each of them get?

Think about what you know and what you need to find.

✓ **Assessment**

22. Franklin says that if he divides 40 by 5, he will get 8. Jeff says that 40 divided by 5 is 9. Who is correct?

Ⓐ Franklin is correct.

Ⓑ Jeff is correct.

Ⓒ Both are correct.

Ⓓ Neither is correct.

23. 16 divided by what number is 4?

Ⓐ 2

Ⓑ 4

Ⓒ 8

Ⓓ 12

Name _____

☆ ☆
Solve & Share

There are 18 children in a ballet class. They are standing in rows of 6 for a dance recital. How many rows of children are there? **Solve the problem any way you choose.**

I can ...
divide by 6 and 7 by thinking about how I multiply with those numbers.

SOL 3.4a; 3.4b

You can use reasoning. How are the numbers in this problem related?

Look Back! **Model with Math** Draw a bar diagram to represent the problem.

Essential Question **How Do You Divide with 6 and 7?**

A

There are 48 dogs entered in a dog show. The judge wants 6 dogs in each group. How many groups will there be?

You can divide to find how many groups of dogs there will be.

B Find 48 ÷ 6.

What You Think	What You Write
What number times 6 is 48? $8 \times 6 = 48$	$48 \div 6 = 8$ There will be 8 groups.

Use a multiplication problem to make sense of a division problem.

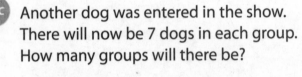

C Another dog was entered in the show. There will now be 7 dogs in each group. How many groups will there be?

Find 49 ÷ 7.

What You Think	What You Write
What number times 7 is 49? $7 \times 7 = 49$	$49 \div 7 = 7$ There will be 7 groups.

Convince Me! **Model with Math** Draw a bar diagram using the numbers 36, 6, and 6. Write the division fact and the related multiplication fact that your bar diagram shows.

Name _____

☆ Guided Practice ☆

Do You Understand?

1. **Reasoning** How can you tell without dividing that 42 ÷ 6 will be greater than 42 ÷ 7?

2. How can 8 × 6 = 48 help you divide 48 by 6?

Do You Know How?

In **3–8**, write the related multiplication fact, and then find each quotient.

3. 36 ÷ 6 = _____   4. 42 ÷ 6 = _____

5. 42 ÷ 7 = _____   6. 18 ÷ 6 = _____

7. $6\overline{)24}$ 8. $6\overline{)30}$

☆ Independent Practice ☆

Leveled Practice In **9–20**, use related multiplication and division facts to find the quotient.

9. 12 ÷ 6 = ?
   What number times 6 is 12?
   6 × ☐ = 12
   12 ÷ 6 = ☐

10. 21 ÷ 3 = ?
    What number times 3 is 21?
    3 × ☐ = 21
    21 ÷ 3 = ☐

11. 30 ÷ 6 = ?
    What number times 6 is 30?
    6 × ☐ = 30
    30 ÷ 6 = ☐

12. $2\overline{)14}$

13. $7\overline{)49}$

14. $6\overline{)60}$

15. $6\overline{)54}$

16. $6\overline{)6}$

17. $7\overline{)28}$

18. Find 49 divided by 7.

19. Divide 54 by 6.

20. Find 35 divided by 7.

Problem Solving

21. A pizza parlor made 88 deep-dish pizzas. It made 10 more thin-crust pizzas than deep-dish pizzas. How many thin-crust pizzas did the parlor make?

22. Higher Order Thinking There are 35 new tires. Each truck will get 6 tires plus 1 tire for a spare. How many trucks will get new tires?

23. Make Sense and Persevere Explain the mistake in the fact family below. Give the correct fact.

$$4 \times 7 = 28 \qquad 7 \times 4 = 28$$
$$7 \div 4 = 28 \qquad 28 \div 7 = 4$$

24. Model with Math Gloria mowed 7 lawns and earned $56. She was paid the same amount for each lawn. How much money did Gloria earn for mowing each lawn? Write an equation to represent this problem.

 Assessment

1 package of 7 red beads

1 package of 5 gold beads

1 package of 6 green beads

25. Andy bought 35 beads. He bought only one color of beads. Which shows the beads he could have bought? Choose all that apply.

☐ 5 packages of red beads

☐ 6 packages of green beads

☐ 7 packages of gold beads

☐ 7 packages of red beads

☐ 7 packages of green beads

26. Cassidy buys only green beads to make a necklace. She buys the exact number of beads that she needs. Which of the following bead amounts could she have bought? Choose all that apply.

☐ 46 beads

☐ 36 beads

☐ 26 beads

☐ 24 beads

☐ 16 beads

Homework & Practice 4-3

Use Multiplication to Divide with 6 and 7

Another Look!

Martha has 63 pine trees to plant on a plot of land. The owner wants 7 rows of trees. How many trees should Martha plant in each row?

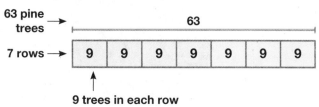

63 pine trees →   63

7 rows → | 9 | 9 | 9 | 9 | 9 | 9 | 9 |

↑
9 trees in each row

Find $63 \div 7$.

You can divide to find how many trees in each row.

What You Think
What number times 7 is 63?
$9 \times 7 = 63$

What You Write
$63 \div 7 = 9$
There will be 9 trees in each row.

In **1** and **2**, draw a bar diagram to find the quotient.

1. Find $56 \div 7$.

2. Find $36 \div 6$.

In **3–13**, find the quotient.

3. $30 \div 6 =$ _____

4. $28 \div 7 =$ _____

5. $42 \div 6 =$ _____

6. $54 \div 6 =$ _____

7. $6\overline{)48}$

8. $7\overline{)56}$

9. $7\overline{)70}$

10. $7\overline{)49}$

11. Divide 60 by 6.

12. Divide 7 by 7.

13. Find 21 divided by 7.

In **14** and **15**, use the picture at the right.

14. Willa is building birdhouses. Each side of the birdhouse will need 9 nails. How many nails does Willa need for each birdhouse?

15. **Number Sense** If Willa uses only 7 nails on each side, how will the total number of nails she uses change?

There are
7 sides on the
birdhouse.

16. **Model with Math** 24 students are going to the zoo. They are going in 4 equal groups. Write and solve an equation to find how many students are in each group.

24

4 groups → | ? | ? | ? | ? |

↑
? students in each group

17. **Higher Order Thinking** There are 42 roses in the garden. Diane picks 7 roses for each bouquet of flowers. How many bouquets can she make? How many more bouquets can Diane make if she uses 6 roses in each bouquet?

✔ **Assessment**

18. Juanita read 48 pages. All chapters are the same length. Choose all the possible pages Juanita could have read.

☐ 6 chapters with 6 pages in each chapter

☐ 6 chapters with 8 pages in each chapter

☐ 8 chapters with 6 pages in each chapter

☐ 8 chapters with 8 pages in each chapter

☐ 8 chapters with 9 pages in each chapter

19. Manny has 28 chapters in a book to read. He reads 7 chapters each week. Choose all of the facts that can help you find how long it will take Manny to read the book.

☐ $28 + 7 = 35$

☐ $4 \times 7 = 28$

☐ $2 \times 2 = 4$

☐ $28 \div 7 = 4$

☐ $7 \times 4 = 28$

Name _____

Solve & Share

An art teacher has 72 crayons. The crayons came in boxes with 8 crayons in each box. How many boxes of crayons were there? *Solve this problem any way you choose.*

You can use reasoning. Which fact family uses the numbers 72 and 8 and could help you solve the problem?

I can ...
divide by 8 and 9 by thinking about how I multiply with those numbers.

SOL 3.4a; 3.4b

Look Back! **Model with Math** Draw a picture you could use to help solve the problem above.

Essential Question **What Multiplication Fact Can You Use?**

A

John has 56 straws. He needs 8 straws to make a spider. How many spiders can John make? Find 56 ÷ 8.

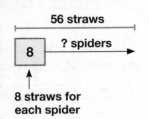

56 straws

8 ? spiders →

↑
8 straws for
each spider

What number times 8 is 56?

To make each spider, you need 8 straws.

7 × 8 = 56

John can make 7 spiders.

B

Luz made 9 animals. She used 54 straws. She used the same number of straws for each animal. How many straws did Luz use for each animal?

Find 54 ÷ 9.

You can divide to find the number of straws Luz used for each animal.

54 straws

| ? | ? | ? | ? | ? | ? | ? | ? | ? |

↑
? straws
for one animal

What You Think	What You Write
9 times what number is 54? 9 × 6 = 54	54 ÷ 9 = 6 Luz used 6 straws for each animal.

Convince Me! **Look for Relationships** Write the related multiplication fact that can be used to complete each division fact.

Division Fact	Related Multiplication Fact
72 ÷ 8 = _____	_____ × _____ = _____
48 ÷ 8 = _____	_____ × _____ = _____
63 ÷ 9 = _____	_____ × _____ = _____

☆ Guided Practice *

Do You Understand?

1. What multiplication fact can you use to find $18 \div 9$?

2. **Construct Arguments** Carla and Jeff each use 72 straws. Carla makes animals with 9 legs. Jeff makes animals with 8 legs. Who makes more animals? Explain.

Do You Know How?

In **3** and **4**, use the multiplication equation to help find each quotient.

3. $16 \div 8 = ?$
   What number times 8 is 16?
   ____ $\times 8 = 16$
   So $16 \div 8 =$ ____.

4. $64 \div 8 = ?$
   What number times 8 is 64?
   ____ $\times 8 = 64$
   So $64 \div 8 =$ ____.

☆ Independent Practice ☆

Leveled Practice In **5–7**, use the multiplication equation to help find each quotient.

5. $24 \div 8 = ?$
   What number times 8 is 24?
   ____ $\times 8 = 24$
   $24 \div 8 =$ ____

6. $45 \div 9 = ?$
   What number times 9 is 45?
   ____ $\times 9 = 45$
   $45 \div 9 =$ ____

7. $27 \div 9 = ?$
   What number times 9 is 27?
   ____ $\times 9 = 27$
   $27 \div 9 =$ ____

In **8–16**, find each quotient.

8. $48 \div 8 =$ ____

9. $72 \div 9 =$ ____

10. $8 \div 8 =$ ____

11. $54 \div 9 =$ ____

12. $72 \div 8 =$ ____

13. $90 \div 9 =$ ____

14. $8\overline{)80}$

15. $8\overline{)32}$

16. $9\overline{)9}$

*For another example, see Set D on page 226.   **Topic 4** | Lesson 4-4   **189**

Problem Solving

17. Model with Math Callie biked 27 miles on Saturday. She biked 9 miles every hour. How many hours did Callie bike? Draw a picture to represent the problem.

18. Math and Science 8 friends decide to test how far 40 paper airplanes with different shapes will fly. If each friend tests the same number of airplanes, how many airplanes does each friend test?

19. Reasoning What other equations are in the same fact family as $18 \div 9 = 2$?

20. Higher Order Thinking Jeremy had 30 gummy bears. He ate 6, then gave the rest to 8 friends. Each friend got the same number of gummy bears. How many did each friend get?

21. What is the value of the 1 in 491? What is the value of the 4? What is the value of the 9?

22. Christopher started with $52. He buys 4 snacks that are $3 each. How much money does Christopher have left?

✔ **Assessment**

23. Mr. Stern spends $36 on tickets. He buys only one type of ticket.

DATA

Playhouse Ticket Prices	
Type of Ticket	**Price of Ticket**
Child	$4
Youth	$8
Adult	$9

Part A

Which types of ticket could he be buying?

Part B

Which type of ticket could Mr. Stern **NOT** be buying? Explain why not.

Homework & Practice 4-4
Use Multiplication to Divide with 8 and 9

Another Look!

Multiplication facts can help you to find division facts when 8 or 9 is the divisor.

There are 32 counters. There are 8 rows of counters. How many counters are in each row?

Think about multiplication facts you know.

Find 32 ÷ 8.

What You Think	What You Write
8 times what number equals 32? $8 \times 4 = 32$	$32 \div 8 = 4$ There are 4 counters in each row.

There are 45 counters. There are 9 equal groups. How many counters are in each group?

Find 45 ÷ 9.

What You Think	What You Write
9 times what number equals 45? $9 \times 5 = 45$	$45 \div 9 = 5$ There are 5 counters in each group.

In **1–3**, use the multiplication equation to help find each quotient.

1. $54 \div 9 = ?$

$9 \times$ _____ $= 54$

So, $54 \div 9 =$ _____.

2. $24 \div 8 = ?$

$8 \times$ _____ $= 24$

So, $24 \div 8 =$ _____.

3. $56 \div 8 = ?$

$8 \times$ _____ $= 56$

So, $56 \div 8 =$ _____.

In **4–12**, find each quotient.

4. $36 \div 9 =$ _____

5. $63 \div 9 =$ _____

6. $80 \div 8 =$ _____

7. $9\overline{)72}$

8. $8\overline{)48}$

9. $9\overline{)81}$

10. $8\overline{)8}$

11. $9\overline{)90}$

12. $9\overline{)27}$

13. Reasoning Maluwa has 9 identical tiles. When she counts the total number of sides on the tiles, she gets 72. Draw a picture of what her tile could look like, and name that shape.

14. Each month Bailey deposits money in her savings account. Over 8 months, she has added $48. If Bailey deposited the same amount every month, how much is one deposit?

15. Construct Arguments The table at the right shows prices for matinee and evening movies. With $63, would you be able to buy more matinee tickets or evening tickets? Explain.

Movie Prices	
Matinee	$7
Evening Movie	$9

16. Model with Math Teri scored 64 points in the first 8 basketball games she played in. She scored the same number of points in each game. Write and solve an equation to find the number of points Teri scored in each game.

17. Higher Order Thinking Adam made 19 paper cranes on Monday and 8 more on Tuesday. He gave all the cranes away to 9 friends so that all the friends had an equal number of cranes. How many cranes did each friend receive? Explain your answer.

✓ **Assessment**

18. Andy earns money washing cars on Monday and Tuesday. He earns $8 for each car that he washes.

Part A

On Monday, Andy earned $40. How can you figure out how many cars Andy washed that day?

Part B

On Tuesday, Andy earned $56. Did he wash more cars on Monday than on Tuesday? Explain how you know without computing.

Name _____

Solve & Share

Prizes for a school fair are packaged with 2 prizes in each package. Which of the prizes listed below can be packaged with none left over? Tell how you decided.

Prize Type	cars	hats	balls	boats	books
Number of Prizes	6	15	23	18	36

I can ...
find and explain patterns for even and odd numbers.

SOL 3.4a, prepares for 5.3b

You can reason. Think about numbers that can be separated into two equal groups.

Look Back! **Look for Relationships** What do you notice about the numbers for the prizes that can be packaged in 2s with none left over? What do you notice about the numbers for the other prizes?

How Can You Explain Multiplication Patterns for Even and Odd Numbers?

A

Nita says that the product of an even number and an odd number is always even. Is she correct?

Even numbers have 0, 2, 4, 6, or 8 in the ones place.

Even numbers are whole numbers that can be divided by 2 with none left over.

Odd numbers are whole numbers that cannot be divided by 2 with none left over.

1	2	3	4	5	6	7	8	9	10
11	12	13	14	15	16	17	18	19	20
21	22	23	24	25	26	27	28	29	30
31	32	33	34	35	36	37	38	39	40

B

Even numbers greater than 0 can be shown as two equal groups.

Think about 2 × 3 and 2 × 5.

2 is an even number.

2 × 3 means 2 equal groups of 3.
2 × 3 = 6

2 × 5 means 2 equal groups of 5.
2 × 5 = 10

There are always 2 equal groups, so the product of 2 times any number is even.

C

You can **generalize**.

All even numbers are multiples of 2.

Think about 4 × 3.

You can think of 4 as 2 groups of 2.

Using properties you can write
4 × 3 = (2 × 2) × 3 as
4 × 3 = 2 × (2 × 3).

So, 4 × 3 = 2 × 6.

There are 2 equal groups of 6. So, the product will be even.

You can write any even number as 2 equal groups. So, Nita is correct: even × odd = even.

Convince Me! **Generalize** Does multiplying by 8 also always result in an even product? Explain.

Name _____

Another Example!

An odd number cannot be divided by 2 with none left over.

Think about 3×5.
3 cannot be divided by 2 with none left over.
5 cannot be divided by 2 with none left over.

$3 \times 5 = 15$

15 is odd.

Both factors are odd. Odd numbers cannot be divided into 2 equal groups with none left over. So: odd $\times$ odd = odd.

☆ Guided Practice

Do You Understand?

1. **Reasoning** If you multiply two even numbers, will the product be even or odd? Explain with an example.

Do You Know How?

Write or circle to complete the sentences. Explain whether the product is even or odd. Then solve.

2. $4 \times 6 = ?$

Can 4 be divided by 2? _____

Can 6 be divided by 2? _____

So 4×6 is $\begin{array}{c} \text{even} \\ \text{odd} \end{array}$.

$4 \times 6 =$ _____

☆ Independent Practice ☆

In **3–5** circle the factors that can be divided by 2.
Then write *even* or *odd* to describe the product and solve the equation.

3. $9 \times 5 = ?$

   9×5 is _____.

   $9 \times 5 =$ _____

4. $8 \times 7 = ?$

   8×7 is _____.

   $8 \times 7 =$ _____

5. $4 \times 8 = ?$

   4×8 is _____.

   $4 \times 8 =$ _____

For another example, see Set E on page 227.   **Topic 4** | Lesson 4-5

Problem Solving

In **6–8**, use the table at the right. Look at the factors. Write *even* or *odd* to describe the product. Then solve.

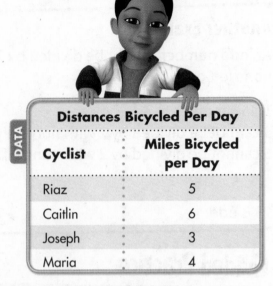

Distances Bicycled Per Day	
Cyclist	**Miles Bicycled per Day**
Riaz	5
Caitlin	6
Joseph	3
Maria	4

DATA

6. How many miles did Joseph bicycle in 6 days?

The product is _____.

7. How many miles did Caitlin bicycle in 8 days?

The product is _____.

8. Make Sense and Persevere
How many miles did Maria and Riaz bicycle in 3 days?

The total is _____.

9. Critique Reasoning Ryan says that the following patterns are true:

even × odd = even
odd × even = odd

Is he correct? Explain.

---

10. Draw a shape with an odd number of sides. Then write the name of the shape.

11. Higher Order Thinking The bakery has 84 muffins. Ms. Craig buys 5 packs of 6 muffins. Did Ms. Craig purchase an even number of muffins or an odd number of muffins? Is the number of muffins left over even or odd? Explain your answer.

✔ **Assessment**

---

12. Choose all of the equations with even products.

- [ ] 7 × 9 = ?
- [ ] 1 × 6 = ?
- [ ] 9 × 2 = ?
- [ ] 7 × 5 = ?
- [ ] 5 × 3 = ?

13. Choose all of the equations that do **NOT** have even products.

- [ ] 5 × 1 = ?
- [ ] 8 × 8 = ?
- [ ] 2 × 7 = ?
- [ ] 6 × 4 = ?
- [ ] 3 × 9 = ?

Name _____

Another Look!

Even numbers have 0, 2, 4, 6, or 8 in the ones place. Odd numbers have 1, 3, 5, 7, or 9 in the ones place.

Think about the numbers 0, 2, 4, 6, and 8. When you divide these numbers by 2, nothing is left over.
These numbers are even.

  0   2   4

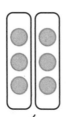 
   6   8

All even numbers can be shown as two equal groups. When multiplying, if one factor is even, the product will be even.

$4 \times 5 = (2 \times 2) \times 5$
$4 \times 5 = 2 \times (2 \times 5)$.

So, $4 \times 5 = 2 \times 10$.
The product is 2 equal groups of 10.

Think about the numbers 1, 3, 5, 7, and 9. When you divide these numbers by 2, there is 1 left over.
These numbers are odd.

   1   3   5

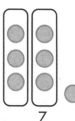 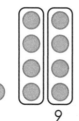
   7   9

You cannot think of odd numbers as 2 equal groups with none left over. When multiplying, if both factors are odd, the product will be odd.

$7 \times 5 = 35$
$1 \times 9 = 9$

In **1–4**, circle the digit in the ones place. Then write *even* or *odd*.

1. 36 is _____.   **2.** 18 is _____.   **3.** 83 is _____.   **4.** 40 is _____.

In **5–7**, circle the factors that can be divided by 2.
Then write *even* or *odd* to describe the product and solve.

5. $7 \times 4 = ?$ **6.** $6 \times 6 = ?$ **7.** $5 \times 9 = ?$

7×4 is _____. 6×6 is _____. 5×9 is _____.

$7 \times 4 = 28$ $6 \times 6 = 36$ $5 \times 9 = 45$

8. Ted bought 1 box of whistles, 1 box of streamers, and 1 box of stickers. How many party favors did he buy in all? Show your work.

Party Favors	
Item	**Number per Box**
Whistles	12
Hats	24
Streamers	48
Stickers	36

9. Critique Reasoning Don says that 9×9 is even. Is he correct? Explain.

10. Generalize Explain why the product of 2 times any number is an even number.

11. Model with Math Sandra has 18 bags of peanuts to hand out to 9 friends. How many bags can she give each friend? Draw a bar diagram to help you solve.

12. Higher Order Thinking Explain whether the product of an **even number × odd number × odd number** is even or odd.

✔ **Assessment**

13. Choose all of the equations with odd products.

☐ $7 \times 3 = ?$
☐ $6 \times 2 = ?$
☐ $1 \times 3 = ?$
☐ $5 \times 7 = ?$
☐ $9 \times 6 = ?$

14. Choose all of the equations with products that are **NOT** odd.

☐ $1 \times 3 = ?$
☐ $3 \times 5 = ?$
☐ $7 \times 1 = ?$
☐ $8 \times 2 = ?$
☐ $6 \times 6 = ?$

Name _____

Solve & Share

Find $5 \div 1$, $0 \div 5$, and $5 \div 5$. Explain how you found each quotient. You can use counters to help.

I can ...
understand the patterns of division with 0 and 1.

SOL 3.4a; 3.4b

Look for relationships. Think about the relationship between division and multiplication. *Show your work in the space below!*

Look Back! **Use Structure** Use your understanding of multiplying by 0 to find $0 \div 7$, $0 \div 4$, and $0 \div 10$. Describe the patterns you see.

Essential Question **How Do You Divide with 1 or 0?**

A

Neil has 3 goldfish. He puts 1 goldfish in each bowl. How many bowls did Neil use? Find 3 ÷ 1.

> Any number divided by 1 is itself.

What number times 1 is 3?

3 × 1 = 3
So, 3 ÷ 1 = 3.

Neil used 3 bowls.

3 put into groups of 1

B **1 as a Quotient**

Find 3 ÷ 3.

> 3 times what number equals 3?

3 × 1 = 3

So, 3 ÷ 3 = 1.

Rule: Any number (except 0) divided by itself is 1.

C **Dividing 0 by a Number**

Find 0 ÷ 3.

> 3 times what number equals 0?

3 × 0 = 0

So, 0 ÷ 3 = 0.

Rule: 0 divided by any number (except 0) is 0.

D **Dividing by 0**

Find 3 ÷ 0.

> 0 times what number equals 3?

There is no such number. So, 3 ÷ 0 can't be done.

Rule: You cannot divide any number by 0.

Convince Me! **Be Precise** Sue wrote 9 invitations.
She put 1 invitation in each mailbox on her street.
How many mailboxes got invitations? Which equation shows the problem and the solution? Explain your thinking.

0 ÷ 9 = 0   9 ÷ 1 = 9

---

200   **Topic 4** | Lesson 4-6

Name _____

☆Guided Practice☆

Do You Understand?

1. How can you tell, without dividing, that 375 ÷ 375 = 1?

2. Describe how you can find 0 ÷ 1.

Do You Know How?

In **3** and **4**, solve the multiplication equation to find each quotient.

3. Find 8 ÷ 8.

   8 × ____ = 8

   So, 8 ÷ 8 = ____.

4. Find 0 ÷ 9.

   9 × ____ = 0

   So, 0 ÷ 9 = ____.

Remember, you cannot divide any number by 0.

Independent Practice ☆

Leveled Practice In **5–7**, solve the multiplication equation to find each quotient.

5. Find 0 ÷ 7.

   7 × ____ = 0

   So, 0 ÷ 7 = ____.

6. Find 4 ÷ 4.

   4 × ____ = 4

   So, 4 ÷ 4 = ____.

7. Find 6 ÷ 1.

   1 × ____ = 6

   So, 6 ÷ 1 = ____.

In **8–18**, find each quotient.

8. 3 ÷ 3 = ____

9. 0 ÷ 8 = ____

10. 5 ÷ 5 = ____

11. 7 ÷ 1 = ____

12. 6)‾6

13. 1)‾5

14. 25)‾25

15. 1)‾13

16. Find 0 divided by 8.

17. Find 9 divided by 1.

18. Find 10 divided by 10.

*For another example, see Set F on page 227.

Problem Solving

In **19–22**, use the picture at the right.

Blue · 3 Miles
White · 5 Miles
Red · 2 Miles
Green · 4 Miles

19. **Reasoning** Addie hiked 3 different trails for a total distance of 11 miles. Which trails did she hike?

20. **Construct Arguments** Marty hikes one of the trails 4 times. In all, he hikes more than 10 miles but less than 16 miles. Which trail does he hike? Explain your answer.

21. **Reasoning** Four teams are tidying the Green trail. They will each tidy an equal distance. How many miles does each team tidy?

22. Fiona hiked on Wednesday and Sunday. Each day she hiked all of the trails. How many miles did Fiona hike?

23. Anthony divided 0 by 6. Jessica used a different equation with even numbers, but got the same answer. What could be an equation Jessica used?

24. **Higher Order Thinking** Yvonne says that $0 \div 21$ and $21 \div 0$ both have a quotient of 0. Is Yvonne correct? Explain.

✓ Assessment

25. Bella had 12 crayons. She used one crayon for each picture she drew. How many pictures did Bella draw? Write the equation that shows the problem and the solution.

26. A group shares 9 stickers equally among 9 friends. Write an equation and solve to show the number of stickers each friend receives.

Name _____

Another Look!

There are special rules to follow when dividing with 0 or 1.

Rule	Example	What You Think	What You Write
When any number is divided by 1, the quotient is that number.	$7 \div 1 = ?$	1 times what number is 7? $1 \times 7 = 7$ So, $7 \div 1 = 7$.	$7 \div 1 = 7$ or $1 \overline{)7}$ with quotient 7
When any number (except 0) is divided by itself, the quotient is 1.	$8 \div 8 = ?$	8 times what number is 8? $8 \times 1 = 8$ So, $8 \div 8 = 1$.	$8 \div 8 = 1$ or $8 \overline{)8}$ with quotient 1
When zero is divided by a number (except 0), the quotient is 0.	$0 \div 5 = ?$	5 times what number is 0? $5 \times 0 = 0$ So, $0 \div 5 = 0$.	$0 \div 5 = 0$ or $5 \overline{)0}$ with quotient 0
You cannot divide a number by 0.	$9 \div 0 = ?$	0 times what number is 9? There is no number that works, so $9 \div 0$ cannot be done.	$9 \div 0$ cannot be done

In **1–8**, write the quotient.

1. $5 \div 1 =$ _____

2. $9 \div 9 =$ _____

3. $0 \div 8 =$ _____

4. $6 \div 6 =$ _____

5. $4 \div 1 =$ _____

6. $1 \overline{)7}$

7. $8 \overline{)8}$

8. $7 \overline{)0}$

In **9** and **10**, use the sign at the right.

9. **Be Precise** Aiden has $20. He spends all of his money on ride tickets. How many ride tickets does Aiden buy?

RIDE TICKETS $1 each

10. Tanji spends $8 on ride tickets and gives an equal number of tickets to 8 friends. How many tickets does each friend get?

11. Explain which of these has the greatest quotient. 6 ÷ 6, 5 ÷ 1, 0 ÷ 3, 8 ÷ 8

12. **Number Sense** Place the numbers 0, 1, 3, and 3 in the blanks so that the number sentence is true.

_____ ÷ _____ > _____ ÷ _____

13. The number of students at Netherwood Elementary School is an odd number between 280 and 300. List all the possible numbers of students there could be.

14. **Higher Order Thinking** Write and solve a story problem that goes with 6 ÷ 6.

 Assessment

15. Lamaar shares 6 pencils equally with himself and 5 friends. Write an equation and solve to show the number of pencils each friend receives.

16. There are 7 ducklings. They sleep in 1 large nest. Write and solve an equation that shows how many ducklings sleep in the nest.

Name _____

Solve & Share

A tour bus to a national park holds 56 people. There are 7 tour guides at the park to lead equal groups of people from the bus. How many people are in each tour group? Each person in a group pays a $2 entrance fee to a tour guide. How much does 1 tour guide collect? *Solve these problems any way you choose.*

I can ...
use patterns and related facts to solve multiplication and division problems.

SOL 3.4a; 3.4b

Model with math. Use any strategies you know to solve. *Show your work in the space below!*

Look Back! **Reasoning** How can 7 × ? = 56 help you find 56 ÷ 7 = ?

Essential Question ## What Fact Can You Use?

A

Sabrina has 28 quarters in her bank. She wants to trade all of them for one-dollar bills. How many one-dollar bills will Sabrina get?

There are 4 quarters in one dollar.

B ## One Way

How many groups of 4 are in 28?

You can draw a bar diagram to help solve the problem.

28 quarters

| 4 | ? |

4 quarters in one dollar

$28 \div 4 = 7$

There are 7 groups of 4 in 28. Sabrina can trade 28 quarters for 7 one-dollar bills.

C ## Another Way

What number times 4 equals 28?

You can use multiplication facts to help solve the problem.

$? \times 4 = 28$

$7 \times 4 = 28$

Sabrina can trade 28 quarters for 7 one-dollar bills.

Convince Me! Construct Arguments
Why can both $28 \div 7 = ?$ and $? \times 7 = 28$ be used to solve the problem above?

Practice Buddy Tools Assessment

☆ Guided Practice *

Do You Understand?

1. Look back at the problem on page 206. Suppose Sabrina put 8 more quarters in her bank. How many one-dollar bills can she trade for the quarters in her bank now?

2. Number Sense Calvin solves the equation $49 \div 7 = \square$. How does this help him complete the equation $7 \times \square = 49$?

Do You Know How?

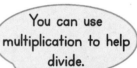

In **3–7**, use a multiplication or a division fact to complete the equations.

3. $45 \div 5 = $ ____

$5 \times $ ____ $= 45$

4. $3 \times $ ____ $= 21$

$21 \div 3 = $ ____

5. $6 \times $ ____ $= 30$

$30 \div 6 = $ ____

6. $24 \div 6 = $ ____

$6 \times $ ____ $= 24$

7. $6 \times $ ____ $= 12$

$12 \div 6 = $ ____

You can use multiplication to help divide.

☆ Independent Practice ☆

Leveled Practice In **8–10**, use fact families to complete the equations.

8. $42 \div 7 = $ ____

$7 \times $ ____ $= 42$

9. $6 \times $ ____ $= 18$

$18 \div 6 = $ ____

10. $9 \times $ ____ $= 72$

$72 \div 9 = $ ____

In **11–19**, find the product or quotient.

11. $36 \div 4 = $ ____

12. ____ $= 8 \times 8$

13. $15 \div 3 = $ ____

14. $6\overline{)36}$

15. $9\overline{)63}$

16. $9\overline{)54}$

17. Multiply 8 times 5. ____

18. Divide 18 by 9. ____

19. Divide 27 by 3. ____

Problem Solving

In **20–22**, use the recipe at the right.

20. **Model with Math** How many cups of peanuts would Eric need to make 5 batches of trail mix?
Write an equation to show your thinking.

Eric's Trail Mix
Makes one batch
Ingredients:
4 cups peanuts
3 cups raisins
2 cups walnuts

21. **Reasoning** How many batches of trail mix can Eric make with 16 cups of peanuts, 15 cups of raisins, and 8 cups of walnuts?

22. **Reasoning** Eric spends $30 to buy the ingredients for 5 batches of trail mix. Find the cost of the ingredients Eric needs for one batch. How much would Eric need for 2 batches?

23. Emilia drew lines to divide these squares into parts. What is a way to name these parts?

24. **Higher Order Thinking** Wilson is thinking of 2 one-digit numbers. When he multiplies them, the product is 27. What is the sum of the two numbers? Explain your answer.

✓ **Assessment**

25. Erin made 32 rings. She gives rings to 8 of her friends. Which two equations could be used to find the number of rings each friend gets?

Ⓐ $32 \div 1 = 32$ and $1 \times 32 = 32$

Ⓑ $8 + 32 = 40$ and $40 - 32 = 8$

Ⓒ $8 \div 2 = 4$ and $4 \times 2 = 8$

Ⓓ $32 \div 8 = 4$ and $8 \times 4 = 32$

26. A tray has 10 plants and costs $7. Jed has $42. How many trays can he buy? How many plants?

Ⓐ 4 trays; 40 plants

Ⓑ 5 trays; 50 plants

Ⓒ 6 trays; 60 plants

Ⓓ 7 trays; 70 plants

Another Look!

A class is making popcorn for a carnival. 10 students each made 3 cups of popcorn. The students put the popcorn in bags that hold 6 cups each. Find the total number of cups. Then find how many bags of popcorn the students made.

You can solve the problems using multiplication and division.

Multiplication	Division
How many total cups of popcorn did they make?	How many groups of 6 are in 30?

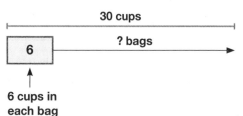

Multiplication

How many total cups of popcorn did they make?

$$10 \times 3 = ?$$

Number of students — Cups each student made — Total number of cups

$$10 \times 3 = 30$$

The students made a total of 30 cups of popcorn.

Division

How many groups of 6 are in 30?

30 cups
6 | ? bags

6 cups in each bag

Divide the total number of cups by the number of cups in each bag:

$$30 \div 6 = 5 \longleftarrow \text{Number of bags}$$

The students made 5 bags of popcorn.

In **1–9**, use multiplication and division to complete the fact family.

1. $21 \div 3 =$ _____

$3 \times$ _____ $= 21$

$21 \div$ _____ $= 3$

_____ $\times 3 = 21$

2. $36 \div 6 =$ _____

$6 \times$ _____ $= 36$

3. $18 \div 9 =$ _____

$9 \times$ _____ $= 18$

$18 \div$ _____ $= 9$

_____ $\times 9 = 18$

4. $54 \div 9 =$ _____

$9 \times$ _____ $= 54$

$54 \div$ _____ $= 9$

_____ $\times 9 = 54$

5. $18 \div 6 =$ _____

$6 \times$ _____ $= 18$

$18 \div$ _____ $= 6$

_____ $\times 6 = 18$

6. $40 \div 5 =$ _____

$5 \times$ _____ $= 40$

$40 \div$ _____ $= 5$

_____ $\times 5 = 40$

7. $14 \div 2 =$ _____

$2 \times$ _____ $= 14$

$14 \div$ _____ $= 2$

_____ $\times 2 = 14$

8. $25 \div 5 =$ _____

$5 \times$ _____ $= 25$

9. $32 \div 4 =$ _____

$4 \times$ _____ $= 32$

$32 \div$ _____ $= 4$

_____ $\times 4 = 32$

In **10** and **11**, use the chart at the right.

10. **Make Sense and Persevere** Ellis asks some classmates to name their favorite color. He records the information in this chart. How many classmates answered the question?

11. Suppose Ellis asked more classmates to name their favorite color. If 4 more classmates named blue this time, how many classmates named blue in all?

Favorite Color	
Red	//// //// /
Blue	//// ////
Green	//// //// ///

12. At a music recital, there are 30 chairs. They are set up in 6 equal rows. Find the number of columns.

13. A music teacher has 4 drum kits. Each kit has 2 drumsticks. Each drumstick costs $3. How many drumsticks does she have? What is the cost to replace them all?

14. **Higher Order Thinking** A chessboard has 8 rows of squares with 8 squares in each row. Two players each put 16 chess pieces on the board, with each piece on its own square. How many squares are empty now? Explain your answer.

 Assessment

15. Tolen has 18 dog treats. He gives the same number of treats to 6 dogs at the animal shelter. Which two equations could be used to find the number of treats each dog gets?

   Ⓐ $18 + 6 = 24$ and $24 - 6 = 18$

   Ⓑ $18 \div 6 = 3$ and $6 \times 3 = 18$

   Ⓒ $18 \div 18 = 1$ and $1 \times 18 = 18$

   Ⓓ $6 \div 3 = 2$ and $6 \div 2 = 3$

16. A pack of pens costs $3. Lynn spent $12 on pens. Each pack has 5 pens. How many packs did she buy? How many pens does she have?

   Ⓐ 3 packs; 15 pens

   Ⓑ 4 packs; 20 pens

   Ⓒ 5 packs; 20 pens

   Ⓓ 6 packs; 30 pens

Name _____

☆ ☆
Solve & Share

24 ÷ 4 is on the right side of the balance
below. What can you write on the left side that will
have the same value as the right side? Write 5 different
multiplication or division problems that will keep the
pans balanced.

I can ...
use multiplication and division
facts to find unknown values in
an equation.

🔺 **SOL** 3.4b; 3.4a, 3.17

You can generalize to
find 5 problems that keep the pans
balanced. What part of the problem is
repeated? *Show your work in
the space below!*

Look Back! **Construct Arguments** Would the problem
$1 \times 3 \times 2 \times 1$ keep the pans above balanced? Explain.

Essential Question **How Do Multiplication and Division Equations Work?**

A The pan balance shows $35 \div 7 = 5$.

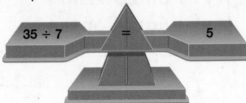

$35 \div 7$ = 5

> Remember, in an equation, the symbol = means "is equal to." It tells you the value on the left is the same as the value on the right.

B These are other examples of equations.

$16 \div 4$ = 2×2

$$16 \div 4 = 2 \times 2$$

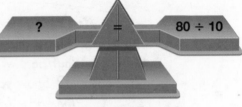

$?$ = $80 \div 10$

$$? = 80 \div 10$$
$$8 = 80 \div 10$$

C Frank has some tubes of tennis balls. Each tube has 4 tennis balls. Frank has 8 tennis balls in all. How many tubes of tennis balls does he have?

> You can write an equation to represent the problem.

$$8 = ? \times 4$$

D Some equations have symbols to represent unknowns. The ? represents the number of tubes of tennis balls Frank has.

$$8 = ? \times 4$$

A multiplication fact that matches this is $8 = 2 \times 4$.

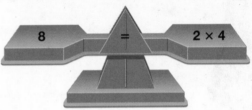

8 = 2×4

The value of ? is 2. So, $? = 2$.

Convince Me! **Reasoning** Use the value of ? in the multiplication equation to write and solve two division equations.

$7 \times ? = 42$ $42 \div ? = \boxed{}$ $42 \div \boxed{} = ?$

Name _____

☆ Guided Practice ☆

Do You Understand?

1. Write an equation that represents the following problem:
   Walt makes some sandwiches. Each sandwich uses 2 slices of bread. He uses 16 slices of bread. How many sandwiches does Walt make? Use ? to represent the number of sandwiches.

Do You Know How?

In **2–5**, find the value for ? that makes the equation true.

2. $9 \times ? = 27$

3. $8 = 40 \div ?$

4. $32 = ? \times 8$

5. $? \div 3 = 6$

☆ Independent Practice ☆

In **6–9**, find the value for ? that makes the equation true.

6. $? \div 4 = 7$

7. $25 = 5 \times ?$

8. $72 = ? \times 9$

9. $4 = 20 \div ?$

In **10–13**, write and solve an equation that represents the problem.

10. Sasha has 21 dimes. She puts them in stacks with the same number of dimes in each stack. In all, she has 3 stacks. How many dimes are in each stack? Use ? to represent the number of dimes in each stack.

11. There were some sheep in a barnyard. Each sheep had 4 legs. There were 24 legs in the barnyard. How many sheep were in the barnyard? Use ? to represent the number of sheep in the barnyard.

12. A football team scored 48 points. The team only scored on touchdowns, worth 6 points each. How many touchdowns did the team score? Use ? to represent the number of touchdowns.

13. There were 6 ladybugs on a leaf. Each ladybug had the same number of spots. There were 36 spots. How many spots were on each ladybug? Use ? to represent the number of spots on each ladybug.

Problem Solving

14. A baker is decorating 5 cakes. He uses 9 chocolate flowers to decorate each cake. How many flowers will he need to decorate all the cakes?

Write an equation to represent the problem, using ? to represent the missing information. Then solve your equation.

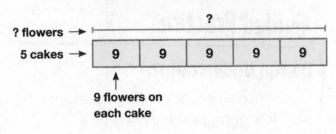

? flowers →
5 cakes →

| 9 | 9 | 9 | 9 | 9 |

9 flowers on each cake

---

15. Be Precise Hal asked 20 people to name their favorite sport. The tally chart shows how many people answered *baseball* and *swimming*. All the other people he asked said their favorite sport was football. Complete the tally chart to show how many people chose football.

Favorite Sport	
Baseball	///
Swimming	ᵗᴴᴸ ////
Football	

---

16. Higher Order Thinking A building has more than 2 stories but fewer than 10 stories. Each story of the building has the same number of windows. The building has 25 windows. Complete the sentence. Then explain how you found your answer.

The building has _____ stories, and each story has _____ windows.

---

17. Claire has 18 strawberries. She wants to give an equal number of strawberries to her 6 friends. How many strawberries should she give to each friend?

Claire says she can write a division equation and a multiplication equation using ? for the unknown value.

Part A

Write and solve a division equation to find the number of strawberries each friend should receive.

Part B

Write and solve a multiplication equation to find the number of strawberries each friend should receive.

Another Look!

Remember that an equation uses an equal sign (=) to show the value on the left is the same as the value on the right.

Some equations have unknown numbers. These numbers may be represented by question marks.

$$10 = 40 \div ?$$

This equation means 10 is equal to 40 divided by some number. You know $40 \div 4 = 10$, so $? = 4$.

You can write equations to represent math problems.

1. Frankie has some nickels. His nickels have a value of 45 cents. How many nickels does Frankie have? Complete the table to write an equation to represent the problem.

Use a ? to represent the number of nickels Frankie has.	?
Nickels are worth 5 cents. You can multiply the number of nickels by 5 to find the total value of the coins.	? × _____
Frankie's nickels are worth 45 cents.	? × 5 = _____

To solve the problem, find the value of ? that makes the equation true: _____ × 5 = 45. Frankie has _____ nickels.

In **2–5**, find the value of ? that makes the equation true.

2. $? \div 5 = 6$

3. $36 = 6 \times ?$

4. $14 = ? \times 2$

5. $81 \div ? = 9$

In **6** and **7**, write and solve an equation for each problem.

6. A restaurant has 24 chairs and some tables. There are 4 chairs at each table. How many tables are there?

7. Suzanne buys 6 paint sets. Each set contains the same number of brushes. She buys 18 brushes. How many brushes are in each paint set?

8. Carlos has a string that is 24 inches long. He wants to divide it into 3 equal parts. Write an equation to find how long each part will be. Use ? to represent the unknown number. Then solve your equation.

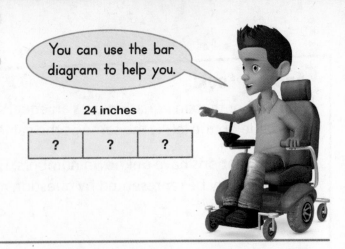

You can use the bar diagram to help you.

24 inches

| ? | ? | ? |

9. **Higher Order Thinking** Hector spent from Sunday to the following Saturday at the beach. Each day he found an equal number of shells. If Hector found 63 shells, how many shells did he find on Tuesday? Explain your answer.

10. **Make Sense and Persevere** Ella solves the equation $32 \div ? = 8$. She says the value of ? is 4. Does Ella's answer make sense? Explain.

11. **Reasoning** Do points A and B represent the same number, or do they represent different numbers? Explain.

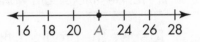

16 18 20 A 24 26 28

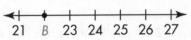

21 B 23 24 25 26 27

12. Bruce arranges 35 pencils on his desk into equal groups of 7. How many groups of pencils are on Bruce's desk?

Bruce says he can write a multiplication equation and a division equation using ? for the unknown value.

Part A

Write and solve a multiplication equation to find the number of groups of pencils.

Part B

Write and solve a division equation to find the number of groups of pencils.

Name _____

☆ ☆
Solve & Share

Two girls and two boys went to the festival. The total cost of their tickets was $20. Each child paid the same amount for a ticket. What was the cost of each ticket? *Solve this problem any way you choose.*

Problem Solving

Lesson 4-9

Make Sense and Persevere

I can ...
make sense of problems and keep working if I get stuck.

 SOL Prepares for 5.4

Thinking Habits

Be a good thinker!
These questions can help you.

- What do I need to find?

- What do I know?

- What's my plan for solving the problem?

- What else can I try if I get stuck?

- How can I check that my solution makes sense?

Look Back! **Make Sense and Persevere** How did you find how many children bought tickets? How did this plan help you solve the problem?

Essential Question
How Can You Make Sense of a Problem and Persevere in Solving It?

A

A store has boxes of video games for sale. In each box, the video games are in 2 rows with 3 video games in each row.

Each video game costs the same amount.

What is the cost of each video game?

To **persevere** you can check your strategy and your work.

What do I need to do?

I need to make sense of the problem before I can solve it. If I get stuck, I need to persevere until I find the cost of each video game.

$54   VIDEO GAMES

B
How can I make sense of and solve this problem?

I can

- identify what is known from the problem.

- look for and answer hidden questions in the problem.

- make a plan to solve the problem.

- check to make sure my work and answer make sense.

C

Here's my thinking...

I know a box costs $54.
There are 2 rows of 3 games in a box.

First, I need to find the total number of games in a box.

I will **multiply** the number of rows by the number of games in each row.

$2 \times 3 = 6$ 6 games are in a box.

Then I will **divide** the cost of a box by the total number of games to find the cost of each game.

$54 \div 6 = $9   Each game costs $9.

Convince Me! **Make Sense and Persevere** How can you check to make sure the work and answer given above make sense?

⭐ Guided Practice *

Make Sense and Persevere

Twelve friends went camping. All except 4 of them went on a hike. The hikers carried 32 water bottles. Each hiker carried the same number of water bottles. How many water bottles did each hiker carry?

1. Tell what you know. Then explain what you need to find first to solve the problem.

If you are stuck, you can persevere. Think: Does the strategy I am using make sense?

2. Tell which operations you will use. Then solve the problem.

Independent Practice ⭐

Make Sense and Persevere

Four students went bowling. They bowled 2 games each. The cost was $5 per game. How much money did the students spend on bowling? Explain.

3. Tell what you know. Then explain what you need to find first to solve the problem.

4. Tell which operations you will use. Then solve the problem.

5. How can you check that your work is correct?

County Fair

The table shows costs at the county fair. Mr. Casey spent $24 on admission tickets for himself and the children in his group. How many children are in his group? Answer Exercises 6–9 to solve the problem.

DATA	County Fair		
Kind of Ticket		**Adult**	**Child**
Admission		$8	$4
Boat Rides		$2	$1

6. **Make Sense and Persevere** What do you know? What are you asked to find?

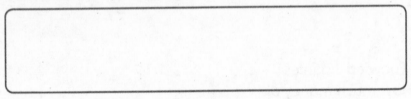

7. **Be Precise** Why is it important to know which kind of tickets Mr. Casey bought?

8. **Critique Reasoning** Dan says there are 6 children in Mr. Casey's group because $24 ÷ $4 = 6. Does Dan's reasoning make sense? Explain.

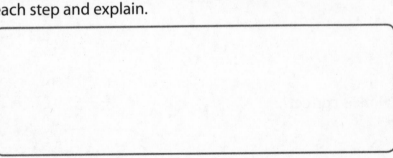

As you make sense of a problem, you can think about whether you have solved a problem like it before.

9. **Use Reasoning** Solve the problem. Write an equation for each step and explain.

Homework & Practice 4-9
Make Sense and Persevere

Another Look!

To solve a two-step problem, you may need to find the answer to a hidden question first. Then you can use that answer to solve the problem.

Sandra has $22 to spend on school supplies. She buys a backpack and spends the rest of her money on notebooks. How many notebooks does Sandra buy?

Tell how to make sense of the problem.

- I can identify what is known from the problem.

- I can look for and answer any hidden questions.

- I can make a plan to solve the problem.

Tell which operations you will use. Then solve the problem.

I will use subtraction and division.

A backpack costs $10. $22 − $10 = $12.

Sandra now has $12 to spend on notebooks. Each notebook costs $3.

$12 ÷ $3 = 4. Sandra can buy 4 notebooks.

> If you are stuck, you can persevere by trying a different strategy.

Make Sense and Persevere

There are 5 players on a basketball team. In a game, 4 players scored 6 points each. The team scored a total of 34 points. How many points did the other player score?

1. Tell how to make sense of the problem.

2. Tell the quantities you know. Then explain what you need to find first to solve the problem.

3. Tell which operations you will use. Then solve the problem.

Zoo Field Trip

The third-grade class at Thomas Elementary School goes on a trip to the zoo. Students are in groups of 6. Mr. Bell's and Ms. Ridley's classes are combined.

Classroom Teacher	Number of Students
Mr. Bell	18
Ms. Ridley	24
Ms. Holtz	17

4. **Make Sense and Persevere** The teachers want to know how many groups will be in the combined classes. What do you need to know to solve?

5. **Use Reasoning** Find the number of groups in the combined classes. Write an equation for each step. Explain how the quantities are related.

Make sense of the information in the problem by identifying the quantities. Think: Is there a hidden question I need to solve first?

6. **Critique Reasoning** Ryan solved the problem above. He says there are 6 groups of 6 students and 1 group of **5** students. What did Ryan do wrong?

7. **Generalize** If you wanted to find the number of groups of 6 students if Mr. Bell's and Ms. Holtz's classes were combined, could you use the same strategy you used in **5**? Explain.

☆ ☆
Find a Match
☆

Work with a partner. Point to a clue.

Read the clue.

Look below the clues to find a match. Write the clue letter in the box next to the match.

Find a match for every clue.

I can ...
add and subtract within 100.

Clues

A Is equal to 59 + 19

E Is equal to 72 − 24

I Is equal to 39 − 17

B Is equal to 13 − 6

F Is equal to 35 + 15

J Is equal to 29 + 44

C Is equal to 48 + 38

G Is equal to 100 − 19

K Is equal to 56 − 47

D Is equal to 57 − 18

H Is equal to 65 + 33

L Is equal to 16 + 35

☐ 73 − 64	☐ 24 + 26	☐ 19 − 12
☐ 37 + 14	☐ 56 − 8	☐ 52 + 26
☐ 47 + 39	☐ 65 − 43	☐ 72 + 26
☐ 48 + 25	☐ 92 − 11	☐ 66 − 27

Vocabulary Review

Glossary

Word List

- dividend
- divisor
- even number
- fact family
- odd number
- product
- quotient

Understand Vocabulary

1. Circle the *divisor* in each equation.

$30 \div 6 = 5$ $24 \div 3 = 8$ $14 \div 2 = 7$ $45 \div 5 = 9$

2. Circle the *dividend* in each equation.

$63 \div 7 = 9$ $4 \div 1 = 4$ $0 \div 5 = 0$ $8 \div 4 = 2$

3. Circle the *quotient* in each equation.

$21 \div 3 = 7$ $54 \div 9 = 6$ $15 \div 5 = 3$ $16 \div 8 = 2$

4. Circle the *even numbers*.

19   24   45   68

5. Circle the *odd numbers*.

21   36   13   47

6. Look at the equations below. Write **Y** if the *product* is 6. Write **N** if the *product* is NOT 6.

$4 \times 6 = 24$ _____ $2 \times 3 = 6$ _____ $6 = 3 \times 2$ _____

7. Look at the equations below. Write **Y** if the group shows a *fact family*. Write **N** if the group does NOT show a *fact family*.

$3 \times 9 = 27$ _____ $12 \div 6 = 2$ _____ $56 \div 8 = 7$ _____

$27 \div 9 = 3$ $2 \times 6 = 12$ $56 \div 7 = 8$

$9 \times 3 = 27$ $12 \div 3 = 4$ $8 \times 7 = 56$

$27 \div 3 = 9$ $6 \times 2 = 12$ $7 \times 8 = 56$

Use Vocabulary in Writing

8. Explain how to find the fact family for 2, 4, and 8. Use at least 2 terms from the Word List in your explanation.

224   **Topic 4** | Vocabulary Review

Name _____

Set A pages 169–174

Monica has 24 chairs to arrange equally in 3 rows. You can use an array to find the number of chairs in each row.

This array shows the relationship between multiplication and division.

3 rows of 8   24 in 3 equal rows
  3 × 8 = 24   24 ÷ 3 = 8

A fact family shows how multiplication and division are related.

Fact family for 3, 8, and 24:

  3 × 8 = 24   24 ÷ 3 = 8
  8 × 3 = 24   24 ÷ 8 = 3

Reteaching

Remember that a fact family is a group of related facts using the same numbers.

In **1–4**, write the other three facts in the fact family.

1. 3 × 7 = 21

2. 5 × 3 = 15

3. 8 × 6 = 48

4. 4 × 5 = 20

Set B pages 175–180

You can use multiplication to solve division problems.

Hector has 24 oranges. He puts 4 oranges in each basket. How many baskets does Hector need for all the oranges?

What number times 4 is 24?
  6 × 4 = 24
  24 ÷ 4 = 6
Hector needs 6 baskets.

Remember that you can use multiplication to help divide.

In **1** and **2**, solve each problem. Write the multiplication fact and division fact you use to solve the problem.

1. Sally has 32 flowers. She puts 8 flowers in each vase. How many vases does Sally need for all the flowers?

2. Jon has 18 peaches. He uses 3 peaches to make a peach tart. How many peach tarts does Jon make if he uses all the peaches?

Brent is putting 42 books on shelves. He puts 6 books on each shelf. How many shelves will Brent need?

What number times 6 is 42?

$7 \times 6 = 42$
$42 \div 6 = 7$

Brent will need 7 shelves.

How many shelves would Brent need if he put 7 books on each shelf?

What number times 7 is 42?

$6 \times 7 = 42$
$42 \div 7 = 6$

Brent would need 6 shelves.

Remember that you can use multiplication facts for 6s and 7s to help you divide by 6s and 7s.

In **1–3**, solve each problem. Write the multiplication fact and division fact you use to solve the problem.

1. There are 36 runners entered in a marathon. They run in groups of 6. How many groups are there?

2. Lani has 35 bird stickers. There are 5 stickers on each sheet. How many sheets of bird stickers does she have?

3. Jake has 18 remote-controlled boats for 6 friends to share equally. How many boats will each friend get?

Lu made 9 bracelets. He used 72 beads. He used the same number of beads for each bracelet. How many beads did Lu use for each bracelet?

72 beads

?	?	?	?	?	?	?	?	?

↑
? beads for
one bracelet

9 times what number is 72?

$9 \times 8 = 72$
$72 \div 9 = 8$

Lu used 8 beads for each bracelet.

Remember that you can use multiplication facts for 8s and 9s to help you divide by 8s and 9s.

In **1–5**, write the related multiplication fact that can be used to complete each division fact. Then find the quotient.

1. $54 \div 9 =$ _____   _____ $\times$ _____ $=$ _____

2. $64 \div 8 =$ _____   _____ $\times$ _____ $=$ _____

3. $36 \div 9 =$ _____   _____ $\times$ _____ $=$ _____

4. $56 \div 8 =$ _____   _____ $\times$ _____ $=$ _____

5. $72 \div 8 =$ _____   _____ $\times$ _____ $=$ _____

Name _____

Set E pages 193–198 _____

A whole number is **even** if it can be divided by 2 with none left over.

A whole number is **odd** if it cannot be divided by 2 with none left over.

Which product is even? Which is odd?

$3 \times 7 =$ odd $5 \times 8 =$ even
        product   product

All even numbers can be thought of as 2 equal groups.

When at least one factor is even, the product is even.

Remember that you can think about dividing by 2 to tell whether a number is even or odd.

In **1–3**, circle the factors that can be divided by 2. Then circle even or odd to describe the product.

1. $6 \times 4 = ?$ **even**   **odd**

2. $9 \times 1 = ?$ **even**   **odd**

3. $8 \times 7 = ?$ **even**   **odd**

Set F pages 199–204 _____

Find $5 \div 1$. Five groups of 1.

What number times 1 is 5?

$5 \times 1 = 5$ So, $5 \div 1 = 5$.

Find $0 \div 8$.

$8 \times 0 = 0$ So, $0 \div 8 = 0$.

Remember that any number divided by 1 is itself. Any number (except 0) divided by itself is 1. Zero divided by any number (except 0) is 0.

In **1–3**, use division to solve.

1. $0 \div 16 =$ _____

2. $10 \div 10 =$ _____

3. Leroy had 4 oranges. He gave one orange to each of his 4 friends. How many oranges did each friend get? Write an equation to show your answer.

Set G pages 205–210 _____

How many groups of 4 are in 24?

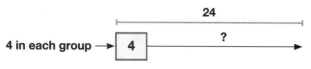

You can use multiplication facts.

$? \times 4 = 24$ $6 \times 4 = 24$

There are 6 groups of 4 in 24.

Remember that you can use bar diagrams or multiplication facts to help solve a division problem.

In **1** and **2**, use related multiplication and division facts to solve.

1. $21 \div 7 =$ _____   2. $5 \times$ _____ $= 45$

   $7 \times$ _____ $= 21$ $45 \div 5 =$ _____

Set H pages 211–216

Look at the equation $3 \times ? = 15$.

The ? stands for an unknown number.

Read the equation like this:

"Multiply 3 by a number. The result is 15."
Then find the value of the unknown.
Think of a fact that uses the numbers in
the equation.

$3 \times 5 = 15$, so the unknown number is 5.

Remember that you can use multiplication
and division facts to find the value of
an unknown.

In **1–6**, find the value of the unknown.

1. $? \div 2 = 6$ 2. $7 \times ? = 42$

3. $20 = 4 \times ?$ 4. $9 = ? \div 3$

5. $16 \div ? = 2$ 6. $24 \div ? = 6$

Set I pages 217–222

Think about these questions to help you
**make sense of problems and persevere in
solving them.**

Thinking Habits

- What do I need to find?
- What do I know?
- What's my plan for solving
  the problem?
- What else can I try if I get stuck?
- How can I check that my
  solution makes sense?

Remember to use the information in each
step to solve the problem.

In **1** and **2**, answer to solve a two-step
problem.

Fourteen friends went to the county fair. All
except 6 of them bought a hot dog. Each
hot dog costs $3. How much did the friends
spend on hot dogs?

1. Tell what you know. Then explain what
   you need to find first to solve the problem.

2. Tell which operations you will use.
   Then solve the problem.

Name _____

1. Heather wrote a multiplication fact and a division fact for the array below. Choose all of the equations that show a fact Heather could have written.

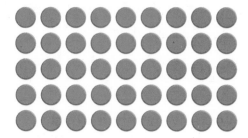

☐ $5 \times 9 = 45$

☐ $5 \times 5 = 25$

☐ $45 \div 5 = 9$

☐ $10 \times 5 = 50$

☐ $50 \div 5 = 10$

2. Colin wrote three equations. What number will make all of Colin's equations true?

$14 = ? \times 2$

$56 \div 8 = ?$

$? \times ? = 49$

3. Betsy and Carlos are sharing a bowl of cherries. They divide the cherries into 2 equal groups. There is 1 cherry left in the bowl. Which number below could be the number of cherries they started with in the bowl?

Ⓐ 37

Ⓑ 48

Ⓒ 24

Ⓓ 18

4. Mrs. Raspa wrote four number sentences. For questions 4a–4d, choose *Yes* or *No* to tell if the equations are true.

4a. $0 \div 8 = 0$ ○ Yes ○ No

4b. $5 \div 1 = 5$ ○ Yes ○ No

4c. $7 \div 7 = 1$ ○ Yes ○ No

4d. $4 \div 0 = 0$ ○ Yes ○ No

5. Mr. Vargas is buying used computer equipment. He buys 3 keyboards and 4 mice. He spends $42. If the items are all the same price, how much does each item cost?

6. Look at the counters below.

Part A

Draw lines around the counters to show $12 \div 6$.

Part B

Find a different multiplication fact where the product is 12. Explain how you can group the counters for the fact.

7. Draw lines to connect equal expressions.

$8 \div 8$		$9 \div 1$
0×7		$0 \div 3$
$24 \div 4$		1×6
$27 \div 3$		$7 \div 7$

8. Peter wrote five numbers. Which of Peter's numbers can be divided into 7 equal groups with 0 left over? Choose all that apply.

☐ 56

☐ 52

☐ 42

☐ 35

☐ 27

9. Crystal drew this bar diagram to model a division problem. Write a multiplication equation Crystal could use to help solve the problem.

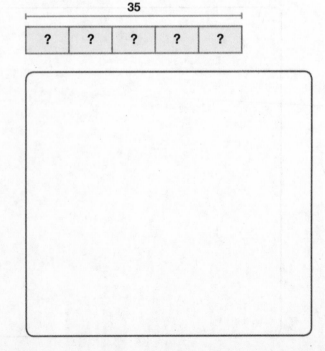

10. Xavier divided his action figure collection into 2 equal groups. There was 1 figure left over. Xavier said he has an even number of action figures. Is he correct? Explain.

11. Mandy is trying to find $6 \div 0$. She says the answer is 6 because $6 \times 0 = 6$. Is Mandy correct? Explain.

12. Luz has 36 pencil toppers. She sorts her pencil toppers into 6 groups. How many are in each group?

13. Kira has 63 sheets of recycled paper. She gives the same number of sheets to each of 9 friends. How many sheets does Kira give to each friend?
Use the bar diagram to help.

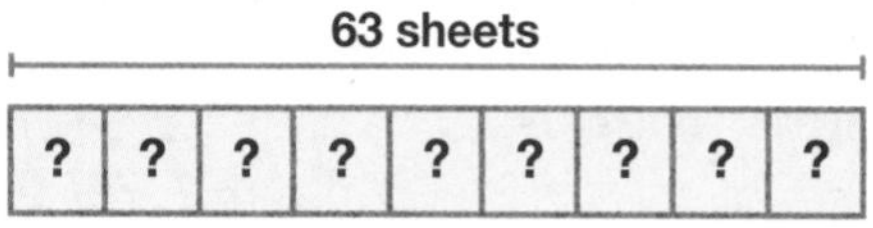

63 sheets

?	?	?	?	?	?	?	?	?

Ⓐ 6

Ⓑ 7

Ⓒ 8

Ⓓ 9

14. Write the fact family for 1, 4, and 4.

15. Gennaro wrote 4 true statements about even and odd products. Choose all of the true statements.

- ☐ An even number times an even number has an even product.
- ☐ An even number times an odd number has an even product.
- ☐ An odd number times an odd number has an odd product.
- ☐ An odd number times an even number has an odd product.
- ☐ If one factor is even, then the product is even.

16. Which number makes both equations true?

$$18 \div 9 = ? \qquad\qquad ? \times 9 = 18$$

17. Anna drew the bar diagram below. Which equations could be used to represent the problem shown in Anna's bar diagram? Choose all that apply.

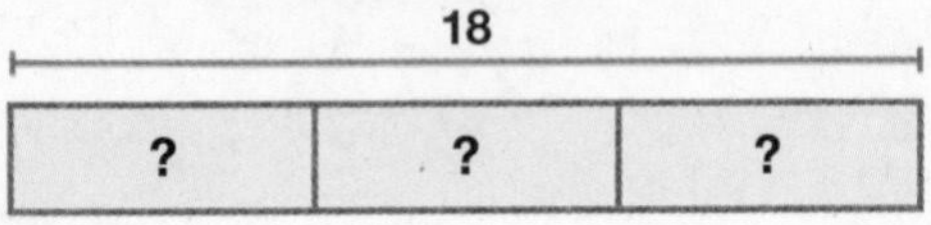

18		
?	?	?

- ☐ $18 \times 3 = ?$
- ☐ $3 \div ? = 18$
- ☐ $18 \div 3 = ?$
- ☐ $? \div 3 = 18$
- ☐ $3 \times ? = 18$

18. A balloon artist wants to make 6 different kinds of balloon animals. She needs 4 balloons to make each animal. If the balloons come in packs of 8, how many packs will she need to buy?

Part A

Explain what you need to find first to solve the problem.

Part B

Tell which operations you will use. Then solve the problem.

Name _____

Relay Race

Mrs. Achilles teaches Physical Education. She is planning a relay race for her school. Each grade forms teams. Each student is on 1 team.

Race Details
• The field is 40 feet wide.
• Each runner gets 1 lane.
• Mrs. Achilles has 7 trophies.

Use the **Race Details** list to answer the following question.

1. Each lane must be an equal width. Mrs. Achilles wants to use the entire width of the field for lanes. How wide will each lane be if Mrs. Achilles sets out 10 lanes? 5 lanes? Use multiplication facts to help you.

Grade Size	
Grade	**Students**
K	24
1	28
2	27
3	24
4	30
5	25
6	32

Use the **Race Details** list and **Grade Size** table to answer the following question.

2. Each grade gets an equal number of trophies. How many trophies does each grade get? Write a division fact and a related multiplication fact you can use to solve this problem.

Use the **Grade Size** table to answer the following question.

3. Mrs. Achilles wonders whether each team can have exactly 2 people. Explain whether or not this is possible.

Use the **Grade Size** and **Grade 3 Possible Team Sizes** tables to answer the following question. Use related multiplication facts to help you.

4. Mrs. Achilles puts more than 2 students on each team. Each team must have an equal number of students.

Grade 3 Possible Team Sizes	
Number of Students on Team	Number of Teams
4	
3	

Part A

Complete the table to show the 4 different ways Mrs. Achilles can form teams for Grade 3.

Part B

Mrs. Achilles tries to make teams of 4 students each. She can do this for some grades but not for all. Which grades can have equal teams of 4?

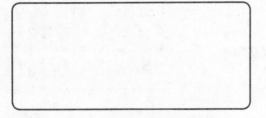

Fill out the table for the grades written above. Use the same-size team for each of these grades.

Team Size			
Grade	Number of Students	Number of Students on Team	Number of Teams
K	24		
1	28		
2	27		
3	24		
4	30		
5	25		
6	32		

Part C

In the **Team Size** table, write the grades that you did **NOT** fill out in Part B.

Choose team sizes that let everyone in these grades participate. Use different sizes for each of these grades. Fill out the rest of the table.

TOPIC 5

Fluently Multiply and Divide within 100

Essential Question: What are strategies to solve multiplication and division facts?

> The weather changes from day to day and from place to place.

> Scientists look for patterns in the weather. These patterns help them understand different climates!

> I predict there will be math in the forecast! Here is a project on weather information and basic facts.

Math and Science Project: Weather Information

Do Research Use the Internet or other sources to find the weather in different places on Earth. Find the weather at different times of day. Write down the temperature for each place. Also write down any conditions such as rain or snow.

Journal: Write a Report Include what you found. Also in your report:

• Tell how many places you checked.

• Tell how many times you checked the weather in one day.

• Write a multiplication or division story using your information. Then find an answer for your story.

Review What You Know

A-Z Vocabulary

Choose the best term from the box.
Write it on the blank.

• dividend   • product
• divisor   • quotient
• factor

1. The answer to a division problem is the _____.

2. A _____ is the answer to a multiplication problem.

3. The _____ is the number in a division problem that is divided into equal groups.

4. Multiply a factor by a _____ to solve a multiplication problem.

Multiplication

5. 6 × 2 = ____

6. 5 × 1 = ____

7. 4 × 10 = ____

8. 7 × 5 = ____

9. 4 × 4 = ____

10. 9 × 3 = ____

11. The oranges in a store are in 7 rows and 8 columns. How many oranges are there?

Division

12. 60 ÷ 6 = ____

13. 25 ÷ 5 = ____

14. 12 ÷ 3 = ____

15. 30 ÷ 6 = ____

16. 14 ÷ 2 = ____

17. 9 ÷ 3 = ____

18. If 28 stamps are arranged into an array with 4 columns, how many rows are there?

The Distributive Property

19. Explain how to use 2s facts to find 4 × 9.

Name _____

Max found $6 \times 8 = 48$. He noticed that $(6 \times 4) + (6 \times 4)$ also equals 48.

Use the multiplication table to find two other facts whose sum is 48.

Use facts that have a 6 or 8 as a factor. What pattern do you see?

I can ...
use structure and properties to explain patterns for multiplication facts.

 SOL 3.4a; 3.4b

×	0	1	2	3	4	5	6	7	8
0	0	0	0	0	0	0	0	0	0
1	0	1	2	3	4	5	6	7	8
2	0	2	4	6	8	10	12	14	16
3	0	3	6	9	12	15	18	21	24
4	0	4	8	12	16	20	24	28	32
5	0	5	10	15	20	25	30	35	40
6	0	6	12	18	24	30	36	42	48
7	0	7	14	21	28	35	42	49	56
8	0	8	16	24	32	40	48	56	64

← These are factors

↑ These are factors   ↑ These are products

You can look for relationships. Use the multiplication table to make connections.

Look Back! **Generalize** How can a multiplication table help you find products that equal 48 when added together?

How Can You Explain Patterns in the Multiplication Chart?

A

Yolanda noticed that 4 × 6 is double 2 × 6. How can you explain this?

You can use a multiplication table to find patterns.

×	1	2	3	4	5	6	7	8	9
1	1	2	3	4	5	6	7	8	9
2	2	4	6	8	10	12	14	16	18
3	3	6	9	12	15	18	21	24	27
4	4	8	12	16	20	24	28	32	36
5	5	10	15	20	25	30	35	40	45
6	6	12	18	24	30	36	42	48	54

B

4 is the double of 2.

So, 4 × 6 is double 2 × 6.

You can use the Distributive Property of Multiplication to explain.

$4 \times 6 = (2 \times 6) + (2 \times 6)$
$4 \times 6 = \quad 12 \quad + \quad 12$
$4 \times 6 = \qquad 24$

C

Look at the highlighted rows.

The product of any number multiplied by 4 will be double the product of that number multiplied by 2.

×	1	2	3	4	5	6	7	8	9
1	1	2	3	4	5	6	7	8	9
2	2	4	6	8	10	12	14	16	18
3	3	6	9	12	15	18	21	24	27
4	4	8	12	16	20	24	28	32	36
5	5	10	15	20	25	30	35	40	45
6	6	12	18	24	30	36	42	48	54

Properties can be used to understand a pattern and check if it is always true.

Convince Me! **Look for Relationships** Look at the highlighted rows of numbers multiplied by 2 or 4. What pattern do you see across the rows?

238   **Topic 5** | Lesson 5-1

Name _____

☆ Guided Practice *

Do You Understand?

1. How are 3×7 and 6×7 related?

2. **Construct Arguments** In the table on page 238, is the pattern that Yolanda found also true for factors that are multiplied by 3 and 6? Explain.

Do You Know How?

In **3** and **4**, use the multiplication table shown below.

3. What pattern do you see in the columns and rows that have 0 as a factor?

4. Explain why this pattern is true.

☆ Independent Practice ☆

In **5–8**, use the multiplication table shown at the right.

5. Look at the shaded products. What pattern do you see?

6. Write the equation for each shaded product.

×	0	1	2	3	4	5	6	7	8	9
0	0	0	0	0	0	0	0	0	0	0
1	0	1	2	3	4	5	6	7	8	9
2	0	2	4	6	8	10	12	14	16	18
3	0	3	6	9	12	15	18	21	24	27
4	0	4	8	12	16	20	24	28	32	36
5	0	5	10	15	20	25	30	35	40	45
6	0	6	12	18	24	30	36	42	48	54
7	0	7	14	21	28	35	42	49	56	63
8	0	8	16	24	32	40	48	56	64	72
9	0	9	18	27	36	45	54	63	72	81

7. Look at the factors you wrote. Explain why the pattern for the products is true.

A multiplication table helps you see lots of products at the same time.

8. Shade a line in the multiplication table to show how this pattern is true for other products.

*For another example, see Set A on page 287.

Topic 5 | Lesson 5-1 239

Problem Solving

9. **Math and Science** How many arms do 9 starfish have if...

   a each starfish has 6 arms? Write a multiplication equation to solve.

   b each starfish has 7 arms? Write a multiplication equation to solve.

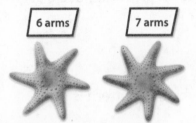

6 arms   7 arms

10. **Higher Order Thinking** Karen found a pattern on the multiplication table. What pattern did she find? Explain why it is true.

×	1	2	3	4	5	6	7	8
3	3	6	9	12	15	18	21	24
6	6	12	18	24	30	36	42	48

11. **Number Sense** The distance from Tom's house to his brother's house is 200 miles. Tom drove 38 miles in the morning and 57 miles in the afternoon. Estimate how much farther Tom has to drive to reach his brother's house.

12. **Look for Relationships** Describe a pattern you see in the 9s row of the multiplication table.

✓ Assessment

13. Shade the 1s row and the 1s column on the multiplication table below.

×	0	1	2	3	4	5	6	7	8	9
0	0	0	0	0	0	0	0	0	0	0
1	0	1	2	3	4	5	6	7	8	9
2	0	2	4	6	8	10	12	14	16	18
3	0	3	6	9	12	15	18	21	24	27
4	0	4	8	12	16	20	24	28	32	36
5	0	5	10	15	20	25	30	35	40	45
6	0	6	12	18	24	30	36	42	48	54
7	0	7	14	21	28	35	42	49	56	63
8	0	8	16	24	32	40	48	56	64	72
9	0	9	18	27	36	45	54	63	72	81

Part A

What pattern do you see?

Part B

Explain why the pattern is true.

Help Practice Tools Games
     Buddy

Another Look!

You can find and explain multiplication patterns.

×	1	2	3	4	5	6	7	8	9
6	6	12	18	24	30	36	42	48	54

You can see that the products of 6 increase by 6 as the other factor increases.

So, you know that 4 groups of 6 is the same as 3 groups of 6 plus 1 more group of 6. You can use the Distributive Property to explain.

$$4 \times 6 = (3 + 1) \times 6$$
$$= (3 \times 6) + (1 \times 6)$$
$$= 18 + 6$$
$$= 24$$

To find patterns, look for things that repeat or are the same.

In **1–5**, use the multiplication table shown at the right.

1. Find the column which has products that are the sum of the yellow shaded numbers in each row. Shade this column.

2. What pattern do you see?

×	1	2	3	4	5	6	7	8	9
1	1	2	3	4	5	6	7	8	9
2	2	4	6	8	10	12	14	16	18
3	3	6	9	12	15	18	21	24	27
4	4	8	12	16	20	24	28	32	36
5	5	10	15	20	25	30	35	40	45
6	6	12	18	24	30	36	42	48	54
7	7	14	21	28	35	42	49	56	63
8	8	16	24	32	40	48	56	64	72
9	9	18	27	36	45	54	63	72	81

3. Explain why this pattern is true.

4. Find a similar pattern using different products. Shade the columns on the multiplication table.

5. Explain how you choose which columns to shade.

6. **Make Sense and Persevere** Teresa bought 3 boxes of chocolate. Each box has 9 pieces of chocolate inside. Teresa gave away 15 pieces of chocolate. How many pieces of chocolate does she have left?

7. **A-Z Vocabulary** Margie divided 24 by 3. The *dividend* is _____. The *quotient* is _____.

8. **Look for Relationships** Look at the multiples of 2. What pattern do you see?

×	1	2	3	4	5	6	7	8	9	10
2	2	4	6	8	10	12	14	16	18	20

9. **Construct Arguments** Look at the table on page 241. Does this table have more even products or more odd products? Explain.

10. **Higher Order Thinking** Chris needs to find the product of two numbers. One of the numbers is 11. The answer also needs to be 11. How will Chris solve this problem? Explain.

✔ **Assessment**

11. Look at the shaded products in the multiplication table shown below.

×	1	2	3	4	5	6	7	8	9
1	1	2	3	4	5	6	7	8	9
2	2	4	6	8	10	12	14	16	18
3	3	6	9	12	15	18	21	24	27
4	4	8	12	16	20	24	28	32	36
5	5	10	15	20	25	30	35	40	45
6	6	12	18	24	30	36	42	48	54
7	7	14	21	28	35	42	49	56	63
8	8	16	24	32	40	48	56	64	72
9	9	18	27	36	45	54	63	72	81

Part A

What pattern do you notice?

Part B

Explain why the pattern works.

Name _____

Solve

Solve & Share

Find 18 ÷ 3 any way you choose.

You can use reasoning. Think about how the quantities in the problem are related.

I can ...
use reasoning and the relationship between multiplication and division to find basic facts.

 SOL 3.4a; 3.4b

×	0	1	2	3	4	5	6	7	8	9	10
0	0	0	0	0	0	0	0	0	0	0	0
1	0	1	2	3	4	5	6	7	8	9	10
2	0	2	4	6	8	10	12	14	16	18	20
3	0	3	6	9	12	15	18	21	24	27	30
4	0	4	8	12	16	20	24	28	32	36	40
5	0	5	10	15	20	25	30	35	40	45	50
6	0	6	12	18	24	30	36	42	48	54	60
7	0	7	14	21	28	35	42	49	56	63	70
8	0	8	16	24	32	40	48	56	64	72	80
9	0	9	18	27	36	45	54	63	72	81	90
10	0	10	20	30	40	50	60	70	80	90	100

Look Back! **Make Sense and Persevere** Describe another way you can find 18 ÷ 3.

How Can You Use a Multiplication Table to Solve Division Problems?

Write a missing factor equation and then use the multiplication table to find 15 ÷ 3.

A

×	0	1	2	3	4	5
0	0	0	0	0	0	0
1	0	1	2	3	4	5
2	0	2	4	6	8	10
3	0	3	6	9	12	15

Look at where rows and columns intersect in a multiplication table to solve a division problem.

$15 \div 3 = ?$

$3 \times ? = 15$

3 times what number equals 15?

B Step 1

You know one factor is 3. Find the 3 in the first column of this multiplication table.

×	0	1	2	3	4	5
0	0	0	0	0	0	0
1	0	1	2	3	4	5
2	0	2	4	6	8	10
3	0	3	6	9	12	15

C Step 2

You know the product is 15. Follow the row the 3 is in until you come to 15.

×	0	1	2	3	4	5
0	0	0	0	0	0	0
1	0	1	2	3	4	5
2	0	2	4	6	8	10
3	0	3	6	9	12	15

D Step 3

Look straight up to the top of that column of the table. The number on the top of the column is 5. The missing factor is 5.

$3 \times 5 = 15$ $15 \div 3 = 5$

×	0	1	2	3	4	5
0	0	0	0	0	0	0
1	0	1	2	3	4	5
2	0	2	4	6	8	10
3	0	3	6	9	12	15

Convince Me! **Reasoning** Write a missing factor equation and use the multiplication table above to solve each division problem.

$6 \div 3 = ?$ $12 \div 3 = ?$ $9 \div 3 = ?$

 Guided Practice *

Practice Buddy   Tools   Assessment

Do You Understand?

1. Where in a multiplication table do you find the two factors in a multiplication problem?

2. How can you rephrase 35 ÷ 7 so you can solve using a multiplication table?

3. Explain how to use a multiplication table to solve a missing factor equation.

Do You Know How?

In **4–11**, find the value that makes the equation correct. Use a multiplication table to help.

4. 24 ÷ 6 = _____

6 × _____ = 24

5. 63 ÷ 9 = _____

9 × _____ = 63

6. 25 ÷ 5 = _____

5 × _____ = 25

7. 42 ÷ 7 = _____

7 × _____ = 42

8. 45 ÷ 5 = _____

5 × _____ = 45

9. 15 ÷ 3 = _____

3 × _____ = 15

10. 12 ÷ 6 = _____

6 × _____ = 12

11. 40 ÷ 5 = _____

5 × _____ = 40

Independent Practice *

Leveled Practice In **12–23**, find the value that makes the equations correct. Use a multiplication table to help.

12. 45 ÷ 9 = _____

9 × _____ = 45

13. 21 ÷ 3 = _____

3 × _____ = 21

14. 36 ÷ 6 = _____

6 × _____ = 36

15. 32 ÷ 4 = _____

4 × _____ = 32

16. 20 ÷ 5 = _____

5 × _____ = 20

17. 21 ÷ 7 = _____

7 × _____ = 21

18. 18 ÷ 9 = _____

19. 35 ÷ 5 = _____

20. 56 ÷ 8 = _____

21. 28 ÷ 4 = _____

22. 14 ÷ 7 = _____

23. 40 ÷ 5 = _____

*For another example, see Set B on page 287.

Topic 5 | Lesson 5-2

Problem Solving

24. Some members of the Bird Club used a tally chart to record how many different birds they each saw one day. Fill in the blanks below to make the sentence correct. _____

saw 4 more birds than _____.

25. Complete the chart to show that Mr. Molina saw 5 fewer birds than Mr. Dobbs and Miss Simmons combined.

Number of Different Birds Seen	
Ms. Chester	ⳁⳁⳁ ‖
Mr. Dobbs	‖‖
Miss Simmons	ⳁⳁⳁ ⳁⳁⳁ ‖
Mr. Molina	_____

---

26. Critique Reasoning Bill used a multiplication table to find the value of 12 ÷ 6. His answer was 3. Do you agree? Why or why not?

27. Algebra Find the value that makes the equation correct.

$$30 \div ? = 5$$
$$? = \underline{\hspace{1cm}}$$

---

28. Higher Order Thinking Brit uses a multiplication table to multiply 2 different factors. She notices that the product is in the same column as the number 35. What is one of the factors in Brit's multiplication problem? Explain your answer.

Think about what you know and what you need to find.

 Assessment

29. Which of the following is the missing number in 21 ÷ ☐ = 7?

Ⓐ 1

Ⓑ 3

Ⓒ 7

Ⓓ 9

×	0	1	2	3	4	5	6	7
0	0	0	0	0	0	0	0	0
1	0	1	2	3	4	5	6	7
2	0	2	4	6	8	10	12	14
3	0	3	6	9	12	15	18	21
4	0	4	8	12	16	20	24	28
5	0	5	10	15	20	25	30	35
6	0	6	12	18	24	30	36	42
7	0	7	14	21	28	35	42	49
8	0	8	16	24	32	40	48	56
9	0	9	18	27	36	45	54	63

Name _____

Another Look!

Find 24 ÷ 6.

You can think of a division problem as a multiplication fact that is missing a factor.

A. Find the factor you already know in the first column of the table. In **6 × ? = 24**, that factor is **6**.

B. Go across the row until you get to the product. In **6 × ? = 24**, the product is **24**.

C. Go straight to the top of that column. The number at the top of the column is 4. So, the missing factor is 4. 24 ÷ 6 = 4

missing factor

×	0	1	2	3	4
0	0	0	0	0	0
1	0	1	2	3	4
2	0	2	4	6	8
3	0	3	6	9	12
4	0	4	8	12	16
5	0	5	10	15	20
6	0	6	12	18	**24**

factor   product

In **1–15**, find the value that makes the equations correct. Use a multiplication table to help.

1. 8 ÷ 2 = _____

  2 × _____ = 8

2. 12 ÷ 4 = _____

  4 × _____ = 12

3. 16 ÷ 8 = _____

  8 × _____ = 16

4. 18 ÷ 6 = _____

  6 × _____ = 18

5. 27 ÷ 3 = _____

  3 × _____ = 27

6. 36 ÷ 4 = _____

  4 × _____ = 36

7. 48 ÷ 8 = _____

  8 × _____ = 48

8. 35 ÷ 7 = _____

  7 × _____ = 35

9. 30 ÷ 5 = _____

  5 × _____ = 30

10. 24 ÷ 8 = _____

11. 49 ÷ 7 = _____

12. 54 ÷ 6 = _____

13. 14 ÷ 2 = _____

14. 24 ÷ 3 = _____

15. 32 ÷ 8 = _____

16. Christina has these two tiles. Draw a new shape she can create with both tiles. Then name the shape and how many sides the new shape has.

17. There are 3 drawers in Mona's dresser. Each drawer has the same number of shirts. Mona has 27 shirts. How many shirts are in each drawer?

18. Model with Math A pet shop has 24 fish in 8 tanks with an equal number of fish in each tank. Which multiplication fact can you use to find how many fish are in each tank?

19. Algebra Ethan went to the farmers market and bought 57 pieces of fruit. He bought 15 pears, 22 apples, and some peaches. Write an equation to help solve the problem. Use an unknown to represent the number of peaches.

20. Math and Science 18 solar panels are put on a house. The solar panels are arranged in 3 equal columns. How many rows of solar panels are on this house? Explain how to use a multiplication table to solve the problem.

21. Higher Order Thinking Mike says he can use a multiplication table to find $5 \div 0$. Is he correct? Explain.

✓ Assessment

22. Using the multiplication table, Jared found the missing number in the equation $63 \div 7 = \boxed{}$. What is the missing number?

    Ⓐ 70

    Ⓑ 56

    Ⓒ 9

    Ⓓ 8

×	0	1	2	3	4	5	6	7	8	9
0	0	0	0	0	0	0	0	0	0	0
1	0	1	2	3	4	5	6	7	8	9
2	0	2	4	6	8	10	12	14	16	18
3	0	3	6	9	12	15	18	21	24	27
4	0	4	8	12	16	20	24	28	32	36
5	0	5	10	15	20	25	30	35	40	45
6	0	6	12	18	24	30	36	42	48	54
7	0	7	14	21	28	35	42	49	56	63
8	0	8	16	24	32	40	48	56	64	72
9	0	9	18	27	36	45	54	63	72	81

Name _____

Solve

Solve & Share

What are the missing factors and products in the table below? Fill in each missing number. **Solve these problems any way you choose.**

I can ...
use reasoning and the relationship between multiplication and division to find basic facts.

SOL 3.4a; 3.4b

You can use reasoning about factors, products, and quotients to find basic facts.

×	7	3	☐	8	4	☐
5		15		40	20	
6	42		36			
2		6				18
☐				56		
4		12			16	
☐					4	

Look Back! **Construct Arguments** How did you find the missing factors in the top row and the first column? Explain using an example.

How Can You Find Multiplication and Division Basic Facts?

A

The table at the right has some missing factors and some missing products. What are the missing numbers in the table?

You can use strategies and reasoning to find missing factors.

×	8	5	
2			
9	72		36
		20	
7			

← These are factors

These are factors

These are products

B

Think multiplication or division to find missing factors.

$36 \div 9 = 4$, so $9 \times 4 = 36$

×	8	5	4
2			
9	72		36
4		20	
7			

$4 \times 5 = 20$
$20 \div 5 = 4$

C

Complete the table.

$2 \times 8 = 16$	$2 \times 5 = 10$	$2 \times 4 = 8$
$4 \times 8 = 32$	$9 \times 5 = 45$	$4 \times 4 = 16$
$7 \times 8 = 56$	$7 \times 5 = 35$	$7 \times 4 = 28$

×	8	5	4
2	16	10	8
9	72	45	36
4	32	20	16
7	56	35	28

Convince Me! **Be Precise** Suppose one factor is 0 and the product is 0. What is the other factor? Tell how you decided.

☆ Guided Practice ☆

Do You Understand?

1. Reasoning When completing a multiplication table, how do you know when you can use division?

Do You Know How?

In **2**, find the missing factors and products.

2.

×	4	□	9
3			
□			54
8		56	
□			81

☆ Independent Practice ☆

In **3–6**, find the missing factors and products.

3.

×	□	5	□
2			
□		25	
6	48		42
□		45	

4.

×	□	□	9
4	12		
□			54
3		6	
□			72

5.

×	□	□	9
2	12		
□			54
3	18	9	
□			45

6.

×	□	7	4
8	16		32
□		42	
□	10		

*For another example, see Set C on page 288.

Problem Solving

7. **Higher Order Thinking** Which missing number do you find first in the multiplication table at the right: A, B, or C? Explain why.

×	B
5	35
A	14
1	C

8. **Algebra** What value of ? makes the equation $5 \times ? = 30$ true?

9. What division equations are in the same fact family as 7×4?

10. **Model with Math** Last week Toby practiced the drums 2 hours each day for 5 days. This week he practiced the drums for 12 hours in all. How many hours did he practice both weeks? Write equations to represent this problem.

11. Jordan is inviting 8 friends to his party. He wants to give each friend 2 maracas and have 2 for himself. Maracas come in boxes of 6. How many boxes does he need to buy?

12. **Number Sense** Fill in the blanks to make the equation correct.

_____ $\times 7 =$ _____ $\times 9$

Think about how multiplication facts are related.

Assessment

13. Complete the sentences below.

Robin has 24 eggs. She wants to put them in 3 baskets with the same number of eggs in each basket. How many eggs should she put in each basket?

$24 \div 3 = \boxed{}$ because $3 \times \boxed{} = 24$.

Robin should put $\boxed{}$ eggs in each basket.

14. Find the missing factors and products.

×	☐	4
2		
☐	63	36

Name _____

Another Look!

What are the missing factors and products in the table?

×	5	9	6
3	15	27	18
2	10	18	12
1	5	9	6
8	40	72	48

$12 \div 2 = 6$

$3 \times 5 = 15, \ 3 \times 6 = 18$

$2 \times 9 = 18$

$9 \div 9 = 1, \ 1 \times 5 = 5, \ 1 \times 6 = 6$

$8 \times 5 = 40, \ 8 \times 9 = 72, \ 8 \times 6 = 48$

Use the given numbers to find the missing numbers. Think multiplication or division.

In **1–4**, find the missing factors and products.

1.

×	□	6	□
0			
□		30	
9	45		63
□		42	

2.

×	□	□	9
2	8		
□			81
3		9	
□			72

3.

×	□	□	6
5	10		
□			48
2	4	0	
□			36

4.

×	3	□	□
4			20
□	18		
1		8	
□			35

5. **Model with Math** Leah has the flowers shown. She wants to put them in 4 vases with the same number in each vase. How many flowers does she need to put in each vase? Tell how you know.

6. **Higher Order Thinking** Bradley is trying to find a missing factor. A product of that factor has a 3 in the ones digit. Is the missing factor even or odd? Explain.

A chart can help you find relationships.

7. **Construct Arguments** George has 7 boxes of 5 pencils. Julio has 3 boxes of 8 pencils. One of the boys arranges all his pencils equally into 2 groups. Was this George or Julio? How many are in each group? Explain.

8. **Critique Reasoning** Ned says he cannot use division to solve a missing factor problem because factors are part of multiplication equations. Do you agree? Explain why or why not.

✓ **Assessment**

9. Complete the sentences below.

Jamal took 72 pictures with his digital camera while on vacation. He wants to put them in 8 folders on his computer. How many pictures should he put in each folder?

$72 \div 8 = \boxed{}$ because $8 \times \boxed{} = 72$.

Jamal should put $\boxed{}$ pictures in each folder.

10. Find the missing factors and products.

×	☐	5
3		
☐	48	40

Name _____

Solve & Share

Alfredo has 3 bags of oranges in each hand. Each bag contains 5 oranges. How many oranges does Alfredo have? *Solve this problem any way you choose.*

You can use structure. Look for relationships when using counters, drawings, skip counting, arrays, or known facts to help solve the problem. *Show your work in the space below!*

I can ...
use different strategies to solve multiplication problems.

SOL 3.4a; 3.4b

Look Back! **Make Sense and Persevere** How do strategies such as skip counting, using known facts, and making arrays help you solve multiplication facts?

A

A scientist on a boat is studying hammerhead sharks. The length of 6 hammerhead sharks lined up nose to tail without gaps is equal to the length of the boat. How long is the boat?

An adult hammerhead shark is 5 yards long.

Drawings, skip counting, tools, and properties of operations are strategies you can use to multiply equal groups.

B **One Way**

Use a bar diagram to find 6×5.

6×5 means 6 groups of 5. Skip count by 5s.

?					
5	5	5	5	5	5

5 10 15 20 25 30

So, $6 \times 5 = 30$.

The boat is 30 yards long.

C **Another Way**

Use counters and properties to find 6×5.

The Distributive Property says you can break the problem into smaller parts. Use 2s facts and 4s facts to help.

$2 \times 5 = 10$

$4 \times 5 = 20$

Then add the two products: $10 + 20 = 30$. The boat is 30 yards long.

Convince Me! **Use Structure** How can knowing the product of 5×6 help you solve 6×5?

Name _____

☆ Guided Practice *

Do You Understand?

1. What two known facts can you use to find 3 × 5?

2. How could knowing 7 × 5 = 35 help you find 9 × 5?

Do You Know How?

In **3–8**, multiply.

3. 6 × 4 = _____   **4.** 4 × 5 = _____

5. 9 × 3 = _____   **6.** 3 × 2 = _____

7.   1
  × 4

8.   9
  × 8

☆ Independent Practice ☆

In **9–25**, use strategies to find the product.

9. 5 × 5 = _____   **10.** 9 × 2 = _____   **11.** 5 × 9 = _____

12. 8 × 7 = _____   **13.** 3 × 6 = _____   **14.** 8 × 4 = _____

15.   10
  × 4

16.   7
  × 6

17.   6
  × 5

18.   2
  × 8

19.   9
  × 0

20.   10
  × 6

21.   4
  × 9

22.   9
  × 7

23. What is 4 × 6? _____   **24.** What is 5 × 8? _____   **25.** What is 10 × 1? _____

*For another example, see Set D on page 288.   **Topic 5** | Lesson 5-4   **257**

Problem Solving

In **26** and **27**, use the pictures below.

26. Make Sense and Persevere
Mr. Marks is studying 3 blacktip sharks and 4 tiger sharks. What is the total length of the 7 sharks? Show your strategy.

27. Critique Reasoning Kent says the total length of 4 blacktip sharks can be found using addition. Is he correct? Explain your thinking.

Blacktip Shark
2 yards long

Tiger Shark
4 yards long

28. Cecilia buys two gifts. One gift costs $57. Cecilia spends $82 in all. How much money does the second gift cost?

$82

$57	$?

29. Higher Order Thinking Show how you can use known facts to find 11×9. Explain how you chose the known facts.

 Assessment

30. Hal counted the number of fish in 3 fish tanks. There were 7 fish in each. How many fish were in the 3 fish tanks?

   Ⓐ 21 fish

   Ⓑ 24 fish

   Ⓒ 27 fish

   Ⓓ 37 fish

31. Bob is starting a sports card collection. He buys 5 packages of sports cards with 9 cards in each package. Which of the following does **NOT** show a way to find how many cards Bob has?

   Ⓐ $9 + 9 + 9 + 9 + 9$

   Ⓑ $(4 \times 5) + (5 \times 5) = 20 + 25$

   Ⓒ $5 \times 9 = 45$, so $9 \times 5 = 45$

   Ⓓ $9 \times (2 \times 5)$

Help   Practice   Tools   Games
       Buddy

Homework & Practice 5-4
Use Strategies to Multiply

Another Look!
Find 6×4.

You can use different strategies to find 6×4.

One Way
Draw a bar diagram and use skip counting.

6×4 means 6 groups of 4.

Each section of the bar diagram is 1 group of 4.

?

4	4	4	4	4	4
4	8	12	16	20	24

Skip count by 4s to solve.

So, $6 \times 4 = 24$.

Another Way
Using the Distributive Property is another way to solve this problem. Use 3s facts to help.

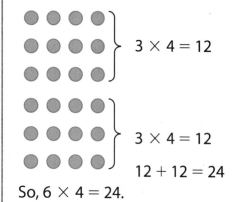

$3 \times 4 = 12$

$3 \times 4 = 12$

$12 + 12 = 24$

So, $6 \times 4 = 24$.

In **1** and **2**, show two different ways to find the product.

1. $3 \times 5 = ?$

?

5	5	
5	10	

$3 \times 5 = $ _____

$2 \times 5 = $ _____

$1 \times 5 = $ _____

$10 + $ _____ $ = $ _____

2. $3 \times 4 = ?$

?

4	4	
4	8	

$3 \times 4 = $ _____

$2 \times 4 = $ _____

$1 \times 4 = $ _____

$8 + $ _____ $ = $ _____

In **3–8**, multiply.

3. $7 \times 2 = $ _____

4. $8 \times 5 = $ _____

5. $6 \times 8 = $ _____

6. $9 \times 7 = $ _____

7. $4 \times 8 = $ _____

8. $7 \times 3 = $ _____

9. **Make Sense and Persevere** The home team scored 3 touchdowns. The visiting team scored 4 field goals. Which team scored more points? Show your strategy.

Football Points	
Type	**Points**
Touchdown	6 points
Field Goal	3 points
Safety	2 points

10. **Critique Reasoning** Rick says, "To find 2×5, I can skip count by 5s: 5, 10, 15, 20, 25. The product is 25." Explain what Rick did wrong.

11. **Algebra** Write the symbols to make the equations correct.

$81 = 9 \boxed{} 9$

$9 \boxed{} 6 = 54$

$9 = 72 \boxed{} 8$

12. **Higher Order Thinking** Jill has 4 bags of marbles. There are 3 red, 5 green, 2 yellow, and 6 black marbles in each bag. How many marbles does Jill have? Show how you found the answer.

13. Mr. Roberts plans to drive a total of 56 miles. He has 29 more miles to go. How many miles has he driven so far?

56 miles	
?	29 miles

✔ Assessment

14. Tia counted the campers and beds in 7 cabins. Each cabin had 9 campers and 12 beds. How many campers were in the 7 cabins?

    Ⓐ 84 campers   Ⓒ 63 campers

    Ⓑ 72 campers   Ⓓ 35 campers

15. Which of the following does **NOT** show a way to find the product of 2×5?

    Ⓐ 5×2

    Ⓑ $5 + 5 + 5$

    Ⓒ $2 + 2 + 2 + 2 + 2$

    Ⓓ $(2 \times 2) + (3 \times 2) = 4 + 6$

Name _____

Solve & Share

At the Fall Fest parade, members of the Cat Lovers Club and the Dog Lovers Club will march in equal rows. There will be 6 members in each row. How many rows of dog lovers will march in the parade? How many total cat lovers will march in the parade?

Complete the table. **Solve the problem any way you choose.**

I can ...
use strategies to solve word problems that involve multiplication and division.

SOL 3.4b; 3.4a

Think about how you can use appropriate tools to help solve the problem.

Pet Club	Number of Members at the Parade	Number of Rows at the Parade
Dog Lovers	24	
Cat Lovers		5

Look Back! Reasoning What operations did you use to solve the problem? Explain your reasoning.

Essential Question

How Can You Solve Word Problems Using Multiplication and Division?

A

Gina has 45 hats. She is packing them by putting 9 hats in each of several boxes. How many boxes will she fill?

Drawing pictures and writing equations can help you when solving multiplication and division problems.

B

45 hats

? boxes

9

9 hats in a box

You can use a bar diagram to show how the numbers are related.

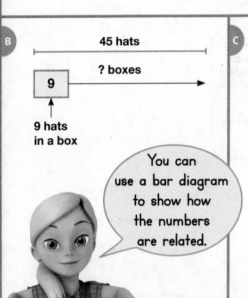

C **One Way**

Think: 45 divided by what number equals 9?

$45 \div 5 = 9$

There are 5 groups of 9 in 45.

Gina can divide 45 hats into 5 boxes of 9 hats each.

D **Another Way**

You can use a related fact.

Think: 9 times what number equals 45?

$9 \times 5 = 45$

So, $45 \div 9 = 5$.

Gina can divide 45 hats into 5 boxes of 9 hats each.

Convince Me! **Generalize** Gina instead has 42 hats. She is putting 6 hats in each of several boxes. Can you find how many boxes she needs using the same strategies as in the example above? Explain.

☆ Guided Practice ☆

Do You Understand?

1. Why can you use division to model the problem on page 262?

2. Casey gives 27 stickers to 3 friends. She writes the equation $27 \div 3 = 9$. What does the 9 represent in this problem?

Do You Know How?

In **3**, represent the problem with an equation or a bar diagram. Then solve.

3. A checkerboard has 64 squares. It has 8 rows. How many columns does it have?

☆ Independent Practice ☆

In **4** and **5**, draw a bar diagram to represent the problem. Then solve.

4. There are 5 pancakes in a stack. Elise makes 40 pancakes. How many stacks does Elise make?

5. A park has 4 swing sets. Each of the sets has 7 swings. How many swings are in the park?

In **6** and **7**, write an equation with an unknown to represent the problem. Then solve.

6. Mrs. Jameson plants 30 tulips in rows. Each row has 6 tulips. How many rows did Mrs. Jameson plant?

7. Bonnie buys 6 paperback books every month. She buys 2 hardcover books every month. How many books does she buy in 4 months?

*For another example, see Set E on page 289.

Problem Solving

8. **Model with Math** Jodie has 24 flowers in her garden. She wants to give an equal number of flowers to 4 families in her neighborhood. How many flowers will each family get? Complete the bar diagram and write an equation to help you solve this problem.

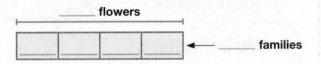

flowers

families

9. **Model with Math** Casey has 2 sisters. He gave each sister 2 pages of stickers. Each page had 9 stickers on it. How many stickers did Casey give in all? Explain what math you used to solve.

10. Jane is thinking about a shape with more than 5 sides. Draw a picture to show which shape Jane could be thinking about.

11. **Higher Order Thinking** 25 students are working in groups on a science project. Each group can have either 2 or 3 students in it. What is the fewest number of groups there could be?

A picture can help you solve a problem!

 **Assessment**

12. 8 vans are going to the zoo. There are 6 children in each van.

Part A

How many children are going to the zoo? Write an equation that could be used to find the answer to this problem. Solve that equation.

Part B

If instead 9 vans go to the zoo, explain how you can use what you know from Part A to find how many children are going to the zoo.

Another Look!

Rico has 32 pine cones. He uses 8 pine cones to make a sculpture in art class. If Rico makes more sculptures with 8 pine cones for each, how many total sculptures can he make?

Draw a bar diagram to represent the problem.

```
|———————— 32 pine cones ————————|
        ? sculptures
┌─────┐  ──────────────────────→
│  8  │
└─────┘
  ↑
Pine cones in
each sculpture
```

A bar diagram can help you see there is more than one way to think about this problem.

Multiply or divide to solve: $8 \times 4 = 32$ or $32 \div 4 = 8$.

So, Rico can make 4 sculptures.

In **1** and **2**, draw a bar diagram to represent the problem. Then solve.

1. Victor buys some six-packs of soda for a party. He buys 42 cans in all. How many six-packs of soda did Victor buy?

2. Lester listens to 8 songs every time he does his exercise routine. He did his exercise routine 3 times this week. How many songs did Lester listen to while exercising this week?

In **3** and **4**, write an equation with an unknown to represent the problem. Then solve.

3. There are 9 players on a baseball team. A club has 9 baseball teams. How many baseball players are in the club?

4. Megan earned $4 for an hour of babysitting. On Saturday, she earned $16. How many hours did she babysit?

5. **Model with Math** Andre is setting up folding chairs for a school assembly. He sets up 4 rows of chairs. Each row has 7 chairs. How many chairs does Andre set up? Complete the bar diagram and write an equation to solve.

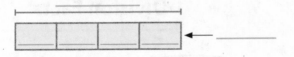

6. **Higher Order Thinking** 36 students ride a school bus route home. The same number of students get off at each stop. Harriet knows how many students got off at one stop. How could she find how many stops the bus made?

7. Mr. Ameda has 4 children. He gives each of them 2 cookies. He spends $40 on the cookies. How much did each cookie cost?

8. Yogesh has 3 quarters, 1 dime, and 2 pennies. How much money does he have?

9. **Critique Reasoning** Neville and Anthony are solving this problem: Barbara bought 3 boxes of pencils with 6 pencils in each box. How many pencils did she buy in all?

Neville says, "I add because of the words *in all*. The answer is 9 pencils." Anthony says, "I multiply because there are equal groups. The answer is 18 pencils." Who is correct? Explain.

 Assessment

10. Garrett uses 5 apples to bake an apple pie. On Sunday, he bakes 2 pies.

Part A

How many apples does Garrett need on Sunday? Write an equation that could be used to find the answer to this problem. Solve that equation.

Part B

On each of the next three days, Garrett will bake the same number of apple pies that he baked on Sunday. Explain how you can use what you know from Part A to find how many apples Garrett needs for those three days.

Name _____

Solve & Share

Write and solve a multiplication story about 4 × 5. Choose one of the phrases below to use in your multiplication story.

Phrases

- 4 equal groups of 5
- 4 rows of 5
- 4 rows and 5 columns

I can ...
write and solve math stories for multiplication equations.

SOL 3.4b; 3.4a

You can make sense of problems. You can write multiplication stories about objects in your classroom.

Look Back! **Reasoning** Why is the answer to your classmate's story the same as the answer to your story?

Essential Question: How Can You Describe a Multiplication Fact?

A

Write a multiplication story for 3 × 6.

Stories can be written to describe multiplication facts.

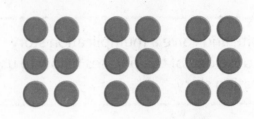

You can draw pictures and use objects to represent joining equal groups.

B Equal Groups

Randy has 3 packs of 6 buttons. How many buttons does he have?

3 × 6 = 18

Randy has 18 buttons.

C An Array

Eliza planted 6 lilies in each of 3 rows. How many lilies did she plant?

3 × 6 = 18

Eliza planted 18 lilies.

D Bar Diagram

A rabbit eats an equal amount of carrots each day for 3 days. If the rabbit eats 6 carrots each day, how many carrots does it eat in all?

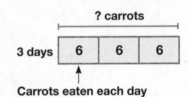

3 × 6 = 18

The rabbit eats 18 carrots.

Convince Me! **Reasoning** Write a multiplication story for 10 × 3 = ☐.

Name _____

 ☆Guided Practice*

Do You Understand?

In **1–3**, use the stories on page 268.

1. How would the story about Randy change if $2 \times 6 = \boxed{}$ were used instead?

2. Could the story about the carrots be written as an addition story? Explain.

3. What equation could be written if Eliza planted 6 lilies in each of 2 rows?

Do You Know How?

In **4** and **5**, write a multiplication story for the equation. Then find the product.

4. $3 \times 5 = \underline{}$

5. $2 \times 4 = \underline{}$

Independent Practice

Leveled Practice In **6–9**, write a multiplication story for each picture or equation. Then find the product.

6.

7.

8. $7 \times 3 = \underline{}$

9. $5 \times 5 = \underline{}$

Problem Solving

10. **Reasoning** Write a multiplication story about these pencils. Write an equation for your story.

Think about how many equal groups will be in your story.

11. **Number Sense** Brian said $42 + 35 + 16$ is greater than 150. Explain why his answer is not reasonable.

12. A soccer team traveled to a game in 4 vans. Each van held 6 players. Two of the players are goalkeepers. How many of the players are not goalkeepers?

13. **Higher Order Thinking** A group of 9 monarch butterflies is getting ready to migrate. Write a multiplication story involving this group. Explain what fact you are using and find the product.

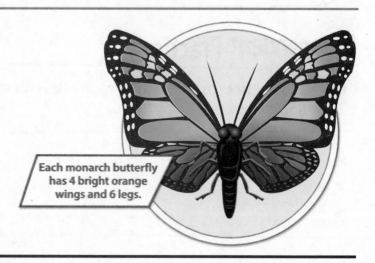

Each monarch butterfly has 4 bright orange wings and 6 legs.

14. Write a multiplication story for 3×9. Then find the product.

15. 7 teams played in a volleyball tournament. There were 6 players on each team. Draw a picture and write a multiplication equation for this story.

Another Look!

Write a story for 4 × 9.

Josephine had 4 friends over for a snack. She gave each friend 9 cherries. How many cherries did Josephine give in all?

$4 \times 9 = 36$

Josephine gave 36 cherries in all.

In **1–6**, write a multiplication story for each equation. Then find the product. You can draw a picture to help.

1. 4 × 3 = _____

2. 5 × 2 = _____

3. 4 × 6 = _____

4. 7 × 5 = _____

5. 8 × 5 = _____

6. 9 × 4 = _____

7. **Reasoning** Write a multiplication story about these tennis balls. Write an equation for your story.

Think about how many objects will be in each equal group in your story.

8. Draw a bar diagram that shows 6×7. How many sections does your bar diagram have? Explain. Then find the product.

9. **Be Precise** Perry counted 8 leaves on each of 9 tree branches. Write a multiplication equation to find how many leaves there are in all. Then use the Commutative Property to find how many leaves there are on 8 tree branches that each have 9 leaves.

10. **Higher Order Thinking** Judy is a dog walker. Some days she walks 4 dogs. Other days she walks 6 dogs. Including Judy's legs, how many legs could be in the group when Judy walks the dogs? Explain how you found the answer.

✓ **Assessment**

11. Write a multiplication story for 4×9. Then find the product.

12. Alvin has 8 bunches of 5 bananas each. Draw a picture to find the total number of bananas. Then write a multiplication equation to describe the problem.

Name _____

Solve & Share

Write a real-world division story for 28 ÷ 4. Then write another real-world story that shows a different way to think about 28 ÷ 4.

You can generalize. What is the same in both of your stories?

I can ...
write and solve math stories for division equations.

SOL 3.4b; 3.4a

Look Back! **Model with Math** Draw a bar diagram and write an equation to represent and solve one of your division stories.

What Is the Main Idea of a Division Story?

A

Mrs. White asked her students to write a division story for 15 ÷ 3.

Mike and Kia decided to write stories about putting roses in vases.

B ## Mike's Story

I have 15 roses. I want to put an equal number of roses in each of 3 vases. How many roses should I put in each vase?

Find 15 ÷ 3 = ☐.

The main idea is "How many are in each group?"

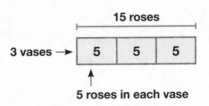

15 roses

3 vases → | 5 | 5 | 5 |

↑
5 roses in each vase

15 ÷ 3 = 5

I should put 5 roses in each vase.

C ## Kia's Story

I have 15 roses to put into vases. I want to put 3 roses in each vase. How many vases will I need?

Find 15 ÷ 3 = ☐.

The main idea is "How many groups are there?"

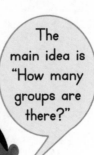

15 roses

? vases → | 3 | 5 vases →

↑
Roses in each vase

15 ÷ 3 = 5

I will need 5 vases.

Convince Me! **Generalize** How are Mike's and Kia's stories alike? How are the two stories different?

☆ Guided Practice ☆

Do You Understand?

1. When you write a division story, what two pieces of information do you need to include?

2. When you write a division story, what kind of information do you ask for?

Do You Know How?

In **3,** plan and write a division story for the equation. Then solve.

3. $8 \div 4 =$ _____

I will write about 8 _____.
They will be in 4 equal groups.

☆ Independent Practice ☆

Leveled Practice In **4–7**, plan and write a division story for each equation. Then use counters or draw a picture to solve.

4. $18 \div 3 =$ _____

I will write about 18 _____.
I will put them in 3 equal groups.

5. $14 \div$ _____ $= 2$

I will write about 14 _____.
I will put them in groups of 2.

6. $24 \div 8 =$ _____

7. $30 \div$ _____ $= 3$

Problem Solving

In **8–11**, use the table at the right. There are 36 third graders who want to play on different teams.

8. **Model with Math** If all the third graders want to play baseball, how many teams will there be? Write a division equation to represent the problem.

9. **Use Appropriate Tools** Explain how you could use a tool to solve **8**.

DATA	Sports Team	Players per Team
	Baseball	9 players
	Basketball	5 players
	Doubles Tennis	2 players

10. Suppose that 20 third graders went swimming and the rest played doubles tennis. How many doubles tennis teams would there be?

11. **Be Precise** Could all 36 third graders play in basketball games at the same time? Explain your answer.

12. **Higher Order Thinking** Hector wrote this division story for 24 ÷ 4:

"There are 24 bears in the woods. Each bear has 4 legs. How many legs are on all the bears in the woods?"

Explain whether you agree with Hector. If so, find the answer. If not, write a correct division story.

13. Kara has 40 activity books. She keeps 25 books and gives the rest to friends as gifts. Each friend gets the same number of books. How many friends get activity books?

COLORING BOOK

5 books for each friend

 Assessment

14. Write a division story for 35 ÷ ? = 7. Draw a picture to represent your story. Then solve.

Help Practice Tools Games
Buddy

Another Look!

Eddie was asked to write a division story using $12 \div 4 = \square$

This is Eddie's story:

Cami has 12 crayons and some cans.
She put 4 crayons in each can.
How many cans did Cami use?

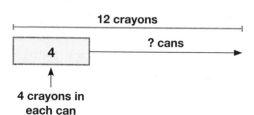

12 crayons

? cans

4

4 crayons in
each can

$12 \div 4 = 3$. So, Cami used 3 cans.

You can draw a bar
diagram to represent
Eddie's story.

In **1** and **2**, write the missing information to plan a division story for
each equation. Write the story. Use counters or draw a picture to solve.

1. $10 \div$ _____ $= 5$

I will write about 10 _____.
I will put them in groups of 5.

2. $21 \div 7 =$ _____

I will write about 21 _____.
I will put them in 7 equal groups.

In **3** and **4**, write a division story for each equation.
Use counters or draw a picture to solve.

3. $48 \div 6 =$ _____

4. $56 \div$ _____ $= 8$

5. **Make Sense and Persevere** Sheila wrote a division story. She wrote about how to divide 24 flowers into equal groups. What information must she give about the groups?

6. **A-Z Vocabulary** Jean wrote the numbers 0, 6, 12, 18, 24, and 30 on a piece of paper. Complete the sentence to describe what each of these numbers has in common with the number 6.

They are all _____ of 6.

7. Vera uses place-value blocks to add two numbers. What addition equation can Vera use?

8. **Be Precise** There are 16 people at a party. They want to set up relay teams with exactly 3 people on each team. Will each person be on a team? Explain.

9. **Higher Order Thinking** Complete the sentences with numbers that make sense. Do not use the number 1. Then write the division equation that matches the story, and draw a picture to solve.

"There are 35 rabbits at the fair. The rabbits are kept in ____ hutches with ____ rabbits in each hutch."

10. Write a division story for 49 ÷ 7. Draw a picture to represent your story. Then solve.

Name _____

Solve & Share

Jacob has started the pattern below. Fill in the blanks to make correct equations and continue the pattern. Explain your thinking.

$$6 \times 1 = 3 \times 2$$

$$6 \times 2 = 3 \times 4$$

$$6 \times 3 = 3 \times \boxed{}$$

$$6 \times \boxed{} = 3 \times \boxed{}$$

$$\boxed{} \times \boxed{} = \boxed{} \times \boxed{}$$

I can ...
use the structure of multiplication and division to compare expressions.

 SOL 3.4b, 3.17

Thinking Habits
Be a good thinker! These questions can help you.

- What patterns can I see and describe?

- How can I use the patterns to solve the problem?

- Can I see expressions and objects in different ways?

Look Back! **Use Structure** Jacob starts this new pattern. Fill in the blank to make the equation true. What do you notice about this pattern compared to the pattern above?

$$3 \times 2 = 6 \times 1$$

$$3 \times 4 = 6 \times 2$$

$$3 \times \boxed{} = 6 \times 3$$

Learn Glossary

Essential Question **How Can You Use the Structure of Mathematics?**

A

How can you tell without computing whether the symbol
>, <, or = should be placed in each circle below?

1. $4 \times 5 \times 2$ ◯ $4 \times 3 \times 5$

2. 6×7 ◯ 7×6

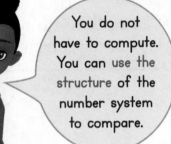

You do not have to compute. You can use the structure of the number system to compare.

What do I need to do to complete the task?

I need to compare the expressions. Instead of doing any calculations, I will look at the values of the factors in each expression.

Here's my thinking...

B **How can I make use of structure to solve this problem?**

I can

- think about properties I know.

- look for patterns and use them as needed.

C Some factors in the expressions are the same and some are different. I will use this to help me compare.

1. I know that I can group factors in any way, so I can rewrite one expression.

$$2 < 3$$

$\underbrace{4 \times 5}_{} \times 2 \qquad \text{◯} < \qquad \underbrace{4 \times 5}_{} \times 3$
$\quad\quad 20 \qquad\qquad = \qquad\qquad\quad 20$

2. I see the factors are the same on both sides. I know this means the products are the same.

6×7 ◯= 7×6

Convince Me! **Use Structure** Dario says, "I can find $9 \times 0 < 3 \times 1$ without computing. I can think about properties that I know." What could he mean?

280 **Topic 5** | Lesson 5-8

☆ Guided Practice*

Use Structure

Hakeem and Nicole each have 48 stickers. Hakeem shared his stickers among 8 friends. Nicole shared her stickers among 6 friends. These expressions show how Hakeem and Nicole shared their stickers.

$48 \div 8 \bigcirc 48 \div 6$

Use structure to compare the values on each side of the circle.

1. Look at the expressions. Explain how you can use what you see to compare without computing.

2. Whose friends each received more stickers? Write the correct symbol $>$, $<$, or $=$ in the circle above.

Independent Practice ☆

Use Structure

Dan has saved $10 each week for 7 weeks. Misha has saved $7 each week for 9 weeks. These expressions show how they saved.

$7 \times \$10 \bigcirc 9 \times \$7$

3. Look at the expressions. Explain how you can use what you see to compare without computing.

4. Who saved more money? Write the correct symbol $>$, $<$, or $=$ in the circle above.

5. Can you use the same symbol you wrote in **4** to compare $\$10 \times 7$ and $\$7 \times 9$? Explain.

Problem Solving

✓ Performance Assessment

Selling Necklaces

Trina wants to find the cheapest way to buy 24 necklaces. She wants to buy only the same type of packages. She has $48. The table shows the number of necklaces in a package and the cost of each package.

Number of Necklaces in a Package	Number of Packages Trina Should Buy	Cost per Package
3	24 ÷ 3 = 8	$4
4	___ ÷ ___ = ___	$5
6	___ ÷ ___ = ___	$6

6. **Model with Math** Complete the table to find the number of packages Trina would need to buy.

7. **Use Structure** Trina can use 8 × $4 to find the cost of enough $4 packages.
Write a similar expression that shows a way to find how much it costs Trina to buy enough $5 packages.

Write a similar expression that shows a way to find how much it costs Trina to buy enough $6 packages.

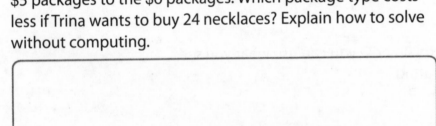

8. **Construct Arguments** Compare the cost of buying the $5 packages to the $6 packages. Which package type costs less if Trina wants to buy 24 necklaces? Explain how to solve without computing.

> When you use structure, you can look for things in common.

9. **Construct Arguments** Compare the costs of buying the $4 packages to the $6 packages. Which package type costs less if Trina wants to buy 24 necklaces? Explain how to solve without computing.

Name _____

Another Look!

How can you tell without computing which of the symbols >, <, or = should be placed in the circle below?

$4 \times 6 \times 2 \bigcirc 6 \times 2 \times 4$

Tell how you can use the structure of mathematics to complete the task.

- I can think about properties I know.

- I can look for patterns and use them as needed.

Look at the expressions. Explain how you can use the factors you see to compare without computing.

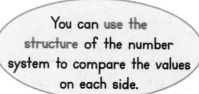
You can use the structure of the number system to compare the values on each side.

The same 3 factors are on each side of the circle. I know that the same factors grouped in a different way have the same product. So, the expressions are equal.

$4 \times (6 \times 2) \bigcirc= (6 \times 2) \times 4$

Use Structure

Maria wrote the expression at the left of the circle below. Riaz wrote the expression at the right of the circle below. Find without computing which of the symbols >, <, or = should be placed in the circle.

Maria   **Riaz**

$4 \times 8 \times 3 \bigcirc 2 \times 3 \times 8$

1. Tell how you can use the structure of mathematics to complete the task.

2. Look at the expressions. Explain how you can use the factors you see to compare without computing.

3. Whose expression has the greater value? Write the correct symbol >, <, or = in the circle above.

Baseball League

Ms. Bush manages a baseball league. She buys the bucket of baseballs shown to share among the teams. She wants to use all the baseballs. The league will have either 6 or 9 teams. There are 14 players on each team. Ms. Bush is trying to decide whether to charge $3 or $4 for each baseball.

36 baseballs in a bucket

4. **Make Sense and Persevere** What information do you know from the problem?

5. **Use Structure** Ms. Bush says each team will get more baseballs if there are 6 teams in the league. Mr. Rosin says each team will get more baseballs if there are 9 teams in the league. Who is correct?

Compare by writing the symbol >, <, or =.
Tell how to decide without computing.

$36 \div 6 \bigcirc 36 \div 9$

6. **Use Structure** Suppose Ms. Bush charges $4 per baseball. Would each team pay more if there are 6 teams or 9 teams?

Compare by writing the symbol >, <, or =.
Tell how to decide without computing.

$(36 \div 6) \times \$4 \bigcirc (36 \div 9) \times \$4$

You can use structure to compare information from different problems.

7. **Construct Arguments** Ms. Bush wants to set up the league so that each team pays the least amount. Should there be 6 or 9 teams? Should each baseball cost $3 or $4? Explain.

Name _____

Find a partner. Get paper and a pencil. Each partner chooses a different color: light blue or dark blue.

Partner 1 and Partner 2 each point to a black number at the same time. Both partners multiply those numbers.

If the answer is on your color, you get a tally mark. Work until one partner has seven tally marks.

I can ...
multiply within 100.

Partner 1

9
5
6
8
4

63	24	40
42	81	28
36	35	56
16	72	30
54	20	48
25	45	32

Partner 2

7
4
5
6
9

Tally Marks for Partner 1

Tally Marks for Partner 2

A-Z
Glossary

Word List

- column
- equation
- even
- fact family
- odd
- row

Understand Vocabulary

For each of these terms, give an example and a non-example.

	Example	Non-example
1. equation	_____	_____
2. odd number	_____	_____
3. even number	_____	_____
4. fact family	_____	_____
	_____	_____

Write *always*, *sometimes*, or *never*.

5. An *even* number can _____ be divided by 2 with none left over.

6. A *fact family* _____ has *odd* numbers.

7. An array _____ has the same number of *rows* and *columns*.

8. The product of an *odd* number times an *odd* number is _____ an *even* number.

Use Vocabulary in Writing

9. Explain the pattern in the green squares. Use at least 2 terms from the Word List in your explanation.

×	0	1	2	3	4	5
0	0	0	0	0	0	0
1	0	1	2	3	4	5
2	0	2	4	6	8	10
3	0	3	6	9	12	15
4	0	4	8	12	16	20
5	0	5	10	15	20	25

Name _____

Set A pages 237–242 _____

You can see patterns in a multiplication table.

×	0	1	2	3	4	5	6	7
0	0	0	0	0	0	0	0	0
1	0	1	2	3	4	5	6	7
2	0	2	4	6	8	10	12	14
3	0	3	6	9	12	15	18	21
4	0	4	8	12	16	20	24	28
5	0	5	10	15	20	25	30	35
6	0	6	12	18	24	30	36	42
7	0	7	14	21	28	35	42	49
8	0	8	16	24	32	40	48	56

In each row, the sum of the green shaded numbers equals the purple shaded number.

$0 + 0 = 0$ $\qquad$ $1 + 6 = 7$

$2 + 12 = 14$ $\qquad$ $3 + 18 = 21$

This is because of the Distributive Property.

A 1s fact plus a 6s fact equals a 7s fact.

Example: $(1 \times 5) + (6 \times 5) = (7 \times 5)$

Remember that properties can help to explain patterns.

In **1** and **2**, use the multiplication table to answer the questions.

×	0	1	2	3	4	5	6	7	8
0	0	0	0	0	0	0	0	0	0
1	0	1	2	3	4	5	6	7	8
2	0	2	4	6	8	10	12	14	16
3	0	3	6	9	12	15	18	21	24
4	0	4	8	12	16	20	24	28	32
5	0	5	10	15	20	25	30	35	40
6	0	6	12	18	24	30	36	42	48
7	0	7	14	21	28	35	42	49	56
8	0	8	16	24	32	40	48	56	64

1. Find the column which has products that are the sum of the green shaded numbers in each row. Shade this column.

2. Explain why this pattern is true.

Set B pages 243–248 _____

Use a multiplication table to find $20 \div 4$.

×	0	1	2	3	4	5	6	7
0	0	0	0	0	0	0	0	0
1	0	1	2	3	4	5	6	7
2	0	2	4	6	8	10	12	14
3	0	3	6	9	12	15	18	21
4	0	4	8	12	16	20	24	28
5	0	5	10	15	20	25	30	35
6	0	6	12	18	24	30	36	42
7	0	7	14	21	28	35	42	49
8	0	8	16	24	32	40	48	56
9	0	9	18	27	36	45	54	63

Find 4 in the first column of the table.

Follow the 4s row until you come to 20.

Then look to the top of that column to find the missing factor: 5. $\qquad$ $20 \div 4 = 5$

Remember how multiplication and division are related.

In **1–12**, use the multiplication table to find each product or quotient.

1. $2 \times 7 =$ _____ $\qquad$ **2.** $5 \times 8 =$ _____

3. $2 \times 10 =$ _____ $\qquad$ **4.** $5 \times 4 =$ _____

5. $3 \times 5 =$ _____ $\qquad$ **6.** $6 \times 5 =$ _____

7. $63 \div 9 =$ _____ $\qquad$ **8.** $56 \div 8 =$ _____

9. $45 \div 9 =$ _____ $\qquad$ **10.** $40 \div 8 =$ _____

11. $35 \div 7 =$ _____ $\qquad$ **12.** $36 \div 6 =$ _____

You can use basic facts and properties to find missing numbers in a multiplication table.

×	4	5	☐	7
3	12	15	18	21
4	16	20	24	28
5	20	25	30	35
6	24	30	36	42
7	28		42	49
8	32	40	48	56

Use multiplication or division to find missing factors.

$42 \div 7 = 6$, so $7 \times 6 = 42$

Use strategies to find products.

$3 \times 5 = 15$ $4 \times 5 = 20$

$5 \times 5 = 25$ $6 \times 5 = 30$

So, $7 \times 5 = 35$

Remember that you can use strategies and reasoning to find missing numbers.

Use multiplication and division strategies to complete the multiplication table. Show your work.

×	☐	5	6	☐
☐	12	15	18	
☐	16	20		28
5	20	25	30	35
6	24	30		42
7		35	42	49
8	32	40	48	

Find 4×7.

There are different strategies you can use when multiplying.

You can use skip counting:
7, 14, 21, 28

You can use known facts:

$2 \times 7 = 14$

$4 \times 7 = (2 \times 7) + (2 \times 7)$

$4 \times 7 = 14 + 14 = 28$

Remember that you can use patterns, known facts, or skip counting to find products.

In **1–8**, use strategies to find the product.

1. $5 \times 9 = $ _____   **2.** $8 \times 10 = $ _____

3. $4 \times 10 = $ _____   **4.** $9 \times 8 = $ _____

5. $6 \times 9 = $ _____   **6.** $7 \times 3 = $ _____

7. $6 \times 5 = $ _____   **8.** $4 \times 9 = $ _____

Set E | pages 261–266

You can solve word problems using multiplication and division.

Aaron has 49 books. His bookcase has 7 shelves. He wants to display an equal number of books on each shelf. How many books can he put on each shelf?

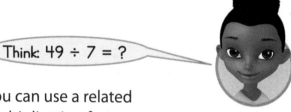

Think: 49 ÷ 7 = ?

You can use a related multiplication fact:

$7 \times 7 = 49$

$49 \div 7 = 7$

Aaron can put 7 books on each shelf.

Remember that multiplication and division use equal groups.

Solve each problem. Show your work.

1. Oksana's dad has 36 batteries in his desk drawer. The batteries come in packs of 4. How many packs of batteries does he have?

2. Every time Lee wins the ring toss at the carnival, he gets 3 prize tickets. Lee needs to win the ring toss 9 times to have enough prize tickets for 1 toy. How many prize tickets does Lee need for 2 toys?

Set F | pages 267–272

Write a multiplication story for 4×7.

You can think of multiplication as equal groups.

Tim has 4 bunches of flowers. Each bunch has 7 flowers. How many flowers does Tim have?

Tim has 28 flowers.

Remember that rows and columns can also represent multiplication.

Write a multiplication story for each equation. Then solve.

1. $3 \times 9 =$ _____

2. $5 \times 6 =$ _____

Set G pages 273–278

Write a division story for 20 ÷ 5.

If 20 children form 5 equal teams, how many children are on each team?

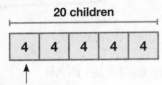

20 ÷ 5 = 4

There are 4 children on each team.

Remember that division stories can ask for the number in each group, or the number of equal groups.

Write a division story for each equation. Then solve.

1. 60 ÷ 10 = ____

2. 32 ÷ 4 = ____

Set H pages 279–284

Think about these questions to help you **look for and make use of structure.**

Thinking Habits

- What patterns can I see and describe?

- How can I use the patterns to solve the problem?

- Can I see expressions and objects in different ways?

Remember that properties can help you understand patterns.

Leroy earns $7 each hour that he works. He works for 8 hours. Rebecca earns $8 each hour that she works. She works for 7 hours. These expressions show the money they earned.

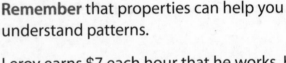

1. Look at the expressions. Explain how you can use what you see to compare without computing.

2. Who earned more money? Write the correct symbol >, <, or = in the circle above.

1. Write and solve a division story for $48 \div 6$.

3. Jesse has 45 apple slices. He bakes 5 apple tarts. How many apple slices are used in each tart? Draw a bar diagram to represent the problem. Then solve the problem.

2. Look at the multiplication table below.

×	□	□	8
0			
□		7	8
2			16
3	18		
□		28	

Part A

Fill in the missing factors and products.

Part B

What pattern do you see in the first row of products in the table? Explain why this pattern is true.

4. Is the product of the following problems greater than 5×7? Choose *Yes* or *No*.

4a. $2 \times 2 \times 7$ ◯ Yes ◯ No

4b. $7 \times 1 \times 5$ ◯ Yes ◯ No

4c. $2 \times 5 \times 7$ ◯ Yes ◯ No

4d. $8 \times 5 \times 0$ ◯ Yes ◯ No

5. Nate has 4 pages of stickers arranged in arrays. The table shows the number of rows and columns on each page. Which page has the most stickers?

Page	Rows	Columns
1	3	5
2	5	4
3	4	3
4	5	3

Ⓐ Page 1 Ⓒ Page 3

Ⓑ Page 2 Ⓓ Page 4

6. Which of the following strategies can help you solve 4×6? Choose all that apply.

- ☐ $(6 \times 6) + (6 \times 6)$
- ☐ $(4 \times 3) + (4 \times 3)$
- ☐ $(5 \times 5) + (4 \times 1)$
- ☐ $(5 \times 4) + (1 \times 4)$
- ☐ $(2 \times 4) + (2 \times 6)$

7. What number is missing from this multiplication table?

×	5	6
2	10	?
3	15	18

- Ⓐ 8
- Ⓑ 9
- Ⓒ 11
- Ⓓ 12

8. Draw lines to match each product or quotient on the left with the equation it solves on the right.

56	$54 \div 6 = ?$
7	$8 \times 7 = ?$
36	$49 \div 7 = ?$
9	$6 \times 6 = ?$

9. Beverly notices a pattern in the multiplication table. She shades some squares orange to show her pattern.

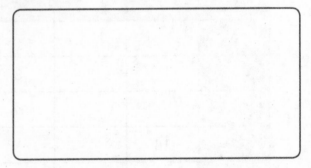

×	4	5	6	7
4	16	20	24	28
5	20	25	30	35
6	24	30	36	42
7	28	35	42	49
8	32	40	48	56

Part A

What pattern could Beverly have seen?

Part B

Explain why this pattern is true.

10. Freddy has 70 books. He puts 7 books in a stack. How many stacks can he make this way?

11. Which of the following stories is about 8 × 4? Choose all that apply.

☐ Billy has 4 columns and 8 rows of stamps. How many stamps does Billy have?

☐ Billy gives away 8 stamps. Each of 4 friends gets the same number of stamps. How many stamps does each friend get?

☐ Billy has 8 stamps. They are in 4 equal rows. How many stamps are in each row?

☐ Billy has a row of 4 stamps and a row of 8 stamps. How many stamps does Billy have in all?

☐ Billy has 8 rows of stamps. Each row has 4 stamps. How many stamps are there in all?

12. Maya has 12 pens that she wants to put into equal groups. Can she put the pens in groups of the following numbers with none left over?

12a. 2   ○ Yes   ○ No

12b. 3   ○ Yes   ○ No

12c. 4   ○ Yes   ○ No

12d. 5   ○ Yes   ○ No

13. Look at these two expressions.

$40 \div 4 \bigcirc 40 \div 8$

Part A

Explain how you can use what you see to compare the expressions without computing.
Then write the correct symbol >, <, or = in the circle above.

Part B

Check your answer by computing both quotients. Write the quotients and the correct symbol >, <, or = below.

____ ◯ ____

14. A kennel has 9 dogs. Each dog gets 3 dog treats. How many treats do all the dogs get together? Write an equation to solve the problem.

15. Which shows a way to solve 5×5?

Ⓐ Skip count 5 times by numbers that end in 5: 5, 15, 25, 35, 45

Ⓑ Use the Distributive Property: $(4 \times 5) + (1 \times 5)$

Ⓒ Look at a multiplication table: Find the 5s row. Go across until you find 5. The product is the number at the top of that column, 1.

Ⓓ Use repeated addition: $5 + 5 + 5 + 5$

16. Write and solve a multiplication story for 9×7.

17. On Saturday, Toni biked to and from the pool. The distance from Toni's house to the pool is 7 miles. How many miles did Toni bike on Saturday?

18. Look at the multiplication table below.

×	4	5	6	7
3	12	15	18	21
4	16	20	24	28
5	20	25	30	35
6	24	30	36	42
7	28	35	42	49
8	32	40	48	56

Part A

Shade the products in the 5s column of the table. What pattern do you see there?

Part B

Explain the pattern you found.

Name _____

Photograph Gallery

Riley is setting up a display. She is hanging photographs on two walls. The photographs are hung in arrays. Riley has to decide how to arrange the photographs. She makes tables to decide which arrangement to use.

1. Use the **Left Wall** table to answer the questions.

   Part A

   Which arrangement on the left wall has the most photographs?

   [ ]

   Part B

   Explain how Riley could find the answer to Part A without calculating the size of each arrangement.

   [ ]

Left Wall

Arrangement	A	B	C	D
Rows	3	3	7	8
Columns	7	9	2	3

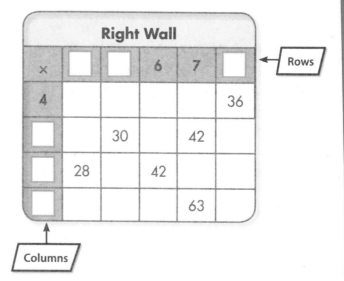

Right Wall

Rows

Columns

Use the **Right Wall** table to answer questions 2 and 3.

2. Fill in the missing columns, rows, and numbers of photographs so that Riley's table is complete.

3. Riley has 42 on her table twice. Is this reasonable? Explain why or why not.

   [ ]

Use the **Right Wall** table to answer questions 4–6.

4. Some of the photographers were men, and some were women. Riley wants the number of photographs taken by men to be equal to the number of photographs taken by women. Shade the squares in the table to show the arrangements that let Riley do this. Explain what pattern you find.

5. Riley shares this table with her friend Leo. Leo is working on a different project. He is **NOT** hanging photographs. For what project could Leo use the table? Explain what 7 × 4 means for Leo's project.

6. Riley also shares this table with her mother. Riley's mother is working on a different project. She is also **NOT** hanging photographs. For what project could Riley's mother use the table? Explain what 30 ÷ 6 means for Riley's mother's project.

Solve   Learn   Glossary   Practice Buddy

Tools   Assessment   Help   Games

TOPIC 6

Connect Area to Multiplication and Addition

Essential Question: How can area be measured and found?

Some designs can help protect buildings from unsafe weather.

This lightning rod on top of the building is connected to the ground. It can direct the electrical current from a lightning strike safely to the ground.

This helps protect the building from being damaged by lightning! Here's a project on building designs and area.

Math and Science Project: Design Solutions

Do Research There are different designs that help protect against weather, such as as lightning rods, flood-defense barriers, and wind-resistant roofs. Use the Internet or another source to gather information about these kind of designs and how they work.

Journal: Write a Report Include what you found. Also in your report:

- Tell how some window or door designs can help protect against weather.

- Use a grid to draw one of the window or door designs. Count the number of unit squares your design measures. Label your drawing to show how the design works to protect against weather.

Name _____

Review What You Know

Choose the best term from the box.
Write it on the blank.

• addend	• equal groups
• array	• multiply

1. When you skip count to get the total number, you _____ .

2. Dividing apples so everyone gets the same amount is an example of making _____ .

3. When you display objects in rows and columns, you make a(n) _____ .

Division as Sharing

4. Chen has 16 model cars. He puts them in 4 rows. Each row has an equal number of cars. How many columns are there?

5. Julie has 24 glass beads to give to 4 friends. Each friend gets an equal share. How many glass beads does each friend get?

Arrays

6. Write an addition equation and a multiplication equation for the array shown at the right.

Relating Multiplication and Division

7. There are 12 team members. They line up in 3 equal rows. Which multiplication equation helps you find how many are in each row?

    (A) $2 \times 6 = 12$ (B) $1 \times 12 = 12$ (C) $3 \times 4 = 12$ (D) $3 \times 12 = 36$

8. There are 20 bottles of juice lined up in 4 equal rows. Explain how you can use a multiplication equation to find out how many bottles of juice are in each row.

My Word Cards

Use the examples for each word on the front of the card to help complete the definitions on the back.

area

You can measure area by counting unit squares.

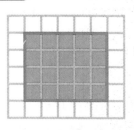

unit square

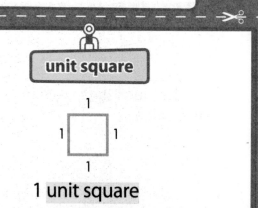

1 unit square

square unit

The area of this shape is 9 square units.

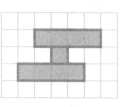

estimate

The area of the circle is about 20 square units.

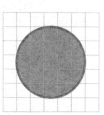

A _____ is a square with sides 1 unit long, used to measure area.

_____ is the number of unit squares needed to cover a region.

To give an approximate number or

answer is to _____.

A unit square has

1 _____ of area.

Name _____

Solve & Share

Look at Shapes A–C on Area of Shapes Teaching Tool. How many square tiles do you need to cover each shape? Show your answers below. Explain how you decided.

I can ...
count unit squares to find the area of a shape.

SOL 3.8b

Shape	Number of Square Tiles
Shape A	
Shape B	
Shape C	

Use tools. Think about how to place your tiles to cover each shape completely.

Look Back! **Be Precise** Can you be sure you have an exact answer if there are gaps between the tiles you used? Explain.

Essential Question **How Do You Measure Area?**

A

Emily made a collage in art class. She cut shapes to make her design. What is the area of this shape?

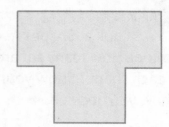

Area is the number of unit squares needed to cover a region with no gaps or overlaps.

A unit square is a square with sides that are each 1 unit long. It has an area of 1 square unit.

This is the unit square for this lesson.

Sometimes you can estimate the area. You can combine partially filled squares to estimate full squares.

B Count the unit squares that cover Emily's shape. The exact count is the area of the shape.

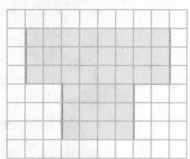

36 unit squares cover the shape. The area of the shape is 36 square units.

C Count the unit squares that cover this shape.

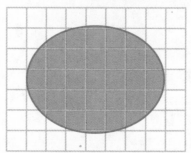

About 27 unit squares cover the shape.

The area of the shape is about 27 square units.

Convince Me! **Construct Arguments** Karen says these shapes each have an area of 12 square units. Do you agree with Karen? Explain.

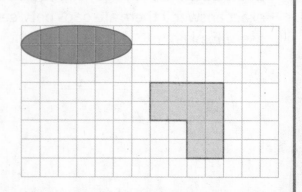

Name _____

Another Example!

Emily wants to cover this octagon.

If she tries to cover it using unit squares, there will be gaps or overlaps.

Emily can break the square into two triangles. She can cover the shape completely using this triangle:

14 triangles cover the octagon. The area of the octagon is 7 square units.

Guided Practice

Do You Understand?

1. **Reasoning** How do you know the area of the octagon is 7 square units?

2. **Be Precise** Explain how finding the area of a shape is different from finding the length of a shape.

Do You Know How?

In **3** and **4**, count to find the area. Tell if the area is exact or an estimate.

3.

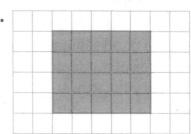

4.

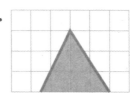

Independent Practice

In **5–7**, count to find the area. Tell if the area is exact or an estimate.

5.

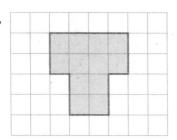

6.

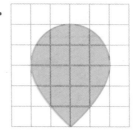

7.

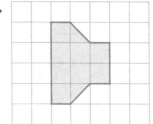

Problem Solving

8. Maggie buys 4 sketch pads. She pays with a 20-dollar bill. How much change does Maggie get back?

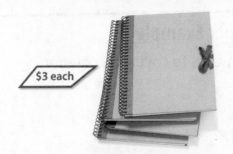

$3 each

---

9. Critique Reasoning Janet covers the red square with square tiles. She says, "I covered this shape with 12 unit squares, so I know it has an area of 12 square units." Do you agree with Janet? Explain.

---

10. Higher Order Thinking Chester drew this picture of a circle inside a square. What would be a good estimate of the green shaded area of the square? How did you calculate your answer?

11. Number Sense Arthur puts 18 erasers into equal groups. He says there are more erasers in each of 2 equal groups than in each of 3 equal groups. Is Arthur correct? Explain.

✔ **Assessment**

12. Daryl draws this shape on grid paper. Estimate the area of the shape Daryl draws. Explain how you estimated.

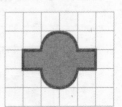

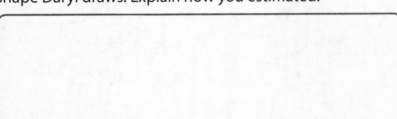

Name

Another Look!

You can find the exact area of the rectangle below by counting the number of unit squares that cover it.

8 unit squares cover the rectangle.

So, the area of the rectangle is 8 square units.

Sometimes you need to estimate area. You can combine partially filled squares to approximate full squares.

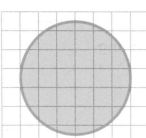

About 28 unit squares cover the shape.

So, the area of the shape is about 28 square units.

Area is the number of unit squares used to cover a region with no gaps or overlaps.

In **1–6**, count to find the area of the shapes. Tell if the area is exact or an estimate.

1.

2.

3.

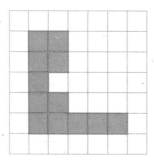

4.

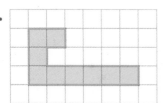

5.

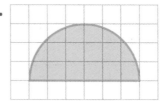

6.

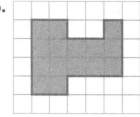

In **7–9**, use the diagram at the right.

7. What is the area of the soccer section of the field?

Use the diagram to help make a plan.

Athletic Field

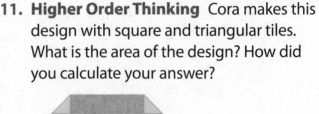

| Soccer | Baseball |
| Tennis | Not Used |

8. What is the area of the field that is **NOT** being used?

9. **Make Sense and Persevere** How many square units of the field are being used?

---

10. **Reasoning** A bookstore has a sale. When customers pay for 2 books, they get another book free. If Pat pays for a box of 16 books, how many books does he get for free? How many books does Pat have? Write division and addition equations to show how the quantities are related.

Buy 2, Get 1 Free!

11. **Higher Order Thinking** Cora makes this design with square and triangular tiles. What is the area of the design? How did you calculate your answer?

---

12. Tyler draws this shape on grid paper. What is area of the shape? Explain how you decided.

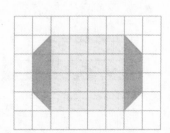

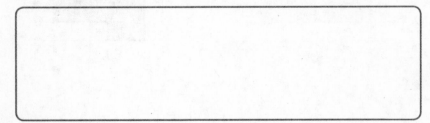

Name _____

Solve & Share

Find the area of the postcard on each grid. What do you notice about the size of the postcard on each grid? What do you notice about the area of the postcard on each grid? Explain.

I can ...
count unit squares to find the area of a shape.

SOL 3.8b

□ = 1 square unit

□ = 1 square unit

Use reasoning to identify relationships. Notice that the same postcard is used for both grids. *Show your work in the space below!*

Look Back! **Be Precise** Are the measurements of the areas of the postcard shown above the same? Explain.

Essential Question

How Can You Measure Area Using Non-Standard Units?

A

Tran designs a bookmark for a paperback book. How can he use unit squares to find the area of the bookmark?

> Unit squares can be different sizes.

B You can count the number of unit squares.

☐ = 1 square unit

There are 32 unit squares.

Area = 32 square units

C You can use a different unit square.

☐ = 1 square unit

There are 8 unit squares.

Area = 8 square units

> The size of the unit square determines the area.

Convince Me! **Reasoning** How are the areas of these two squares alike and how are they different?

☆ Guided Practice ☆

Do You Understand?

1. Which of these shapes has an area of 5 square units? How do you know?

Do You Know How?

2. Draw unit squares to cover the figures and find the area. Use the unit squares shown.

 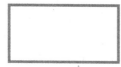

= 1 square unit   = 1 square unit

☆ Independent Practice ☆

In **3–5**, draw unit squares to cover the figures and find the area. Use the unit squares shown.

3.

 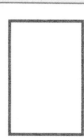

☐ = 1 square unit   ☐ = 1 square unit

4.

☐ = 1 square unit   ☐ = 1 square unit

5.

☐ = 1 square unit   ☐ = 1 square unit

*For another example, see Set B on page 345.

Topic 6 | Lesson 6-2   **309**

Problem Solving

6. **Be Precise** Ben finds the area of this figure is 14 square units. Draw unit squares to cover this figure.

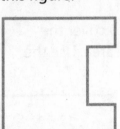

Think about the size of the unit squares you need to use.

7. **Reasoning** Luke eats 6 grapes from the bowl. Then Juan and Luke equally shared the grapes that are left. How many grapes does Juan eat? Show how you used reasoning to solve the problem.

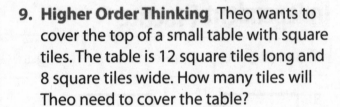

24 grapes

8. **Construct Arguments** Riaz estimates the area of this figure is 45 square units. Martin estimates the area is 48 square units. Whose estimate is closer? Explain.

 = 1 square unit

9. **Higher Order Thinking** Theo wants to cover the top of a small table with square tiles. The table is 12 square tiles long and 8 square tiles wide. How many tiles will Theo need to cover the table?

10. Rick found the area of this shape is 21 square units. If he used a larger unit square, would his measurement be greater than 21 square units or less than 21 square units? Explain.

☐ = 1 square unit

Another Look!

A unit square is a square with sides that are each 1 unit long.

Unit squares can be different sizes. The size of the unit square you use determines the area of a figure.

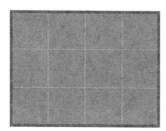

> You can measure area by counting the unit squares that cover a figure.

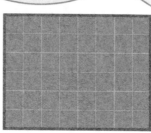

☐ = 1 square unit

There are 12 unit squares.

The area of this figure is 12 square units.

☐ = 1 square unit

There are 48 unit squares.

The area of this figure is 48 square units.

In **1** and **2**, draw unit squares to cover the figures and find the area. Use the unit squares shown.

1.

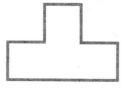

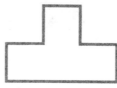

☐ = 1 square unit

☐ = 1 square unit

> Remember to look at the size of the unit squares that are used for each figure.

2. 10 square units

☐ = 1 square unit

☐ = 1 square unit

3. Be Precise Inez finds the area of this figure is 9 square units. Draw unit squares to cover this figure.

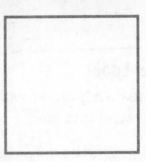

4. **Vocabulary** Fill in the blanks: Yasmeen can cover a figure with 7 rows of 8 _____ to find the figure's _____.

5. Number Sense Paula is making gift bags for each of her 5 friends. Each bag will have 6 markers. How many markers will Paula need? Skip count by 5s to find the answer. Then write a multiplication equation to represent the problem.

6. Higher Order Thinking Helen makes the rectangle on the right from colored tiles. Each tile is 1 unit square. Helen says the green tiles cover more area than the blue tiles. Do you agree? Explain.

7. Rick found the area of this shape is 15 square units. If he used a smaller unit square, would his measurement be greater than 15 square units or less than 15 square units? Explain.

☐ = 1 square unit

Name _____

Solve & Share

Draw a square to represent 1 unit square. Use your unit square to draw a rectangle that has an area of 8 square units. Compare your shape with a partner's shape. What is the same? What is different?

I can ...

measure the area of a shape using standard units.

SOL 3.8b

Be precise. Check your shape to make sure you have used the correct number of unit squares.

Look Back! **Reasoning** Is the size of your shapes something that is the same or something that is different? Explain.

Essential Question

How Can You Measure Area Using Standard Units of Length?

A

Meg bought this sticker. What is the area of the sticker in square centimeters?

You can measure area in standard units. A square centimeter is a standard unit of area.

B

Here are some standard units of length and area.

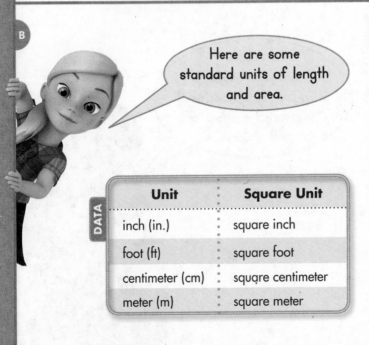

Unit	Square Unit
inch (in.)	square inch
foot (ft)	square foot
centimeter (cm)	square centimeter
meter (m)	square meter

C

Count the unit squares.

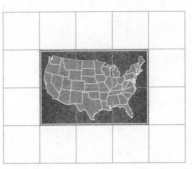

□ = 1 square centimeter

6 unit squares cover the sticker. The sticker is measured in square centimeters.

So, the area of the sticker is 6 square centimeters.

Convince Me! Be Precise If square inches rather than square centimeters were used for the problem above, would more unit squares or fewer unit squares be needed to cover the shape? Explain.

☆ Guided Practice ☆

Do You Understand?

1. If Meg's sticker on page 314 measured 2 inches by 3 inches, what would its area be?

2. Zoey paints a wall that measures 8 feet by 10 feet. What units should Zoey use for the area of the wall? Explain.

Do You Know How?

In **3** and **4**, each unit square represents a standard unit. Count the shaded unit squares. Then write the area.

3. 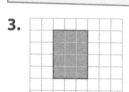 ☐ = 1 square ft

4. 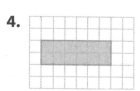 ☐ = 1 square m

☆ Independent Practice ☆

In **5–10**, each unit square represents a standard unit. Count the shaded unit squares. Then write the area.

5.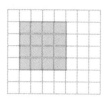
☐ = 1 square in.

6.
☐ = 1 square ft

7.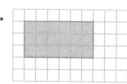
☐ = 1 square in.

8.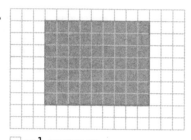
☐ = 1 square m

9.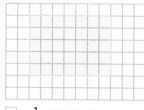
☐ = 1 square cm

10.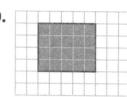
☐ = 1 square ft

For another example, see Set C on page 346.

Problem Solving

11. Reasoning Mr. Sanchez grows three types of vegetables in his garden. What is the area of the garden that Mr. Sanchez uses to grow lettuce and cucumbers? Explain how to use the units in this problem.

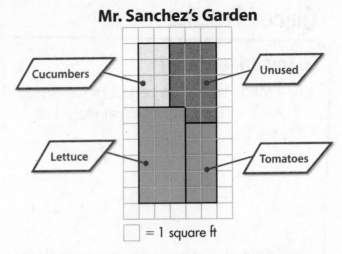

Mr. Sanchez's Garden

Cucumbers
Unused
Lettuce
Tomatoes

☐ = 1 square ft

---

12. Lisa received 34 text messages on Monday and 43 text messages on Tuesday. She received 98 text messages on Wednesday. How many more text messages did Lisa receive on Wednesday than on Monday and Tuesday combined?

13. Construct Arguments Monica buys a postage stamp. Is the area of the stamp more likely to be 1 square inch or 1 square meter? Explain.

---

14. Algebra Which operation can you use to complete the equation below?

$8 = 56 \boxed{} 7$

15. Higher Order Thinking Brad says a square that has a length of 9 feet has an area of 18 square feet. Is Brad correct? Why or why not?

✓ **Assessment**

16. Each of these unit squares represents 1 square foot. Does each figure have an area of 40 square feet? Choose *Yes* or *No*.

A 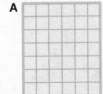 B   C

Shape A   ○ Yes   ○ No

Shape B   ○ Yes   ○ No

Shape C   ○ Yes   ○ No

Help Practice Buddy Tools Games

Another Look!

Count how many unit squares cover this figure.

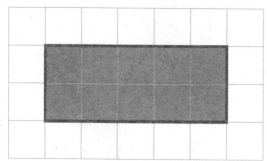

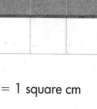 = 1 square cm

You can use standard units of length to help measure area.

- 10 unit squares cover the figure.
- Each unit square equals 1 square centimeter.

The area of the figure is 10 square centimeters.

In **1–6**, each unit square represents a standard unit. Count the shaded unit squares. Then write the area.

1.

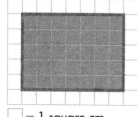

☐ = 1 square cm

2.

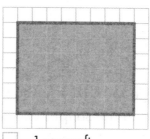

☐ = 1 square ft

3.

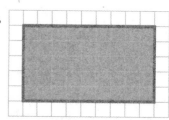

☐ = 1 square m

4.

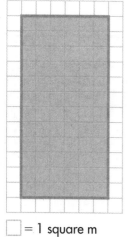

☐ = 1 square m

5.

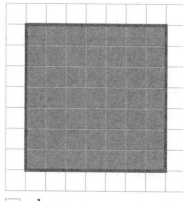

☐ = 1 square cm

6.

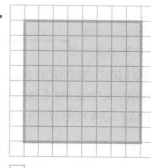

☐ = 1 square in.

In **7** and **8**, use the diagram at the right.

7. **Be Precise** What is the area of Tom's photo? Explain how you know which units to use.

Sue's photo

Ali's photo

Tom's photo

☐ = 1 square in.

8. What is the area in square inches of all the photos? Explain.

9. **Construct Arguments** Is the area of a desk more likely to be 8 square feet or 8 square inches? Explain.

10. Michele has 5 coins worth $0.75 in all. What coins does she have?

11. **Higher Order Thinking** Sam made the shape at the right from colored tiles. What is the area of the shape? Explain how you found your answer.

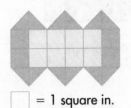

☐ = 1 square in.

12. Each of these unit squares represents 1 square meter. Does each figure have an area of 24 square meters? Choose *Yes* or *No*.

A  B C

Shape A	○ Yes	○ No
Shape B	○ Yes	○ No
Shape C	○ Yes	○ No

Name _____

★ ☆ ★
Solve & Share

Jorge is carpeting a square room. One side of the room is 6 meters long. How many square meters of carpet does Jorge need? *Solve this problem any way you choose.*

I can ...
find the area of squares and rectangles by multiplying.

SOL Prepares for 4.7

You can generalize. What do you know about squares that can help you find the number of square meters of carpet Jorge will need?

6 m

Look Back! **Reasoning** If the sides of the room were 6 feet long, how would the answer to the problem change?

Essential Question **How Can You Find the Area of a Figure?**

A

Mike paints a rectangular wall in his room green. The picture shows the length and width of Mike's wall. A small can of paint covers 40 square feet. Does Mike need more than one small can to paint the wall of his room?

6 ft

8 ft

1 can covers
40 square feet

B One Way

Count the unit squares to find area.

6 ft

8 ft

That's a lot of squares to count!

There are 48 unit squares. The area of Mike's wall is 48 square feet.

C Another Way

Count the number of rows and multiply by the number of squares in each row. There are 8 rows and 6 squares in each row.

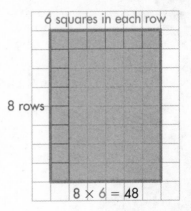

6 squares in each row

8 rows

$8 \times 6 = 48$

The area of Mike's wall is 48 square feet. He will need more than one small can of paint.

Convince Me! **Model with Math** Mike plans to paint a wall in his living room blue. That wall measures 10 feet tall and 8 feet wide. What is the area of the wall Mike plans to paint blue?

Another Example!

The area of another wall in Mike's room is 56 square feet. The wall is 8 feet high. How wide is the wall?

$56 = 8 \times ?$

You can use division. $56 \div 8 = ?$

$56 \div 8 = 7$

The wall is 7 feet wide.

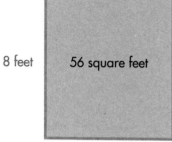

8 feet   56 square feet

? feet

Guided Practice

Do You Understand?

1. Suji's garden is 4 yards long and 4 yards wide. What is the area of Suji's garden?

2. The area of Michi's garden is 32 square feet. The garden is 8 feet long. How wide is Michi's garden?

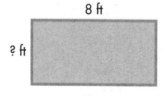

8 ft

? ft

Do You Know How?

In **3** and **4**, find the area of each figure. Use grid paper to help.

3.
7 in.

3 in.

4.
9 ft

6 ft

Independent Practice

In **5** and **6**, find the area. In **7**, find the missing length. Use grid paper to help.

5.
3 cm

1 cm

6.
4 ft

9 ft

7.
7 in.

? in.   35 square in.

Problem Solving

8. **Construct Arguments** Jen's garden is 4 feet wide and has an area of 28 square feet. What is the length of Jen's garden? How do you know?

9. **Make Sense and Persevere** Briana has 2 grandmothers. She mailed 2 cards to both of them. In each card she put 6 photographs. How many photographs did Briana mail in all?

10. **Generalize** Kevin thinks he found a shortcut. He says he can find the area of a square by multiplying the length of one side by itself. Is Kevin correct? Why or why not?

11. **Higher Order Thinking** Ryan measures a rectangle that is 9 feet long and 5 feet wide. Teo measures a rectangle that has an area of 36 square feet. Which rectangle has the greater area? Explain how you found the answer.

 Assessment

12. Marla makes maps of Lower Falls Garden. One map is shown at the right.

    Part A

    Complete the boxes in the equation to show the area of the map at the right.

    $\boxed{} \times \boxed{} = \boxed{}$ square feet

    Part B

    Another map has an area of 27 square feet. If the length is 9 feet, how wide is the other map? How do you know?

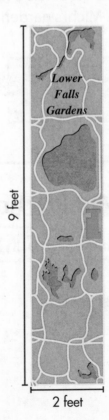

9 feet

Lower Falls Gardens

2 feet

Help Practice Tools Games
Buddy

Another Look!

What is the area of this rectangle?

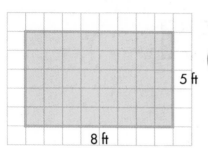

5 ft

8 ft

You can count
squares or multiply
to find the area.

A. You can count the number of unit squares.

There are 40 unit squares.
Each unit square is 1 square foot.

The area of the rectangle is 40 square feet.

B. You can count the number of rows, and multiply by the number of squares in each row. There are 5 rows, and 8 squares in each row.

$5 \times 8 = 40$

The area of the rectangle is 40 square feet.

In **1–3**, find the area.

1.
2 m
9 m

2.
6 in.
4 in.

3.
3 cm
8 cm

In **4–6**, find the missing length of one side. Use grid paper to help.

4.
9 ft
? ft
54 square ft

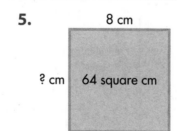

5.
8 cm
? cm
64 square cm

6.
? m
6 m
42 square m

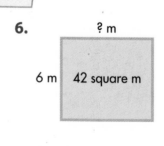

7. Number Sense Rachel's family went on a car trip. They traveled 68 miles the first day. They traveled 10 fewer miles the second day. They traveled 85 miles the third day. How many miles did they travel?

8. Critique Reasoning Diane says that the area of this shape is 32 square inches, because $4 \times 8 = 32$. Do you agree? Explain.

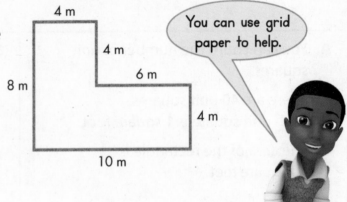

8 in.

4 in.

9. Higher Order Thinking Rubin drew this diagram of his garden. How can you divide the shape to find the area? What is the area of the garden?

4 m

4 m

6 m

8 m

4 m

10 m

You can use grid paper to help.

 Assessment

10. Part A

Jerry builds 5 shelves. Complete the equations to show the area of Shelf A.

□ × □ = □ square feet

Part B

Which is the largest shelf? What is its area? Explain the strategy you used.

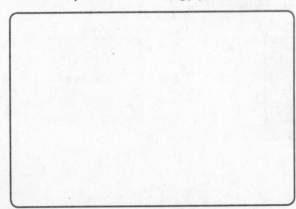

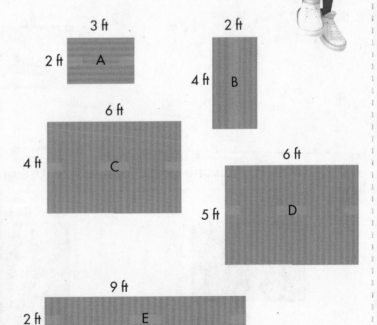

3 ft

2 ft   A

2 ft

4 ft   B

6 ft

4 ft   C

6 ft

5 ft   D

9 ft

2 ft   E

324   Topic 6 | Lesson 6-4

Name _____

Solve & Share

The new reading room floor is a rectangle that is 8 feet wide by 9 feet long. Mrs. Wallace has a rectangular rug that is 8 feet wide by 5 feet long. What area of the reading room floor will not be covered by the rug? *Solve this problem any way you choose.*

I can ...
use properties when multiplying to find the area of squares and rectangles.

SOL Prepares for 4.7

You can draw rectangles on the grid to model with math. *Show your work in the space below!*

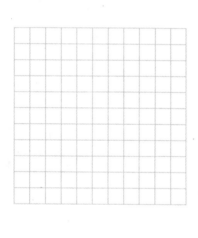

Look Back! **Make Sense and Persevere** Does your strategy change if the rug is in the corner of the room or in the center? Explain why or why not.

Essential Question

How Can the Area of Rectangles Represent the Distributive Property?

A

Gina wants to separate this rectangle into two smaller rectangles. Will the area of the large rectangle equal the sum of the areas of the two small rectangles?

You can use the Distributive Property to break apart facts to find the product.

Area = 7 × 8

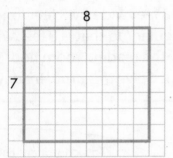

B Separate the 8-unit side into two parts.

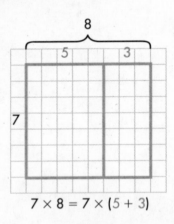

$7 \times 8 = 7 \times (5 + 3)$

C $7 \times 8 = 7 \times (5 + 3) = (7 \times 5) + (7 \times 3)$

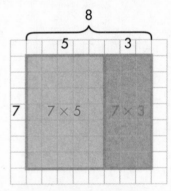

So, the area of the large rectangle is equal to the sum of the areas of the two small rectangles.

Convince Me! **Generalize** Find another way to separate this rectangle into two smaller parts. Write an equation you can use to find the areas of the two smaller rectangles. Is the area of the large rectangle still the same? What can you generalize?

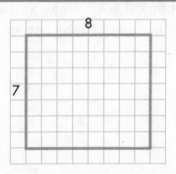

☆ Guided Practice*

Do You Understand?

1. Describe a way to separate a 6 × 6 rectangle into two smaller rectangles.

2. What multiplication facts describe the areas of the two smaller rectangles you identified in Exercise 1?

Do You Know How?

Complete the equation that represents the picture.

3.

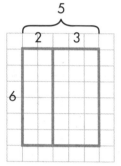

$6 \times \boxed{} = 6 \times (2 + \boxed{})$

$= (\boxed{} \times 2) + (6 \times \boxed{})$

☆ Independent Practice ☆

In **4** and **5**, complete the equation that represents the picture.

4.

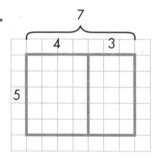

$5 \times \boxed{} = 5 \times (4 + \boxed{})$

$= (\boxed{} \times 4) + (5 \times \boxed{})$

5.

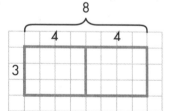

$3 \times \boxed{} = \boxed{} \times (4 + \boxed{})$

$= (\boxed{} \times 4) + (\boxed{} \times \boxed{})$

6. Write the equation that represents the picture.

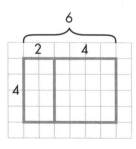

You can use the Distributive Property to help find areas of rectangles.

*For another example, see Set E on page 347.

Problem Solving

7. Model with Math Claudia sold 3 shells last week for $5 each and 2 more shells this week for $5 each. Show two ways to determine how much money Claudia made in the two weeks.

8. Math and Science Amit wants to replace the roof of his dog house with a new wind-resistant material. The roof has two rectangular sides that are 6 feet by 4 feet. What is the total area of the roof?

9. Use Structure Chiya has an 8 × 6 sheet of tiles. Can she separate the sheet into two smaller sheets that are 8 × 4 and 8 × 2? Do the two smaller sheets have the same total area as her original sheet? Explain.

10. Higher Order Thinking List all possible ways to divide the rectangle at the right into 2 smaller rectangles.

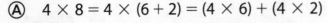

Assessment

11. Which equation represents the total area of the green shapes?

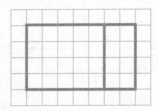

Ⓐ $4 \times 8 = 4 \times (6 + 2) = (4 \times 6) + (4 \times 2)$

Ⓑ $4 \times 7 = 4 \times (3 + 4) = (4 \times 3) + (4 \times 4)$

Ⓒ $4 \times 7 = 4 \times (4 + 3) = (4 \times 4) + (4 \times 3)$

Ⓓ $4 \times 7 = 4 \times (5 + 2) = (4 \times 5) + (4 \times 2)$

Name _____

Another Look!

You can use the Distributive Property to break apart multiplication facts to find the product.

You can separate a rectangle into two smaller rectangles with the same total area.

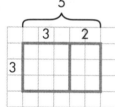

You can write the multiplication fact that represents the area of the large rectangle.

$$4 \times 5 = 20$$

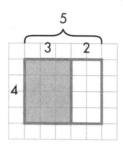

You can write the multiplication facts that represent the area of each of the smaller rectangles.

$$4 \times 5 = 4 \times (3 + 2)$$
$$4 \times 5 = (4 \times 3) + (4 \times 2)$$
$$4 \times 5 = 12 + 8 = 20$$

In **1–4**, complete the equation that represents the picture.

1.

$3 \times \square = \square \times (3 + \square)$

$3 \times \square = (3 \times \square) + (\square \times 2)$

$3 \times \square = \square + \square = 15$

The areas of the large rectangles are equal to the sum of the areas of the smaller rectangles.

2.

$\square \times 7 = \square \times (\square + 4)$

$\square \times 7 = (\square \times 3) + (4 \times \square)$

$\square \times 7 = \square + \square = 28$

3.

$3 \times \square = \square \times (2 + \square)$

$3 \times \square = (3 \times \square) + (\square \times 4)$

$3 \times \square = \square + \square = 18$

4.

$\square \times 6 = \square \times (\square + 3)$

$\square \times 6 = (\square \times 3) + (5 \times \square)$

$\square \times 6 = \square + \square = 30$

5. Tina divided the rectangle at the right into two smaller parts. Show another way to divide the rectangle into two smaller parts. Write the equation you could use to find the area of the two smaller rectangles.

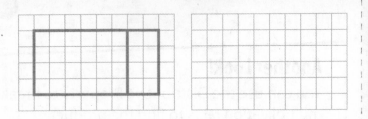

6. **Critique Reasoning** Lee wants to place 48 photographs on a wall at school. He puts the photographs into 8 equal rows. How many photographs are in each row?

7. **Higher Order Thinking** George had 1 sheet of paper. He cuts it into 6 inches by 5 inches, and 3 inches by 6 inches. What were the dimensions and total area of his original sheet of paper? Explain.

8. **Use Structure** Darren has a piece of wood that is 7 inches by 8 inches. Explain how he could divide this large rectangle into two smaller rectangles.

Break apart a problem into smaller problems!

9. Which equation represents the total area of the green shapes?

Ⓐ $3 \times 10 = 3 \times (3 + 6) = (3 \times 3) + (3 \times 6)$

Ⓑ $3 \times 9 = 3 \times (4 + 5) = (3 \times 4) + (3 \times 5)$

Ⓒ $3 \times 9 = 3 \times (3 + 6) = (3 \times 3) + (3 \times 6)$

Ⓓ $3 \times 9 = 3 \times (2 + 7) = (3 \times 2) + (3 \times 7)$

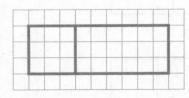

Name _____

Solve & Share

Mrs. Marcum's desk is shaped like the picture below. The length of each side is shown in feet. Find the area of Mrs. Marcum's desk. **Solve this problem any way you choose.**

You can look for relationships. Think about how you can break the problem into simpler parts. *Show your work in the space below!*

I can ...
use properties to find the area of irregular shapes by breaking the shape into smaller parts.

SOL Prepares for 4.7

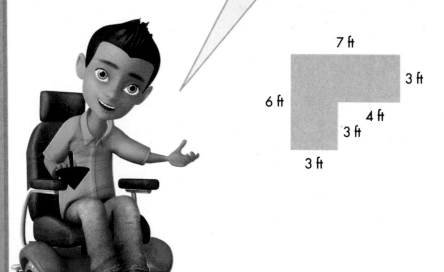

7 ft

3 ft

6 ft

4 ft

3 ft

3 ft

Look Back! **Make Sense and Persevere** How can you check your answer? Is there more than one way to solve this problem? Explain.

How Can You Find the Area of an Irregular Shape?

A

Mr. Fox is covering a miniature golf course putting green with artificial grass. Each artificial grass square is 1 square foot. What is the area of the putting green that Mr. Fox needs to cover?

Look for relationships. Think about smaller shapes that are part of the larger shape.

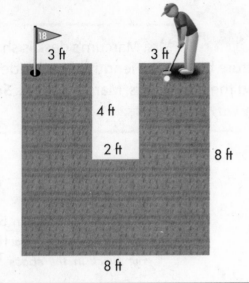

3 ft   3 ft

4 ft

2 ft   8 ft

8 ft

B One Way

You can draw the figure on grid paper. Then count the unit squares to find the area.

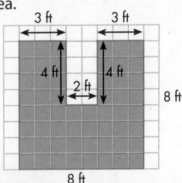

3 ft   3 ft

4 ft   2 ft   4 ft

8 ft

8 ft

The area of the putting green is 56 square feet.

C Another Way

Divide the putting green into rectangles. Find the area of each rectangle. Then add the areas.

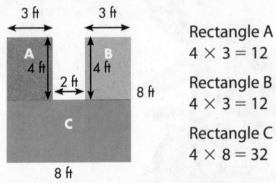

3 ft   3 ft

A   4 ft   2 ft   B   4 ft

C   8 ft

8 ft

Rectangle A
$4 \times 3 = 12$

Rectangle B
$4 \times 3 = 12$

Rectangle C
$4 \times 8 = 32$

$12 + 12 + 32 = 56$. The area of the putting green is 56 square feet.

Convince Me! **Use Structure** Find another way to divide the putting green into smaller rectangles. Explain how you can find the area of the putting green using your smaller rectangles.

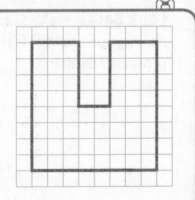

☆Guided Practice *

Do You Understand?

1. Explain why you can find the area of the putting green on page 332 using different rectangles.

2. **Generalize** Explain what operation you use to find the total area of the smaller rectangles.

Do You Know How?

In **3**, and **4**, find the area of each figure. Use grid paper to help.

3.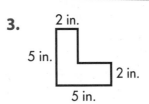

4.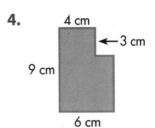

Independent Practice ☆

In **5–8**, find the area of each figure. Use grid paper to help.

5.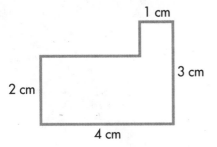

6.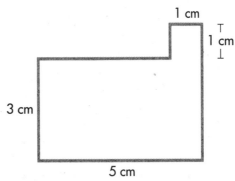

7.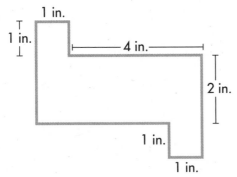

8.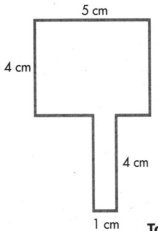

*For another example, see Set F on page 348.   **Topic 6** | Lesson 6-6   **333**

Problem Solving

9. **Reasoning** Mr. Kendel is making a model house. The footprint for the house is shown at the right. What is the total area? Explain your reasoning.

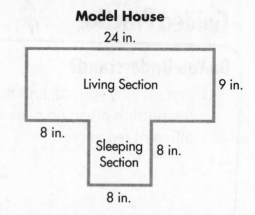

Model House

24 in.

Living Section   9 in.

8 in.

Sleeping Section   8 in.

8 in.

10. **⇄ Vocabulary** Fill in the blanks. Mandy finds the _____ of this shape by dividing it into rectangles. Phil gets the same answer by counting _____.

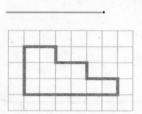

11. **Algebra** Use a question mark to represent the unknown quantity in the phrase "six times a number is 24." Solve the equation.

12. **Higher Order Thinking** Mrs. Delancy used 3-inch square tiles to make the design at the right. What is the area of the design she made? Explain how you found it.

3 in.

✓ **Assessment**

13. Jared drew the figure to the right. Draw lines to show how you can divide the shape to find the area. What is the area of the figure?

☐ square inches

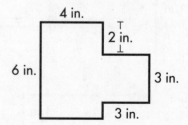

4 in.

2 in.

6 in.

3 in.

3 in.

Name _____

Another Look!

How can you find the area of the irregular shape below?

You can count unit squares, or divide the shape into rectangles.

Place the shape on grid paper. Then you can count unit squares.

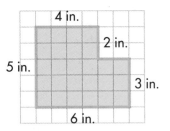

The area of the irregular shape is 26 square inches.

You can divide the shape into rectangles. Find the area of each rectangle. Then add the areas.

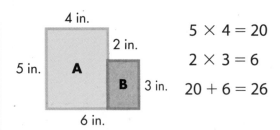

$5 \times 4 = 20$

$2 \times 3 = 6$

$20 + 6 = 26$

The area of the irregular shape is 26 square inches.

In **1–4**, find the area of each irregular shape. Use grid paper to help.

1.

2 in.
2 in.
6 in.
2 in.
5 in.

2.

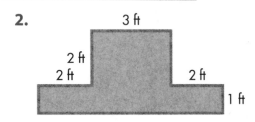

3 ft
2 ft
2 ft
2 ft
1 ft

3.

5 cm
3 cm
2 cm
4 cm

4.

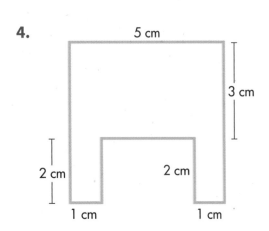

5 cm
3 cm
2 cm
2 cm
2 cm
1 cm
1 cm

5. Reasoning Tony made this diagram of his vegetable garden. What is the total area? Explain your reasoning.

Vegetable Garden

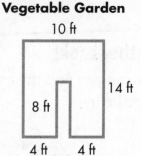

10 ft

14 ft

8 ft

4 ft   4 ft

6. Math and Science Mr. Thomson wants to protect his garage by installing a flood barrier. He connects 2 barriers side by side. Each barrier is 9 feet long by 2 feet high. What is the combined area of the barriers?

7. Number Sense Hadori made this solid figure by paper folding. What is the name of the figure she made? How many faces, edges, and vertices does it have?

8. Higher Order Thinking Jordan made this design from three pieces of square-shaped cloth. What is the total area of the design Jordan made? Explain how you found your answer.

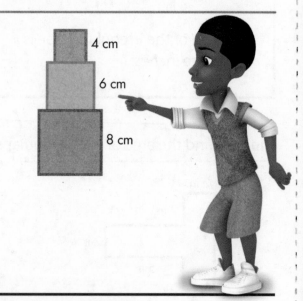

4 cm

6 cm

8 cm

✓ **Assessment**

9. Daniel drew the figure on the right. Draw lines to show how you can divide the figure to find the area. What is the area of the figure?

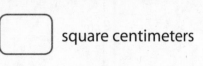
square centimeters

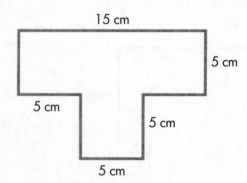

15 cm

5 cm

5 cm

5 cm

5 cm

Solve

Solve & Share

Mr. Anderson is tiling his kitchen. He will not need tiles for the areas covered by the kitchen island or the counter. How many square meters of tiles does Mr. Anderson need?

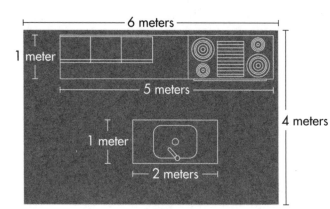

6 meters

1 meter

5 meters

4 meters

1 meter

2 meters

I can ...
use the relationships between quantities to break a problem into simpler parts.

 SOL Prepares for 4.7

Thinking Habits
Be a good thinker!
These questions can help you.

- What patterns can I see and describe?

- How can I use the patterns to solve the problem?

- Can I see expressions and objects in different ways?

Look Back! **Use Structure** Is the tiled area greater than or less than the total area of the kitchen?

Essential Question **How Can You Use Structure to Solve Problems?**

A

Janet is painting a door. She needs to paint the entire door except for the window.

What is the area of the part of the door that needs paint?

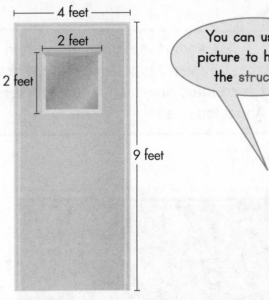

├── 4 feet ──┤

├── 2 feet ──┤

2 feet

9 feet

You can use the picture to help see the structure.

What do I need to do to solve this problem?

I need to find the area of the door without the window.

B **How can I make use of structure to solve this problem?**

I can

- break the problem into simpler parts.

- find equivalent expressions.

C

Here's my thinking...

I will subtract the area of the window from the total area.

<u>Find the area of the whole door.</u>
4 feet × 9 feet = 36 square feet

<u>Find the area of the window.</u>
2 feet × 2 feet = 4 square feet

<u>Subtract to find the area that needs paint.</u>
36 − 4 = 32 square feet

The area of the part of the door that needs paint is 32 square feet.

Convince Me! **Use Structure** Janet thinks of a different way to solve the problem. She says, "I can divide the area I need to paint into 4 smaller rectangles. Then I will find the areas of these 4 smaller rectangles." Does Janet's strategy make sense? Explain.

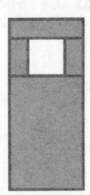

---

338 **Topic 6** | Lesson 6-7

☆ Guided Practice*

Use Structure

Lil glued beads on the border of the frame. What is the area of the part she decorated with beads?

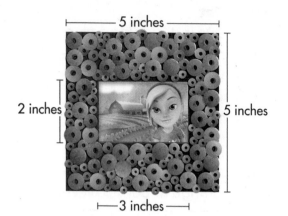

5 inches

2 inches   5 inches

3 inches

1. How can you think about the total area of the frame?

2. Use what you know to solve the problem.

A picture can help you see equivalent expressions. Think about the structure.

Independent Practice ☆

Use Structure

A keypad has 10 rubber buttons. Each button is 1 centimeter by 2 centimeters. The rest is made out of plastic. Is the area of the plastic greater than the area of the rubber buttons?

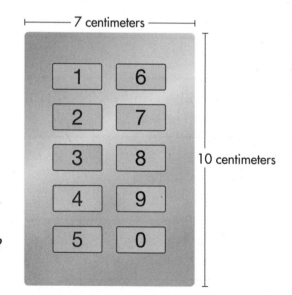

7 centimeters

10 centimeters

3. How can you break the problem into simpler parts? What is the hidden question?

4. How can you find the area of all the rubber buttons?

5. Use what you know to solve the problem.

Place Mat

Genevieve is designing a placemat. The center measures 8 inches by 10 inches. A 2-inch border goes around the center. Genevieve cuts the corners to make the placemat an octagon. She wants to find the area of the placemat.

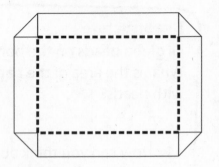

6. **Use Structure** What are the lengths and widths of each rectangular border piece?

7. **Use Appropriate Tools** How can Genevieve find the exact area of the 4 corner pieces using grid paper?

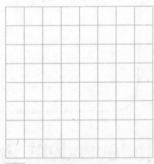

 = 1 square in.

8. **Model with Math** What equation can Genevieve use to find the area of the center? Find the area of the center using your equation.

Use structure to simplify a problem.

9. **Reasoning** How are the quantities in this problem related?

10. **Be Precise** Solve the problem. Explain what unit you used for your answer.

Name _____

Another Look!

How can you find the area of the shaded part of the figure at the right?

Tell how you can use structure to solve the problem.

- I can break the problem into simpler parts.

- I can find equivalent expressions.

8 cm

5 cm

2 cm
3 cm

Solve the problem.

> Use structure to think of a complex shape as simpler shapes.

The shaded area equals the total area minus the non-shaded area.

Find the area of the large rectangle.	$5 \times 8 = 40$ square in.
Find the area of the small rectangle.	$2 \times 3 = 6$ square in.
Subtract to find the area of the shaded part.	$40 - 6 = 34$ square in.

The area of the shaded part is 34 square inches.

Use Structure

A tablet computer has a 1-inch border of plastic around the screen. What is the area of the plastic border?

10 inches

7 inches

1. Tell how you can use structure to solve the problem.

2. Find two different ways to express the area of the screen.

3. Use these equivalent expressions to solve the problem.

Playground

Mr. Velasquez built a playground. It has one section with a slide and another section with a swing set. A pathway connects the two areas. The slide is 2 meters high. The areas and the pathway are covered in asphalt. Mr. Velasquez wants to know how much of the playground is covered in asphalt.

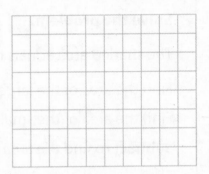

Section	Length (meters)	Width (meters)	Area
Swing set	8	3	
Slide	8	2	
Pathway	5	1	

4. **Reasoning** Fill in the table above to show the area of each section. Use the grid to draw a possible diagram of the playground.

5. **Construct Arguments** Find the total area covered in asphalt. Explain your reasoning using math.

6. **Make Sense and Persevere** Did you use addition or subtraction to solve this problem? Could you have used the other operation instead? Explain.

Use structure to find different ways of looking at areas.

7. **Use Structure** Find the area on the grid that is not covered in asphalt. Use this to check your work.

Name _____

Shade a path from **START** to **FINISH**. Follow the quotients that are odd numbers. You can only move up, down, right, or left.

I can ...
divide within 100.

Start				
15 ÷ 5	45 ÷ 5	40 ÷ 8	36 ÷ 4	6 ÷ 3
28 ÷ 7	12 ÷ 2	90 ÷ 9	63 ÷ 9	0 ÷ 8
48 ÷ 8	50 ÷ 5	81 ÷ 9	9 ÷ 3	56 ÷ 7
20 ÷ 5	48 ÷ 6	42 ÷ 6	10 ÷ 5	6 ÷ 1
30 ÷ 3	16 ÷ 8	35 ÷ 7	45 ÷ 9	56 ÷ 8

Finish

TOPIC 6 · Vocabulary Review

A-Z
Glossary

Understand Vocabulary

Choose the best term from the Word List. Write it on the blank.

1. A(n) _____ has sides that are each 1 unit long.

2. _____ is the number of unit squares that cover a region or shape.

3. You can use the _____ to break apart facts and find the _____.

4. A unit square has an area of 1 _____.

5. When you _____, you give an approximate answer.

Write *always, sometimes,* or *never.*

6. *Area* is _____ measured in square meters.

7. *Multiplication* _____ involves joining equal groups.

8. The *area* of a shape can _____ be represented as the sum of the *areas* of smaller rectangles.

Use Vocabulary in Writing

9. What is the area of this rectangle? Explain how you solved the problem. Use at least 3 terms from the Word List in your answer.

Set A pages 301–306

A unit square has sides that are 1 unit long.

Count the unit squares that cover the shape. The exact count is the area of the shape.

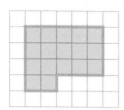 ☐ = 1 unit square

17 unit squares cover the shape. The area of the shape is 17 square units.

Sometimes you need to estimate to find the area. First count the full squares. Then estimate partially filled squares.

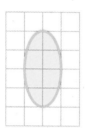 About 6 unit squares cover this shape.

Remember area is the number of unit squares needed to cover a region with no gaps or overlaps.

In **1** and **2**, count to find the area. Tell if the area is exact or an estimate.

1.

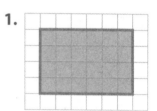

2.

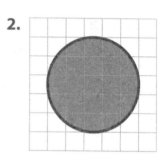

Set B pages 307–312

Unit squares can be different sizes. The size of a unit square determines the area.

 16 unit squares

 4 unit squares

☐ = 1 square unit   ☐ = 1 square unit

Area = 16 square units   Area = 4 square units

The measurements are different because different sizes of unit squares were used.

Remember that you can use unit squares to measure area.

Draw unit squares to cover the figures and find the area. Use the unit squares shown.

1.

☐ = 1 square unit

2.

☐ = 1 square unit

The unit squares below represent square inches.

What is the area of the figure below?

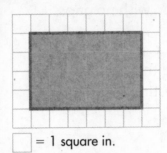

☐ = 1 square in.

24 unit squares cover the figure.
The area of the figure is measured in square inches.

So, the area of the figure is 24 square inches.

Remember that you can measure using standard or metric units of length for unit squares.

In **1** and **2**, each unit square represents a standard unit. Count the unit squares. Then write the area.

1.

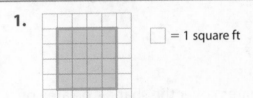

☐ = 1 square ft

2.

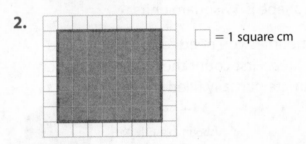

☐ = 1 square cm

You can find area by counting the number of rows and multiplying by the number of squares in each row.

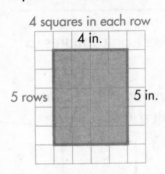

There are 5 rows.
There are 4 squares in each row.

5 × 4 = 20

The area of the figure is 20 square inches.

Remember that you can multiply the number of rows by the number of squares in each row to find the area.

In **1–3**, find the area of each figure. Use grid paper to help.

1.

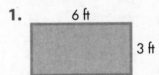

2.

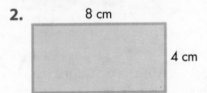

3.

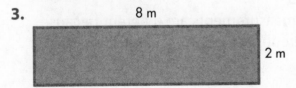

Set E pages 325–330

You can use the Distributive Property to break apart facts to find the product.

Separate the 5 unit side into two parts.

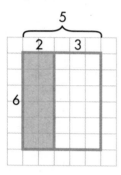

Area of the large rectangle: $6 \times 5 = 30$

Areas of the small rectangles:

$6 \times 2 = 12$

$6 \times 3 = 18$

Add the two areas: $12 + 18 = 30$

You can write an equation to show that the area of the large rectangle is equal to the sum of the areas of the two small rectangles.

$6 \times 5 = 6 \times (2 + 3) = (6 \times 2) + (6 \times 3)$

When you divide a rectangle into two smaller rectangles, the total area does not change!

Remember that you can separate a rectangle into two smaller rectangles with the same total area.

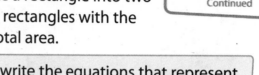
In **1–3**, write the equations that represent the total area of the red shapes. Find the area.

1.

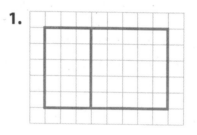

2.

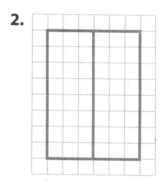

3.

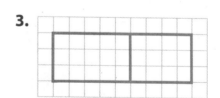

Find the area of this irregular shape.

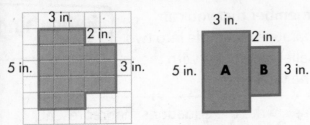

You can place the shape on grid paper and count the unit squares. The area of the shape is 21 square inches.

You can also divide the shape into rectangles. Find the area of each rectangle and add.

$5 \times 3 = 15$ square inches

$3 \times 2 = 6$ square inches

$15 + 6 = 21$ square inches

Remember that you can add smaller areas to find a total area.

In **1** and **2**, find the area of each shape.

1.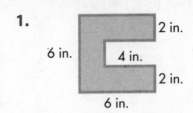

2.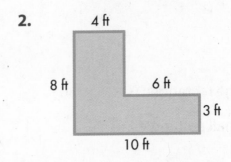

Think about these questions to help you use **structure** in solving problems.

Thinking Habits

- What patterns can I see and describe?

- How can I use the patterns to solve the problem?

- Can I see expressions and objects in different ways?

Remember to look for simpler ways of representing an area.

Debra made this design from 1-inch square tiles. What is the area of the blue tiles?

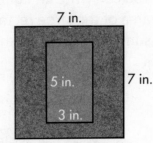

1. How can you express the area of the blue tiles?

2. Solve the problem. Explain how you solved.

1. Count to find the area of the shape. Tell if the area is exact or an estimate.

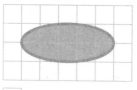

☐ = 1 unit square

3. Lewis says that the figure below has an area of 4 square meters. Is he correct? Explain.

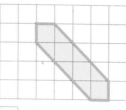

☐ = 1 square cm

2. Choose all of the ways to break apart the area of the large rectangle into the sum of the areas of two smaller rectangles.

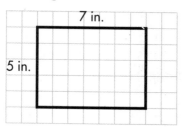

7 in.

5 in.

☐ $5 \times 7 = 5 \times (1 + 5) = (5 \times 1) + (5 \times 5)$

☐ $5 \times 7 = 5 \times (3 + 4) = (5 \times 3) + (5 \times 4)$

☐ $5 \times 7 = 5 \times (2 + 3) = (5 \times 2) + (5 \times 3)$

☐ $5 \times 7 = 5 \times (1 + 6) = (5 \times 1) + (5 \times 6)$

☐ $5 \times 7 = 5 \times (2 + 5) = (5 \times 2) + (5 \times 5)$

4. Use the Distributive Property to write the equation that represents the picture.

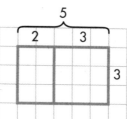

5

2   3

3

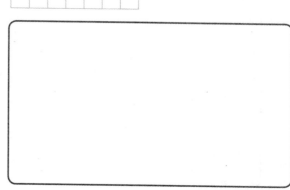

5. Ms. Blanca makes a design with square inches of colored paper shown below. What is the total area of the design?

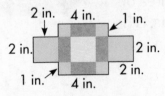

(A) 16 square inches

(B) 20 square inches

(C) 24 square inches

(D) 32 square inches

6. Jared draws a rectangle. Explain how to find the area.

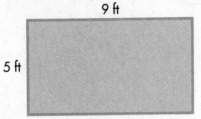

7. Fran has a square garden. One side of the garden is 3 feet long. What is the area of Fran's garden?

(A) 9 square feet

(B) 10 square feet

(C) 12 square feet

(D) 14 square feet

8. Find the missing side length. Then find the area.

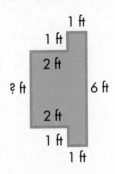

9. Stella draws a rectangle with an area of 56 square centimeters. She labels one side 7 centimeters, but she forgot the other side. What is the missing length?

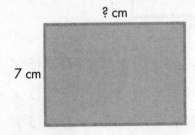

(A) 5 cm

(B) 6 cm

(C) 7 cm

(D) 8 cm

10. What is the area of Ron's figure?

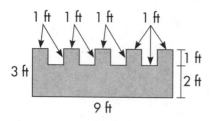

Ⓐ 20 square feet

Ⓑ 23 square feet

Ⓒ 32 square feet

Ⓓ 36 square feet

11. Maddie makes a mosaic with 1-inch glass squares, as shown below. Which color of glass has the greatest area in Maddie's mosaic?

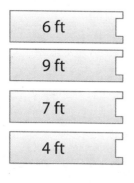

12. Draw lines to match each side length of a square to its area.

6 ft		16 square feet
9 ft		49 square feet
7 ft		81 square feet
4 ft		36 square feet

13. Ryan and Jodie each make a rectangle on grid paper. Explain how to find the area of each rectangle.

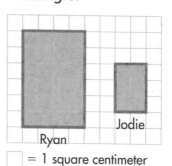

□ = 1 square centimeter

14. Some students in Springfield make a parade float with the letter *S* on it. Draw lines to divide the shape into rectangles. Then find how many square feet the letter is.

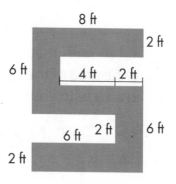

Ⓐ 28 square ft   Ⓒ 56 square ft

Ⓑ 54 square ft   Ⓓ 90 square ft

15. Max draws a rectangle with an area of 24 square centimeters. For questions 18a–18d, choose *Yes* or *No* to tell if the lengths are possible side lengths of Max's rectangle.

18a. 4 cm by 7 cm   ○ Yes ○ No

18b. 4 cm by 6 cm   ○ Yes ○ No

18c. 4 cm by 5 cm   ○ Yes ○ No

18d. 3 cm by 8 cm   ○ Yes ○ No

16. A community center builds a new activity room in the shape shown below. Explain how to find the area of the room, and solve.

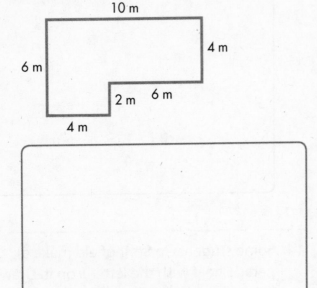

17. Show 2 different unit squares that you can use to measure the area of these rectangles. Find the area with your unit squares.

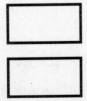

18. Ethan wants to know the area of the yellow part of this design.

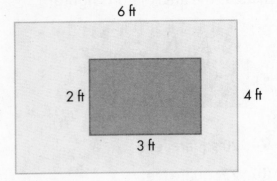

Part A

Explain how you can break this problem into simpler problems.

Part B

Find the yellow area. Show your work.

Name _____

Banner Design

Jessie is designing a banner that has red, blue, and white sections.
The **Banner Details** list shows the rules for each color.
The **Jessie's Banner** diagram shows the different sections of the banner.

Banner Details

- Red sections must have a total area greater than 40 square inches.
- Blue sections must have a total area greater than 30 square inches.
- The white section must have an area less than 40 square inches.

Use the **Jessie's Banner** diagram to answer Question 1.

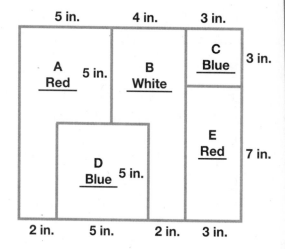

1. To check if his banner fits the rules, Jessie started this table. Complete the table. Use multiplication and addition as needed.

Section	Color	Show How to Find the Area	Area
A	Red		
B	White		
C	Blue		9 square inches
D	Blue		
E	Red	7 × 3	

Use the table above and the **Banner Details** list to answer Question 2.

2. Is Jessie's banner within the totals in the **Banner Details** list? Explain.

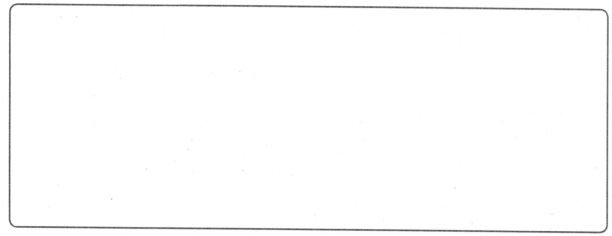

3. Jessie makes a square patch to go on top of the banner.

Jessie's Patch

Part A

Draw unit squares to cover the patch. How many unit squares cover the patch?

Part B

Jessie says if he checks the area by multiplying, the area will be the same as if he counts each unit square. Is he correct? Explain.

☐ = 1 square cm

4. Jessie uses two colors to make the patch. The colors have different areas.

Part A

Explain how to separate the square into two smaller rectangles with different areas. Use multiplication to find the areas of each of the smaller rectangles.

Part B

Is the area of the square equal to the total area of the two smaller rectangles? Use an equation to explain.

Represent and Interpret Data

Essential Question: How can data be represented, interpreted, and analyzed?

Digital Resources

Solve   Learn   Glossary   Practice Buddy

Tools   Assessment   Help   Games

The weather and temperature can change a lot during different seasons.

The seasons can have a huge impact on how we lead our daily lives.

I better prepare for the upcoming season! Here's a project on seasons and data.

Math and Science Project: Seasons

Do Research Use the Internet or other sources to find information about patterns of temperature in the different seasons where you live. Include information about the average monthly temperatures and the record low and high temperatures.

Journal: Write a Report Include what you found. Also in your report:

- For one week, record the daily high and low temperatures in the area where you live. Make a graph displaying this information.

- Find the difference between the highest and lowest daily temperatures from your graph.

Name _____

Review What You Know

A-Z Vocabulary

Choose the best term from the box.
Write it on the blank.

| • multiplication | • number line |
| • equal groups | • multiples |

1. _____ have the same number of items.

2. 0, 2, 4, 6, and 8 are _____ of 2.

3. _____ is used to find a total when joining equal groups.

Multiplication

In **4** and **5**, complete the equation.

4. $5 \times 3 =$ ____

5. $3 \times$ ____ $= 21$

6. Make a bar diagram to represent 4×6.

Multiplication on the Number Line

7. Ed bought 2 bags of grapefruit. There are 6 grapefruit in each bag. How many grapefruit did he buy? Draw jumps on the number line to find the answer.

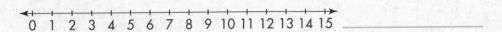

8. Show the multiplication fact 3×4 on the number line. Write the product.

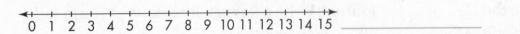

Finding Area

9. Count to find the area of the rectangle.

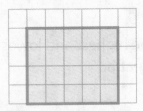

☐ = 1 square inch   _____

356   **Topic 7** | Review What You Know

My Word Cards

Use the examples for each word on the front of the card to help complete the definitions on the back.

scaled picture graph

Plants Sold at the Garden Shop

April	🌱 🌱 🌱 🌱 🌱
May	🌱 🌱 🌱 🌱 🌱 🌱

Each 🌱 = 5 plants.

key

Plants Sold at the Garden Shop

April	🌱 🌱 🌱 🌱 🌱
May	🌱 🌱 🌱 🌱 🌱 🌱

Each 🌱 = 5 plants. ← **key**

scaled bar graph

Favorite Activities

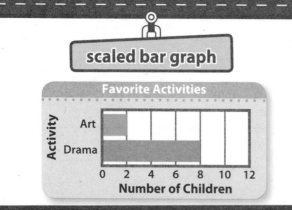

scale

Favorite Activities

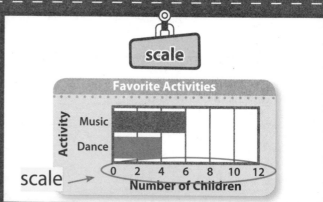

scale →

frequency table

frequency

Simon's Book Shop

Kind of Book	Number Sold
Fiction	25
Nonfiction	40

DATA

data

Rico's Paper Chains

Number of Paper Chains	Length
3	6 in.
2	7 in.

DATA

data →

survey

Favorite Color

Red	Green	Yellow	Blue	Orange
ℍℍ	ℍℍ	//	ℍℍ	ℍℍ
ℍℍ	//			ℍℍ
ℍℍ				

My Word Cards

Complete each definition. Extend learning by writing your own definitions.

A _____ explains what each symbol represents in a picture graph.

A graph using pictures or symbols to show data is called a

_____.

The numbers that show the units used

on a graph are called a _____.

A graph using bars to show data is called a

_____.

Pieces of information are called

_____.

A table used to show the number of times something occurs is called a

_____.

Collecting information by asking a number of people the same question and recording their answers is called a

_____.

Name _____

☆ ☆
Solve & Share

Students in Jorge's class took a survey of their favorite cereals and made this graph to show the results. Name at least three facts about the information in the graph.

I can ...
use picture graphs and bar graphs to answer questions about data sets.

SOL 3.15b

You can use structure. How can you find the number of votes for each type of cereal?

Favorite Cereals	
Berry Crunch	✕ ✕ ✕ ✕ ⟍
Honey Granola	✕ ✕
Corn Puffs	✕ ✕ ✕ ⟍
Nuts and Wheat	✕ ✕ ✕ ✕ ✕

Each ✕ = 2 votes. Each ⟍ = 1 vote.

Look Back! **Be Precise** What do the two different symbols on the graph stand for?

Essential Question: How Can You Read Picture Graphs?

A

How many teams are in the East Falls League?

Information you collect is called data. A scaled picture graph uses pictures or symbols to show data.

The scale is the number each picture or symbol represents.

Number of Hockey Teams in Each League

East Falls	✕ ✕ ✕ ╱
North Falls	✕ ✕ ╱
South Falls	✕ ✕
West Falls	✕ ✕ ✕ ✕ ✕ ╱

Each ✕ = 2 teams.
Each ╱ = 1 team.

The key explains the scale used in the graph.

B Use the key.

Look at the data for East Falls League.

There are 3 ✕ and 1 ╱ .

The 3 ✕ represent $3 \times 2 = 6$ teams.

The 1 ╱ represents $1 \times 1 = 1$ team.

$6 + 1 = 7$

There are 7 teams in the East Falls League.

C How many more teams does the East Falls League have than the South Falls League?

Use the picture graph to write equations and compare the two rows.

East Falls ✕ ✕ ✕ ╱
$3 \times 2 + 1 = 7$

South Falls ✕ ✕
$2 \times 2 = 4$
Subtract: $7 - 4 = 3$

The East Falls League has 3 more teams than the South Falls League.

Convince Me! **Be Precise** Tell something about each league you can find out from the picture graph.

Another Example

A scaled bar graph uses bars to represent and compare information. This bar graph shows the number of goals scored by different players on a hockey team. The scale shows the units used.

On this bar graph, each grid line represents two units. Every other grid line is labeled: 0, 4, 8, and so on. For example, the line halfway between 4 and 8 represents 6 goals.

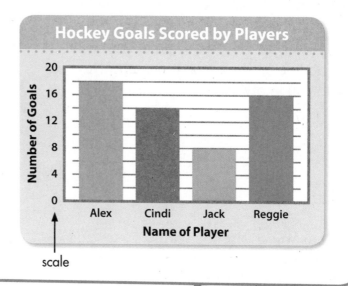

scale

☆ Guided Practice *

Do You Understand?

In **1** and **2**, use the bar graph above.

1. How many goals in all did Alex and Reggie score?

Do You Know How?

2. Explain how to find how many more goals Alex scored than Cindi.

☆ Independent Practice ☆

In **3–5**, use the picture graph.

3. Which area has lights on for the most hours each week?

4. Which area has lights on for exactly 50 hours each week?

5. In one week, how many more hours are lights on in the exercise room than in the swimming pool?

Hours of Light Usage at Sports Center
Number of Hours Lights Are on Each Week

Exercise Room	🔆🔆🔆🔆🔆🔆🔆🔅
Locker Room	🔆🔆🔆🔆🔆🔆🔆🔆
Swimming Pool	🔆🔆🔆🔅
Tennis Court	🔆🔆🔆🔆🔆

Each 🔆 = 10 hours. Each 🔅 = 5 hours.

Problem Solving

In **6–8**, use the bar graph at the right.

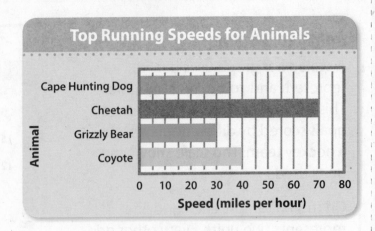

Top Running Speeds for Animals

6. **Be Precise** How many units does each grid line on the graph represent? How do you know?

7. **Reasoning** Use the symbols >, <, or = to show two ways to compare the top speeds of the cheetah and the coyote.

8. **Higher Order Thinking** The top running speeds of which two animals, when added together, equal the top running speed of a cheetah?

✓ **Assessment**

In **9** and **10**, use the picture graph.

9. For which days can you use the equation 9 × 7 to find how many points were scored? Choose all that apply.

   ☐ October 3
   ☐ October 10
   ☐ October 17
   ☐ October 24
   ☐ None of the days

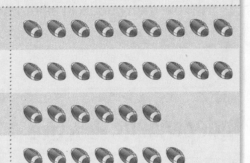

Football Team Scores

October 3	🏈🏈🏈🏈🏈🏈🏈🏈🏈
October 10	🏈🏈🏈🏈🏈🏈🏈🏈🏈
October 17	🏈🏈🏈🏈🏈
October 24	🏈🏈🏈🏈🏈🏈

Each 🏈 = 7 points.

10. On which days did the football team score fewer than 50 points? Choose all that apply.

    ☐ October 3
    ☐ October 10
    ☐ October 17
    ☐ October 24
    ☐ None of the days

Basic facts can help you read a picture graph!

Name _____

Help Practice Tools Games
       Buddy

**Homework
& Practice** 7-1
Read Picture Graphs
and Bar Graphs

Another Look!

You can use a picture graph
or a bar graph to represent
and interpret data.

Picture graphs use pictures or parts of
pictures to represent data.

Gold Medals Won at 2010 Vancouver Winter Olympics

Sweden	🪙 🪙 🪙 🪙 🪙
France	🪙 🪙
Switzerland	🪙 🪙 🪙 🪙 🪙 🪙
Russia	🪙 🪙 🪙

Each 🪙 = 1 gold medal.

Picture graphs have keys to explain the
scale being used and what each picture
represents.

Bar graphs use bars to represent data.

Bar graphs have scales that show the
units used.

Each line in this bar graph represents
2 medals.

In **1–4**, use the picture graph at the right.

1. How many houses were built in City B?

2. How many houses were built in City B
   and City F?

3. How many more houses were built in
   City D than in City E in 1 year?

4. Put the cities in order from fewest
   houses built to most.

Number of Houses Built in 1 Year

City A	🏠 🏠 🏠 🏠 🏠
City B	🏠 🏠 🏠 🏠
City C	🏠 🏠 🏠
City D	🏠 🏠 🏠 🏠 🏠 🏠 🏠
City E	🏠 🏠 🏠 🏠 🏠
City F	🏠 🏠 🏠 🏠 🏠 🏠

Each 🏠 = 10 houses. Each 🏠 = 5 houses.

In **5–8**, use the bar graph at the right.

5. **Higher Order Thinking** How many more people chose football or soccer than baseball or basketball?

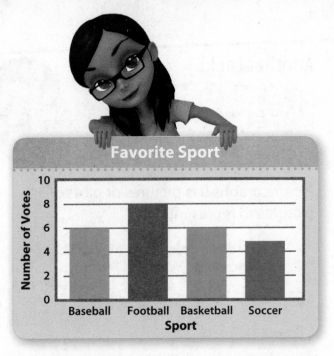

Favorite Sport

6. Compare the votes for football and the combined votes for baseball and soccer. Use the symbol >, <, or =.

7. Which sports received the same number of votes? How can you tell?

8. **Generalize** By just looking at the bars, how can you tell which sport got the most votes? The fewest votes? Which sports were they?

✔ **Assessment**

In **9** and **10**, use the picture graph at the right.

9. Which students read more books than Phil? Choose all that apply.

☐ Anders   ☐ Miguel

☐ Jamal   ☐ Tamika

☐ Nancy

10. Which students read fewer than 12 books? Choose all that apply.

☐ Anders   ☐ Miguel

☐ Jamal   ☐ Tamika

☐ Nancy

Books Read

| Nancy |
| Tamika |
| Jamal |
| Phil |
| Anders |
| Miguel |

Each ☐☐ = 4 books.   Each ☐ = 2 books.

Name _____

☆ ☆
Solve & Share

Mary is helping her teacher count school playground equipment. She records the data in a frequency table. Use the data in the table to complete the picture graph. Write two statements about your completed graph.

I can ...
make a picture graph to record information and answer questions about a data set.

 SOL 3.15a

DATA

School Playground Equipment		
Equipment	**Tally**	**Number**
Basketballs	𝟚𝟙 𝟚𝟙	10
Jump Ropes	𝟚𝟙 𝟚𝟙	10
Bats	𝟚𝟙	5
Soccer Balls	𝟚𝟙 𝟚𝟙 𝟚𝟙	15

_____

Basketballs	
Jump Ropes	
Bats	
Soccer Balls	

Each 🏀 = 2 items.   Each 🏀 = 1 item.

You can make sense of problems. How can the tally marks and the key help you represent the data in the picture graph?

Look Back! **Be Precise** How did you know the number of symbols to draw for jump ropes?

Essential Question # How Do You Make a Picture Graph?

A

Sam recorded the number of each kind of bicycle a store sold during one month. He made a frequency table. Use the table to make a picture graph.

You can also collect data with a survey by asking people questions.

DATA

Kinds of Bicycles Sold		
Kind of Bicycle	**Tally**	**Number**
Road	𝍷𝍷𝍷𝍷 𝍷𝍷𝍷𝍷	10
Track	𝍷𝍷𝍷𝍷 𝍷𝍷𝍷𝍷 𝍷𝍷𝍷𝍷 𝍷𝍷𝍷𝍷	20
Training	𝍷𝍷𝍷𝍷 𝍷𝍷𝍷𝍷 𝍷𝍷𝍷𝍷	15
Racing	𝍷𝍷𝍷𝍷 𝍷𝍷𝍷𝍷	10

B

Write a title for the picture graph.

The title is "Kinds of Bicycles Sold."

Choose a symbol for the key. Decide what each whole symbol and half-symbol will represent.

Each △ means 10 bicycles.

Each ◣ means 5 bicycles.

A half-symbol is used to represent 5 bicycles because 5 is half of 10.

C

Set up the graph and list the kinds of bicycles. Decide how many symbols you need for each number of bicycles sold. Draw the symbols.

Kinds of Bicycles Sold	
Road	△
Track	△ △
Training	△ ◣
Racing	△

Each △ = 10 bicycles.
Each ◣ = 5 bicycles.

Convince Me! **Model with Math** Suppose 25 mountain bicycles were also sold. Draw symbols to show a row in the picture graph for mountain bicycles. Explain how you decided.

☆ Guided Practice *

Do You Understand?

In **1** and **2**, use the picture graph on page 366.

1. **Reasoning** Explain the symbols that were used for the number of training bicycles sold.

2. If the scale used in the key were ▲ = 2 bicycles, how many symbols would be used for the number of road bicycles sold? For the number of track bicycles sold?

Do You Know How?

3. Use the table to complete the picture graph.

Favorite School Lunch		
Lunch	**Tally**	**Number**
Taco	//	2
Pizza	THL ///	8
Salad	///	3

Favorite School Lunch	
Taco	
Pizza	
Salad	

Each 🛍 = 2 votes.
Each 🛍 = 1 vote.

☆ Independent Practice ☆

In **4–6**, use the data in the chart.

4. Complete the picture graph.

Cubs	
Hawks	
Lions	
Roadrunners	

Each ● = __ goals. Each ◖ = __ goals.

5. Which two teams scored more goals, the Cubs and the Lions or the Hawks and the Roadrunners?

Goals Each Team Has Scored		
Team Name	**Tally**	**Number**
Cubs	THL THL	10
Hawks	THL THL THL THL	20
Lions	THL THL THL THL THL THL	30
Roadrunners	THL THL THL	15

6. Explain how you decided the number of each symbol to draw to show the goals for the Roadrunners.

Problem Solving

In **7–9**, use the frequency table at the right.

7. Model with Math Make a picture graph to show the data in the table.

Favorite Vegetables

DATA

Kind	Tally	Number
Corn	////	4
Green Beans	//	2
Tomatoes	//// /	5

8. Ask six students in your class which of the three vegetables is their favorite. Record the answers in your picture graph.

9. Make Sense and Persevere What is the difference between the odd number and the sum of the even numbers in the table?

10. Higher Order Thinking Suppose you are going to make a picture graph to show the data in the Simon's Book Shop table. Choose a symbol to stand for 5 books sold. Draw the row for fiction books sold. Justify your drawing.

Simon's Book Shop

DATA

Kind of Book	Number Sold
Fiction	25
Nonfiction	40
Poetry	20
Dictionary	15

✓ Assessment

11. The Garden Shop sold 30 plants in May, 35 plants in June, and 25 plants in April. Complete the picture graph for this data. Choose the symbols you will use.

Plants Sold at Garden Shop

April	
May	
June	

Each ____ = 10 plants.   Each ____ = 5 plants.

Help Practice Tools Games
      Buddy

Another Look!

The frequency table shows items that were ordered for lunch. Follow the steps below to learn how to make a picture graph.

> Data in a table can be shown in a picture graph.

Items Ordered

Food	Tally	Number
Pasta	ⷧⷧ I	6
Salad	IIII	4
Casserole	ⷧⷧ ⷧⷧ	10
Fish	ⷧⷧ IIII	9

Items Ordered

Pasta

Salad

Casserole

Fish

Each ▭ = 2 meals.
Each ▭ = 1 meal.

Step 1

Write a title that explains what the picture graph shows.

Step 2

Choose a symbol and a scale.

Step 3

Draw in the graph the number of symbols that are needed for each item.

---

1. Complete the frequency table to show how Ms. Hashimoto's class voted for their favorite type of movie.

Favorite Type of Movie

Type	Tally	Number
Action	ⷧⷧ III	
Comedy	III	
Drama	ⷧⷧ I	
Animated	ⷧⷧ ⷧⷧ	

Which two types of movies had more votes, comedy and animated or action and drama?

2. Use the table in Exercise 1 to complete the picture graph.

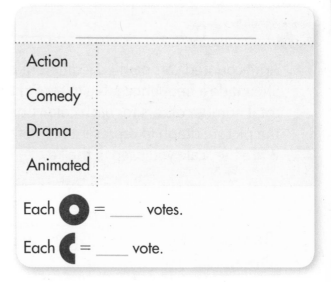

How did you choose the number that each symbol represents?

3. **Math and Science** There are 61 days in March and April. Mrs. Dorsey recorded 18 sunny days in March and 12 sunny days in April. How many days were not sunny?

4. **A-Z Vocabulary** A _____ can also be used to represent and compare the same data set using bars instead of pictures or symbols.

In **5–7**, use the picture graph at the right.

5. **Critique Reasoning** Pamela made this picture graph showing 14 students' favorite drinks. She drew 3 glasses to represent the 6 students who chose chocolate milk. Is her picture graph correct? Explain.

6. **Higher Order Thinking** How would Pamela's picture graph change if 12 students chose grape juice as their favorite?

7. **Make Sense and Persevere** How would the scale have to change if her picture graph showed the favorite drinks of 70 students?

✔ **Assessment**

8. April counted cars painted 4 different colors. She made a frequency table to record the total number of cars for each color. Complete the picture graph to represent her data. Write the scale you used in the key.

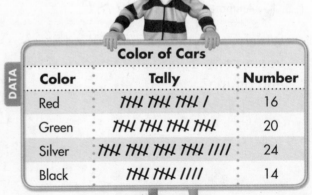

Color of Cars	
Red	
Green	
Silver	
Black	

Color of Cars		
Color	**Tally**	**Number**
Red	⊣⊦⊦⊦ ⊦⊦⊦⊦ ⊦⊦⊦ /	16
Green	⊦⊦⊦⊦ ⊦⊦⊦⊦ ⊦⊦⊦⊦ ⊦⊦⊦⊦	20
Silver	⊦⊦⊦⊦ ⊦⊦⊦⊦ ⊦⊦⊦⊦ ⊦⊦⊦⊦ ////	24
Black	⊦⊦⊦⊦ ⊦⊦⊦⊦ ////	14

Name _____

Solve

Solve & Share

Use the data in the table below to complete the bar graph. What conclusions can you make by analyzing the bar graph?

I can ...
make a bar graph to record information and answer questions about a data set.

SOL 3.15a

DATA

Daily Reading Log

Student's Name	Number of Pages Read
Yoma	13
Don	10
Bonita	10
Adam	6

You can use reasoning. You can use the data in the table to help draw the bars on the graph.

Daily Reading Log

Number of Pages Read
18
16
14
12
10
8
6
4
2
0

Yoma   Don   Bonita   Adam
Student's Name

Look Back! Use Appropriate Tools How can tools such as a ruler help you create a bar graph?

A

Greg made a table to show the amount of money he saved each month from tutoring. Use the data in the table to make a bar graph.

DATA

Amount Greg Saved Each Month

Month	Amount Saved
January	$25
February	$50
March	$65
April	$40

A bar graph can make it easy to compare data.

B

Write a title. Use the same title as in the table.

The title of this bar graph is **Amount Greg Saved Each Month.**

Choose the scale. Decide how many units each grid line will represent.

Each grid line will represent $10.

C

Set up the graph with the scale, each month listed in the table, and labels. Draw a bar for each month.

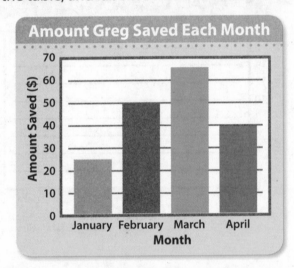

Amount Greg Saved Each Month

Convince Me! **Be Precise** Write new amounts for how much Greg saved in 4 other months. Consider the scale.

In May, Greg saved _____.

In June, Greg saved _____.

In July, Greg saved _____.

In August, Greg saved _____.

Draw bars on the graph to show your new data.

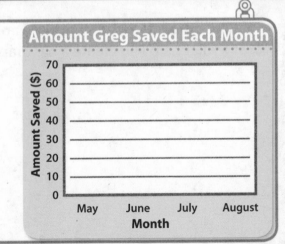

Amount Greg Saved Each Month

☆ Guided Practice ☆*

Do You Understand?

In **1–3**, use the bar graph on page 372.

1. **Reasoning** Explain why the bar for January ends between 20 and 30.

2. Suppose Greg saved $35 in May. Between which grid lines would the bar for May end?

3. How can you tell how much more Greg saved in February than in April?

Do You Know How?

4. Use the table to complete the bar graph.

Number of People Signed Up for Classes

Class	Tally	Number of People
Chess	⫫⫫⫫	6
Guitar	⫫⫫⫫ ⫫⫫⫫	10
Painting	⫫⫫⫫	7
Writing	⫫⫫⫫ ⫫⫫⫫⫫	9

☆ Independent Practice ☆

In **5**, use the table at the right.

5. Complete the bar graph to show the data.

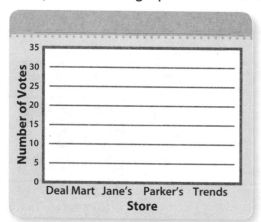

Favorite Store for Clothes

Store	Tally	Number of Votes
Deal Mart	⫫⫫⫫ ⫫⫫⫫ ⫫⫫⫫	15
Jane's	⫫⫫⫫ ⫫⫫⫫ ⫫⫫⫫ ⫫⫫⫫ ⫫⫫⫫ ⫫⫫⫫	30
Parker's	⫫⫫⫫ ⫫⫫⫫ ⫫⫫⫫ ⫫⫫⫫	20
Trends	⫫⫫⫫	5

Problem Solving

In **6–8**, use the table at the right.

6. **Model with Math** Make a bar graph to show the data.

Favorite Kind of Movie				
Kind of Movie	Adventure	Cartoon	Comedy	Science Fiction
Number of Votes	16	7	10	6

7. **Construct Arguments** Which two kinds of movies received about the same number of votes? Explain how to use your bar graph to find the answer.

8. **Make Sense and Persevere** Each movie ticket costs $8. Jo buys tickets for the number of people who voted for science fiction. How much change does she get from $50?

9. **Higher Order Thinking** Suppose you are going to make a bar graph to show the data in the table at the right. What scale would you choose? Explain.

Speed of Birds	
Kind of Bird	**Flying Speed (miles per hour)**
Frigate Bird	95
Peregrine Falcon	180
Spin-Tailed Swift	105

 Assessment

10. Which information is needed to complete the graph?

Ⓐ How many friends wore pink shoes

Ⓑ The color of shoes with the longest bar

Ⓒ The color of shoes worn by exactly 8 friends

Ⓓ The color of shoes worn by exactly 7 friends

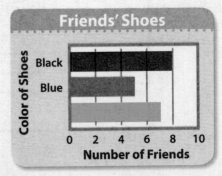

Name _____

Another Look!

The table below shows the number of birds that visited a bird feeder.

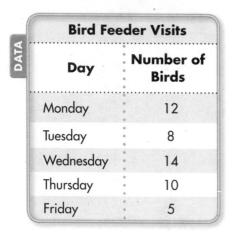

Bird Feeder Visits	
Day	**Number of Birds**
Monday	12
Tuesday	8
Wednesday	14
Thursday	10
Friday	5

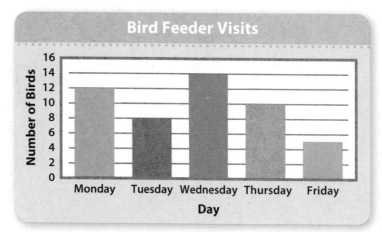

Follow the steps below to learn how to make the bar graph at the right.

Step 1	**Step 2**	**Step 3**	**Step 4**
Write each of the days and label the bottom of the graph "Day."	Choose a scale. Number the scale. Label the scale "Number of Birds."	Draw a bar for each day. Check that the bar lengths match the number in the table.	Give the graph a title.

For **1–3**, use the table at the right.

1. Complete the bar graph to show the data. Remember to add a title.

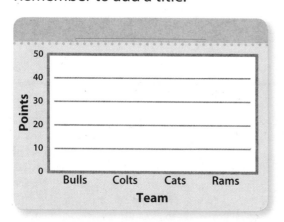

Field Day Results	
Team	**Points**
Bulls	45
Colts	30
Cats	25
Rams	40

2. Explain how to use your bar graph to find the team with the most points.

3. Which team has the shortest bar in your bar graph? Why?

In **4–6**, use the table at the right.

4. **Model with Math** Make a bar graph to show the data.

Favorite States to Visit

State	Number of Votes
New York	25
Florida	35
California	30
Hawaii	20

5. **Construct Arguments** Explain how to use your bar graph to find the state with the least number of votes. Which state is it?

6. **Algebra** The total number of votes for two states can be represented by the equation $35 + ? = 65$. Which state's number of votes makes this statement true?

7. **Math and Science** Dawn made a paper airplane and measured the distance it flew in feet for 30 tosses. The longest distance she measured was 45 feet. The shortest distance was 28 feet. How many more feet is the longest distance than the shortest distance?

8. **Higher Order Thinking** Kim makes a bar graph to record votes for the choice of a class pet. Each grid line represents 4 votes. Fish got 10 votes. The bar for hamster is 3 grid lines higher than the bar for fish. How many votes did hamster get?

✓ **Assessment**

9. **Math and Science** The table at the right shows the average monthly snowfall where Mr. Walker lives. Which would be the best number to use for a scale on a bar graph of the data?

Ⓐ 1

Ⓑ 2

Ⓒ 5

Ⓓ 10

Average Snowfall

Month	Snowfall (Inches)
November	2
December	8
January	12
February	10
March	2

Name _____

Solve

Solve & Share

The students in Ms. Seymour's class voted for their favorite kind of sandwich. How many more students voted for peanut butter than cheese? How many fewer students voted for tuna than peanut butter?

I can ...
use graphs and other tools to solve word problems.

SOL 3.15b

Think about what you are trying to find out to make sense of this problem.

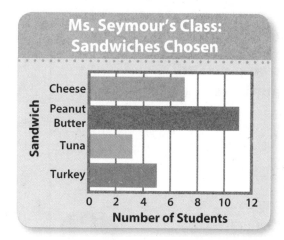

Ms. Seymour's Class: Sandwiches Chosen

Sandwich
- Cheese
- Peanut Butter
- Tuna
- Turkey

Number of Students
0 2 4 6 8 10 12

Look Back! **Be Precise** What is the scale for this graph? How do you know the number of votes a bar represents when it is between two lines on this graph?

Essential Question # How Can You Solve Problems Using Graphs?

A

Angela wants Karli and Monique to have a total of 60 paper cranes. The bar graph shows how many paper cranes her friends already have. How many more paper cranes does Angela need to make for Karli and Monique have 60 paper cranes in all?

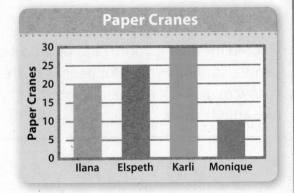

This problem has a hidden question!

B Solve the hidden question.

How many paper cranes do Karli and Monique already have?

Use the scale to find how many paper cranes Karli and Monique each have. Then add.

Karli has 30 paper cranes.
Monique has 10 paper cranes.

$30 + 10 = 40$

Together they have 40 paper cranes.

Remember you still need to answer the main question.

C Solve the main question.

How many paper cranes does Angela need to make?

Subtract the number of cranes the friends already have from the total.

$60 - 40 = 20$

Angela needs to make 20 paper cranes.

Convince Me! **Critique Reasoning** Angela says, "I want Ilana and Elspeth to also have 60 cranes in all. I can subtract two times to find how many more cranes I need to make for them." Is Angela correct? Explain.

378   **Topic 7** | Lesson 7-4

Copyright © Savvas Learning Company LLC. All Rights Reserved.

☆Guided Practice*

Practice Buddy   Tools   Assessment

Do You Understand?

1. Look at the graph on page 378. Explain whether you would add, subtract, multiply, or divide to find how many more paper cranes Karli already has than Monique.

2. How does a bar graph help you compare data?

Do You Know How?

In **3**, use the bar graph.

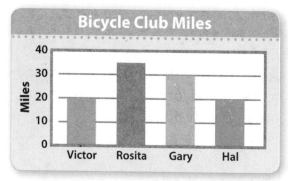

3. How many more miles did Hal and Victor ride than Rosita?

Independent Practice ☆

In **4–6**, use the picture graph at the right.

4. How many more red T-shirts were sold at Ultimate T than at Jazzy's?

5. How many fewer green T-shirts were sold at Jazzy's than at Ultimate T?

6. How many more blue and red T-shirts were sold at Jazzy's than green T-shirts were sold at Ultimate T?

T-Shirt Sales	Jazzy's	Ultimate T
Blue	👕👕❘	👕
Red	👕👕	👕👕❘
Green	❘	👕👕👕

Each 👕 = 10 T-shirts. Each ❘ = 5 T-shirts.

*For another example, see Set C on page 393.

Problem Solving

In **7–9**, use the bar graph at the right.

7. **Number Sense** How many people voted for their favorite type of exercise? How can you find the answer?

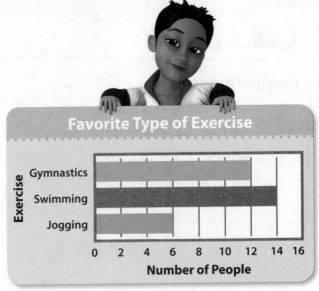

Favorite Type of Exercise

8. **Construct Arguments** How many more people voted for gymnastics than for jogging? How do you know?

9. How many fewer people voted for swimming than for gymnastics and jogging?

---

10. **Make Sense and Persevere** Leslie delivers papers on weekdays and Saturdays. She delivers 6 papers each weekday and 16 papers on Saturday. How many papers does Leslie deliver during the entire week?

11. **Higher Order Thinking** What kinds of comparisons can you make when you look at a bar graph or a picture graph?

 Assessment

12. Daryl made a bar graph to record the number of books read by each member of a reading club.

    How many fewer books did Alice read than Sandra and Daryl? Explain.

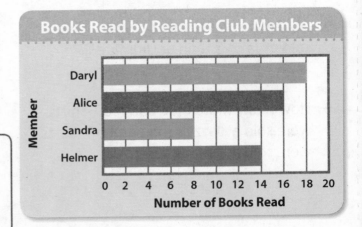

Books Read by Reading Club Members

Help   Practice   Tools   Games
Buddy

Another Look!

Students were asked to name their favorite type of dog. The picture graph shows the results of the survey.

Students' Favorite Dogs	
Dog	**Number Counted**
Beagle	🐕 🐕 🐕
Collie	🐕 🐕 🐕 🐕 🐕
Shepherd	🐕 🐕 🐶
Poodle	🐕
Dalmatian	🐕 🐕

Each 🐕 = 2 votes. Each 🐶 = 1 vote.

> You can use graphs to compare data and draw conclusions.

Some conclusions you can draw from the picture graph include:

- Shepherd was chosen by exactly 5 students.
- 2 fewer students chose dalmatian than chose beagle.
- 2 more students chose collie than chose beagle or poodle.

In **1–4**, use the bar graph at the right.

1. How many more votes did punch get than water?

2. How many fewer votes did milk get than juice and water?

3. How many more votes did juice get than punch and water?

4. What is the difference between the number of votes for juice and the number of votes for water and milk combined?

In **5** and **6**, use the picture graph at the right.

5. **Generalize** Which type of shoe was sold least at Just Shoes? How do you know?

6. **Construct Arguments** How many more pairs of boots than pumps were sold at Just Shoes? How did you find your answer?

In **7** and **8**, use the bar graph at the right.

7. **Higher Order Thinking** Jared, Alicia, Lydia, and Tray are cousins. Jared is 8 years older than Alicia. Lydia is 4 years younger than Tray. Tray is 18 years younger than Jared. Alicia is 22. Complete the graph to show their ages.

8. How many years older is Jared than Lydia?

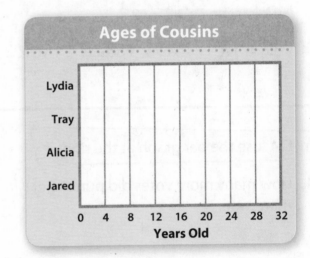

✓ **Assessment**

9. Students at King Elementary School washed cars to raise money for a school trip.

How many more cars did the 4th graders and the 6th graders wash than the 5th graders? Explain.

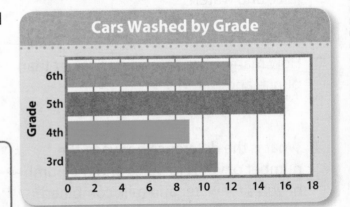

382 **Topic 7** | Lesson 7-4

Name _____

Solve

☆ Solve & Share ☆

Action books and mystery books cost $5 each. Biography books cost $10 each. A librarian has $100 to spend on new books. She collected some information about the kinds of books that students checked out to read last month.

How should the librarian spend the money? Use math words and symbols to explain your thinking.

I can ...
be precise when solving math problems.

SOL 3.15b

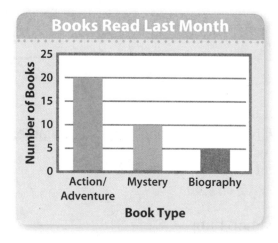

Thinking Habits

Be a good thinker! These questions can help you.

- Am I using numbers, units, and symbols appropriately?

- Am I using the correct definitions?

- Am I calculating accurately?

- Is my answer clear?

Look Back! **Be Precise** How did you use words and symbols to explain your answer?

Essential Question

How Can You Be Precise When Solving Math Problems?

A

Bella has a bakery. She will use the bakery items at the right to make a gift basket worth $40. Bella wants the basket to have more than one of each bakery item. Show one way to make a gift basket.

Bakery Items Available

Wheat Loaves ($4 each)	
Cinnamon Buns ($2 each)	
Muffins ($1 each)	

Each 🍞 = 2 items

What do I need to do to make a gift basket?

I need to be precise. I will decide how many of each item to put in a basket so the total is exactly $40.

B

How can I be precise in solving this problem?

I can

- correctly use the information given.

- calculate accurately.

- decide if my answer is clear and appropriate.

- use the correct units.

C

Here's my thinking...

I will start with $40.
I know how many of each item is available.

3 wheat loaves × $4 = $12
$40 − $12 = $28

9 cinnamon buns × $2 = $18
$28 − $18 = $10

10 muffins × $1 = $10
$10 − $10 = $0

All calculations are correct. My gift basket has 3 wheat loaves, 9 cinnamon buns, and 10 muffins. The total is exactly $40.

Convince Me! **Be Precise** Is there another way to make a gift basket that totals exactly $40? Explain.

Practice Buddy   Tools   Assessment

☆Guided Practice*

Be Precise

Use the graph on page 384. Suppose Bella wanted to make a gift basket worth $25 instead. The gift basket must also have more wheat loaves than muffins. Show one way Bella can make the gift basket.

To be precise, you need to check that the words, numbers, symbols, and units you use are correct and that your calculations are accurate.

1. What given information will you use to solve?

2. Show and explain one way Bella can make the gift basket.

Independent Practice*

Be Precise

Derek is making a tile pattern that will be 30 inches long. The graph shows how many of each length of tile Derek has. He wants to use more than one of each length of tile in his pattern. Show one way to make the pattern.

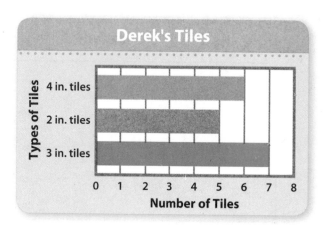

Derek's Tiles

3. What given information will you use to solve?

4. Show and explain one way Derek can make the pattern.

Problem Solving

Picture Planning

Marta has $50 to spend on sketches. She wants to display them in an array of 3 rows, with 4 sketches in each row. Marta wants to include each type of sketch at least two times in her array.

Sketch Types and Pricing

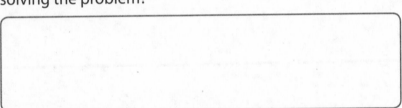

Landscape ($2 each)	
Animal ($4 each)	
Portrait ($10 each)	

Each □ = 2 sketches in stock.
Each ⊏ = 1 sketch in stock.

5. **Reasoning** How many sketches does Marta want?

6. **Make Sense and Persevere** What is a good plan for solving the problem?

7. **Be Precise** Show one way Marta can buy sketches to make the array. Use math words and symbols to explain.

Be precise when analyzing the symbols, words, and numbers displayed in a picture graph.

8. **Use Structure** Suppose Marta wants to make an array of 4 rows, with 3 sketches in each row. Would your answer still work? Explain.

Help   Practice Buddy   Tools   Games

Another Look!

Wynton made a picture graph to record the music he would like to download. He has $35 to spend on music. He wants to buy at least 1 of each type of item. He wants to buy more singles than albums. What is one way Wynton can spend $35 on music?

Tell how you can be precise when solving this problem.

- I can correctly use the information given.

- I can make sure my calculations are accurate.

Solve. Use math words and symbols to explain your thinking.

5 singles × $2 = $10   35 − 10 = $25 left

3 albums × $6 = $18   25 − 18 = $7 left

1 collection × $7 = $7   7 − 7 = $0 left

Wynton has spent exactly $35.
He has bought more singles than albums.

When you are precise, you use math symbols and language correctly.

Music to Download	
Singles ($2)	♩ ♩ ♩ ♩
Albums ($6)	♩ ♩ ♩
Collections ($7)	♩ ♩

Each ♩ = 3 items.

Be Precise

Casie made a picture graph to record the points that third-grade students scored on a test. Mrs. Wilson's group scored 40 points in all. There are 11 students in Mrs. Wilson's group. What is one way Mrs. Wilson's group may have scored 40 points?

1. Tell how you can be precise when solving this problem.

2. Solve. Use math words and symbols to explain your thinking.

Test Scores	
Point Types	**Number of Students**
2 points	😀 😀 😀 😀
4 points	😀 😀 😀
6 points	😀 😀 😀

Each 😀 = 3 students.

Pizza Party!
Ms. Chavez is planning a class party. There are 28 students at the party. She wants to get at least 1 of each type of pizza and have enough pizza so each student gets 2 slices. Delivery takes 20 minutes. Ms. Chavez has $55 to spend.

Ready To Go Pizza Delivery

Pizza Type	Number of Pizzas Available
Cheese ($6 each)	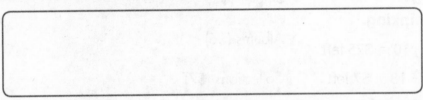
Pepperoni ($8 each)	
Supreme ($10 each)	

Each  = 8 slices.

3. Reasoning How many slices of cheese pizza are available? How do you know?

4. Make Sense and Persevere How many slices of pizza does Ms. Chavez need? Explain.

5. Model with Math Show how to find the number of pizzas Ms. Chavez should order.

Be precise. Make sure your answer is clear and appropriate.

6. Be Precise Show one way Ms. Chavez can order enough pizzas. Use math words and symbols to explain your thinking.

7. Make Sense and Persevere Which information did you not need to help you solve the problem?

Find a partner. Get paper and a pencil. Each partner chooses a different color: light blue or dark blue.

Partner 1 and Partner 2 each point to a black number at the same time. Both partners multiply those numbers.

If the answer is on your color, you get a tally mark. Work until one partner has seven tally marks.

I can ...
multiply within 100.

Partner 1

| 5 |
| 8 |
| 4 |
| 3 |
| 10 |

48	90	35	20
50	72	27	9
60	30	12	15
45	18	27	25
36	28	21	56
40	56	70	24

Partner 2

| 7 |
| 3 |
| 9 |
| 5 |
| 6 |

Tally Marks for Partner 1

Tally Marks for Partner 2

Vocabulary Review

Word List

- data
- frequency table
- graph
- key
- scale
- scaled bar graph
- scaled picture graph
- survey

Understand Vocabulary

Rainy Days

| April | ☂ ☂ ☂ ☂ ☂ ☂ |
| May | ☂ ☂ ☂ ☂ |

Each ☂ = 2 days

Graph A

Complete each sentence with *scaled picture graph*, *scaled bar graph*, *key*, or *scale*.

1. The _____ in Graph A shows that each umbrella represents 2 days.

2. Graph A is a _____.

3. The _____ in Graph B increases by 5.

4. Graph B is a _____.

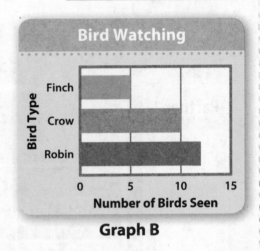

Graph B

Write T for *True* or F for *False*.

_____ **5.** A survey is the only way to collect data.

_____ **6.** A scaled bar graph has a key.

_____ **7.** Data from a frequency table can be used to make a scaled bar graph.

Use Vocabulary in Writing

8. Suppose you found out the number and type of pets your classmates have. Explain how you can display that information. Use at least 3 terms from the Word List in your answer.

Set A pages 359–364

Picture graphs use pictures or parts of pictures to represent data.

The scale is the number each picture represents. The key explains the scale that is used.

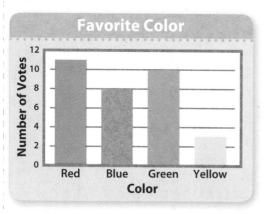

Caps on Sale

Baseball	🧢 🧢 🧢 🧢
Basketball	🧢
Racing	🧢 🧢

Each 🧢 = 10 caps.   Each 🧢 = 5 caps.

Bar graphs use bars to represent data. You can use a scale to find how much a bar represents.

Favorite Color

Each line in this bar graph represents 2 votes.

Remember to use a key or scale. The number of pictures in picture graphs and the lengths of bars in bar graphs help to compare data.

In **1–3**, use the picture graph on the left.

1. How many more baseball caps are on sale than racing caps?

2. How many more baseball caps are on sale than basketball and racing caps?

3. How many fewer basketball caps are on sale than baseball caps?

In **4–7**, use the bar graph on the left.

4. Which color got the most votes? How many votes did that color get?

5. How many fewer votes were for yellow than for green?

6. How many more votes were for red than for blue?

7. What is the difference between the votes for red and the votes for blue and yellow combined?

This frequency table shows data about the number of coins Mark has.

Mark's Coins

Coin	Tally	Number of Coins
Penny	𝍢𝍢 ///	8
Nickel	𝍢𝍢 𝍢𝍢	10
Dime	𝍢𝍢 /	6

You can use the data to make a picture graph. Picture graphs include a title, symbol, and a key to show the scale.

Mark's Coins

Coin	Number of Coins
Penny	⬤ ⬤ ⬤ ⬤
Nickel	⬤ ⬤ ⬤ ⬤ ⬤
Dime	⬤ ⬤ ⬤

Each ⬤ = 2 coins.

In this picture graph, each symbol equals 2 coins.

You can also use the data to make a bar graph.

1. Label the bottom and side of the graph.

2. Choose a scale.

3. Draw a bar for each type of coin.

4. Include a title.

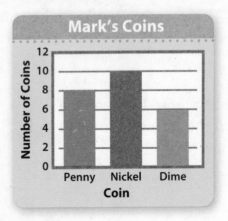

Remember a frequency table includes tally marks or numbers. A picture graph uses pictures to show data.

In **1** and **2**, use the frequency table below.

Dan's class voted for their favorite pet. The results are shown in this frequency table.

Favorite Pet

Pet	Tally	Number
Bird	////	
Dog	𝍢𝍢 𝍢𝍢 ////	
Fish	𝍢𝍢 /	
Cat	𝍢𝍢 ///	

1. Complete the frequency table.

2. Use the data in the frequency table to make a picture graph.

3. Use the data in the table to make a bar graph.

Set C pages 377–382

Reteaching
Continued

You can use data from bar graphs or picture graphs to draw conclusions.

In a picture graph Erica recorded the number of magazines she read. How many more magazines did she read in April and May than in June?

You can solve 2-step data problems.

There are 6 symbols for April and May. There are 3 symbols for June.

$6 - 3 = 3$. There are 3 more symbols for April and May.

Each symbol represents 2 magazines.
$3 \times 2 = 6$. Erica read 6 more magazines in April and May than in June.

Remember you can use tables and graphs to make comparisons. Sometimes you need to find and answer hidden questions.

In **1–6**, use the picture graph below.

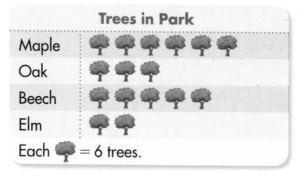

1. How many more maple trees than elm trees are there?

2. How many fewer beech trees are there than maple trees?

3. How many trees are **NOT** maple trees?

4. How many more maple and beech trees are there than oak trees?

5. How many fewer oak trees are there than beech and elm trees?

6. If the city wants to have 24 elm trees, how many more elm trees does it need to plant? Explain how to solve.

Think about these questions to help you **attend to precision**.

Thinking Habits

- Am I using numbers, units, and symbols appropriately?

- Am I using the correct definitions?

- Am I calculating accurately?

- Is my answer clear?

Use the bar graph below to solve **1** and **2**.

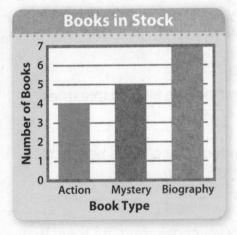

Remember to use words, numbers, and symbols to show your reasoning.

In **1** and **2**, use the bar graph at the left to solve.

Jackie has $50 to spend on books. She has made a bar graph to show the number of each type of book the store has in stock. Jackie wants to buy at least 2 of each type of book. Show one way Jackie can spend $50 on books.

Action books cost $5.

Biographies cost $10.

Mysteries cost $5.

1. What given information will you use to solve the problem?

2. Show one way Jackie can spend $50 on books. Use math words and symbols to explain your thinking.

1. Use the data from the frequency table to make a picture graph.

Favorite Sandwiches		
Sandwich	**Tally**	**Frequency**
Turkey	ʇʜʇ ʇʜʇ ////	14
Ham	ʇʜʇ /	6
Tuna	//	2
Egg	////	4

Part A

Circle the key you will use.

🥪 = 1 sandwich   🥪 = 2 sandwiches

🥪 = 3 sandwiches   🥪 = 4 sandwiches

Part B

Draw a picture graph.

2. Use the data from the picture graph you made in Question 1. How many students did **NOT** choose turkey as their favorite sandwich?

Ⓐ 10   Ⓒ 13

Ⓑ 12   Ⓓ 14

3. Jamie's class made a picture graph to show how many hours they volunteered each week. In which week or weeks did the class volunteer 9 hours?

Each 🕐 = 2 hours. Each 🕐 = 1 hour.

Ⓐ Week 1   Ⓒ Week 3

Ⓑ Week 2   Ⓓ Weeks 1 and 3

4. Look at the picture graph above. How many total hours did the class volunteer?

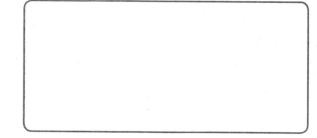

5. How many more hours did the class volunteer in Weeks 2 and 3 than in Week 1?

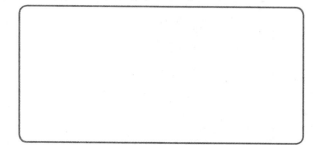

6. Mr. Thomas's class made a bar graph of the number of brothers and sisters each student has. How many students in the class have 1 brother or sister?

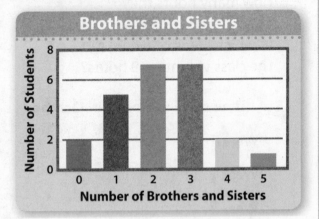

Brothers and Sisters

Ⓐ 2

Ⓑ 5

Ⓒ 7

Ⓓ 1

7. Choose the number of brothers and sisters that are most common in Mr. Thomas's class. You can pick more than one answer.

☐ 0
☐ 1
☐ 2
☐ 3
☐ 5

8. How many students in the class have 2 or more brothers and sisters?

9. Beth is making a bar graph to compare how many marbles of each color she has. She has 25 blue marbles, 35 red marbles, 5 green marbles, and 15 yellow marbles. Which scale makes the most sense for Beth to use with her graph?

Ⓐ Each grid line equals 1 marble.

Ⓑ Each grid line equals 2 marbles.

Ⓒ Each grid line equals 5 marbles.

Ⓓ Each grid line equals 20 marbles.

10. Use the information in Question 9 to make a bar graph of Beth's marbles.

11. For questions **11a–11d**, choose *Yes* or *No* to tell if each sentence is true.

11a. Beth has more green and yellow marbles than blue ones.

○ Yes   ○ No

11b. Beth has more red marbles than blue and green ones.

○ Yes   ○ No

11c. Beth has fewer yellow marbles than blue and green ones.

○ Yes   ○ No

11d. Beth has fewer red marbles than green and yellow ones.

○ Yes   ○ No

12. The school had a fundraiser in the first part of the school year. In which month did the school make the most money?

Fundraiser Earnings

Dollars
60
50
40
30
20
10
0
Sep   Oct   Nov   Dec
Month

(A) September

(B) October

(C) November

(D) December

13. Look at the bar graph above. Suppose $45 was raised in January. Where would the bar end?

14. Did the school earn more money in September and October than in November? Explain.

15. The frequency table below shows the time Kelly jumped rope during the week. Use the data to make a picture graph.

Minutes Kelly Jumped Rope		
Day	Tally	Number of Minutes
Monday	ⅢⅢ ⅢⅢ ⅢⅢ	15
Tuesday	ⅢⅢ ⅢⅢ ⅢⅢ ⅢⅢ	20
Wednesday	ⅢⅢ ⅢⅢ	10
Thursday	ⅢⅢ	5
Friday	ⅢⅢ ⅢⅢ ⅢⅢ ⅢⅢ	20

Part A

Circle the key you will use.

= 2 minutes   = 5 minutes

= 10 minutes   = 15 minutes

Part B

Draw a picture graph.

Minutes Kelly Jumped Rope	
Monday	
Tuesday	
Wednesday	
Thursday	
Friday	

16. Look at the picture graphs below. Which type of book was chosen by the same number of students in each class?

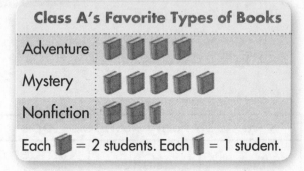

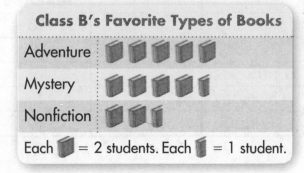

Ⓐ Adventure

Ⓑ Mystery

Ⓒ Nonfiction

Ⓓ Not here

---

17. In Class A how many fewer students like mystery than adventure and nonfiction combined?

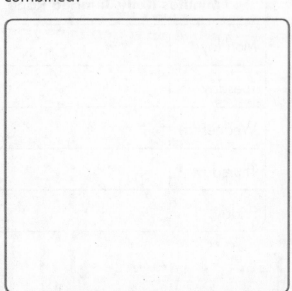

18. Ellie has $22 to spend on art supplies. She wants to buy at least one canvas, one tube of paint, and one brush. Which art supplies can she buy if she spends all of her money?

Part A

What given information will you use to solve the problem?

Part B

Explain your thinking and show the supplies she can buy on the bar graph.

Name _____

Twisting Balloons

Miles twisted balloons into different animals at his daughter's birthday party. The **Balloons Used** picture graph shows the different color balloons he used.

Use the **Balloons Used** picture graph to answer Questions 1 and 2.

1. How many more green balloons than yellow balloons did Miles use? Explain.

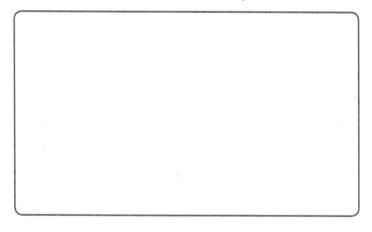

Balloons Used

Blue	🎈 🎈 🎈 🎈 🎈
Brown	🎈 🎈
Green	🎈 🎈 🎈
Yellow	🎈 🎈

Each 🎈 = 2 balloons

2. How many fewer blue balloons were used than all of the other colors combined? Explain.

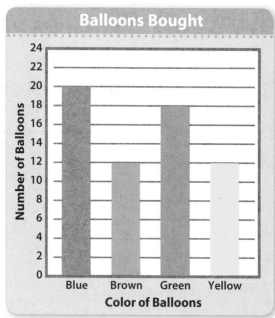

Balloons Bought

Use the **Balloons Used** picture graph and the **Balloons Bought** bar graph to answer Question 3.

3. How many balloons does Miles have left? Complete the table below.

Color	Bought	Used	Left
Blue			
Brown			
Green			
Yellow			

Use your response to Question 3 to answer Question 4.

4. Complete the bar graph to show how many balloons are left.

The **Balloon Shapes and Colors** table shows the number and color of balloons Miles needs to use to make each balloon animal. Use your response to Question 4 and the **Balloon Shapes and Colors** table to answer Question **5**.

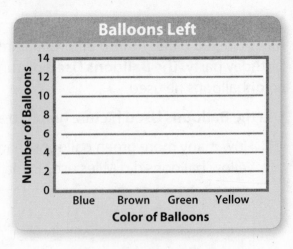

Balloons Left

5. Miles plans to use all of the balloons that are left and wants to make at least one of each balloon animal. Make a picture graph to show one way Miles can finish using the balloons.

Part A

Circle the key you will use.

 = 1 balloon animal   = 2 balloon animals

 = 3 balloon animals   = 4 balloon animals

Part B

Complete the picture graph and explain how you solved the problem.

Balloon Shapes and Colors	
parrot	2 blue
monkey	1 brown 1 yellow
frog	2 green
dolphin	1 blue

Balloon Animals	
Parrot	
Monkey	
Frog	
Dolphin	

Glossary

A.M. The time between midnight and noon.

acute angle An angle that is open less than a right angle.

addends Numbers added together to give a sum.
Example: $2 + 7 = 9$
↑ ↑
Addend Addend

angle A figure that is formed where two sides meet.

angle measure The degrees of an angle.

area The number of unit squares needed to cover a region.

array A way of displaying objects in equal rows and columns.

Associative (Grouping) Property of Addition The grouping of addends can be changed and the sum will be the same.

Associative (Grouping) Property of Multiplication The grouping of factors can be changed and the product will be the same.

benchmark fraction A commonly used fraction such as $\frac{1}{4}, \frac{1}{3}, \frac{1}{2}, \frac{2}{3}$, and $\frac{3}{4}$.

capacity (liquid volume) The amount a container can hold measured in liquid units.

centimeter (cm) A metric unit of length.

column An arrangement of objects or numbers, one above another.

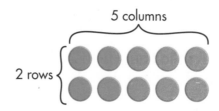

5 columns

2 rows

Commutative (Order) Property of Addition Numbers can be added in any order and the sum will be the same.

Commutative (Order) Property of Multiplication Numbers can be multiplied in any order and the product will be the same.

compare To decide if one number is greater than or less than another number.

compatible numbers Numbers that are easy to add, subtract, multiply, or divide mentally.

compensation Choosing numbers close to the numbers in a problem to make computation easier and then adjusting the answer for the numbers chosen.

compose To combine different parts.

conjecture A statement that is believed to be true, but it has not been proven.

cone A solid figure with a circle as its base and a curved surface that meets at a point.

cube A solid figure with 6 same-size squares as its faces.

cylinder A solid figure with 2 circular bases.

D

data Pieces of information.

decompose Breaking a number into parts.
Example: $\frac{2}{5}$ can be broken into $\frac{1}{5} + \frac{1}{5}$.

degrees (°) A unit of measure for angles.

denominator The number below the fraction bar in a fraction, which shows the total number of equal parts.

difference The answer when subtracting one number from another.

digits The symbols 0, 1, 2, 3, 4, 5, 6, 7, 8, and 9 used to write numbers.

Distributive Property A multiplication fact can be broken apart into the sum of two other multiplication facts.
Example: $5 \times 4 = (2 \times 4) + (3 \times 4)$

dividend The number to be divided.
Example: $63 \div 9 = 7$

↑
Dividend

division An operation that tells how many equal groups there are or how many are in each group.

divisor The number by which another number is divided.
Example: $63 \div 9 = 7$
$\uparrow$
Divisor

dollar sign A symbol ($) used to indicate money.

edge A line segment where 2 faces meet in a solid figure.

eighth One of 8 equal parts of a whole.

elapsed time The total amount of time that passes from the starting time to the ending time.

equal (equality) When the two sides of an equation have the same value.

equal groups Groups that have the same number of items.

equation A number sentence that uses an equal sign (=) to show that the value on its left side is the same as the value on its right side.

equilateral triangle A triangle with all sides the same length.

equivalent fractions Fractions that name the same part of a whole or the same location on a number line.

estimate To give an approximate number or answer.

even number A whole number that can be divided by 2 with none left over.

expanded form A number written as the sum of the values of its digits.
Example: $476 = 400 + 70 + 6$

face A flat surface of a solid that cannot roll.

fact family A group of related facts using the same numbers.

factors Numbers that are multiplied together to give a product.
Example: $7 \times 3 = 21$
$\uparrow \quad \uparrow$
Factor Factor

foot (ft) A customary unit of length. 1 foot equals 12 inches.

fourth One of 4 equal parts of a whole.

fraction A symbol, such as $\frac{1}{2}$, used to name a part of a whole, a part of a set, or a location on a number line.

frequency table A table used to show the number of times something occurs.

gram (g) A metric unit of mass, the amount of matter in an object.

half (halves) One of 2 equal parts of a whole.

half hour A unit of time equal to 30 minutes.

hexagon A polygon with 6 sides.

hour A unit of time equal to 60 minutes.

Identity (Zero) Property of Addition The sum of any number and zero is that same number.

Identity (One) Property of Multiplication The product of any number and 1 is that number.

inch (in.) A customary unit of length.

intersecting lines Lines that cross at one point.

inverse operations Two operations that undo each other.

key The explanation for what each symbol represents in a pictograph.

kilogram (kg) A metric unit of mass, the amount of matter in an object. One kilogram equals 1,000 grams.

kilometer (km) A metric unit of length. One kilometer equals 1,000 meters.

line A straight path of points that is endless in both directions.

line plot A way to organize data on a number line.

line segment A part of a line that has 2 endpoints.

liter (L) A metric unit of capacity. One liter equals 1,000 milliliters.

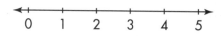

mass A measure of the amount of matter in an object.

meter (m) A metric unit of length. One meter equals 100 centimeters.

mile (mi) A customary unit of length. One mile equals 5,280 feet.

milliliter (mL) A metric unit of capacity.

millimeter (mm) A metric unit of length. 1,000 millimeters = 1 meter.

minute A unit of time equal to 60 seconds.

mixed number A number with a whole number part and a fraction part. *Example:* $2\frac{3}{4}$

multiple The product of a given whole number and any non-zero whole number. *Example:* 4, 8, 12, and 16 are multiples of 4.

multiplication An operation that gives the total number when you join equal groups.

nearest fourth inch A measurement that ends with a $\frac{1}{4}$, $\frac{2}{4}$, $\frac{3}{4}$, or full inch.

nearest half inch A measurement that ends with a $\frac{1}{2}$ or full inch.

not equal When two sides of a number sentence do not have the same value.

number line A line that shows numbers in order using a scale. *Example:*

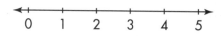

numerator The number above the fraction bar in a fraction, which shows how many equal parts are described.

obtuse angle An angle that is open more than a right angle.

octagon A polygon with 8 sides.

odd number A whole number that cannot be divided by 2 with none left over.

open number line A number line which only displays the numbers being computed.

order To arrange numbers from least to greatest or from greatest to least.

ounce (oz) A customary unit of weight.

P.M. The time between noon and midnight.

parallel lines Lines that never cross each other.

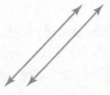

parallel sides Sides of a polygon that go in the exact same direction; if the sides cross when they are made longer, they are not parallel.

parallelogram A quadrilateral with 2 pairs of parallel sides.

pentagon A polygon with 5 sides.

perimeter The distance around a figure.

perpendicular lines Two intersecting lines that form right angles.

pint (pt) A customary unit of capacity. One pint equals 2 cups.

place value The value given to the place a digit has in a number.
Example: In 946, the place value of the digit 9 is *hundreds*.

point An exact position often marked by a dot.

polygon A closed figure made up of straight line segments.

pound (lb) A customary unit of weight. One pound equals 16 ounces.

product The answer to a multiplication problem.

quadrilateral A polygon with 4 sides.

quart (qt) A customary unit of capacity. One quart equals 2 pints.

quarter hour A unit of time equal to 15 minutes.

quotient The answer to a division problem.

ray A part of a line that has one endpoint and continues endlessly in one direction.

rectangle A parallelogram with 4 right angles.

rectangular prism A solid figure with 6 rectangular faces.

regroup (regrouping) To name a whole number in a different way.
Example: 28 = 1 ten 18 ones

remainder The number that is left over after dividing.
Example: 31 ÷ 7 = 4 R3

Remainder

rhombus A parallelogram with all sides the same length.

right angle An angle that forms a square corner.

round To replace a number with a number that tells about how much or how many to the nearest ten, hundred, thousand, and so on.
Example: 42 rounded to the nearest 10 is 40.

row An arrangement of objects or numbers, one to the side of another.

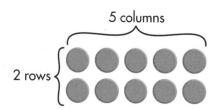

S

scale The numbers that show the units used on a graph.

scaled bar graph a graph that uses bars to show data.

scaled picture graph a graph that uses pictures to show data.

second A unit of time. 60 seconds equal 1 minute.

side A line segment forming part of a polygon.

sixth One of 6 equal parts of a whole.

solid figure A figure that has length, width, and height.

sphere A solid figure in the shape of a ball.

square A parallelogram with 4 right angles and all sides the same length.

square unit A measure of area.

standard form A way to write a number showing only its digits.
Example: 845

straight angle An angle that forms a straight line.

sum The answer to an addition problem.

survey To collect information by asking a number of people the same question and recording their answers.

T

tally mark A mark used to record data on a tally chart.
Example: |||| = 5

third One of 3 equal parts of a whole.

time interval An amount of time.

trapezoid A quadrilateral with only one pair of parallel sides.

triangle A polygon with 3 sides.

triangular prism A solid figure with two triangular faces.

unit angle An angle with a measurement of 1 degree.

unit fraction A fraction representing one part of a whole that has been divided into equal parts; it always has a numerator of 1.

unit square a square with sides 1 unit long, used to measure area.

unknown A symbol that stands for a number in an equation.

vertex of a polygon The point where two sides of a polygon meet.

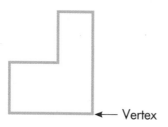

Vertex

week A unit of time equal to 7 days.

weight A measure of how heavy an object is.

word form A number written in words. *Example:* 325 = three hundred twenty-five

yard (yd) A customary unit of length. One yard equals 3 feet or 36 inches.

Zero Property of Multiplication The product of any number and zero is zero.

Photographs

Photo locators denoted as follows: Top (T), Center (C), Bottom (B), Left (L), Right (R), Background (Bkgd)

F34 Eric Isselée/Fotolia; **001** Gemenacom/Shutterstock; **028** Corbis; **057** Jacek Chabraszewski/Fotolia; **105** pk7comcastnet/Fotolia; **165** Christopher Dodge/Shutterstock; **297** Marques/Shutterstock; **355** Barbara Helgason/Fotolia; **401** Erni/Shutterstock; **436** Corbis; **456** Rabbit75_fot/Fotolia; **471** Arnold John Labrentz/ShutterStock; **488** KennStilger47/Shutterstock; **494B** imagebroker/Alamy; **494TL** hotshotsworldwide/Fotolia; **494TR** imagebroker/Alamy; **496T** John Luke/Index open; **508** David R. Frazier Photolibrary/Alamy; **535** Sam D'Cruz/Fotolia; **542** Palou/Fotolia; **571** Nancy Gill/ShutterStock; **605** B.G. Smith/Shutterstock; **669** Cathy Keifer/ShutterStock; **742B** Getty Images; **742T** Getty Images; **759TL** photolibrary/Photos to go; **759TR** Simple Stock Shot; **760BR** Simple Stock Shot; **768** Jenoe/Fotolia; **771BL** Jupiter Images; **771CL** Getty Images; **771TR** Stockdisc/Punch Stock; **805** Amy Myers/Shutterstock; **843** Photocreo Bednarek/Fotolia; **856** Jupiterimages/ThinkStock; **916** Oleksii Sagitov/ShutterStock; **932** Photos to go.

GRADE 3 LESSONS EXCLUSIVELY FOR VIRGINIA

You will use these lessons throughout the year.

Learn Glossary

Virginia Lesson 1
Numbers to 10,000

I can... read, write, and represent place values in numbers to 10,000.

 SOL 3.1a

Essential Question **How Can You Represent Numbers to 10,000?**

A

A two-humped camel weighs between 1,000 and 1,450 pounds. What are different ways you can show the weight of this camel at the right?

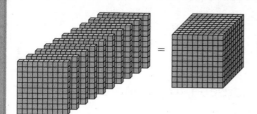

Remember, ten hundreds equal one thousand.

This camel weighs 1,350 pounds.

B You can use a model, like place-value blocks.

1 thousand   3 hundreds   5 tens   0 ones

You can use a place-value chart.

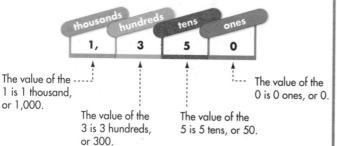

The value of the 1 is 1 thousand, or 1,000.

The value of the 3 is 3 hundreds, or 300.

The value of the 5 is 5 tens, or 50.

The value of the 0 is 0 ones, or 0.

C You can also use one of these forms to write the number.

Word form:

one thousand, three hundred fifty

Write a comma between the thousands and the hundreds.

Standard form:

1,350

Write a comma between the thousands and the hundreds.

Expanded form:

1,000 + 300 + 50

Convince Me! **Reasoning** How could you represent 2,345?

Guided Practice

Do You Understand?

1. Write the 4-digit number with 5 as the tens digit, 2 as the hundreds digit, and 6 for each of the other digits.

2. How could you show 1,350 with place-value blocks if you do not have a thousand block?

3. **Reasoning** Explain why you do not need to use tens blocks to show 6,802 with place-value blocks.

Do You Know How?

For **4–6**, write each number in standard form.

4.

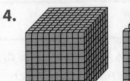 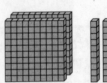

5. $8,000 + 500 + 30 + 9$

6. Two thousand, four hundred sixty-one

Independent Practice

For **7–9**, complete the table. You can use a place-value chart to help.

	Model	Standard Form	Expanded Form	Word Form
7.				
8.		3,201		
9.				five thousand, three hundred seventy-four

Problem Solving

10. The record for the world's largest pumpkin keeps changing as heavier pumpkins are grown. Write the weight of the pumpkin at the right in word form and in expanded form. Then, draw place-value blocks to show the weight.

This record setting pumpkin weighed 2,323 pounds.

---

11. **Reasoning** Explain the value of each 2 in 2,323.

12. **Number Sense** Write the greatest possible number and the least possible number using the four digits 5, 2, 8, and 1.

---

13. **Higher Order Thinking** Marianna says two thousand, four hundred is the same amount as twenty-four hundred. Is Marianna correct? Explain.

14. **Make Sense and Persevere** Nina picked 48 pounds of tomatoes this summer. Josh picked 37 pounds of tomatoes. Their father said he would buy them a scooter if they pick 100 pounds of tomatoes in all. How many more pounds of tomatoes do they need to pick? Explain.

 Assessment

15. Which is the word form of 2,406?

Ⓐ   twenty-four thousand, six

Ⓑ   two thousand, four hundred six

Ⓒ   two thousand, forty-six

Ⓓ   two hundred forty-six

16. Which is the standard form of $9,000 + 500 + 70$?

Ⓐ   957

Ⓑ   9,057

Ⓒ   9,507

Ⓓ   9,570

For **1–3**, complete the table. You can use a place-value chart to help.

	Model	Standard Form	Expanded Form	Word Form
1.				
2.		5,009		
3.				four thousand, seven hundred twelve

---

4. Write the number that matches all the clues in the riddle.

What Number Am I?
- My thousands digit is 1 more than my tens digit.
- My ones digit is 1 less than my hundreds digit.
- My hundreds digit is 8.
- My tens digit is 4.

---

5. **Higher Order Thinking** Regina made 1,240 pot holders. She wants to sell them in packages of 10. How many packages will she have? Explain your thinking.

Think about how many tens are equal to 1,240 to help solve this problem.

Name _____

Virginia Lesson 2
Greater Numbers

I can... tell the value of each digit in a six-digit number.

SOL 3.1a

Essential Question **How Can You Read, Write, and Name Greater Numbers?**

A

Yosemite National Park in California covers 748,036 acres of land. How can you read, write, and name 748,036 in different ways?

Place-Value Chart

A period is a group of 3 digits in a number, starting from the right.

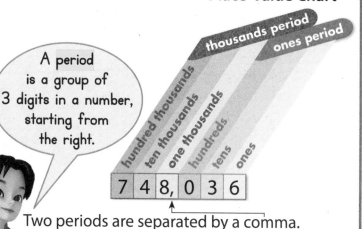

Two periods are separated by a comma.

B **Standard form:**
748,036

Expanded form:
700,000 + 40,000 + 8,000 + 30 + 6

Word form:
seven hundred forty-eight thousand, thirty-six

Guided Practice

Do You Understand?

1. Raymond says the value of the digit 5 in 365,420 is 50,000. Do you agree? Why or why not?

2. Describe how 530,434 and 434,035 are alike and how they are different.

Do You Know How?

In **3–6**, write each number in standard form.

3. nine hundred ninety-nine thousand, nine hundred ninety-nine

4. three hundred ninety-eight thousand, three hundred twenty

5. 600,000 + 20,000 + 600 + 90 + 3

6. 70,000 + 8,000 + 700 + 40 + 2

Independent Practice and Problem Solving

7. Write 598,326 in a place-value chart, and then write it in expanded, standard, and word forms.

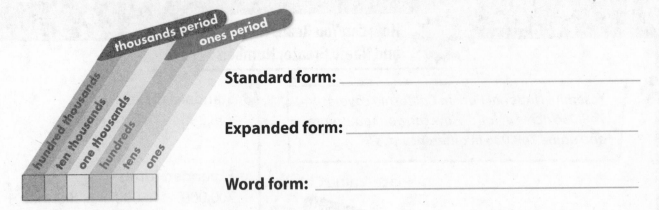

Standard form: _____

Expanded form: _____

Word form: _____

---

8. Write seven hundred twenty-seven thousand, five hundred fifty in standard form.

9. Write 646,374 in expanded form.

For **10–13**, find the missing numbers.

10. 30,000 + _____ + 600 + 3 = 34,603

11. 80,000 + 3,000 + _____ + 20 + 1 = 83,921

12. 20,000 + _____ + _____ = 22,300

13. _____ + _____ + 400 + _____ + _____ = 250,412

---

14. Big Bend National Park in Texas covers a large number of acres of land. What is the value of the 8 in the number of acres?

15. **Higher Order Thinking** Write how many hundred thousands, ten thousands, and thousands there are in the number of acres of land Big Bend National Park covers.

Welcome to Big Bend National Park 801,163 acres

Name _____

Virginia Lesson 3
Compare Whole Numbers

> **I can** ... compare whole numbers to 10,000.
>
> **SOL** 3.1c

Essential Question **How Can You Compare Two Numbers to 10,000?**

A

Which class collected more cans?

Number of Cans Collected

Grade 2: 3,456
Grade 3: 3,482

Use these symbols to compare numbers.

DATA

Symbol	Meaning
<	is less than
>	is greater than
=	is equal to

B One Way

You can use place-value blocks to compare.

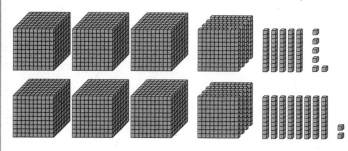

So, 3,482 **is greater than** 3,456.

3,482 > 3,456

Grade 3 collected more cans.

C Another Way

You can use a place-value chart.
Line up the digits by place value.
Compare the digits, starting from the left.

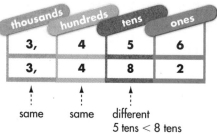

thousands	hundreds	tens	ones
3,	4	5	6
3,	4	8	2

same   same   different
                   5 tens < 8 tens

So, 3,456 **is less than** 3,482.

3,456 < 3,482

Grade 3 collected more cans.

Convince Me! **Reasoning** The fourth-grade class collected 3,395 cans.
Is 3,395 greater than the number of cans the third-grade class collected, since
9 tens > 8 tens? Explain why or why not.

Another Example!

You can order numbers two ways. Look at the numbers in the place-value chart.

Write the numbers from **greatest to least**:
6,450   5,783   5,729

Write the numbers from **least to greatest**:
5,729   5,783   6,450

thousands	hundreds	tens	ones
6,	4	5	0
5,	7	2	9
5,	7	8	3

6 > 5
So 6,450 is the greatest.

7 = 7
Compare the tens.

2 < 8
So 5,729 is the least.

Guided Practice

Do You Understand?

1. **Construct Arguments** How do the place-value blocks on the previous page show 3,482 > 3,456?

2. **Critique Reasoning** Arna said that any number with 4 digits is greater than any number with 3 digits. Is Arna correct? Explain.

Do You Know How?

In **3–8**, compare the numbers. Use <, >, or =.

3.

1,234 ◯ 1,243

4. 2,561 ◯ 825   5. 6,807 ◯ 6,807

6. 3,722 ◯ 4,099   7. 1,001 ◯ 999

8. 8,968 ◯ 8,986

Independent Practice

For **9-14**, compare the numbers. Use <, >, or =.

9. 679 ◯ 4,985   10. 9,642 ◯ 9,642   11. 5,136 ◯ 5,163

12. 8,204 ◯ 8,402   13. 3,823 ◯ 3,853   14. 2,424 ◯ 2,242

Problem Solving

15. Write the number of feet above sea level Mount Rogers is in word form.

16. Which is greater, the highest point in Virginia or the highest point in Kentucky? Write a number sentence with > or < to explain.

Highest Points in Several States

State	Highest Point	Feet Above Sea Level
Illinois	Charles Mound	1,235
Kentucky	Black Mountain	4,145
Ohio	Campbell Hill	1,550
Virginia	Mount Rogers	5,729

17. Write the heights of the highest points in order from least to greatest. Then write which point is the highest.

18. **Higher Order Thinking** What is the least number of additional feet the highest point in Ohio would need to be, so that it would be higher than the highest point in Kentucky?

19. **Reasoning** Suppose you are comparing 1,272 and 1,269. Do you need to compare the ones digits? Explain.

20. **Make Sense and Persevere** Tomas and Gerta hiked Beecher Hill. They hiked 475 feet before lunch and 328 feet more after lunch. How many more feet did they need to hike to reach 900 feet in all? Explain.

✔ Assessment

21. Which comparisons are correct? Select all that apply.

- ☐ 6,342 > 6,432
- ☐ 5,295 < 5,380
- ☐ 4,578 = 4,597
- ☐ 3,120 > 871
- ☐ 7,707 < 7,770

22. Which comparisons are correct? Select all that apply.

- ☐ 3,837 > 3,873
- ☐ 1,010 < 995
- ☐ 7,200 < 7,209
- ☐ 2,215 > 2,125
- ☐ 3,454 = 3,454

In **1–8**, compare the numbers. Use $<$, $>$, or $=$.

1. 2,093 ◯ 2,120 **2.** 3,376 ◯ 2,380

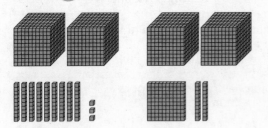

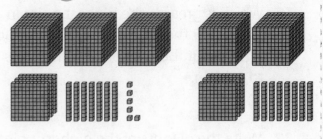

3. 4,916 ◯ 4,216 **4.** 868 ◯ 1,008 **5.** 5,035 ◯ 5,350

6. 6,730 ◯ 6,730 **7.** 2,427 ◯ 2,417 **8.** 9,126 ◯ 9,216

A scientist measured the heights that flocks of geese were flying. The height they were flying at is called altitude.

9. Construct Arguments Explain how to compare the altitude of Flock 1 to the altitude of Flock 3.

10. Make Sense and Persevere Write the order the flocks of geese were flying from highest altitude to lowest altitude.

Altitudes of Canadian Geese	
Flock	**Altitude in Feet**
1	1,954
2	3,345
3	1,594
4	2,045

11. Draw a picture to explain how to compare 1,240 to 1,420.

12. Higher Order Thinking Explain why any 4-digit number is less than 10,000.

Name _____

12. What is the value of the 2 in 2,765?

Ⓐ 2,000

Ⓑ 200

Ⓒ 20

Ⓓ 2

---

13. Write the number that the model below represents in standard form, expanded form, and word form.

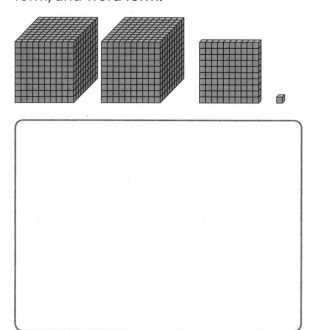

---

14. Write the number six hundred forty-two thousand, seven hundred fifty-three in standard form.

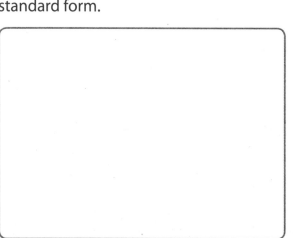

15. Which symbol makes the comparison true? Write the correct symbol from the box to compare the two numbers below the box.

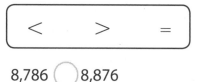

| < | > | = |

8,786 ◯ 8,876

---

16. Write a comparison for 4,036 and 4,063. Explain how you compared the two numbers.

17. Write the numbers shown below in order from greatest to least.

6,579 5,999 6,601

18. Which shows six hundred fifty-two thousand, seven hundred sixty-three in standard form?

Ⓐ 6,763

Ⓑ 65,763

Ⓒ 625,763

Ⓓ 652,763

19. Richard says the value of the digit 9 in 895,024 is 900,000? Do you agree? Why or why not?

Learn   Glossary

Virginia Lesson 4
Patterns: Number Rules

I can ... identify and make number patterns.

 SOL 3.16

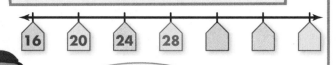 **How Can You Extend Number Patterns?**

A

The houses on a street are in a pattern. If the pattern continues, what are the next three numbers?

| 16 | 20 | 24 | 28 | | | |

This is a growing pattern. These numbers grow by the same amount. The rule is Add 4.

$28 + 4 = 32$

$32 + 4 = 36$

$36 + 4 = 40$

The next three numbers are 32, 36, 40.

B

Here is a different type of number pattern. If this pattern continues, what are the next three numbers?

1, 4, 7, 1, 4, 7, 1, 4, 7, _____, _____, _____

1, 4, 7 is the part that repeats. This is a repeating pattern.

The next three numbers are 1, 4, 7.

☆ Guided Practice

Do You Understand?

1. In the first example above, if 16 is the 1st number in the pattern, what is the 9th number?

2. Describe this pattern using words.

   15, 18, 15, 18, 15, 18, 15, 18

Do You Know How?

In **3–6**, write the next three numbers to continue each pattern.

3. 12, 17, 22, 27, _____, _____,

   _____

4. 4, 8, 8, 4, 8, 8, 4, 8, 8, 4, _____,

   _____, _____

5. 3, 6, 3, 6, 3, 6, 3, 6, _____,

   _____, _____

6. 16, 14, 12, 10, _____, _____,

   _____

Independent Practice and Problem Solving

For **7–10**, write the next three numbers to continue each pattern.

7. 7, 6, 7, 6, 7, 6, 7, _____, _____, _____

8. 1, 3, 5, 7, _____, _____, _____

9. 1, 3, 6, 9, 1, 3, 6, 9, 1, 3, 6, 9, 1, _____, _____, _____

10. 26, 23, 20, 17, 14, 11, _____, _____, _____

For **11** and **12**, write the missing numbers for each pattern.

11. 8, 12, 16, 8, _____, 16, _____, 12, 16

12. 31, 26, 21, 16, _____, 6, _____

13. Write your own growing pattern.

14. Write your own repeating pattern.

15. This is an input/output table. The rule tells what to do to the **input** to get the **output**. Complete the table.

16. How did you know which numbers to write in the Output column?

Rule: Add 6	
Input	Output
4	
6	12
9	
10	

17. Jane is using "subtract 4" as her rule to make a pattern. Fill in her missing numbers. Then continue the pattern.

31, _____, _____, _____, 15,

_____, _____, _____

18. Higher Order Thinking Complete the input/output table.

Rule: Add 3	
Input	Output
7	
	13
	18
	20

14. Draw lines to connect the pattern with the number that continues the pattern.

7, 6, 5, 7, 6, 5, 7, 6, 5, 7,		5
2, 5, 8, 11, 14,		6
11, 9, 7, 5, 3,		1
1, 5, 5, 1, 5, 5, 1, 5, 5, 1,		17

15. Peter correctly wrote three numbers to continue this pattern. Which numbers did he write?

16, 19, 22, 25,

Ⓐ 26, 27, 28

Ⓑ 26, 28, 30

Ⓒ 28, 30, 32

Ⓓ 28, 31, 34

16. Complete the Output column for this table.

✓ **Assessment**

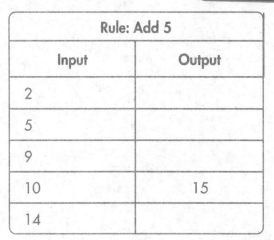

Rule: Add 5	
Input	Output
2	
5	
9	
10	15
14	

Explain how you knew which numbers to write.

17. Choose *Yes* or *No* to tell if these patterns are growing patterns.

a. 6, 7, 8, 9, 10

○ Yes   ○ No

b. 6, 7, 6, 7, 6, 7

○ Yes   ○ No

c. 9, 12, 15, 9, 12, 15, 9, 12, 15

○ Yes   ○ No

d. 14, 11, 8, 5

○ Yes   ○ No

Name _____

Virginia Lesson 5
Understand Probability and Outcomes

I can ... use probability to describe events.

 SOL 3.14

Essential Question **How Can You Describe the Chance That an Event Will Happen?**

A

Probability is the measurement of chance that an event will happen.

An event is *likely* if it will probably happen. It is *unlikely* if it will probably not happen.

An event is *certain* if it is sure to happen. It is *impossible* if it will never happen.

 Think of events in a tropical rainforest.

Certain event: seeing green plants

Impossible event: seeing a polar bear

Likely event: seeing colorful birds

Unlikely event: seeing dry soil

B A possible result of a game or experiment is called an **outcome**.

When you spin the spinner, the outcome might be blue, red, yellow, or green.

It is certain you will spin a color.

It is likely you will spin red.

It is unlikely you will spin green.

Blue Green Yellow Red

It is impossible to spin orange.

It is equally likely you will spin green or yellow.

Convince Me! **Construct Arguments** If you spin the spinner above, is it equally likely you will spin red or green? Why or why not?

Do You Understand?

1. What is the difference between a certain event and a likely event?

2. What is the difference between an impossible event and an unlikely event?

Do You Know How?

A **1–6** number cube has 6 faces. You roll the number cube.

3. List all the possible outcomes.

4. Which outcomes are equally likely?

5. Name an outcome that is impossible.

6. Is it certain you will roll a number 6 or less? Explain.

☆ Independent Practice ☆

For **7–10**, use the spinner at the right.

7. List all the possible outcomes.

8. What outcomes are equally likely?

9. Name an outcome that is certain.

10. Name an outcome that is impossible.

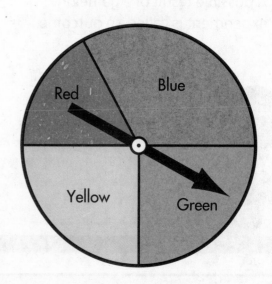

Problem Solving

11. This is the heads side of a quarter. The other side is tails. What are the possible outcomes of flipping the coin?

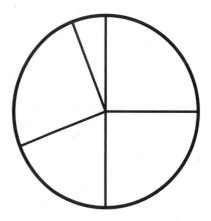

12. Reasoning Is one of the outcomes you listed in Exercise 11 unlikely? Explain.

---

13. Draw any 4 pattern blocks. List the outcomes if you were to choose one of your pattern blocks from a bag.

Describe how likely one of the outcomes will be.

14. Eric is running a race. There are 12 people in the race. What are the possible outcomes for where Eric will finish in the race?

---

15. Higher Order Thinking Color the spinner so that it is:

- unlikely you will spin red
- impossible you will spin blue
- equally likely you will spin green and yellow

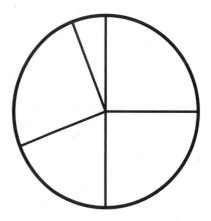

 Assessment

16. Mary chooses one paper clip from a box. She has 8 green paper clips, 12 red paper clips, 7 yellow paper clips, and 8 blue paper clips.

Which colors does Mary have an equally likely chance of choosing?

Ⓐ Green and red

Ⓒ Green and blue

Ⓑ Red and blue

Ⓓ Red and yellow

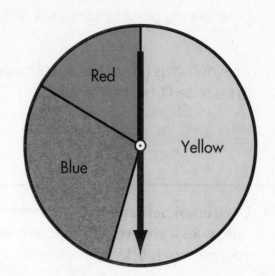

For **1–4**, use the spinner at the right.

1. List all the possible outcomes.

2. Which outcomes are unlikely?

3. Name an outcome that is impossible.

4. Name an outcome that is certain.

---

5. **Construct Arguments** Helena puts 9 red counters and 2 blue counters in a bag. If she picks 1 counter without looking, is she *certain* or *likely* to pick out a red counter? Explain.

6. How could you change the spinner above to make it likely to spin blue?

---

7. **Higher Order Thinking** Circle the spinner that matches all these clues.

   1. Certain to spin red, green, blue, or a line.

   2. Equally likely to spin red or blue.

   3. Likely to spin green.

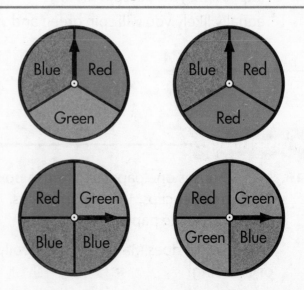

19. How likely are these outcomes if you were to spin this spinner? Draw lines to match the outcome with the word that describes how likely it is to happen.

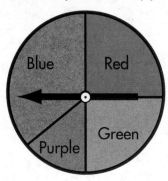

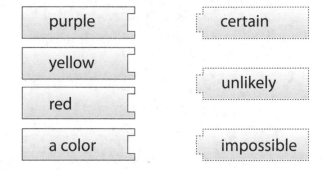

purple		certain
yellow		unlikely
red		
a color		impossible

20. How would you change the spinner above to make it likely to spin green?

21. Each student in Ms. Lin's class voted for the city they would most like to visit. There were:

6 votes for Orlando,
8 votes for Dallas,
6 votes for New York,
4 votes for Chicago.

If Ms. Lin picks a paper vote without looking, which two cities is she equally likely to pick?

Ⓐ Dallas and Chicago

Ⓑ Orlando and New York

Ⓒ Dallas and New York

Ⓓ Orlando and Dallas

22. A sports team has 11 jerseys numbered 1 through 11. Yasmin picks one jersey without looking. List all the possible outcomes for the jersey number she picks.